The Politics of Lawmaking in Post-Mao China

Studies on Contemporary China

The Contemporary China Institute at the School of Oriental and African Studies (University of London) has, since its establishment in 1968, been an international centre for research and publications on twentieth-century China. *Studies on Contemporary China*, which is edited at the Institute, seeks to maintain and extend that tradition by making available the best work of scholars and China specialists throughout the world. It embraces a wide variety of subjects relating to Nationalist and Communist China, including social, political, and economic change, intellectual and cultural developments, foreign relations, and national security.

Series Editor

Dr Frank Dikötter, Director of the Contemporary China Institute

Editorial Advisory Board

Dr Robert F. Ash
Professor Hugh D. R. Baker
Professor Elisabeth J. Croll
Dr Richard Louis Edmonds
Mr Brian G. Hook

Professor Christopher B. Howe
Professor Bonnie S. McDougall
Professor David Shambaugh
Dr Julia C. Strauss
Dr Jonathan Unger
Professor Lynn T. White III

The Politics of Lawmaking in Post-Mao China

Institutions, Processes and Democratic Prospects

MURRAY SCOT TANNER

CLARENDON PRESS · OXFORD

This book has been printed digitally and produced in a standard specification in order to ensure its continuing availability

OXFORD
UNIVERSITY PRESS

Great Clarendon Street, Oxford OX2 6DP
Oxford University Press is a department of the University of Oxford.
It furthers the University's objective of excellence in research, scholarship,
and education by publishing worldwide in
Oxford New York
Auckland Bangkok Buenos Aires Cape Town Chennai
Dar es Salaam Delhi Hong Kong Istanbul Karachi Kolkata
Kuala Lumpur Madrid Melbourne Mexico City Mumbai Nairobi
São Paulo Shanghai Singapore Taipei Tokyo Toronto
with an associated company in Berlin

Oxford is a registered trade mark of Oxford University Press
in the UK and in certain other countries

Published in the United States
by Oxford University Press Inc., New York

© Murray Scot Tanner 1999

The moral rights of the author have been asserted
Database right Oxford University Press (maker)

Reprinted 2002

All rights reserved. No part of this publication may be reproduced,
stored in a retrieval system, or transmitted, in any form or by any means,
without the prior permission in writing of Oxford University Press,
or as expressly permitted by law, or under terms agreed with the appropriate
reprographics rights organization. Enquiries concerning reproduction
outside the scope of the above should be sent to the Rights Department,
Oxford University Press, at the address above

You must not circulate this book in any other binding or cover
and you must impose this same condition on any acquirer

ISBN 0-19-829339-9

Acknowledgements

Since I first became interested in China's legislative system during Kenneth Lieberthal's China Research Seminar more than ten years ago, I have accumulated a daunting list of intellectual and personal debts on the way to writing this book. This short note can barely begin to acknowledge, let alone repay, those obligations.

The research for this study would have been impossible without generous support provided by the Committee on Scholarly Communications with China, which made possible two trips to China in 1989 and 1995, and by Western Michigan University's Faculty Research and Creative Activities Support Fund, which underwrote part of the research expenses for my 1992 Beijing trip. Beijing University's Foreign Affairs Office and its Law Department (now Law School) graciously hosted me as a visiting scholar on all three of these occasions and provided wonderful research support. I hope some day a book can be written lauding the untold acts of bureaucratic wizardry and personal heroism these fine people performed for us foreign scholars and students when the shooting began on that terrible night in June 1989.

I owe a terrific debt of gratitude to the members of my doctoral committee at the University of Michigan for their comments and guidance on the original dissertation. Michel Oksenberg was an intellectually engaging and terrifically resourceful co-chairman, patiently reading and commenting on innumerable rough drafts, and always pressing me to take the analysis of policy-making further. Whitmore Gray's expertise on and contacts within the Chinese legal system greatly facilitated the research. John Kingdon's lively mind and deep intuition about how politicians think enlightened me more about Chinese politics than I suspect he will ever believe. Finally, Kenneth Lieberthal, my other co-chair, was the best kind of encouraging sceptic—pushing me hard to prove my case that something important was changing in the Chinese political-legal system, and to think seriously about how to reconcile China's promising political changes with its brutal realities. Along the way, he also taught me a great deal about how to be a responsible scholar, colleague and friend.

In addition, a number of colleagues have read and provided extensive comments on all or part of various drafts of this book, including William Alford, Richard Baum, Jim Butterfield, Donald Clarke, Kevin Corder, Anthony Dicks, James Feinerman, Frances Hoar Foster, Merle Goldman, Guo Daohui, Carolyn Lewis, Stanley Lubman, Roderick MacFarquhar, Melanie Manion, Kevin O'Brien, Neil Pinney, Pitman Potter, Lucian Pye, William Ritchie, Chet Rogers, Dorothy Solinger, Anne Seidman, Robert

Seidman, David Shambaugh, Zhou Wangsheng, and two anonymous reviewers for Oxford University Press. I am particularly grateful to Ken Lieberthal, Merle Goldman, David Shambaugh, and Anne and Bob Seidman for organizing seminars at which various parts of the research were presented and discussed.

Two successive Chairmen of the WMU Political Science Department, Professors Ernie Rossi and Chet Rogers, dreamed up countless administrative manoeuvres to facilitate my research on this book. WMU doctoral student Chen Ke was a resourceful, diligent and careful research assistant for many parts of the research, and without his patient efforts the valuable voting data in Chapter 5 could not have been pulled together. Alison Surry of the School of Oriental and African Studies did a swift, first-rate job editing my often wooden prose into more readable text. Dotty Barr patiently typed changes to the penultimate draft of the manuscript and along the way good-humouredly made me aware of many stylistic inconsistencies. Sharon Myers patiently made innumerable logistical arrangements for research trips and conferences for a professor whose mind was usually far more on his writing than on the necessary paperwork. Ms. Linda Thai did a fine job preparing the index. I am very grateful to them all.

There are several others to whom I owe more personal debts for their support of my study. This list must begin with my longtime friend Bruce Adams, and also includes Joe Fewsmith and Irene Kiedrowski, Bob Hunter, Jiang Ci, George Kish, Chris Lansing, Alan Liotta, Jolene McNamara, Ann and Barney McCullom, Harriet Mills, Marty Petersen, Linda Sarnoff, Bob Suettinger, William P.Y. Ting, and Lori and Bill Wagoner. Kimberley Wheat Condas was a constant source of love, support and encouragement while I was writing the original dissertation, which is rightfully dedicated to her. The present volume is dedicated to my parents, Duncan Tanner and Jean Lund Tanner, my brother Cam Tanner, and my sister Ellen Tanner Wise, with all my love and gratitude.

Finally, I deeply regret that like generations of sinologists before me, I cannot acknowledge by name several dozen Chinese colleagues and friends who assisted me during my research trips to Beijing. Many undertook significant costs and risks to help a foreigner understand their system better, with no apparent prospect of personal reward or recompense. I can only hope that I have done justice to them by writing a balanced, careful account.

With so many friends and colleagues having supplied so much help, it only remains for me to absolve all of them of any responsibility for the remaining errors of fact or interpretation. These mistakes are entirely my responsibility, and doubtless would be far more numerous without the help of such fine friends.

Contents

	PART I: THEORETICAL CONSIDERATIONS	1
1.	Introduction: The New Importance of Lawmaking Politics in China	3
2.	Bureaucracies, 'Organized Anarchies', and Inadvertent Transitions: Towards New Models of Chinese Lawmaking	12
	PART II: LAWMAKING INSTITUTIONS	41
3.	The Emergence of China's Post-Mao Lawmaking System	43
4.	The Erosion of Party Control over Lawmaking	51
5.	The Rise of the National People's Congress System	72
6.	The State Council's Lawmaking System	120
	PART III: CASE STUDIES IN LAWMAKING	133
7.	The Case of the Enterprise Bankruptcy Law	135
8.	The Case of the State-owned Industrial Enterprises Law	167
	PART IV: CONCLUSIONS	207
9.	Stages and Processes in Chinese Lawmaking	209
10.	Lawmaking Reforms and China's Democratic Prospects	231
	Selected Bibliography	253
	Index	283

PART I
Theoretical Considerations

1
Introduction: The New Importance of Lawmaking Politics in China

*A Chinese Puzzle: The Surprising Difficulty
of 'Rubber Stamping' a Law*

In December 1978 Deng Xiaoping, in his pivotal address to the Communist Party Central Committee meeting that set the course for China's reform movement, called for the government to draft a law on factories that would help reform China's chronically money-losing state-owned enterprises. Armed with Deng's public endorsement, a senior Party economic planner in charge of enterprises set straight to work drafting the law and hammering out a consensus policy among the government ministries, unions, Party officials and legislators concerned with the project. Finally the bill that China's top leader called for was passed into law—*ten years later*.

In March 1989 Communist Party General Secretary Zhao Ziyang addressed a briefing session for key delegates to the annual meeting of China's legislature, the National People's Congress. Zhao told the attendees, all of whom were loyal Party members, that the top leadership wanted that year's meeting to show unity and obedience to Central directives. But when the piece of legislation most important to Zhao came up for discussion and vote (a bill designed to give the south-eastern Special Economic Zone of Shenzhen greater freedom to enact experimental laws promoting economic reform), there was terrific debate and resentment among the delegates. Led primarily by legislators and officials from Guangdong province (where Shenzhen is located), over 40% of the delegates present either voted 'no' or abstained on the resolution, which then limped embarrassingly to passage.

In autumn 1997 Jiang Zemin, Zhao's successor as Party General Secretary, anxious to secure his position after paramount leader Deng Xiaoping's death, skilfully manoeuvred to remove his chief rival Qiao Shi from the organizational positions that made him a threat. Over the past decade Qiao had occupied several of the cornerstone posts in China's Leninist power hierarchy, including head of Party organization and personnel, overseer of Party discipline, and chief of internal security and intelligence. But even the most cynical, tough-minded China watchers in the Hong Kong press corps acknowledged that in many ways, what made Qiao Shi most threatening to Jiang Zemin's authority was that for five years Qiao had been 'the man who wields the "rubber stamp"'—Chairman of the Standing Committee of the National People's Congress.

As the popular saying goes, 'Something is *very wrong* with this picture.'

Until very recently, discussions of lawmaking and the legislature in China were regularly greeted by scholars, journalists and policy makers with tough questions such as 'why should we care how laws are made in China?' Few could be convinced that law, lawmaking politics and legislatures matter in single-party authoritarian systems such as China. And surely more than one reader who opened this book had to overcome some justifiable scepticism before doing so. Because even though the politics of the lawmaking process have been a staple of the study of American, British, or even Japanese politics for well over a quarter of a century, much of what we know (or *think* that we know) about China and other Marxist-Leninist or one-party systems suggests law, lawmaking, and legislatures are not important research topics. For years many leading textbooks on China only visited these topics briefly, as part of a scholarly 'duty dance' description of the government's formal constitutional authority structure. They would state that according to the Constitution the National People's Congress (NPC) was China's 'highest organ of state authority'. Almost invariably, however, these texts would then make a flat, dismissive concluding assertion that lawmaking institutions and processes are little more than a showpiece, and are irrelevant to the realities of Chinese power politics. Even today many news reports still refer to the NPC as 'China's rubber-stamp parliament' (indeed, scholars in the field have come to regard it as a minor victory when such reports refer to the Congress as 'China's *historically* rubber-stamp parliament').[1] As recently as ten years ago a book such as this one on Chinese lawmaking politics might have caught the eye of a scholar of Asian law, but for most political scientists it would have held scant interest, since their principal fascination is the study of power.

So where is the proof that something important in China has quietly changed, and lawmaking and the legislature now merit the attention of students of power? As the three examples cited above illustrate, nothing justifies a study of 'how a bill becomes a law' in Beijing quite so well as the fact that from the early 1980s, the Chinese lawmaking system simply began behaving in ways that were radically at odds with the earlier models, images and assumptions. Under pressure at home and abroad to develop a legal

---

1. Many of the dominant undergraduate textbooks on China still have relatively brief discussions of either the NPC or lawmaking: Townsend and Womack (1986), 100–1. Pye (1984) 178, 328–9 and Pye (1991), 180–1; Saich (1981) 120–2; Domes (1985) ch. 6; and Dreyer (1993) 111–13, and ch. 8. For some recent texts with relatively sophisticated discussions of the NPC and lawmaking, see Ogden (1992), 184, 236–7; Lieberthal (1995), 162, 223, 319–20; and Wang (1992), 111–16.

system, Chinese began drafting many policy documents on major issues that had historically been issued as administrative regulations of the State Council (China's cabinet) or as Communist Party 'Central Committee Documents' (called *zhongfa*), in the form of 'laws' which were also submitted to the scrutiny of the NPC. Now, quite routinely, when such laws come before the NPC or its Standing Committee, even though they already bear the endorsement 'in principle' of the highest Party ofices, they are subjected to extended, repeated subcommittee review and serious floor debate. Most surprisingly, it is now quite common for the NPC and its Standing Committee to seriously delay, amend, table or return bills to their drafters and insist upon major changes. In recent years the NPC has from time to time voted down proposed State Council amendments to their own draft laws, and some NPC sources even report two cases of the NPC Standing Committee voting down Party-approved draft laws, although these actions have not yet been publicized. Gone forever, it would seem, are the days before 1979 when the NPC would hear a brief summary of a bill, move to an immediate vote and then invariably pass it unanimously.

Yet, as fascinating, new and counterintuitive as some of this behaviour is, there is very little explanation for it within either the general literature on comparative politics or in the specific literature on Chinese policy-making. Mostly, this is because of some complementary shortcomings in these two literatures. The comparative politics literature on legislatures has tended to ignore the overall process of lawmaking, while the Chinese politics literature on policy-making processes has tended to overlook the growing importance of law as a form of policy and the emergence of the NPC as a policy-making institution.

The many fine studies of legislatures in developing countries, that for decades were steeped in the relativist theories of structural-functionalism, often looked past such questions of policy-process and power. With regard to the developing world, there really was not a process-oriented literature on 'comparative lawmaking politics,' but rather a structural-functional literature on 'comparative legislatures'. These legislative studies rarely examined the entire political process of how a law was drafted, inquiring what role the legislature played as one of several lawmaking institutions. And faced with the often grim reality of legislative irrelevance or repression, there was frequently good reason for this omission. Instead, these studies tended to focus on legislatures more or less in isolation as institutional structures that served a variety of other political functions. The overwhelming verdict of such scholarship was that lawmaking is a top-down process dominated by actors and institutions elsewhere in the system, such as the ruling Party or the executive branch.[2] Developing country legislatures play little or no significant role as policy makers, or even as

---

2. I will later refer to this view as the 'Command model' of lawmaking. See Chapter 2.

6   The Politics of Lawmaking in Post-Mao China

important adjunct arenas of political warfare.[3] Consequently the principal aim of much of the comparative legislatures literature was often to explicate the most significant *non*-policy-making functions of legislatures, such as political socialization, elite recruitment, or national integration.[4] By contrast, the new importance of China's lawmaking politics and the NPC's increasingly assertive role in the process provide an unusual opportunity to trace how a legislature in a one-party authoritarian system can emerge from irrelevance and gradually come to play a significant role in genuinely important policy-making activities.

Sinologists, on the other hand, have over the past two decades produced an enormous array of studies that are filling in the still-sketchy picture of Chinese policy-making processes. But to this point these studies have largely neglected one of the fastest growing bodies of 'policy' in the system: law. And with a few rare exceptions, most notably Kevin O'Brien's major study *Reform Without Liberalization*, China scholars have overlooked the growing influence of the National People's Congress. These are important omissions. Ever since the 1978 Third Plenum of the Eleventh Chinese Communist Party (CCP) Central Committee called for more rapid development of 'socialist democracy' and rule by law, lawmaking has become an increasingly large, important and contentious part of policy-making. Examples abound. When former Premier Zhao Ziyang and other radical economic reformers wanted to light a fire under non-performing state enterprises, one of the key vehicles was the 1986 Enterprise Bankruptcy

---

3. G. R. Boynton and Chong Lim Kim, in summarizing the results of a series of studies on legislatures in developing countries, divide potential legislative functions into three categories: 'goal-setting' (drafting, amending or changing laws); 'structuring political content'; and 'integrating political systems'. They find that legislatures play the greatest role in integrating systems. With respect to the lawmaking role of legislatures, they note succinctly, 'If one wants to find their [legislature's] significance in these political systems, one must look elsewhere'. Boynton and Kim (1975), 18. Another study of legislatures in developing countries notes they 'often appear to have only an insignificant role in the making of public policy'. See Kim, Barkan, Turan and Jewell (1984), 5–6. Similarly, Nelson and White's (1982, 1) important comparative study of legislatures in communist states notes that 'there . . . still are strong indications that legislatures in communist states do not "legislate" in the ordinary sense of that word. Where they come closest to doing so, in Yugoslavia and Poland, their activites appear to have an impact only at the periphery of "rule-making".'

4. The structural functional orientations of this literature are reflected in the institutional research designs of such studies, most of which focus solely on the roles or functions of the legislature as an institution, rather than examining the process of 'lawmaking' as an aspect of 'policy-making'. It is the present study's contention that one of the best methods for gaining a more precise and realistic understanding of any legislature's true role and influence in a political system is to examine the entire process of lawmaking, examining not only the role of the legislature, but also the roles of all the other institutions involved in that process. On the 'integrative' and other non-policy-making functions of legislatures in developing and one-party states, see the following: Boynton and Kim (1975); Loewenberg and Patterson (1979); Patterson (1978); Smith amd Musolf (1979). On communist systems in particular, see Nelson and White (1982); and on China, O'Brien (1987 and 1990). For a dissenting view that argues that the true importance of the legislature can only be assessed by looking at its lawmaking/policy-making roles, see Sisson and Snowiss (1979).

The New Importance of Lawmaking Politics in China 7

Law, and the most prominent point of opposition was the NPC. After the 1989 Tiananmen massacre, orthodox Leninists in the state bureaucracy, frightened by the Democracy Movement, responded in part by delaying passage of one law which they feared would loosen social control (the Press Law) and ramming through a more restrictive version of another which they hoped would tighten control (the Public Demonstrations Law).[5] In late 1992, when Beijing wanted to head off increasing pressure from the United States Congress to expand intellectual property protection for foreign businesses, the result was a major revision to the Patent Law.

Consequently, when the NPC Standing Committee in 1986 tabled, delayed, amended and ultimately gutted the State Council's highly touted Bankruptcy Law, that act should have caused Western analysts to reconsider many conceptions of the policy-making process and of the roles lawmaking bodies play in that process. Western scholars' new interest in Chinese law and lawmaking did spawn a few excellent case studies of individual laws; and O'Brien's pathbreaking work greatly expanded our knowledge of the NPC's numerous evolving institutional roles. But important issues remained unaddressed by each of these bodies of literature. Studies of Chinese policy-making have still tended to ignore lawmaking.[6] The available case studies of individual laws revealed much about debates over their content, but little about the relative power of the leaders and institutions in the drafting process.[7] And so, despite the acknowledged importance of the topic and the rich and expanding separate literatures on Chinese *law* and Chinese *policy-making* processes, there is still no comprehensive English-language study of the Chinese lawmaking system and process.[8] Multi-functional studies of the NPC, which did not analyse in detail its lawmaking interactions with the Party's Central offices and the State Council, necessarily tended to be more general on the crucial question of whether the NPC really had significant influence over policy content, or was still just ratifying decisions made elsewhere in the system.

This book takes a very different approach to these questions of lawmaking and the lawmaking institutions. It looks at the entire lawmaking process and assesses the power of the full array of actors and institutions involved in the various stages of that process, including the Party Centre,

---

5. Judy Polumbaum has provided excellent case studies of both of these laws. See Polumbaum (1991 and 1994).
6. Among the most influential such studies have been Lieberthal and Oksenberg (1988), Lampton (1987), Hamrin (1990), Lieberthal and Lampton (1992) and Fewsmith (1994). An early exception is Solinger (1982).
7. See, for example, Klein (1987) and Chang Ta-Kuang (1987).
8. Regarding China's post-Mao legal reforms in general, see Edwards (1984), Leng and Chiu (1985), Baum (1986), Feinerman (1989), Dicks (1989), Feinerman (1991), Alford (1993), Potter (1993), Keith (1994), Lubman (1995), Clarke (1995), Alford (1995) and Tanner (1995). For an excellent regularly updated bibliography of recent English-language studies on Chinese law, see Johnson (1990 and subsequent editions available from the Library).

the NPC and the State Council and its ministries. This focus on the process and the various institutions involved in it not only reveals more about lawmaking in China, it also provides a unique base of evidence for understanding and evaluating how much real influence the NPC has relative to other institutions in making law. By studying the historical development and policy roles of the three key sets of institutions involved in lawmaking, and then examining specific case studies of how these institutions work (or fight) together to draft laws, this book attempts to sketch out the evolving power relations in the system. With respect to the NPC, this approach sacrifices an understanding of many of its non-policy-making functions, but in return reveals much more clearly and concretely the sources and limitations of its emerging influence over policy.

But of course the importance of the NPC's growing power in lawmaking goes far beyond what it can tell us about how policies are hammered out in Beijing. A study of lawmaking in China is not just another study of the policy-making process, because in a one-party authoritarian system, 'law' is not just any policy and the legislature is not just any policy-making institution. An understanding of lawmaking and the legislature is essential in order to assess the prospects that China, or any other state, can make a transition from Leninism to a political system that is more open, consultative, and ultimately, perhaps, democratic. This book begins and ends with some considerations about what impact the growth of China's lawmaking system, and especially the growing influence of the NPC, might have on China's prospects for initiating a genuine democratic transition.

When Leninist systems begin drafting more key policies in the form of laws to be considered by the legislature, something most of them began doing during their 'post-totalitarian' phases, these legal transitions often have important institutional consequences. The shift away from policy-making by Party edict to increasing 'rule by law' means the Party-state's rules for social behaviour are clearer and more predictable, and may even herald the beginnings of a contractual state–society relationship. At very least it marks the decline of relatively random unpredictable terror as the Party-state offers society an agreement that says that if citizens do not engage in certain clearly proscribed activities or challenge the Party-state's core values, they may expect that the Party-state will not attempt to punish or sanction them.[9] At early stages, this is merely an agreement to 'rule by law', rather than the liberal constitutionalist notion of 'rule of law', in which law defines a series of actions the state may not take, even though it might otherwise possess the raw power necessary to do so. The dramatic history of the last decade, however, suggests that the process is very difficult to freeze at this early stage. Very gradually, the Leninist Party-state may

---

9. The classics in this genre are Dallin and Breslauer (1970); Moore (1954); Lowenthal (1970); and Baum (1986).

The New Importance of Lawmaking Politics in China 9

recognize that in order to lure low-cost, voluntary mass compliance with its policies, it must increasingly submit to being voluntarily bound by its own legal rules, and must consult a broader array of social interests in making those rules. This process is most apparent in the economic sector, where foreign and domestic entrepreneurs can insist on an increasingly predictable, well-defined economic and legal environment or otherwise withdraw their investments. Leninist states are unlikely to succeed in erecting such an economic-legal infrastructure unless they consult these newly important economic actors and provide them with institutional avenues by which they can influence the drafting of laws.

Even though the top Party leadership's commitment to 'rule by law' in such systems is usually uneven at best, the growth of new lawmaking organs, especially the rise of the legislature, often has powerful unintended institutional implications. The Party leadership almost invariably tries to keep tightly unified control over lawmaking. But as Chapter 2 argues, this requires the Party leadership to prevent its own internal factional, personal, bureaucratic and policy-based disagreements from spilling over into the more open and accessible state lawmaking institutions such as the legislature. Legal and economic reforms in Leninist systems are inherently highly conflictual processes, and these conflicts cannot help finding their way into all the policy-making arenas in which these reforms are considered. Even though leadership posts in the legislature are initially restricted to 'reliable' Party-state officials, central control over lawmaking usually tends to fray and dissipate as various cleavages within the Party find new and more public institutional expression in the legislature.

History also demonstrates that this opening of the legislative process need not await the collapse of one-party rule and the establishment of a relatively fully developed civil society. Legislatures often become politically powerful long before either their societies or policy-making systems become more fully democratic.[10] The Soviet, Polish and Hungarian legislative reforms of 1988–90 dramatically demonstrate that a significant expansion in the power, assertiveness and corporate identity of the legislature can still take place even though the key officials in these institutions are still Party members nominally subject to increasingly abstract notions of 'Party discipline'.

Of course only a political Pollyanna would assume that the rise of lawmaking and the decentralization of policy-making power will inexorably lead to a transition towards a more consultative or democratic system. In bureaucratically-established authoritarian systems, temporary cycles of

---

10. For the U.S. and Europe, this point is made in Palmer (1959) and Shepsle (1988). On the former USSR and Eastern Europe, see especially the works of Hahn (1989, 1990 and 1996); also White (1992), Sabbat-Swidlicka (1990a, 1990b, 1991a, 1991b), de Weydenthal (1991), Rahr and Pomeranz, (1991) Gwertzman and Kaufman (1990), Steele (1994), and Lijphart and Waisman (1996).

10   The Politics of Lawmaking in Post-Mao China

policy-making decentralization which end in a reassertion and recentralization of regime power are quite common. For changes in policy process to translate into system transition, they must first become institutionalized, settled and resistant to change. Secondly, they must link up with other system-changing processes in the broader society, such as the emergence of politically active, influential civil society groups. The rise of law, lawmaking and the legislature are key parts of the picture, but they are only parts.

Key Research Questions and the Layout of the Book

This book focuses on two major sets of questions. The first, 'what are the politics of the lawmaking process in post-Mao China?' occupies the central chapters of the book, which examine China's national-level law-making institutions and processes. Chapter 2 critically analyses the assumptions, images and models which until now have guided Western sinologists' thinking about lawmaking and the NPC. The chapter compares and evaluates four competing models of the process drawn from Western political science literature. The 'Command model' and the 'Leadership Struggle model' have dominated discussions of lawmaking to this point. This study argues that the system now much more closely resembles the politics of an 'Organizational Politics model' and the unfortunately-named but perceptive 'Garbage Can model'. Chapters 3 to 6 focus on the historical development, policy-making roles and power sources of China's major lawmaking institutions—the Party Central apparatus, the National People's Congress (including its Standing Committee, permanent bureaucracy, and subcommittees), and the State Council (including its ministries). There are two key unifying themes in these chapters. The first concerns the erosion of centralized Communist Party control over lawmaking, and the corresponding rise of strong, competing legislative bureaucracies within the State Council, its ministries, and the NPC. The second theme is that as a result of this erosion and fragmentation of centralized control, each of these three systems should be seen as a separate lawmaking 'arena' characterized by a different constellation of powers and interests. Chapters 7 and 8 illustrate the changing politics of lawmaking using two quite highly detailed case studies of major recent Chinese laws—the 1986 Enterprise Bankruptcy Law and the 1988 State-Owned Industrial Enterprises Law.[11]

11. It is important to note that these case studies do not examine the true 'final' stage of the process: the politics of actually implementing the draft law. Instead, I have traced the laws' progress only through the stage of 'explicating' the law: that is, drafting a set of 'implementing regulations' or some similar interpretive document. Such explication, though important, represents only the beginning of the process of translating a law into a set of more precise bureaucratic instructions that can be implemented by lower levels. The reasons for not tracing the implementation of these laws are largely practical, since a proper study of how laws are implemented would involve extensive further interviewing, much of it at the local level, and

The New Importance of Lawmaking Politics in China 11

These case studies devote a great deal of attention to documenting and explaining, as reliably as possible, how the content of each law changed during the process, and the actual influence that various actors and processes had on the content. For the scholarly observer, such changes are the most reliable and verifiable indicators of real influence in the policy-making process. This requires a good deal of rather tedious comparison of multiple drafts of each law (which, fortuitously, are available for both cases). Whatever the stylistic shortcomings of such comparisons, they allow us to speak more precisely of the real political influence of such political actors as top Party leaders, State Council ministries and the NPC. Chapter 9 summarizes the lessons of the institutional chapters and case studies, and sketches out the different ways in which each of China's lawmaking institutions are influential in the various 'stages' of the lawmaking process.

The second major set of questions shifts the focus from policy process to the institutional politics of system transition. Chapters 2 and 10 ask what impact the rise of China's post-Mao lawmaking institutions, in particular the evolving Party–NPC relationship, is having upon China's prospects for a transition to a system that is more consultative, open and perhaps ultimately democratic. The theoretical transition between policy-making questions and system transition issues turns out to be a surprisingly difficult one because overwhelmingly the models of policy-making which have been employed to analyse China and other communist states have not been used to generate forecasts about a post-communist system transition. But the institutional evolution of the lawmaking system is creating pressure for significant further decentralization of power and is opening up windows for new public 'constituencies' to get involved in policy-making. Since there is no evidence that the Party leaders who designed this system intended it to create such pressures for transition, I argue that the emergence of the legislative system may be pushing China towards an 'inadvertent transition'. The nature and limitations of these pressures towards an 'inadvertent transition' are introduced in the latter half of Chapter 2 and discussed again in greater detail in Chapter 10.

would also make two already lengthy case studies unmanageably long. Still, this research design decision is an important flaw, since recent studies increasingly stress that the process of policy implementation frequently involves protracted battles that often change the content of a policy, or undermine it altogether (see Lampton, 1987). Hence, although there are perfectly defensible practical reasons for omitting this stage of the process, the reader should be aware that an important part of the story of these laws is being omitted.

2

Bureaucracies, 'Organized Anarchies' and Inadvertent Transitions: Towards New Models of Chinese Lawmaking

Chapter 1 argued that the politics of China's lawmaking process have changed greatly since 1979. Lawmaking is now a far more important part of the policy-making process, is far more conflictual and is fought out among a far greater array of institutions and arenas than ever before. It also argued that by better understanding lawmaking politics analysts can better appreciate the prospects for an eventual democratizing transition in China, and the role which the NPC might play in the process. But neither the theoretical images from comparative legislative studies nor those from current studies of the Chinese policy-making process have prepared scholars for these changes. This chapter attempts to provide some new theoretical images of the lawmaking process; it then considers how these new images might help us better understand the prospects for system tranformation in China.

Efforts to account for the new importance and rancorousness of lawmaking have been burdened by outmoded models and images of the lawmaking system. Generally, a long period has elapsed between the time that scholars and journalists began to apply increasingly sophisticated policy-making models to the Chinese system as a whole, and the time they began to acknowledge similarly sophisticated patterns in lawmaking and the role of the legislature. It was many years after leadership factional models came to dominate the study of Chinese politics before authors such as Frances Hoar Foster and Dorothy Solinger became the first to identify similar patterns in the legislative system. Likewise, scholars of bureaucratic and organizational politics who took charge of the field in the mid-1980s have, since that time, seemed to apply that perspective to almost every sector of Chinese governance except lawmaking. This lag is not entirely the fault of Western analysts, and a large part of the reason for it lies in the fact that the legal system as a whole was crushed during the Cultural Revolution and only gradually recovered after 1978. But it is also true that many scholars, and even more journalists, have been genuinely reluctant to acknowledge increasingly undeniable evidence that the lawmaking institutions, especially the NPC, were growing in importance as policy-making bureaucracies and arenas of political conflict. At most times since 1978, Western observers have clung to the belief that these institutions and

Bureaucracies, 'Organized Anarchies' and Inadvertent Transitions 13

the battles which appeared to rage there were, in reality, being more tightly controlled by the top Party leadership than they actually were.

This chapter analyses the evolution of Western images of China's lawmaking system, focusing on the two models which have dominated such understanding: the Command model and the Leadership Struggle model. The first of these, I argue, is no longer defensible as a way of analysing the lawmaking process, while the second must be supplemented with insights from two other models derived from Western policy-making process studies: the Organizational Politics model, and Cohen, March and Olsen's horrifically-named Garbage Can model.

Towards the end, the chapter switches back to the long-term issue of how the rise of the legislative system, especially the NPC, might contribute to China's transition towards a more open and consultative system. This requires an effort to forge an analytical link between policy process models and the forces which might promote a system transition. As it happens, the insights of the last two models suggest some important ways in which the institutional growth of the NPC, coupled with changes in other political institutions, are gradually deconcentrating power in the system, opening up linkages between ranking officials and a variety of popular constituencies, and institutionalizing elite tolerance for moderate, 'normal' levels of policy dissent. While these changes still leave many key prerequisites of a true democratizing transition unfulfilled, they also create significant forces which may help China in the direction of a 'quiet revolution from within' the Party-state, or an 'inadvertant transition' away from Leninism. These forces, moreover, are all nested in an institution which is far less alarming to devout Leninists, and hence might ease a future liberalizing transition.

Policy Process Models and China

Previous Western scholarly work on law, lawmaking and the legislature in China has been strongly influenced by one of two assumed models or images of the policy-making process. Like most policy-process models, these are simply an interrelated set of assertions concerning: where real power lies in the system; the major 'battlelines' or lines of cleavage in the system; the nature of the policy-making behaviour which characterizes lawmaking (such as top-down orders, factional struggle, incremental consensus-building, sudden major policy changes); and any substantive or content biases the process tends to impose on the policies it produces. This chapter very briefly examines the central premises of these models, how they have affected Western studies of Chinese lawmaking and their strengths and weaknesses as tools for helping towards an understanding of lawmaking politics in post-Mao China.

The most dominant image of lawmaking in China is still based on a

14   The Politics of Lawmaking in Post-Mao China

Command model historically developed for and applied to the study of Soviet-style systems. In the past decade this view has gradually been supplemented by a second, more conflict-oriented Leadership Struggle model. But several key institutional developments in the Chinese lawmaking system since 1978 have seriously attenuated most of the value these two models may once have had. Two other models of the policy-making process, both drawn from discussions of Western policy-making, provide better insights into China's post-Mao lawmaking system. Although the third model, the Organizational Politics model, has come to dominate recent studies of the Chinese policy-making process, its principal adherents have not yet suggested its careful application to the study of the legal system. The fourth model, the Garbage Can model, was originally developed for the analysis of complex organizations in the West, and is a useful corrective to the Organizational Politics model's sometimes excessive focus upon gradual, incremental policy-making.

Like most models of policy-making, these four models sometimes provide perspectives on the process which are not entirely mutually exclusive. Rather, as Graham Allison's apt metaphor of a 'conceptual lens' suggests, each model focuses attention on certain key elements and processes in the system, sometimes at the cost of obscuring or overlooking others.[1] These models are also not always strictly comparable. Some, such as the Leadership Struggle and Organizational Politics models, try to posit the key actors in the policy-making process, and illuminate their motivations, power resources and the key political cleavages in the system. Others, such as the Garbage Can model, focus attention on key processes rather than actors and their motivations. Accordingly, they need not always be treated strictly as competitors, but also as complementary. Hence these four models are not presented in the belief that through testing one single model will emerge as the best description of Chinese lawmaking. Rather, the analyst probably does best to pick and choose among elements of the models, stressing those key aspects of each which provide the most useful insights into the politics of lawmaking. Also, a discussion of these models is a useful reminder that previous studies of Chinese law, lawmaking and the legislature have always been influenced by particular implicit models of how Chinese law is made.

All four models provide fairly clear 'behavioural predictions'—forecasts about the type of policy-processes and political behaviour one would expect to see in the system, as well as those processes and behaviour that would *not* be expected if the key assumptions of that model are correct. They are not all strictly descriptive, however. Some take a theoretical step further and suggest ways in which the lawmaking *process* might affect the *content* of the laws it produces. Some suggest, however tentatively, that the

1. Allison (1971).

nature of the policy-making process biases the system in the direction of producing particular types of policies, while others give little guidance concerning the types of policies the system is likely to produce. In discussing these models, therefore, this chapter stresses any forecasts they suggest concerning the effect of process upon policy content.

The Command Model and the Image of the 'Rubber Stamp'

During the Maoist period and the early Deng years, before the NPC became the scene of rancorous debates, Western writings on the Chinese legislative system were generally so few and so brief that they barely justified the term 'model'. Nevertheless, these few early studies did share certain images and assumptions about power and process which I have chosen to label a Command model of policy-making. Lacking the empirical data necessary to flesh out a discussion of the real lawmaking process, Western scholars tended to focus far more on the constitutional formalities of the system, even while noting the harsher realities of power. Until the 1980s, moreover, the NPC's placidity did not seem to justify any such data gathering efforts.[2]

When they did discuss the actual process, however, Western and some Chinese scholars sketched power and process in very rigid terms, portraying lawmaking as a unified, tightly-run, top-down process in which political conflict is either assumed away or treated as unknowable for analytical purposes. The principal and agent in this reified model of lawmaking are the Party and the NPC. These institutions are often treated as distinct and separate, with the Party completely dominating and manipulating the legislature as one tool of political rule in much the same fashion that a carpenter employs a saw or a screwdriver. The Party exercises this control over the legislature principally through its power of appointments (the *nomenklatura* system), which ensures that only politically pliant delegates, behold to the Party, will gain seats in the legislature. The Command model stresses the fact that historically, regular people's congress delegates have been nominated by Party committees[3] to run in controlled elections at their respective local and national levels, and are not chosen through free, competitive elections.[4] In addition, the senior leaders of the NPC are either Communist Party elders or politically trustworthy non-Party luminaries. The image of the lawmaking process under the Command model is equally

---

2. See, for example, Ginsburgs (1963) and Cohen (1978).
3. Actually, a key question is which level of Party Committee selects the NPC delegates, since this may have an impact upon the degree of diversity among the delegates.
4. An excellent discussion of the mechanisms of Party control over People's Congress elections, and its resilience in the face of recent efforts by democracy activists to weaken this control, is in Nathan (1985), ch. 10.

16   The Politics of Lawmaking in Post-Mao China

straightforward: the law springs forth fully formed from the Party leadership and is dutifully ratified by the NPC, usually by unanimous vote. As a question of political mechanics and intra-Party division of labour, some authors who adhere to this viewpoint sometimes go so far as to suggest that the NPC is controlled specifically by the leaders of the Party Central Committee's Political-Legal Committee.[5] These leaders commission their staffs to draft the desired laws and submit them to the NPC or the State Council for passage.

> The Communist Party sets the whole [lawmaking] process in motion by issuing a directive calling for the introduction of legislation to regulate or safeguard a particular principle (e.g., democratic rights) or area (e.g., economic relations) . . . in response, the Politburo member Chairman of the Legislative Affairs Commission of the National People's Congress appoints a Special Committee for drafting the specific piece of legislation.[6]

> Whenever any important issue occurs in state affairs, what the party says goes. The NPC simply 'puts up a show' and 'unanimously approves', and that is all.[7]

Influenced by 'structural-functionalist' literature on comparative legislatures, some authors in the 1980s began to stress the political importance of the NPC as an organ of 'inclusion' and highlighted the 'rationalizing' effect of the NPC's non-policy-making functions.[8] These studies focused on the NPC's role as a symbol of regime legitimacy, or as a 'united front organ' expanding the Party's base of support by incorporating non-Party intellectuals, national minorities and other social notables into the formal machinery of the state. According to this image, the formalities of legislative debate are an important safety valve for the system, even if these debates do not ultimately affect the content of policy. NPC sessions allow interested parties to let off steam by voicing their opinions in a Party-controlled, Party-sanctioned forum.

> Essentially, the NPC has been a forum for learning about, supporting, and ratifying actions of the central leadership; it symbolizes the popular base of the regime and honors the politically favored deputies elected to it, but it has no real political power.[9]

---

5. This organization has also at times gone by the name 'Political-Legal Leading Group' (*Zhengfa Lingdao Xiaozu*). The Committee is discussed in Chapter 4.

6. Foster (1982), 411–14. In fact, Foster alternates between treating the Party as a unified actor, and stressing the impact which intra-elite struggle can have on overall codification policy. Two other important studies which assign a major role to the Central Political-Legal Committee are Hsia and Johnson (1986) and O'Brien (1987).   7. Wu Jialing (1980).

8. In the language of this literature, the NPC fits the model of a Third World or communist 'legitimizing legislature' which has a 'minimal' role in policy-making. See Loewenberg and Patterson (1979), 198. Several studies have stressed the rationalizing, inclusive or united front functions of the NPC's non-lawmaking functions. See Townsend (1974), 85, Gasper (1982), Baum (1986), O'Brien (1987 and 1989), Tsou Tang (1986a) and Womack (1984).

9. Wu Jialing (1980).

Inadequacies of the Command Model

The major shortcoming in Command model analyses is that they usually treat the Party Centre, implicitly or explicitly, as though it were basically united in its general conceptions about the lawmaking process, and capable of resolving specific legal drafting issues 'in-house'. The NPC was seen neither as a significant arena for the resolution of policy-making conflicts, nor as an organization led by a group of Party leaders with their own distinct policy agendas, anxious to advance those agendas by enhancing the NPC's role.[10] Instead it was largely assumed that law-related policy conflicts, if they arose, could be resolved within the confines of the Party apparatus, without recourse to the state lawmaking organs as adjunct arenas of political struggle. As a behavioural prediction, the Command model does not lead one to expect that lawmaking will be a conflictual process, especially in the NPC. One would certainly never expect to see the legislature vote down, significantly amend or greatly delay any draft which the CCP leadership—especially the Politburo—had already approved. Nor would the NPC be regarded as a notable avenue of political influence, and no politically sophisticated Chinese actor would be likely to waste their time trying to influence an important policy decision through the NPC. Instead, they would focus their attention and efforts where the real power lay, in the CCP apparatus and the State Council.

The Command model's indifference to lawmaking is in part rooted in an assumption that enacted laws are something distinct from, and inferior to, the real policy by which the Party rules society. A number of legal scholars and a few political scientists have discussed the Chinese cultural preference for uncodified norms rather than enacted law as a tool of social control. But these scholars by and large did not discuss the relationship between enacted law and national-level policy.[11] Some political scientists have highlighted the use of laws to confirm policy.[12] Others have stressed the symbolic aspect of laws, seldom if ever treating them as genuine vehicles for communicating policy. Rare is the discourse which assumes that an enacted law would be the documentary vehicle by which the Party leadership would actually chose to consider, debate and adopt a major *policy* departure. Yet this is precisely what has begun to happen in China since 1979.

---

10. This is largely the result of these authors' academic focus. The vast majority of authors on Chinese law have been legal scholars rather than political scientists, and have focused their research on the evolving constitutional mechanics of lawmaking and the substance of legal policy, rather than the role of political conflict in the lawmaking process. Two excellent examples of this type of analysis are Hsia and Johnson (1986), and Cohen (1978).
11. There are numerous studies of this distinction between social control by enacted law (*fa*) and by learned or inculcated social propriety (*li*). The classics are Schwartz (1957), Chu T'ung-tsu (1961), Li (1971), Leng Shao-chuan and Chiu Hungdah (1985) and Baum (1986).
12. O'Brien (1987), 292.

18   The Politics of Lawmaking in Post-Mao China

The 1980s: New Departures, but Some Lingering Images

Recent research on the NPC's history by O'Brien and others does indeed suggest that during the Maoist era, the lawmaking system did, in fact, function in a manner consistent with the Command model. The only notable challenge came during the 1956–57 Hundred Flowers Campaign, when some non-Party NPC delegates tried to expand radically the role of the NPC above and beyond CCP control. These efforts were crushed after July 1957 during the Anti-Rightist Campaign.[13]

Many aspects of the Command model retain their hold today, despite the evolution of an understanding of Chinese law and the Chinese policymaking process. And even though a handful of Western scholars undertook a reformulation of the NPC's role in the wake of the 1980s legislative debates, most writing on the topic nevertheless still rests on several key assumptions of the Command model or the image of the NPC as a 'united front' organ. Recent studies have, for example, stressed the clearer formal delineation of authority between legislative institutions, and the increased respect for the consultative procedures which are contained in the 1982 PRC State Constitution. Without actually invoking the name of Max Weber, these authors have characterized the NPC's new role as representing an important step toward a more 'rational-legal' style of governance in China, portraying the system as increasingly rational, regular, legalized, predictable, and inclusive, though not yet liberal.[14]

But despite widespread recognition that the NPC has expanded its role, few writings have directly addressed the question of the real allocation of influence among the NPC and the various other lawmaking organs in the Chinese system. Implicitly or explicitly, Western scholarship has largely maintained the top-down image of the process, even while stressing what appears to be a clearer, more regular and legalized division of labour between the Party, government and state apparatus. In the end, therefore, the behavioural predictions based on this 'new' image of the lawmaking system would not differ greatly from those based upon the 'old' image. One might expect there to be more public debates and a heightened attention to the formal rules in the lawmaking process. But for the disgruntled Chinese political actor, the NPC still would not look like a worthwhile arena of influence over policy. The assumption remains that policy disputes can still be resolved within Party arenas before they are sent down to the NPC, which accepts them with little complaint. And the Party leadership is still

---

13. On NPC involvement in this period see O'Brien (1987, 43–90, 145–77) and MacFarquhar (1960). For a sample of some of these dissident views, see the self-criticisms by Lo Lung-chi (1965) and Chang Po-chun (1965).

14. Womack (1984), Baum (1986), Tsou Tang (1986) and O'Brien (1987 and 1990). Partial exceptions are Solinger (1982) and La Dany (1984). On the concept of 'inclusiveness' in Marxist regimes, see Jowitt (1975).

portrayed as having a relatively clear, unified conception of the proper current and future role of the NPC in the lawmaking system.

However, the NPC debates of the mid-1980s, particularly the bitter public fights over the 1986 Bankruptcy Law, the 1986 Land Management Law[15] and the State-Owned Enterprise Law, made it clear that Western analysts of lawmaking and the legislature now required a different, more conflict-oriented set of assumptions. Conflict-oriented models raise a whole host of additional questions about policy-making. Who are the key actors? What are the main lines of cleavage in the system? Which issues are at stake and how are they resolved? The principal response of analysts was to embrace a new model which acknowledged this conflict, but preserved the tight top-down view of lawmaking and the NPC.

The Leadership Struggle Model

By the mid-1980s a few Western analyses of lawmaking and the NPC began to catch up with the rest of the field of Chinese political studies by employing 'factional' or Leadership Struggle models which had dominated the field since the onset of the Cultural Revolution. This shift represented an explicit acknowledgement that even though the Communist Party does, in some sense, 'control' the legislature (a truism), the Party leadership is nevertheless so split over policy issues that the legislative system could still serve as a significant adjunct arena for leadership political debate.[16]

Like the Command model, the Leadership Struggle model also assumes that the distribution of power in the system is very top-heavy, and policy-making is still very much a top-down process. The key actors who dominate policy-making are the senior thirty-five or so Central leaders. Western analysts have built a rich literature debating the complex of forces which motivate these senior leaders, including psycho-cultural orientations, personal jealousies, factional loyalties, bureaucratic-organizational ideologies and, of course, policy goals.[17] Regardless of what motivates the leaders,

---

15. I am indebted to Andrew Claster for pointing out the case of the Land Management Law, whose passage was delayed during the summer of 1985 owing to NPC resistance.
16. Solinger (1982).
17. The finest recent discussions of Chinese elite politics today characteristically combine two analytical models which were once considered distinct. The first model—called a 'factional model'—tends to be rooted in notions of paternalism in Russian or Chinese culture, and emphasizes the personal element in politics. Factional models treat elite struggle as the often amoral contention of top leaders and their patronage networks (the landmark studies are Pye [1981]; Nathan [1973]; Tsou Tang [1986b]; and MacFarquhar [1974 and 1983]). These networks, which penetrate various organizational, generational or geographic bases, are bound by ties of mutual obligation and dependence (*guanxi*). The various authors writing in this tradition differ greatly over whether or not such a factional system can reach a stable 'equilibrium' similar to the factional system of Japan's Liberal Democratic Party. The second model, with its roots in the study of Soviet politics, is Franklyn Griffiths 'tendency analysis'.

this model portrays lower levels as tightly bound to various central leaders (through factional or organizational networks), and highly responsive to their superiors' wishes. Policy formulation and deliberation within the government are dominated by the views of the central leaders who oversee a particular issue area, rather than the permanent organizational interests of the career bureaucrats who regularly deal with those issues. Issues rise and fall on the agenda in response to the political mood in Beijing. Policy proposals languish within the bureaucracy until a central leader pulls an idea to the top of the agenda in an effort to promote his or her own policy package. A relatively sophisticated form of the Leadership Struggle model might concede that lower levels of the government promote their own organizational interests and policy proposals, but would nevertheless portray these career bureaucrats as obsessive 'Peking-watchers'—unwilling to make a move without central blessing, quickly and carefully trimming their sails to the prevailing political winds coming from the Politburo. Stronger formulations of the elite politics model treat ministries, NPC delegates and establishment intellectuals as little more than 'stalking horses' for their respective central patrons.[18]

Despite this large set of common assumptions, scholars employing a leadership struggle paradigm to analyse the NPC and the lawmaking system have differed over the role of the NPC and its leadership in elite politics. Frances Hoar Foster, in the first Western study of post-Mao Chinese lawmaking, documented that the state of play in elite politics had a direct effect on the central leadership's overall attitude towards reliance upon enacted law, rather than Party edict, as a tool of governance.[19] Dorothy Solinger's pathbreaking study of leadership economic policy debates at the late 1970s–early 1980s NPC sessions was the first Western study to argue that the NPC had become a serious arena for political conflict and policy debate among top leaders.[20] Her work revealed how senior leaders were using the public occasion of an NPC session to attack the economic policies of their opponents. Solinger's research aim, however, was not to analyse lawmaking politics or the political orientations of the NPC leadership itself. Nor was her work directed at identifying any distinctive policy-making role for the NPC.

Later, however, journalists and some academics began portraying the top

---

Griffiths de-emphasizes the personal element and portrays elite political disputes as conflicts between enduring alternative policy packages, or 'patterns of articulation.' In contrast to tight factional or patronage networks, Griffiths posits only the existence of loose coalitions of like-minded leaders at various levels of the system and argues that officials are 'unlikely to be fully aware of the common thrust and consequences of their activity'. Griffiths model has the advantage of demanding fewer data about the private attitudes, personal ties and organizational bases of the top leaders. See Griffiths (1971), Lieberthal (1974 and 1978), Oksenberg and Goldstein (1974), Solinger (1982 and 1984).

18. For analyses of this type see Parris Chang (1975) and Goldman (1981).
19. Foster (1982).   20. Solinger (1982).

NPC leadership as key actors in a continuing 'two-line struggle' over China's political and economic reforms since 1978. This was seen as a complex struggle in which calls for increased rule by law and an enlivened lawmaking process became unique weapons for attacking opponents and their policies. In late 1978 and 1979 Deng Xiaoping, Peng Zhen and others revived the NPC lawmaking apparatus and pushed China's long-awaited first Criminal Code through to completion. In the process, they further undercut the authority of party Chairman Hua Guofeng, Vice-Chairman Wang Dongxing and other members of the so-called Public-Security Left leadership faction which had directly succeeded Mao.[21] But Deng and Peng's co-operation was fragile, and by the middle and late 1980s, legislative politics were often portrayed as a duel between a 'reformist' State Council, led by Deng's erstwhile protégé, Premier Zhao Ziyang, and a 'conservative' NPC led by Standing Committee Chairman Peng Zhen. Deprived of power in the State Council and increasingly weak in the Politburo, Peng and several other 'conservative' Party elders took advantage of the NPC's strengthened role as an organ of 'socialist democracy', and fanned popular opposition to key economic reforms. Journalists and scholars at this time who adhered to the elite politics model tended to portray the NPC, especially its Standing Committee, as a rather pliant tool of Peng Zhen and his allies.[22] After Tiananmen the two-line interpretation was revived, this time with the political orientations of the NPC leaders reversed. Now, younger conservatives such as Jiang Zemin and Li Peng were locked in struggle with politically and economically more reformist NPC leaders including Wan Li and Qiao Shi.

The Leadership Struggle Model: Strengths and Weaknesses

Certainly there is good deal of truth to the elite politics view, and personal relations among top leaders do help define the political relations between the institutions they lead. These relations also influence the political 'mood' in which all forms of policy-making are carried out.

But the Leadership Struggle model has always required some rather farfetched assumptions about policy-making. As Lieberthal and Oksenberg have argued, this model overstates the centrality of amoral struggles over naked power, and understates the significance of debates over ideas or organizational interests (indeed, they choose to refer to this model simply as the Power model).[23] Also, with its top-down view of policy-making, this

---

21. For examples of studies which analyse the NPC debates in terms of their use in leadership factional struggles, see Parris Chang (1983 and 1987), Foster (1982), 411–13, Domes (1985), 169, LaDany (1986) and Delfs (1987).
22. For reports emphasizing this 'reformer-conservative' line and the role of Peng Zhen, see especially La Dany (1986), Delfs (1987) and Parris Chang (1987).
23. Lieberthal and Oksenberg (1987), 13–16.

model inevitably exaggerates the senior leaders' attention to, understanding of, involvement in and—most importantly—*control over* the lengthy and detailed process of building a major policy. The case studies researched here provide ample evidence to indicate that there are limits on all these sources of the top leadership's power.

The elite politics model, because of its focus on amoral power rather than policy as an object of struggle, also does not yield very clear or precise insights about the content of the policies such a process is likely to produce. The only thing that can be said for certain is that this process is likely to produce policies which are calculated to enhance the power of the key central leaders involved in policy-making. But this statement, of course, borders on tautology, since virtually any policy produced could be interpreted as serving the interests of one or another top leaders.[24]

Perhaps, by stressing power over policy as an object of struggle, the elite politics model best reveals the 'symbolic' aspects of policy-making or lawmaking. Policies or laws are important only as they enhance the power of a leader or a faction, regardless of how effective they are in addressing 'real' problems in society. This model, therefore, suggests many symbolic political aspects of law which contribute to leadership struggles: the passage of a particular law can serve as a *milestone* which publicizes the progress a leader has made in promoting their policy programme; or as a *scorecard* indicating which leader is ahead in a power struggle; or, as in the December 1978 battles between Deng Xiaoping and then-Party Chief Hua Guofeng, 'law' can be a *slogan* whose very mention is certain to erode the legitimacy of leaders such as Hua whose power rests conspicuously on other than legal bases.

The Organizational or Bureaucratic Politics Model

Increasingly in the 1980s, students of policy-making in China and other socialist states began to borrow from Western studies of the influence of 'bureaucratic' or 'organizational politics' on policy-making. The organizational politics theorists focused on bureaucratic cleavages and inter-agency tension as a source of 'bounds' on the 'rationality' or 'coherence' of policy-making. They posited ministries, bureaus and territorial governments as the key actors in the system and focus on how they employ their power bases in pursuit of their political goals. The goals of ministries and bureaus are usually a function of relatively stable organizational 'missions' or 'ideologies,' which define the organization's role in the system, the problems which it considers important, the preferred range of methods for dealing with

---

24. As a theoretical matter, this unfalsifiability alone should alert us to the limits of this particular model.

those problems and the terms by which it judges its success or failure.[25] The motivations of political leaders in territorial bureaucratic units (in China, provincial and local level Party Committees and governments) are more difficult to capture with a single appealing characterization such as an 'organizational mission'. These motivations include, among others: local economic growth and development; 'kingdom building' (increased individual power at the local level coupled with greater local autonomy from Central authorities); increased access to Central resources; and local leaders' desire to promote their careers by impressing Central authorities.[26]

In contrast to elite-dominated models, which assume a great concentration of power at the Central level, the Organizational Politics model highlights the fragmentation of power and authority among ministries, bureaus and territorial units. Each organization has its own unique and fluctuating package of power resources, including unequal bureaucratic ranks, and unequal access to bargaining resources such as money, goods, territory, personnel and access to top leaders. The Central leadership is by no means lacking in resources to control policy, of course. The Chinese Central leadership can call upon ideology, the civilian and military coercive apparatuses, financial and propaganda apparatuses, various meeting and document systems, personnel management systems (the *nomenklatura* system), and a variety of overlapping and competing policy implementation networks, to achieve compliance with its directives.[27] The allocation of power, moreover, is not only complex and multi-dimensional, but also constantly shifting. In the post-Mao era, for example, the Central leadership has witnessed a terrific decline in the effectiveness of its ideological and financial control levers, but has been partially compensated by a tremendous increase in the information resources available to it (in the form of statistics and feasibility studies, for example).[28] Recent studies have also moved away from a simple 'centralization–decentralization' model of this allocation of power, and are suggesting a more curvilinear model of power distribution: the fragmentation of power is greatest in the middle levels of the system (at the ministerial and provincial level), but at the Central and sub-provincial levels, 'this is a system characterized by extraordinary concentrations of power'.[29]

25. Simon (1964), Mohr (1973). More generally, see Downs (1967) and Allison (1971). On organizational missions and ideologies in Chinese bureaucracy, see Oksenberg (1983).
26. The literature on the powers and motivations of territorial units in China is far too big to be surveyed here. For representative recent studies of the range of territorial officials' goals and political motivations, see Solinger (1986), Naughton (1987) and Lampton (1987). For some classic discussions, see the following debate over the degree of Central versus local control over financial resources: Donnithorne (1972) and Donnithorne and Lardy (1976). On the topic of local officials and their strategies for getting ahead, see Oksenberg (1970).
27. For a discussion of power in Chinese bureaucracies, see Lieberthal and Oksenberg (1987), 135–68.   28. See Lieberthal, 'Introduction' in Lieberthal and Lampton (1992).
29. *Ibid.*, 31.

Yet, even while noting these concentrations of power at the Centre, the organizational politics theorists are distinguished from other students of China by the stress they place upon the limits on Central power, and the corresponding constraints on the top leadership's ability to develop coherent policies and promote their implementation. The emerging image of the policy-making process is distinctly less totalitarian or top-down than the view assumed by either the Command or Leadership Struggle models. The top Central decision-makers face persistent dilemmas of forging policy in this divided system. These top leaders are alternately advised and lobbied by a variety of senior advisors and key organizational players, who vie for leadership attention in a relatively free-wheeling game of 'competitive persuasion'.[30] On the one hand, the Centre's policies must be as clear, coherent and consensus-based as possible, in order to heighten their chances of being obeyed at lower levels. On the other hand, ministries and localities often show great tenacity in defending and promoting their own policy preferences and forestalling the concessions needed to forge such a clear consensus position. Consequently, despite the apparent coercive resources available to the Central leadership, studies of China's economic policy-making and implementation have increasingly highlighted the limits of coercive implementation, stressing instead the Centre's inevitable preference for bargaining over tangible resources, co-optation of lower levels and consensus-building.[31] David Lampton, a major exponent of the Organizational Politics model, succinctly summarizes the difference between this and the elite politics view, arguing that the Chinese system is 'not one in which the few at the top generally choose to unilaterally impose their solutions on large subordinate bureaucracies and territorial units'.[32]

Effects on the Content of Policy

More than either the Command or Leadership Struggle models, the Organizational Politics model provides a relatively clear, recognizable and even falsifiable set of forecasts about the nature of the policy-making process and the types of policies the system is prone to produce. Actual policy proposals appear on the agenda not because they are 'rational' from the standpoint of any vaguely defined 'public good', but because they are 'rational' from the standpoint of satisfying the goals and missions of the sponsoring organizational unit.[33] Given the heavy stress the model places on bargaining and consensus-building, policy-making, predictably, is slow, plodding and cumbersome. Policy differences are resolved through near

---

30. The term 'competitive persuasion' has been coined by Nina Halpern. See Halpern (1986) and her contribution to Lieberthal and Lampton (1992).
31. Lampton (1987), Lieberthal and Oksenberg (1987 and 1988), and Lieberthal and Lampton (1992).   32. Lampton (1983), 17.
33. Downs (1967), Allison (1969), Simon (1957 and 1964) and Lindblom (1959).

endless lobbying, compromise, consultation, negotiation, side-payments and groping for acceptable alternatives among many organizations.[34] Incremental policy change predominates, and sudden, radical policy changes are rare and difficult indeed. As Lieberthal and Oksenberg's case studies of major energy projects indicate, this process can be agonizingly slow, often taking decades.[35] Lampton argues, in fact, that in such a system, immobilism is often so great that a crisis can actually play a constructive role as a consensus-inducing condition.[36]

The Organizational Model: Strengths and Weaknesses

With its stress upon the important role of bureaucracies, in particular the State Council's ministries, Central Party Offices and the NPC permanent bureaucracy, the Organizational Politics model has greatly enlightened understanding of the lawmaking system, its power and politics. This study relies heavily upon this viewpoint in Chapters 3 to 6 as it sketches out the institutional development and sources of power in China's post-Mao lawmaking system. One of its central arguments is that much of the NPC's growth in power can be better understood in organizational-bureaucratic terms than as a result of a liberalizing preference for the rule of law. Bureaucratic cleavages and inter-organizational consensus-building are also frequent, recurrent processes in the politics of the lawmaking process. To anticipate the discussion somewhat, the case studies will show quite clearly that the largest share of the basic contents of Chinese laws is defined during the inter-agency bargaining stage of the process, and not the Party or NPC reviews. Yet the few recent Western studies of lawmaking have paid little attention to the important place of the inter-organizational consensus-building process in determining the content of laws, often preferring to look at the NPC in isolation from the State Council and the rest of the system. Moreover, as predicted by the organizational politics theorists, this process of 'internal fermentation' (*neibu yunniang*) is extremely prone to stalemate and immobilism, and inter-ministerial review periods of over a decade are not uncommon.

The Organizational Politics model also helps reveal several key cleavages in the lawmaking system which hamper consensus-building. One such cleavage which plays a particularly important role throughout the lawmaking system is the tension between codifying organizations and reforming or restructuring organizations. When post-Mao Chinese discuss the concept of law, one meaning they often attach is that of a policy which is explicit, codified, relatively stable and resistant to the whims of individual leaders.

---

34. Lampton (1974, 1983 and 1986), Oksenberg (1982) and Lieberthal and Oksenberg (1987 and 1988). 35. Lieberthal and Oksenberg (1986).
36. Lampton (1983).

26   The Politics of Lawmaking in Post-Mao China

Those organizations whose mission it is to codify laws are often concerned with creating a policy document which can remain unchanged for a long time.[37] But during periods of rapid economic and political structural reform, there may be inherent contradictions between organizations whose mission is to promote rapid economic and political reform,[38] and organizations such as the NPC Standing Committee whose mission is to debate, review and revise draft laws carefully in an effort to produce 'stable', 'authoritative', codified policy documents. The former organizations, as these case studies show, prefer flexibility in policy-making, and fear that excessively precise and stable laws may preclude their ability to innovate.[39] As revealed below, this bureaucratic cleavage became particularly acute during the latter stages of drafting the State-Owned Industrial Enterprises Law.

While the Organizational Politics model clearly provides a wealth of potential insights into the politics of lawmaking, it is also not without serious shortcomings. For example, it is unclear what is the most appropriate way to apply this perspective, with its assumption that ministries are more or less unitary actors with their own coherent cultures, goals and ideologies, in analysing the role of a broad-based legislature with nearly 3,000 members. Can a legislature, even a legislature whose members are all approved by the ruling Party, truly have a common 'mission'? As suggested above, it is true that legislative organs as codifying bodies may have certain procedural orientations, including a preference for proper legal procedure, prolonged discussion and careful drafting of stable, relatively unchanging policy documents. And it might be reasonable, on the other hand, to describe some of the permanent and specialized subcommittees and staff under the NPC Standing Committee as organizations with missions. But the evidence about delegate activities and voting patterns in this study clearly contradict any notion that the NPC or its Standing Committee could have specific policy orientations similar to a ministerial mission.[40]

The Organizational Politics model's image of the policy process, the ebb and flow of policy-making, presents a second and more serious problem. Its focus on inter-agency consensus building, with a strong bias toward incrementalism, is only half right. It is undeniably true, and the case studies in this book make clear, that the lawmaking process does include a prolonged period of tedious inter-ministerial negotiation. What is more, it is this glacial process which carves the basic outlines of a given law's content.

37. See, for example, Chen Pixian (1988).
38. For example, the State Commission for Restructuring the Economic System (SCRES).
39. This issue of how precisely to codify a piece of 'reform' legislation became an important source of concern to SCRES officials in the latter stages of the debate over the State-Owned Industrial Enterprise Law. This point is discussed at some length in Chapter 8.
40. Unfortunately, limits on access and the time available for interviewing made it impossible to address this interesting question of NPC subcommittee 'missions'.

But not all politics is stultifying slow negotiation, even in China. Nor is all policy change incremental. Major new departures and innovations do occur. Yet the Organizational Politics model is at its worst when trying to explain non-incremental, radical policy innovations and major surges and reversals in the policy-making process. Efforts to explain such rapid changes within an organizational politics paradigm often seem to require the analyst to invoke actors, events and situations which actually fall well outside the core elements of the organizational paradigm. These may include the intervention of an extremely powerful individual leader, or a systemic crisis, or international forces, or the activities of groups or policy networks which transcend the bureaucratic system and its more narrow organizational interests.[41] Analysts of legislation in the U.S. Government have increasingly pointed out this flaw in the classic incrementalist view.[42] Incrementalist theories fail to capture the fluidity of politics, and therefore cannot explain why 'political lightning' can sometimes strike, transforming a long-dead policy proposal and pushing it to the top of the agenda.[43]

By focusing the analyst's attention on bureaucratic actors and their relationships to the exclusion of most other types of actors, the Organizational Politics model suggests that all policy-making must take place under a bureaucratic roof, and every idea must have a bureaucratic 'owner'. Neither the individual policy entrepreneur nor the idea itself occupy any significant place in this model. It does not suggest that policy ideas can have a 'life of their own' apart from their organizational patron. The policy proposal is seen as an object, a tool, a means to an end, a servant of the organizational actor—used by the organization to serve its own purposes. Using only this model, it is not possible to account for ideas spreading freely, to account for a policy proposal which simply catches fire on its own, independent from any particular organization and its goals, cropping up again and again as the proposed solution for a variety of perhaps unrelated problems. There is no 'diffusion' of ideas, only the tedious bureaucratic door-to-door salesmanship of the organization's policy product.[44]

---

41. A concrete example may help clarify this argument. In this study, we would be hard pressed to account for the appearance of so radical a departure as a bankruptcy law solely on the basis of organizational politics, since none of the organizations really saw the proposal as central to its mission. Inter-ministerial negotiation might account for how the law evolved during its drafting, but it cannot explain how such an unprecedented proposal got on the agenda in the first place.

42. Kingdon (1984), 8–88. See also Schulman (1975).   43. Kingdon (1984), 85–8.

44. One possible explanation for such a diffusion of ideas within the organizational politics paradigm would be the existence of 'policy communities' or 'issue networks'—groups of policy analysts or advocates whose common interest in government policy on a particular issue leads them to establish enduring ties which cut across organizational lines. Hugh Heclo (1977 and 1978) has suggested that in the U.S. system, such issue networks are an important corrective to ministerial parochialism, and such networks are especially common among staff officials (e.g. budget, financial, personnel officials) because of the executive branch's strong interest in promoting common procedures for these tasks. Such networks, which increased in number

The 'Garbage Can' Model

One recent Western model of policy-making which suggests a more fluid image of the process is Cohen, Olsen and March's Garbage Can model of organizational choice.[45] This model admittedly rests on some organizational assumptions which do not always accurately describe the Chinese case. At the same time, it highlights some interesting core features of the legislative system, focuses attention on some interesting questions of policy process, and explains certain unusual types of policy-making behaviour which cannot be accounted for by the three previous models. This rather complex model is therefore presented, in part, as a heuristic device.

The authors of the Garbage Can model begin by questioning three traditional assumptions about most complex organizations, such as governments, and how they make decisions. The key assumptions are that organizations are vehicles for solving well-defined problems, and that they have 'well-defined goals', 'well-defined [decision-making] technology', and 'substantial participant involvement in the affairs of the organization'. The Garbage Can model, by contrast, is intended to apply to a certain type of complex organization which the authors call an 'organized anarchy'. They argue that no organization approximates an organized anarchy all the time, but almost all organizations approximate one some of the time, perhaps even a good deal of the time.

An organized anarchy has three defining features. First, its goal preferences are unclear, even to the organization itself. It is also unable to establish a clear ranking among the numerous goals being simultaneously pursued by the organization and its various subunits (it lacks a single utility function). Rather than establishing its goals in advance and then developing a strategy to pursue them, a variety of potential goals (or problems requiring resolution) coexist, competing for the attention of the various parts of the organization. Secondly, the organization's decision-making system is 'ambiguous', that is, it lacks relatively clear rules and procedures for making decisions. Even long-standing participants do not

---

and importance during Zhao Ziyang's tenure as Premier, could certainly be a conduit for the freer propagation of policy proposals which were not parochially tied to one organization. My objection (and perhaps it is no more than a semantic objection) to including them as part of a model of organizational politics or institutional pluralism is that such extra-agency or cross-agency networks seem to come from outside the central tenets of organizational politics model—like crises, powerful interventionist leaders and international forces. These networks are indeed 'pluralistic' in their ability to put forward new demands from outside traditional channels. But are they really 'institutional' or 'organizational'? Or are we bending the organizational politics model to account for an important new behaviour which the model did not foresee?

45. Kingdon (1984), especially chs. 1,4,6 and 8. The origins of this conception are in Cohen, March and Olsen (1972). For non-specialist readers, Smith (1988), chs. 1 and 3 presents a similar conception of politics, which he calls a 'power float'.

necessarily know in advance how a given issue may be resolved, by which actors, in which decision-making arenas or by which procedures. The future agenda of a potential decision-maker or decision-making arena is also unpredictable. Thirdly, the key decision-makers in the organized anarchy are not all sustained or regular participants in the process. At any given time, or with respect to any given problem, it is difficult to predict which of the potential participants will be available to take part in the decision, and how serious their involvement will be.

In a nutshell, the organized anarchy lacks clear and predictable direction, rules and leadership. Yet, work goes on. Decision-makers and other workers show up each day and involve themselves in meetings and tasks which are advanced—perhaps even completed—towards some end. All this activity, quite naturally, must produce something. What it principally produces, according to the authors of the Garbage Can model, is more of the stuff of organizational activity: recognized problems, potential solutions, opportunities to make choices (decisions), and potential decision-makers anxious to get involved in making them.

At this point, Cohen, March and Olsen take a giant step away from these traditional decision-making models. 'Rational' or 'bounded rationality' (including Organizational Politics) models all posit a common decision-making sequence: problem recognition; ranking of goals and values; evaluation of alternatives, and selection of a value-maximizing (or satisficing) solution. Such structured, sequential decision-making is by definition impossible for an organized anarchy. And so, taking their metaphor of 'fluidity' a step further, the authors instead suggest thinking of the decision-making process in these systems in the image of three or four more or less independent 'streams' produced by the organization: problems, potential solutions, and opportunities for choice. For purposes of analysing governments, John Kingdon has also suggested a fourth, slightly different stream: of political moods or balances of power.[46]

Stated in more concrete terms, governments constantly face a stream of problems, some of which are viewed as especially urgent or ripe for solution at any given time, some of which go largely unnoticed for long periods. Fortunately the system also produces, more or less independently, a stream of available solutions (policy proposals). These solutions could be used to address one, two or perhaps even more of the currently recognized problems. Needless to say, any complex organization such as a government also has a stream of opportunities for making choices or decisions. These include meetings, legislative sessions, elections, annual budgets, five-year plans, major projects, regular annual legislative bills which are awaiting passage, and so on.

Under ideal circumstances, the organization actually resolves a problem

---

46. Kingdon (1984), 92, 93.

30 The Politics of Lawmaking in Post-Mao China

when the various streams intersect or 'flow together'. For this to happen, a problem must be perceived as urgent and solvable. Simultaneously, a suitable policy solution must be available, the political mood (or balance of power) must be propitious for attacking the problem with the preferred solution, and an appropriate opportunity for choice must be at hand. Unfortunately, such an auspicious mix of circumstances is rare indeed. Most of the time, the organization (or government) produces only some of the conditions necessary for a successful choice. This leads to some interesting, even bizarre political behaviour which violates key assumptions of 'rational' or even 'bounded rationality' decision-making. Cohen, March and Olsen note some examples of this behaviour:

... (organized anarchies) can be viewed ... as collections of choices looking for problems, issues and feelings looking for decision situations in which they might be aired, solutions looking for issues to which they might be the answer, and decision makers looking for work.

For the purposes of this study, the most interesting aspects of the model are the research questions and insights it generates about the process which arises in an organized anarchy. For example, while these streams of problems, proposals, choice opportunities and political moods are described as 'independent', this does not mean the system is governed largely by chance.[47] Quite the contrary, some of the most interesting insights and questions generated by this model concern the politics of just how the various streams of problems, policies, political moods and choice opportunities are brought together. The model leads us to ask, for example, how a long latent problem finally begins to receive attention. How does an old policy proposal get linked to a newly recognized problem? Why does an issue get addressed in one of several potential decision-making arenas? And how is the involvement of one particular set of decision-makers, rather than another, accounted for in deciding a problem?

One example of how the Garbage Can model can focus attention on interesting aspects of the policy process is Kingdon's study of agenda-setting in the U.S., which illustrates the important role performed by 'policy entrepreneurs' in linking streams of policy proposals (potential solutions) to streams of recognized problems. These policy entrepreneurs, whose chief defining characteristic is persistent, obsessive devotion to selling their pet policy proposal ('the ability to talk a dog off a meatwagon', in Kingdon's words), work patiently to forge a link in the public mind between their policy proposal and a high profile problem. Commonly these entrepreneurs will try to convince policy makers facing a variety of seemingly unrelated problems that the entrepreneur's pet solution is the

---

47. Though one advantage of the Garbage Can model is that—unlike many organizational politics theories—it clearly recognizes the importance of political luck.

answer to all their prayers. In another approach, legislative entrepreneurs will often seize on a choice opportunity, such as a popular legislative bill which seems certain to pass (for example, in the U.S., the annual defence authorization bill), and try to attach a rider amendment supporting the entrepreneur's pet cause, regardless of that cause's intrinsic connection to the subject of the original bill.

With respect to the effect of lawmaking process on the content of laws, the Garbage Can model provides a useful corrective to the all-pervasive incrementalism and gradualism forecast by the Organizational Politics model. Its treatment of problems, solutions, moods and choice opportunities as analytically separate means that the Garbage Can model is far more open to explaining non-incremental policy change than is the Organizational Politics model. By not automatically linking all the problems and solutions 'floating about' in the system to specific bureaucratic organizations, the model sensitizes the analyst to the importance of ideas themselves, and to the possibilities for individual entrepreneurship. In an era of rapid reform, this is an important analytical plus.

The Chinese Lawmaking System as an 'Organized Anarchy'

Without a doubt, the biggest problem with trying to apply the Garbage Can model to the Chinese lawmaking process is portraying the Chinese system as an organized anarchy. To declare suddenly that the Chinese Communist Party-state is really best described as lacking clear leadership, policy goals or decision-making processes requires an extremely long stride away from the traditional images of the People's Republic; images which have been so heavily influenced by hierarchical, ideologically-charged 'totalitarian' or 'Mao-in-command' models.

There are also powerful empirical arguments to support the current predominance of elite-centred and bureaucratic models of the Chinese policy-making process. Tiananmen and the 'one child per couple' policy brutally illustrate that, at least on some key issues, the senior Chinese leadership can reach a clear decision and arrange for it to be carried out. The leadership also has a great deal of influence over which problems will find a place on the government's agenda and, in particular, which will remain 'non-issues'.[48] Many, perhaps most policy proposals (solutions) do not seem to circulate freely outside the control of central bureaucrats—at least not nearly as freely as they do in countries with less censored media. Obviously, not all Chinese policy-making is likely to be as wide-open, non-incremental and serendipitous as the Garbage Can model would suggest.

There are other shortcomings of the Garbage Can model which require, at a minimum, that it is augmented with other models, in particular the

---

48. On the concept of a 'non-issue', see Bachrach and Baratz (1962).

Organizational Politics model. Unlike the Leadership Struggle and Organizational Politics models, the Garbage Can model does not give any clear insights into which are the key actors in the system. Nor does it suggest any particular motivation for an actor's behaviour, let alone one with the commonsense appeal of the 'organizational mission'. At the same time, I would argue that a number of aspects of China's current lawmaking system do closely approximate the characteristics of an organized anarchy. As the political and legal reforms of the 1980s and 1990s have eroded and decentralized China's policy-making system, and made the boundaries of that system increasingly permeable to more political actors, many of the political processes of lawmaking begin to approximate the behaviour suggested by the Garbage Can model. The following quick points are discussed in greater detail later in the book.

First, I would argue that the Chinese lawmaking system does indeed have an increasingly ill-defined (that is, high ambiguous) set of decision-making institutions and processes.[49] Formal constitutional provisions and the institutional division of labour among lawmaking institutions remain highly unclear, despite considerable efforts at development since 1979. Moreover, with these lawmaking institutions evolving rapidly and seeking to establish new and more influential roles for themselves, few informal rules or norms have developed either. Nowhere is this procedural ambiguity better illustrated than in the relationships between China's various state and Party policy documents, including laws, and the organizations which promulgate them. Decisions over which types of policy issues are to be decided in which of the various decision-making arenas (such as the Party Centre, the State Council, the NPC, its Standing Committee or the Supreme People's Court), must be separately negotiated for each issue. The formal constitutional ambiguities of lawmaking are discussed in much greater detail in Chapter 3.

This ambiguity is exacerbated by the ill-defined relationship between the formal legal system and the Communist Party. The perennial debate over the relative authoritativeness of 'laws' versus Party 'policy', a debate which has raged since the earliest years of the People's Republic, has never been resolved with any useful clarity. Many Party leaders and legal scholars have argued that laws possess a special authoritativeness and stability because they reflect the Party's distilled wisdom and experience, developed in carrying out a policy over a long period.[50] Since 1978, more and more important

---

49. I develop this argument about the 'ambiguity' of the lawmaking system in Chapter 3. As I argue in that chapter, it may be the case that the lawmaking system has a more 'ill-defined' or 'ambiguous' decision-making system than many other sectors of the Chinese decision-making system, in large part because of the rapidly growing yet still ill-defined role of the NPC and its Standing Committee.
50. For some excellent examples of this important debate, see Gao Wenxiang (1979), Sun Guohua (1979) and Zhang Jin (1979).

Bureaucracies, 'Organized Anarchies' and Inadvertent Transitions 33

policy issues which used to be addressed by Party edict are being addressed by state laws. But the Party has never resolved this authoritativeness debate by taking the above assertion to its appropriate logical conclusion and officially declaring state law superior to Party policy.[51] In procedural terms, just exactly what is meant by the truism that 'the Party leads lawmaking work' is increasingly unclear, as shown in Chapter 4.

There is also considerable ambiguity and disagreement among China's lawmaking leaders and institutions concerning the appropriate roles for these lawmaking organs. One issue, alluded to above, concerns the degree of legislative detail and precision which is appropriate for lawmaking in a developing or reforming system. Senior Party leaders who have also held high-ranking posts within the NPC, such as the late NPC Vice-Chairman Chen Pixian, have often stressed the need to enhance the 'stability' and 'authoritativeness' of law by approaching the task with care, deliberation and precision. Chen in particular stressed what Chinese legal scholars call the 'experience-based theory of lawmaking' (*jingyan lifa lun*), which argues that lawmaking should lag well behind reform experience. By contrast, Deng Xiaoping's remarks on lawmaking often seemed almost cavalier by comparison, calling for China to adopt quickly a number of general, flexible laws, which could be revised later as experience is gained.[52] Is it the NPC's duty to try to foresee a wide variety of contingencies and address them specifically in the draft laws it reviews? Or should the NPC pass codes which are more vague, and abdicate the power over the details to other policy-making and implementing bodies?

More concretely, NPC activism in recent years has proven quite controversial within the senior leadership, and has evoked considerable resentment, particularly within China's executive branch, the State Council. In a 1986 internal address to the NPC Standing Committee, the late Politburo Member and NPC Standing Committee Chairman Peng Zhen noted with some pride that the NPC was no longer a 'rubber stamp' legislature as in the past. In fact, Peng alluded derisively to 'some comrades' who 'wished' the NPC would be 'more of a rubber stamp'.[53] More recently, such senior leaders as Party Chief Jiang Zemin, and former NPC Standing Committee Chairmen Wan Li and Qiao Shi have voiced conflicting views on the NPC and its role. Clearly, there is a great deal of ambiguity in the system concerning the evolving roles of the NPC and other lawmaking bodies.

---

51. The current official formulation, as stated in the 1982 Communist Party Constitution, is simply that 'the Party carries on its activities within the bounds of law', a formulation which takes advantage of the ambiguity in the Chinese over the question of whether the Party actually *does* obey the law or simply *should* obey the law. Thus, it still begs the question of how to resolve any clear conflict between Party policy and the law.

52. For a comparison of Chen and Deng's remarks on the subject, see Chen (1988) and Deng's speech to the 1978 Third Plenum. Again, for an example of this problem in action, see Chapter 8 on the State Enterprises Law.

53. Peng's speech is analysed at length in Chapter 4.

As a result of the muddying of organizational relationships since 1978, the lawmaking system is looking less and less like a coherent system. Not only has the NPC been able to build itself as an increasingly autonomous institution under ever less well-defined Party leadership, the system as a whole is increasingly fragmenting into a set of inter-related decision-making 'arenas'. The three major arenas through which all major laws must pass—the State Council, the Party Centre, and the NPC—are all characterized by their own unique constellations of powers and interests. This is not to suggest these three arenas are equal in importance—the Party Centre is still by far the most important. But as the case studies illustrate, lawmaking decisions coming out of the Party Centre are far less carefully defined than in the past, and are far less likely to be 'the final word' on the topic. As the Garbage Can model would forecast, this increasing ambiguity among lawmaking arenas invites those actors who lose in one arena to try again to win in another. The policy which is turned down in the State Council and Politburo arenas may be reinstated while the law is under consideration by the NPC. Likewise, those actors who dislike the way a law has been amended in the NPC may also seek to kill the implementation of the offending passages when the law is turned back to the State Council or local governments for implementation.

More generally, during the 1980s and 1990s the larger Chinese policymaking system began to develop a somewhat freer stream of policy proposals (solutions). Policy proposals became much easier to float, and less tightly wedded to individual ministries and their missions than in the past, in large part due to the rise of policy think-tanks and an unprecedentedly open popular and academic press. This important development of the post-Mao era, which is often overlooked in the popular press reporting on China, has encouraged a much more entrepreneurial style of policymaking, especially on the part of policy intellectuals.[54] Chapter 7 on the drafting of the Bankruptcy Law provides an illustration of this new policy entrepreneurialism which is truly dramatic.

As these points illustrate, the Chinese legislative system, despite its many closed and hierarchical features, does in many ways approximate an organized anarchy as described by the authors of the Garbage Can model. Organizational goals are often unclear, decision-making processes and inter-organizational relationships are ill-defined and rapidly evolving, and the stream of policy proposals flows more freely than ever. Consequently, as the case studies show, the process of lawmaking on many occasions looks very much like the politics suggested by the Garbage Can model. The insights of this model will also help to explain better those

---

54. The best recent work on this point has been the studies of Chinese economists done by Nina Halpern, who apparently has also found the Garbage Can model a useful heuristic device. See, for example, Halpern (1986 and 1992).

moments when the system produces non-incremental policy change of a type which is not well explained by the Organizational Politics model. They also spotlight several new, more open features of China's policy-making system which encourage consideration of the system's long-term evolution and prospects for fundamental change.

'Inadvertant Transition'?: Policy-making Changes, Institutional Growth and Democratic Prospects

Most sinologists are not interested in China's lawmaking institutions and processes solely because of what they reveal about China's broader policy-making system, but because of the insights they can provide concerning China's potential for moving towards a less autocratic system. Models of the policy process, however, are not typically formulated in a manner which generates many insights into how authoritarian systems might make the transition to more open or liberal systems. Most models, including those used here, tend to treat political systems as static, and focus more on the statist elements of the policy apparatus than the forces which change state–society relations or expand participation and accountability. This lack of a well-developed theoretical link between studies of policy-making and studies of system transition is as ironic as it is unfortunate, for the link between the two seems fairly natural. Much of what scholars and laypersons really mean by the 'democratization' of an authoritarian system involves making fundamental changes in the patterns of policy-making: by institutionalizing a more decentralized process, opening up debate, enhancing transparency, broadening popular consultation and participation, and establishing formal and informal accountability of policy makers to the citizenry.

This is not meant to reduce the definition of democratization to mere policy-making reform. Democratization also requires a full range of reforms toward qualitatively much broader and equitable popular participation and effective accountability anchored in free, fair, competitive elections. Obviously China, like other authoritarian states, will continue to fall far short of social scientists' notions of democracy until top policy makers, including legislators, are genuinely electorally accountable to the public. Just as obviously, the decision to cross such an electoral rubicon, if it is ever crossed at all, will have to be taken by Party-state leaders and institutions which are far more powerful than China's legislature is at present (though legislative leaders and institutions would almost certainly be involved). Still, short of electoral reform, many of the key institutional changes in legislative politics which this study spotlights through its use of the Organizational Politics and Garbage Can models are drawing the Chinese system closer to fundamental transformation, and perhaps may make such a transformation much less daunting to power holders when it comes.

The legislative changes discussed here are not of the dramatically liberalizing order of a major electoral reform or a 'capture' of the Party-state by dissident intellectuals and civil society—the two scenarios which have figured so prominently in many recent studies of democratization in Eastern Europe. This is because the strengthening of China's legislative institutions thus far has been focused principally on institutionalizing legislative influence over governance, and has been driven overwhelmingly by political forces from within the Party-state, rather than by citizen resistance in society. To borrow from Andrew Walder's *The Waning of the Communist State*, these changes represent far more of an institutional 'quiet revolution from within' the Party-state than the sort of societal 'quiet revolution from below' which has to date failed in China.[55] Nevertheless, as Chapters 3 to 6 of this study show, the organizational-institutional transformation of the lawmaking system has substantially deconcentrated policy-making power and processes, opened new access channels to lower-level influence, and along the way produced institutional and attitudinal barriers to recentralization of power which neither the late Deng Xiaoping nor Jiang Zemin have shown much capacity to roll back.

The major legislative contributions towards system transformation are largely an unintended consequence of the Party's efforts to restore its legitimacy by overcoming the worst problems left over from its more centralized and totalitarian period. This analysis is also very much in keeping with the processes analysed by Walder and his coauthors, though they prefer to posit departures from central economic planning as the 'master process' driving the types of political changes on which they focus.[56] It is true that the post-Mao leadership's desire to build the legal system did, in part, result from its need to reassure reluctant foreign investors and encourage limited domestic market reforms. But the 'political-legal' reforms in Leninist states, including lawmaking reforms, have been driven far more by these countries' other great post-totalitarian yearning: the desire to heal the social traumas of unpredictable totalitarian violence, re-establish stability and institutionalize rule by law. In China's case, of course, the social wounds of Cultural Revolution lawlessness were awesome and profound even by the historical standards of modern communism; and they planted in many Party leaders an especially powerful desire to revive the 1950s' dream of establishing legitimacy through a well-controlled but more law-based state—a sort of 'Leninist *rechtsstaat*'. Such a state would still be authoritarian and imposed by the Party-state on society rather than contractual. But it would also be far more predictable, procedurally less arbitrary, and would involve greatly increased consultation both within the Party elite and between the Party-state and society.

While it seems clear enough how economic reforms could inadvertently

55. Walder (1995), 6–7.   56. *Ibid.*, 3–4

Bureaucracies, 'Organized Anarchies' and Inadvertent Transitions 37

contribute to system transformation by undermining the material bases of centralized Party-state control over lower-level officials and society, how could the revival of formal lawmaking set off any analogously powerful processes? Students of Chinese culture and law universally concur that historically, both enacted laws and the legislative institutions which promulgate them have been a weak, shifting-sand base on which to establish real political power. In the classical architecture of Chinese politics it has not been obedience to law, but rather the power of bureaucratic organizations which has always constituted the solidest of foundations on which to construct enduring political power. If China's prospects for a more open, consultative system, anchored around a relatively powerful and accessible legislature, were rooted only in the sporadic clarion calls of a few top leaders and liberal intellectuals for greater 'rule of law', there would be little cause for optimism that such a system could be constructed on Chinese soil any time soon.

But this study argues that the pressure for change has come less from the laws themselves than from the growth of the institutional structures which were built to draft, interpret and implement them. As argued in Chapters 3 to 6, the *bureaucratic development* of China's lawmaking system since 1978 has become a powerful force for the largely inadvertent opening up and decentralization of policy-making power. In this case, the 'master process' was not so much the liberalizing power of law, but the decentralizing power of organizational growth, bureaucratic-institutional rivalry, and the resulting rise of multiple 'arenas' in which the political struggles of the reform era could be fought out. Chapters 3 and 4 describe how the internal fragmentation of the post-Cultural Revolution Party leadership, coupled with its policy need for rapid legal drafting to support reform, have hastened the bureaucratic erosion of centralized Party control over the lawmaking system. As Lieberthal says, the Centre must speak with a clear, insistent voice in order to overcome the system's powerful fissiparous tendencies. But in the lawmaking system, the notion of a unified Party 'Centre' which can provide strong, clear, regular and detailed leadership over the multi-year process of drafting a major piece of legislation has become increasingly remote over the past two decades. Instead, the Garbage Can model's image of an 'ambiguous' decision-making system of unclear leadership, mixed values and ill-defined processes has been looming ever larger. New adjunct policy-making arenas have sprung up (including the NPC) and a number of other political actors have rushed into the newly emerging institutional freespace. Chapter 6 details the common efforts of two ideologically very different Chinese Prime Ministers, Zhao Ziyang and Li Peng, to rebuild and expand a centralized legislative drafting system centred in the State Council's Legislative Affairs Bureau (the *Fazhi ju*), which could impose orderly, planned, legal-economic development upon China's Hydra-headed ministerial bureaucracy. The result has been the rise of the State Council as the institutional arena with the greatest impact on the actual content of most legislation. But it is also an arena in which an enormous array of interests get consulted in the drafting of new legislation.

Chapters 4 and 5 tell the even more bizarre bureaucratic tale of the rise of a Leninist legislature. During the early post-Mao years, many influential Party elders were eased out of their historically powerful offices in the government and at the Party Centre into NPC posts. Increasingly, they saw the NPC Standing Committee as the principal formal conduit for their power, and as a useful venue in which to construct an influential policy-making bureaucracy to pursue their various personal, factional, institutional and policy goals. These Party leaders, many of whom were restless senior revolutionaries, took the NPC's institutional development and its prerogatives as a lawmaking arena very seriously, particularly when these forces could be harnessed to serve their own factional and policy agendas. Like good bureaucrats, the NPC leadership dramatically built up the legislature's permanent bureaucracy and subcommittee system after 1978 to the point where it now exercises far more influence over policy-making than might ever be expected of a Leninist legislature. As a spin-off effect, the institution they built provided powerful political protection for much more open policy debate than the People's Republic has ever seen before. Most importantly, because the NPC's growth was originally rooted in such traditional sources of organizational-bureaucratic power, its influence is showing powerful signs of staying power—of institutionalization. Perhaps the greatest irony of this story is that the principal builders of China's chief organ of 'socialist democracy' have not been the so-called 'bourgeois liberal' intellectuals within the Party, but rather a group of men from precisely that sector of the Communist Party which is the very essence of classical totalitarianism: the 'Political-Legal System'. But then, just as 'only Nixon could go to China', perhaps only the sworn defenders of the Leninist Party-state could build the NPC into an increasingly influential policy-making bureaucracy while insisting on a significant place for it as an arena for political debate.

Of course, as a process for eroding authoritarianism, bureaucratic development and institutional rivalries can only go so far, and several potential limitations of this process in promoting system transition are apparent. For example, power and access within the various concerned lawmaking organizations could in principle remain tightly held by a relatively small number of Party members and bureaucrats who remained loyal to an only moderately reformed version of the Leninist Party-state system. Then, even though rule *by* law might play a bigger role in how China is governed, and lawmaking authority might be formally decentralized, the overall political system might still be stopped well short of genuine liberalization and evolve no further that the one which Kenneth Lieberthal has labelled 'fragmented authoritarianism' or the ones others have labelled 'semi-democracy'.

In this study, however, there is modest but important evidence that just as the economic structural reforms have eroded the underpinnings of CCP economic control over lower levels of government and society, the institutional transformation of lawmaking politics is leading to more far-reaching, potentially liberalizing, change. Windows are being opened and frameworks built through which portions of the Party-state leadership can establish links to China's evolving society, and groups within that society can strengthen their influence over government. This prolonged institutional metamorphosis has produced more than a simple relocation of policy-making power; it means that more decisions, and increasingly important decisions, are being hammered out in what has emerged as the most open, permeable and therefore potentially risky policy arena of the Party-state. And although genuine legislative accountability must await direct, competitive elections, the erosion of centralized Party control increasingly permits legislators, even Party-selected legislators, gradually to begin reconsidering who constitutes their true 'constituency'—that is, whose interests it is they are trying to represent. Many are less concerned with trying to please Central leaders and more concerned with linking up with and representing an increasingly broad selection of bureaucratic, sectoral, regional and societal interests even before electoral reform forges a genuine link of social accountability.

There is even stronger evidence that well before the Party has shown any willingness to tolerate openly organized opposition, the NPC's growth is providing an arena and a set of institutional practices which are acclimatizing the Party to much more open debate and criticism, albeit with the life-or-death issues of the Party-state's existence off the table. As the newly available NPC voting data in Chapter 5 show, an ever-wider spectrum of policy debate, criticism and dissent is gradually seen as less threatening and more 'normal'. Certainly, 'in-house' debate within a one-Party system need not lead to Party acceptance of a transition to a multi-party system. In the post-Deng era, however, it may gradually undercut the regime hardliners' fears about the risks of liberalization and eventually create an institution in which moderate critics could stretch the boundaries of the politically permissible, and regime reformers and moderate critics could manage the compromises of transition. Recent research on democratic transition and consolidation has spotlighted a number of cases in which similar institutional patterns have resulted in stable, albeit slow, 'elite dominated' or 'pacted' transitions. The final chapter argues that at a minimum, this 'normalization of moderate dissent' represents a powerful and underappreciated change in the norms of China's elite political culture, and could help overcome the 'zero-sum' attitude towards open policy debate which has been such an intractable obstacle to democratization throughout this century.

Even the principals involved in this nearly twenty-year process of legislative blossoming cannot tell how much of this institutional evolution has been driven by the Party's own sporadic and uncertain quest for rule by law, and how much by far less noble processes of factional infighting, generational transition, bureaucratic kingdom building and an incipient politics of interest-group competition. Certainly as a morality play of how Chinese autocracy may erode, it pales in comparison with the heroically principled and self-sacrificing efforts of China's dissident intellectuals. But the academic question of which motivations might drive such an 'inadvertant transition' may, in the end, be moot. As this study shows, the rise of the lawmaking system is causing the politics of policy-making within the Party-state to change quietly, but substantially. Ironically, it may be that twenty years hence, analysts of a prospective Chinese democratic transition will see a greater impact from the inadvertent institutional changes wrought by battles among current power holders than from the deliberate efforts of avowed democrats.

PART II
Lawmaking Institutions

3

The Emergence of China's Post-Mao Lawmaking System

When Deng Xiaoping, at the December 1978 Third Plenum of the Eleventh Central Committee, called upon China's lawmaking system to draft a bold, far-ranging package of reform-oriented legislation, there was, in reality, virtually no lawmaking system out there to answer his call. The State Council, China's cabinet, had not had a legislative drafting office since the Great Leap Forward year of 1959, when the last such office was abolished and its director, Premier Zhou Enlai's close aide Tao Xijin, was exiled to manual labour in remote rural Guizhou. Nor could the National People's Congress meet the challenge, having at that time no drafting offices and a total staff of less than thirty. Even within the Party Central Committee offices, which by a combination of hoarding and default had achieved a virtual monopoly on major policy-making over the past decade, lawmaking was but a third-rate concern of one committee: the Central Political-Legal Group. In the twenty-one years between the onset of the Anti-Rightist Campaign and the Third Plenum, through a combination of legal nihilism, anti-intellectualism, Party-led campaigning, and displacement of Party and state authority by Maoist cult, the gauze-thin fabric of China's fledgling legal order had been shredded. In an effort to ensure that it never recovered, every one of the organizations charged with weaving that legal order had been destroyed, and their personnel scattered, imprisoned or killed.

Against such an historical backdrop, the organizational rebirth and growth of China's lawmaking system over the past nineteen years has been dramatic. The system now encompasses a large number of increasingly powerful, expanding bureaucracies, boasting at least a couple of thousand staff. This organizational evolution is the subject of the next four chapters. Chapter 4 focuses on the Party's declining role in lawmaking, while the latter two chapters look at the corresponding organizational growth of the National People's Congress' and the State Council's lawmaking offices.

To place these chapters in context, there follows a brief overview of the formal and informal organizational trends in China's post-Mao lawmaking system.

Background: Defining the National Lawmaking System

At the national level, the Chinese lawmaking system mainly comprises three groups of organizations, which may also be thought of as increasingly separate arenas or battlegrounds where lawmaking politics take place:

(1) *The Communist Party Central Committee*, including its Politburo, Secretariat, Leading Groups and Departments.
(2) *The State Council*, including its Standing Committee (China's cabinet, headed by the Premier) and a couple of dozen extremely powerful ministries, commissions, bureaus and corporations, The State Council's chief lawmaking office is the powerful Legislation Bureau, which oversees much legislative drafting and drafts China's one and five-year legislative plans.
(3) *The National People's Congress*, China's legislature. The full NPC, containing almost 3,000 representatives, meets annually. The smaller and more powerful NPC Standing Committee meets several times a year. The NPC is really led by its Committee Chairmen's Group, which contains the NPC's CCP Party Group (see Chapters 4 and 5) and leads the work of the NPC's growing permanent bureaucracy and its eight subcommittees.

The Formal System: The Myth of Unity, and an Invitation to Struggle

Most Chinese scholarly analyses of the lawmaking system place primary emphasis upon its formal constitutional development as a source of organizational growth. But in China, the formal constitutional system is not, and has never been, a leading determinant of real legislative power. It is undeniable that changes in the system since 1982 have at least begun to remove some important obstacles to organizational development, particularly the development of the NPC Standing Committee. But the current constitutional delineation of lawmaking authority between the State Council, the NPC and its Standing Committee remains ill-defined and highly ambiguous, and the resulting system is still far more of an invitation to organizational struggle than a clear blueprint for lawmaking procedure.

The first of China's four state constitutions, adopted in 1954, decreed that the plenary session of the National People's Congress was the 'highest organ of state authority', and assigned to the NPC the sole authority to promulgate laws (*falu*). The NPC Standing Committee, on the other hand, was not empowered to pass laws. Rather, it could issue decrees (*faling*) and interpret laws (*jieshi falu*) promulgated by the NPC.[1] In 1955, the Standing

---

1. Constitution of the People's Republic of China (1954).

Committee was granted the vague power to adopt partial (*bufenxing*) or individual legal regulations (*danxing fagui*), but it still lacked the authority to promulgate laws.[2] Numerous changes in the status of the NPC were enshrined in the radical 1975 Constitution, most notably the explicit assertion that the NPC exercised its authority under the leadership of the CCP. Nevertheless, with respect to the narrow issue of lawmaking authority, the powers granted to the NPC and its Standing Committee remained, for the most part, unchanged through the 1975 and 1978 Constitutions.[3]

The rapid acceleration of legal codification after the 1978 Third Plenum of the Eleventh CCP Central Committee quickly showed up the constitutional bottleneck created by centralizing formal legislative authority in the NPC plenary session. With the establishment of several new legislative drafting organs under the NPC and the State Council (most notably Peng Zhen's NPC Legislative Affairs Commission), the system could produce legislation much more quickly than it could be promulgated by the annual NPC plenary meetings. Moreover, NPC plenary sessions would be forced to consider major laws so quickly and superficially that the situation was incompatible with efforts to expand the NPC's consultative power. In part to alleviate this stress on the agenda, the revised 1982 Constitution redivided and clarified legislative authority between the NPC and its Standing Committee.[4]

The 1982 Constitution gave the NPC plenary session a more circumscribed grant of authority, declaring that it had sole authority to enact and amend those 'basic laws' (*jiben falu*) which dealt with 'criminal offences, civil affairs, the state organs and other matters'. The authority of the NPC Standing Committee, on the other hand, was expanded enormously. It was for the first time empowered to promulgate and amend laws, 'with the exception of those which should be enacted by the National People's Congress'. The State Council, as in previous constitutions, could adopt 'administrative measures ... administrative laws and regulations (*xingzheng fagui*) ... and orders in accordance with the Constitution and laws (*falu*)'. The State Council could also refer draft laws to the NPC and its Standing Committee for adoption.

Since 1982, the NPC has additionally authorized the State Council to promulgate temporary legislation (*zhanxing tiaoli, zhanxing guiding*) on issues of economic reform and restructuring, and opening to the outside. The stated justification for this grant of authority is to allow the State Council greater freedom to experiment with innovative new policies. But

---

2. Wu Daying *et al.* (1984), 100–2.
3. See Constitution of the People's Republic of China, 1975, articles 17 and 18, and 1978, articles 22 and 25.
4. The author's political suspicions suggest a third reason for expanding the Standing Committee's legislative authority. Peng Zhen and other Standing Committee leaders may have wanted to vest greater authority in the institution they could more easily influence: the Standing Committee.

the legal status of this 'empowered legislation' (*shouquan fa*) and the time limits on its effectiveness remain ill-defined.[5]

In their published works, many of China's most influential legal scholars have lauded the legislative provisions of the 1982 Constitution for making major breakthroughs in decentralizing and clarifying legislative authority.

This provision [of the 1982 Constitution] broke out of the traditional model under which only the NPC could exercise legislative authority, and not the NPC and its Standing Committee. This change is of decisive significance for the perfection of lawmaking and the strengthening of lawmaking.[6]

While conceding that great progress has been made since 1977 in clarifying and codifying Chinese legislative authority and procedures, one should not lose sight of the most important, most basic nature of the system. The key lines of authority and procedures between the major lawmaking institutions are still only very vaguely defined. Chinese law still gives only the most general guidance on the question of which legal documents should be promulgated by the State Council, which by the NPC Standing Committee and which by the NPC plenary session. Moreover, interviews with Chinese legal scholars—including some who have publicly praised the breakthroughs of the 1982 Constitution—indicate that there are very few informal rules or norms to clarify these relationships.

Interviews conducted among the Chinese legal community reveal considerable criticism of the unclear delineation of legislative authority (*lifa quanxian*). The key, of course, lies in terms such as 'basic law'. As one legislative scholar has noted, so long as the term 'basic law' remains undefined, the powers of the NPC plenum are also undefined. According to this and other scholars, under article 62, only six major codes could indisputably be considered 'basic laws': the Criminal Law, the Civil Code, the Administrative Code, and the accompanying Procedural Codes for each. Beyond these, there are no regulations to define which laws the NPC, as opposed to the Standing Committee, must promulgate.

The result is a system which is unclear even to those officials who work within it. Party, State Council and NPC officials must separately negotiate, for each law, which state organ will promulgate it. Not surprisingly, all three legislative organs are anxious to maximize their sphere of influence, and jurisdictional disputes are not uncommon. One NPC staffer was highly critical of the division of labour within the legislative system, describing it as 'chaotic' (*fengong luan*).[7] In this ongoing dispute between the State

---

5. On this 'empowered' or 'temporary' reform legislation, see Peng Zhen's remarks, Beijing Xinhua Domestic Service (BXDS) 23 January 1985; also *Renmin Ribao* 24 January 1985, 2. In the above speech, Peng argues that '[temporary] . . . does not mean lasting one or two years'.
6. Liu Shengping (1988), 5. Similar viewpoints are expressed in Wu Daying, *et al.* (1984); Sun Chenggu (1983) and Zhang Youyu (1983).
7. 12-32-17/34-19-28/ABE, Beijing, May 1989.

The Emergence of China's Post-Mao Lawmaking System 47

Council and the NPC Standing Committee, representatives of each side tend to perceive the other side as having a great deal of autonomy and influence in deciding who gets to see which law. Consider the following: [8]

In this regard (deciding which organ promulgates a law), the State Council Legislation Bureau has too much power
—An NPC Adviser.

... the NPC Legislative Affairs Commission and the (State Council) Legislation Bureau decide together on which laws they will place on the plan for the next year ... the NPC ... has a great deal of freedom to choose which laws it will examine during the course of a year
—A Legislation Bureau Staffer.

Seen in this light, the issue of the NPC 'empowering' the State Council to promulgate temporary regulations on major issues for an undefined period takes on even greater political significance. On controversial reform issues, many members of the NPC Standing Committee have been openly critical of State Council-sponsored innovations when they came before the Standing Committee in the form of draft laws, and have tried radically to amend these proposals. Faced with such opposition, the State Council (and sometimes the Party Secretariat under the late Hu Yaobang) has declined to submit such reform policies to the NPC Standing Committee's scrutiny, and has simply continued to implement the policy under the documentary rubric of a Party Central Document or a State Council 'temporary regulation'.[9]

In earlier times, when the NPC was indeed acting like a 'rubber stamp', such procedural ambiguities were not significant legal or political problems. But over the past decade they have become politically significant, because the State Council and the NPC are now behaving like distinct political arenas, with separate policy processes, and incorporating different configurations of powers and interests. As direct Party Centre involvement has become less detailed and more irregular, this procedural ambiguity has become even more pronounced.

Real Power Trends Since 1978: A Fragmented, 'Multi-arena' Process

Even this brief discussion of the formal constitutional process should be sufficient to dispel the notion that Chinese lawmaking involves a unitary, tightly hierarchical, well-ordered, top-down system. Based on the evolving

---

8. Sometimes consensus on the promulgating institution is reached relatively easy. Indeed, one surprising result of my interviewing was that disagreements of this sort are not universal. For example, while my sources were able to cite numerous cases of disagreement on other laws, none indicated that there was any serious disagreement over which bodies would pass the Bankruptcy and Enterprise Laws.

9. This seems to be precisely what happened in the case of the 'manager responsibility system' enshrined in the State-Owned Industrial Enterprises Law. See Chapter 8.

real distribution of power, it is now better thought of as a 'multi-arena' process. As a draft law works its way through the system, the primary location for political battles over it shifts around among the three key organizational arenas: the Party Centre, State Council and NPC. A very rough schematic for many laws would be as follows: first drafting is led either by the State Council or one of its ministries, or by the NPC Standing Committee bureaucracy; this is followed by prolonged inter-agency review, mostly by the concerned State Council ministries; then the Party Centre (in effect, the Politburo) must approve the bill 'in principle' before it can go to the NPC or its Standing Committee for debate, vote and promulgation (which is formally signed by the President); then the law is sent back either to the State Council ministries or, increasingly, to the Supreme People's Court, for translation into implementing regulations, which are turned over to the relevant ministries, local governments and courts to be carried out.

Power and authority relationships between these arenas have been evolving rapidly over the last fifteen years. Power resources within the system are fragmented among the various leaders and bureaucracies involved in drafting a given law, and an organization's or a leader's power varies from stage to stage in the process.[10] The precise configuration of powers and interests in the lawmaking system also varies from one institutional arena to another. That is, the balance of power and the access of interests within the State Council arena is very different from that within the National People's Congress arena, and both differ from that in the Party Centre. Thus, even though all the key players in the system are Party members, not all of them find it advantageous to try to resolve their lawmaking disagreements within the confines of the top Party decision-making organs. Actors involved in lawmaking will try to steer key legislative proposals into the arenas where they enjoy the greatest influence, and away from those in which their adversaries predominate. This process, not surprisingly, further erodes and decentralizes Party control over lawmaking.

Since 1978, the relations between China's three key lawmaking organizations (arenas) have been marked by four major power trends. First, Communist Party Central Committee organs' involvement in and influence over the lawmaking process has been eroded substantially. As the next chapter shows, this decline is in part due to deliberate efforts by some senior Party leaders (most notably Deng Xiaoping, former Premier and Party Chief Zhao Ziyang, and former NPC Chief Wan Li) to reduce their influence and direct control over policy-making in general and lawmaking in particular. The Party decision-making organs' chronic difficulty in

---

10. This basic view of the Chinese policy-making system as one of 'fragmented authoritarianism' and inter-agency bargaining is heavily influenced by the work of Kenneth Lieberthal, Michel Oksenberg and David Lampton. See, in particular, Lieberthal and Oksenberg (1988); also Lieberthal and Lampton (1992).

reaching policy consensus 'in-house' has also frequently led these bodies to abdicate their influence in lawmaking.

Secondly, within the *state* system, the formal constitutional lines of authority between the three state organs empowered to promulgate laws (the NPC, the NPC Standing Committee and the State Council) have been clarified to some extent since 1982, and are now more clearly delineated than at any time in PRC history. This has been a boon to the NPC Standing Committee in particular. Nevertheless, the current constitutional system is still extremely vague and ill-defined, and creates incentives for all three state legislative organs to try to expand their spheres of influence at the expense of the other two.

Thirdly, the State Council Standing Committee has resumed the trend, begun in the 1950s under the late Premier Zhou Enlai, of expanding and strengthening its inter-ministerial legislative co-ordinating office, the Legislation Bureau (*Fazhi ju*). Because of their vast resources and organizational memories, however, the commissions, ministries and think-tanks under the State Council still retain their dominance over the content of most legislation. For the majority of Chinese laws, the most significant arena for determining their policy content is the State Council, not the Party or the NPC; and the most significant and intractable political process affecting legislative content is consensus-building among State Council and other agencies.

Finally, the National People's Congress, especially the NPC Standing Committee and its permanent bureaucracy and subcommittees, is an increasingly influential actor in determining the content of laws. Now, if a political actor loses a legislative battle in the Party and State Council arenas, it is still possible to block or significantly amend a major law within the NPC. For these actors, politicking within the NPC is no longer a waste of time. There are several sources of this power. Most notably, recent elite turnover policies have forced many senior leaders to focus their influence through NPC channels; as a result, the NPC has been greatly strengthened as a bureaucracy.

From 'Party Leadership' to an 'Ambiguous' System

The central theme woven through this discussion of China's lawmaking organs concerns the increasingly blurred authority relationships and the concurrent decentralization of power within the lawmaking system over the last twenty years. Both the formal and informal 'rules' of lawmaking which might define the relationship between Party, government and NPC organs have remained unclear, even to the system's experts and practitioners. Organizational power trends during this period have accelerated the trend towards decentralized power and authority. A gradual but persistent erosion of the Party Centre's organizational control over lawmaking has been coupled with tremendous bureaucratic development within the State Council and NPC staff offices responsible for lawmaking work. In part this reflects a conscious decision to decentralize power. In part it reflects Deng's apparently backfired strategy to ease aging rivals from more traditional avenues of power. And in part it reflects the natural result of good old fashioned Chinese-style bureaucratic kingdom-building. As a result, power within the lawmaking system, just as in other sectors of the Chinese policy-making system, is fragmented among numerous individuals and organizations.[11] The various lawmaking organizations continue to evolve their own unique packages of power resources which allow them to influence lawmaking in differing degrees, at different stages of the process. The result, in the words of Garbage Can model proponents, is a lawmaking system with an increasingly 'ambiguous decision-making technology', and with multiple arenas in which political struggle can be carried out.

Advocates of a top-down model of lawmaking might object that the Politburo could, if it so chose, end much of this confusion by recentralizing power, since it does have the authority of prior approval over laws. But the top Party leaders often fail to exercise their influence fully, either because they cannot reach consensus, or because they lack the training or the interest to concern themselves with the details of a draft bill. Government ministries, on the other hand, have enormous influence over the detailed content of legislation and its implementation, but are often forced into important compromises either with other ministries or increasingly with the NPC and its Standing Committee. In such a system, political actors who are dissatisfied with the current consensus on a draft law will unavoidably be drawn to resume the battle in another, more sympathetic arena.

Against this background of organizational power trends, the next chapter focuses on forces eroding Party control over lawmaking.

11. See Lieberthal and Oksenberg (1988).

4

The Erosion of Party Control over Lawmaking

This chapter focuses on the structure and evolution of Communist Party control over lawmaking institutions and the lawmaking process in post-Mao China. In particular, it charts the erosion and decentralization of that control which has accompanied the rise of lawmaking since 1978. The unity of Party control over lawmaking has frayed and dissipated dramatically in these years, as more and more important policy issues are resolved outside the arena of the Party's Central decision-making organs (the Politburo, the Secretariat and so on). The decentralization of Party control, in turn, has been matched by a corresponding increase in the institutional power, autonomy and assertiveness of more permeable policy-making arenas, most notably the legislature, but also including the State Council lawmaking offices.

Efforts to institutionalize the decentralization of Party control over lawmaking reached a milestone in early 1991 with the promulgation of a major confidential Party document, Central Committee Document Number 8 [1991]. Central Document 8 represents the first time the Communist Party has ever attempted to define in writing the respective lawmaking roles of the Party Centre, the NPC and the State Council. Central Document 8, which was intriguingly and rather deceptively entitled 'Several Opinions of the Central Committee on Strengthening Leadership over Lawmaking Work', delimits Central Party lawmaking authority.[1] It also grants the leadership of the Chinese legislature greater operational autonomy than it has ever enjoyed before.

Despite a recent explosion in Western studies of both law and the policy-making process in China, Western scholars still know very little about the 'commanding heights' of the system, the Party's role in lawmaking and the nature of its leadership over the legislature. Many key questions about Party leadership over lawmaking remain unanswered. By what organizational means is Party leadership maintained? How unified and complete is this Party leadership? Does Party leadership mean centralized, highly detailed control over the content of lawmaking, or is it limited to ensuring a general control over basic policy issues enshrined in laws? How have the forms and degree of Party leadership changed over

---

1. 'Zhonggong Zhongyang guanyu Jiaqiang dui Lifa Gongzuo Lingdao de Ruogan Yijian' ('Several Opinions of the CCP Central Committee on Strengthening Leadership over Lawmaking Work'), CCP Central Committee Document (*Zhongfa*) Number 8 [1991].

time? All these process-related questions lead back to the key question of system transition: has the decentralization of Party leadership over lawmaking during the 1980s opened a window sufficiently large that China's legislature might some day begin to play as assertive a role in any prospective 'transitional China' as its Russian and Polish counterparts played during their societies' transitions?

The purpose of this chapter is to give at least partial answers to these important questions by examining the key Communist Party institutions involved in lawmaking, and their evolving structures and roles since 1978. The chapter begins by discussing the origins of decentralized Party control over lawmaking since 1978. Next, it examines in some detail the organization of Party control over lawmaking and the legislature, and discusses the erosion of that organizational control over the last nineteen years. This section ends with a discussion of the contents of Central Document Number 8 and an assessment of its significance. In conclusion, the chapter addresses the issue of how firmly established these changes have become, and briefly discusses the impact of lawmaking decentralization on China's prospects for a transition towards a more open, consultative system.

Forces for Decentralizing Party Control Over Lawmaking

There are several forces or processes which have contributed to the decentralization of Party control over lawmaking in China. Some reflect the Party leadership's desire for a new policy-making system after Mao's death. The institutions established to carry out this new system, in turn, developed a life of their own as a result of factional infighting and bureaucratic empire-building.

First, in the immediate post-Mao years, the Party's top leadership recognized that the Cultural Revolution had forced an unmanageably large number of policy decisions into its own hands.[2] Institutionalized Party and state decision-making authority at all levels of the system had been destroyed. Policy-making had degenerated into factional struggles for the blessing of a deified, aging and unpredictable Chairman, with purge or even death being the stakes of losing. In this tense and stalemated policy environment, leaders throughout the system, quite rationally, kicked any remotely controversial issue up to higher levels for decision, ultimately reaching the level of the Premier, the Politburo or the Chairman himself. This period correlates with the dissolution of the legislature and other state lawmaking organs, and an almost complete end to the use of law as a

---

2. Deng Xiaoping's clearest discussion of the evils of overcentralized decision-making power is 'On the Reform of the System of Party and State Leadership', in Deng Xiaoping (1984), 302–26.

The Erosion of Party Control over Lawmaking 53

policy-making vehicle. As Lieberthal has meticulously documented, the Party was instead forced to rely excessively upon its most authoritative policy documents, the Politburo-approved Central Documents (*zhongfa*), for even highly routine and specific decisions.[3]

Secondly, the scars left by this period renewed the desire among both Party leaders and society to create an institutionalized, stable, predictable system of rule by law (*fazhi*) and socialist democracy (*shehuizhuyi minzhu*); a goal first evinced in the post-revolutionary years of the mid-1950s. This desire initially focused on two areas: the build-up of the people's congress system and the predictable, codified administration of criminal law. While a certain cynicism must attend any post-Tiananmen discussion of CCP commitment to law, one nevertheless senses a genuine yearning for more legal stability, predictability and consultativeness in the early post-Mao speeches of veteran Chinese leaders such as Peng Zhen, himself a victim of Red Guard lawlessness. As late as 1986 Peng, the architect of China's new lawmaking system, still mentioned 'a personal understanding of the Cultural Revolution' prominently when listing those personal attributes which he felt best qualified senior Party leaders to serve in the National People's Congress and help build China's legal system.[4]

Thirdly, Deng Xiaoping and many of his fellow economic reformers probably valued an open legislature more instrumentally—as a vehicle to forge consensus behind economic reform—than intrinsically, as a proper way to make policy. The establishment of an increasingly open and consultative legislature with the power to criticize state bureaucrats who resisted reform or committed malfeasance would be a powerful institutional impetus for sustaining and accelerating economic reform. It seems clear that Deng, at least, did not especially desire that the legislature become a very wide-open, autonomous lawmaking institution. His speeches after 1978 invariably stressed that his goal in strengthening the legislature was not the creation of an American-style tripartite system of checks and balances.[5] Nevertheless, Deng did enjoy periodically using the legislature to attack his factional opponents and light a fire under recalcitrant bureaucrats. This occurred in 1979 when the NPC became the focal point for the attack upon the leaders of the so-called 'Petroleum Faction'

3. Lieberthal (1976).
4. See Potter, (1986), 21–50; see also Peng Zhen, 'Jiaqiang Minzhu yu Fazhi Jianshe, Jiaqiang Renda Changweihui Gongzuo' ('Strengthen Construction of Democracy and the Legal System, Strengthen the Work of the NPC 'Standing Committee'), speech at an NPC Standing Committee delegates work meeting, 27 June 1986, in Peng Zhen (1989), 324–31. See also Deng Xiaoping's December 1978 Third Plenum address, 'Emancipate the Mind, Seek Truth from Facts, and Unite as One in Looking to the Future', in Deng Xiaoping (1984), especially 157–8.
5. 'In political reforms, we can affirm one thing: we have to insist on implementing the system of the National People's Congress and not the American system of the separation of three powers.' Deng's speech to the military commanders in Beijing, 9 June 1989, *Beijing Review* 10–16 July 1989, 18–21.

who dominated the state planning apparatus and resisted Deng's more market-oriented reforms.[6]

Fourthly, since Mao's death, the lawmaking system has benefited from a strong strain of thinking within the Chinese leadership which held that policy choices could be made more correctly and 'scientifically' (*kexue*) by making the system more open and consultative. In conceiving 'democracy', numerous CCP and other modern Chinese leaders have overlooked the existence of irreducible conflicts of interest in society. Instead, they take it on faith that an open, wide-ranging and well-intentioned debate of different policy proposals can overcome differences of interest, and universal consensus can eventually emerge upon a single 'correct' policy, which all people may be educated to embrace and support.[7] In using such terms, the CCP leaders often seem to regard the goal of policy-making 'rationality' as far more serious and attainable than Western social scientists have for several decades. Lawmaking and the legislature are key parts of this process, by which the Party can stay in touch with the people and avoid policy mistakes.

Wan Li, who succeeded Peng Zhen as Chairman of the NPC Standing Committee (from 1988 to 1993), has probably been the Party's most persistent and outspoken advocate for strengthening the legislature in order to make Party-led policy-making more scientific. In a major speech on political structural reform in 1986, Wan called for much greater tolerance of divergent policy advice and an end to the persecution of well-intentioned policy specialists whose views were rejected in policy debates.[8] In the wake of the 1989 Democracy Movement and the Tiananmen Massacre, Wan Li forcefully argued that the roots of the movement lay in the Party's increasing distance from the populace, and that such errors could only be avoided in the future if the Party would heed the voice of the NPC.[9] Chinese legal sources confirm that in arguing this last point, Wan Li was engaged in a public debate with Party General Secretary Jiang Zemin over the proper relationship between the Party and the NPC, a point explored later in this chapter.

Inevitably, these various ideological arguments for decentralizing power within the lawmaking system have been reinforced and accelerated by leadership, factional and bureaucratic interests. Party leaders such as Peng Zhen, Wan Li, Chen Pixian, Peng Chong, Qiao Shi, Tian Jiyun and Wang Hanbin, all of whom have been tasked with serving in the legislature, have pushed hard to strengthen China's lawmaking organizations, even though they are men of hugely varied ideological views. Doubtless they

---

6. See, for example, Solinger, (1982), 1238–75; also Lieberthal and Oksenberg (1988), 252–4.
7. For an excellent discussion of this assumption that all interests can be made compatible through the democratic process, see Nathan (1985), especially 45–66.
8. See Wan Li, (1986), translated in Foreign Broadcast Information Service, *China: Daily Report* (hereafter FBIS-CHI), 19 August 1986, K-22.   9. Wan Li (1990).

did this, at least in part, to strengthen their own power bases. But the strengthening of these organizations is not all cynical power manipulation, and my own interviewing strongly suggests that the Party's legislative leaders have by and large come to value an increasingly open and consultative policy-making process for its own sake.[10] Consequently, as a matter of course, they have greatly strengthened the NPC and other lawmaking units as bureaucracies, increasing their manpower, budgets, staff offices and other bureaucratic resources. The result since 1978 has been a dramatic shift in the location of day-to-day control and influence over lawmaking away from the Party's Central offices into the offices of the State Council and the NPC permanent bureaucracy. This organizational transformation constitutes, in my view, the most important force for institutionalizing the decentralization of lawmaking power in China, for it allows this decentralization to sink deep roots in the Chinese tradition of bureaucratic power and better guards it against any possible efforts to recentralize.

In reforming this policy-making process to make it more compatible with other reforms, Party leaders face several dilemmas. In a nutshell, the Party needs to strike a balance between maintaining the most important of Deng's Four Cardinal Principles—Communist Party leadership over society—and promoting a level of policy-making decentralization which is necessary to rationalize the process, undermine reform opponents and defuse some of the inevitable disagreements in the reform process. There has been tremendous disagreement among political, academic and legal-sector leaders over the proper balance between these goals. In addition, groups both inside and outside the legislative system, particularly those, such as the official trade unions and other mass organizations, who feel their interests have not received sufficient protection, have exerted pressure to expand access to the system.[11]

The (Dis-) Organization of Party Control Over Lawmaking: Key CCP Organs in the Lawmaking Process

The key CCP organizations involved in lawmaking are: the Politburo (and its Standing Committee), and the various 'leading groups' directly under the Politburo;[12] the Party's Central Secretariat, which is responsible for much policy planning work; and the various departments under the

---

10. This was especially stressed by interview 26-17-13-33/TWS, Beijing, 1992.
11. This was stressed by a high-ranking trade union legal scholar, and is discussed in depth in the two case studies in Chapters 7 and 8. Interview 27-22-13-33/TSE, Beijing, 1989 and 1992.
12. These leading groups (*lingdao xiaozu*), divided up by issue-area, are usually chaired by the Politburo member holding the appropriate policy portfolio, and bring together leading policy specialists in that issue area.

56 The Politics of Lawmaking in Post-Mao China

Secretariat (such as the Organization, Propaganda and United Front Work Departments). Nearly all Western studies on the Chinese lawmaking system have attributed great power to the Central Political-Legal Leading Group.[13] But all the Chinese sources consulted for this project suggest that this group's power over lawmaking has been greatly exaggerated in the past, and has in any case declined markedly since 1978. Party leadership over lawmaking takes four dominant organizational forms: organizational penetration of the NPC leadership and control over key NPC appointments through the NPC Party Group system and the *nomenklatura* system; control over meeting agendas, as well as heavy influence (but not complete control) over the general tone of legislative debate; organizational oversight of legal drafting, some of which was previously performed by the Central Political-Legal Leading Group; and Politburo and Secretariat pre-approval of draft laws to be promulgated by the NPC.

This system of Party control, while indeed impressive in comparative perspective, is nevertheless not nearly so unified or organized as it once was, nor as Western scholars have often conceived it to be. Party control over NPC agendas and meetings has not prevented a secular increase in the acrimoniousness of NPC debate and the number of 'no' votes and abstentions. Control through the *nomenklatura* system is watered down through post-Mao unofficial norms of NPC delegate selection which allocate seats to representatives of virtually every notable bureaucratic, regional and sectoral interest. In legislative review, the Party Centre's influence is often vague and ill-defined, and has eroded significantly since 1978. Most importantly, on several key post-Mao legislative issues, the leadership voice from the Party Centre has not been sufficiently unified or potent to inoculate the legislature effectively against the contagious effects of intra-Party disagreement. As a result, the legislature and other state and government organs have more leeway to assert themselves in lawmaking, and play a more influential, though less well defined, role.

The Party's Nomenklatura System

Central Party control over NPC Standing Committee appointments is the basic system for preventing Standing Committee delegates from threatening the core values of the regime.[14] The *nomenklatura* list of NPC appoint-

---

13. The organization's title has changed twice since 1978. Until 1979 it was called the Central Political-Legal Group (*Zhongyang Zhengfa Xiaozu*); that name was changed to the Central Political-Legal Commission (*Zhongyang Zhenfga Weiyuanhui*) in late 1979. In 1988, the name changed again to the Central Political-Legal Leading Group (*Zhongyang Zhengfa Lingdao Xiaozu*).
14. This section relies in particular on interveiws 11-19-13-33/OKE, Beijing, 1989; 11-19-13-33/ADH, Beijing 1989 and 1992; and 26-17-13-33/TWS, Beijing, 1992.

ments which must be approved by the Party Centre includes all members of the NPC Standing Committee Party Group (*dangzu*), plus all the approximately 125 members of the NPC Standing Committee, as well as the top officials of all the special committees under the Standing Committee.[15] The final list of candidates for the Standing Committee must be approved by the Politburo. In 1988 the Politburo, in an unprecedented effort to give NPC delegates a greater choice in voting, approved 144 possible candidates for the 135 posts on the Seventh NPC Standing Committee. It did not, however, approve multiple candidates for the twenty top Standing Committee posts, the members of the agenda-setting Committee Chairmen's Group, from whose Party members the Standing Committee Party Group is formed.[16]

Yet it remains an open question how much control the *nomenklatura* system provides the Party. In a much-publicized case in 1989, Standing Committee Member Hu Jiwei was expelled from the Standing Committee for his democracy movement activities, most notably circulating a petition among other Standing Committee members which called for an emergency NPC meeting which could have repealed Prime Minister Li Peng's martial law order. After 4 June, the Standing Committee forced Sichuan (Hu's home delegation) to recall Hu from the legislature. Although procedural proprieties were strictly observed, Hu Jiwei's expulsion dramatically underscores the Party leadership's willingness to use the *nomenklatura* system to suppress truly heterodox thinking by NPC delegates. Yet, at the same time, Hu's case is also a reminder that in times of rapid political change or crisis, not even the *nomenklatura* system is a foolproof way of preventing potential political radicals from entering the Standing Committee. Most importantly, the system certainly cannot prevent once-disciplined Party member delegates from becoming radicalized once they have already been elected to the Standing Committee.

Moreover, in non-crisis situations, Central approval of Standing Committee members by no means guarantees that NPC and Standing Committee delegates hold uniform opinions on substantive policy issues, or even that they will always comply with Central suggestions on how to vote on a given issue. On the contrary, during the 1980s, the Party Centre seems to have established an unofficial norm in delegate selection which favours choosing delegates representing a broad spectrum of factional, organizational, geographical and social interests. Certain groups and mass organizations—such as women, national minorities, trade unions, as well as

---

15. According to 1984 and 1990 Central Committee *nomenklatura* lists obtained by John P. Burns, the Central Committee's control extends no lower than the NPC Standing Committee and its chief staff officers. *Nomenklatura* control over the nearly 3,000 regular NPC delegates is unclear, but is probably worked out in consultation between the Centre and the provincial Party committees and the PLA, since the delegates are formally elected to the National Congress at the provincial/army level. See Burns (1989), 122, 123; also Burns (1994).

16. Beijing Xinhua English (BXE), 1 April 1988 in FBIS-CHI, 1 April 1988, 11.

virtually every ministry of the State Council and every provincial level unit—are *de facto* guaranteed at least one place on the Standing Committee. On the NPC Special Committees, which were established under the Sixth, Seventh, Eighth and Ninth NPC Standing Committees, the norm is to choose at least one committee member from each of the State Council ministries and mass organizations which regularly deal with that policy issue-area. In interviews, members of some of these constituencies, such as the trade unions, admit that they feel under-represented within the State Council and Party hierarchies. Consequently, these groups take their NPC Standing Committee and Special Committee positions very seriously, attempting to make the most of them politically to lobby for group interests.[17] Their activism and assertiveness has the effect of further diluting any centralized Party control over the legislature.

The NPC Party Groups

The system of Party Groups (*dangzu*) within the NPC is the principal reporting conduit connecting the NPC leadership to the Party Centre. Laws and motions under consideration by the NPC Standing Committee which require Party approval are reported through the Committee Chairmen's Group to the Standing Committee Party Group (which, since at least 1988, has comprised essentially all the CCP members on the Committee Chairmen's Group) to the Party Secretariat. Although in theory these Party Groups are supposed to centralize the Party's organizational leadership within the NPC, in reality they have at times compounded organizational overlap within the legislative bureaucracy. One internal history of the CCP's organization work indicates that during the first decade after 1978, the Party Centre established at least three different Party Groups within the NPC Standing Committee bureaucracy.[18] Interview sources report that these three Party Groups lacked any clear lines of subordination, and tended to exacerbate organizational divisions among the staffs of the NPC General Office, the Legislative Affairs Commission and the Special Committees.[19] The three Party Groups were:

(1) *The NPC Standing Committee Party Group.* This group has historically been chaired by the current Chairman of the NPC Standing Committee, usually with assistance from the NPC Secretary-General. Hence, from 1981 until (probably) July 1983 it was led by Ye Jianying. Ye was

17. Interview 27-22-13-33/TSE, Beijing, 1992.
18. This information is taken from CCP Central Organization Department Research Office (comp.), *Dang de Zuzhi Gongzuo Dashiji, 1978–1988 (A Chronology of Major Events in the Party's Organizational Work, 1978–1988)* (Beijing: Beijing Daxue Chubanshe, 1990).
19. Interviews 26-17-13-33/TWS, and 15-21-31-33/AEDH, Beijing, 1992.

succeeded by Peng Zhen, who chaired the Group until April 1988. Wan Li chaired the Group until March 1993, with Secretary-General Peng Chong as his deputy.

(2) *The NPC Standing Committee Organs Party Group.* This group oversaw the permanent bureaucracy under the NPC General Office. It was led from August 1981 to July 1983 by Yang Shangkun, and from 1983 until its abolition in April 1988 by NPC Secretary-General Wang Hanbin.

(3) *The NPC Standing Committee Legislative Affairs Work Committee Party Group.* (The Party history indicates the existence of this Party Group, but not its leadership).

In July 1987, after chairing a nine-month investigation of how to improve the NPC permanent bureaucracy, Standing Committee Vice-Chairman Peng Chong presented a major report which called for strong measures to end bureaucratic overlap and unify the work of the General Office, the Legislative Affairs Commission and the special committees.[20] As a result, during the April 1988 transition to the Seventh NPC, the new NPC leadership centralized and streamlined the NPC's Party Group structure. The Party Groups in the Legislative Affairs Work Committee and the Standing Committee Work Organs were abolished. They were replaced by a more powerful Standing Committee Party Group, chaired by Wan Li, whose membership included all the Standing Committee Vice-Chairmen who were Party members, plus NPC Deputy Secretary General Cao Zhi.[21] The membership of the Eighth NPC Standing Committee Party Group was apparently not reported publicly. But if the past system is followed, the Group Chairman was almost certainly Standing Committee Chairman Qiao Shi, with Secretary General Tian Jiyun as Vice-Chairman, and including all the Party member Vice-Chairpersons and the Secretary General, plus perhaps one or more of the Deputy Secretaries General.[22]

Preparatory Meetings of Party Member NPC Delegates

In addition to the Party Groups, which are permanent organizations, the CCP leadership convenes a meeting of all NPC delegates who are Party members before each annual NPC plenary session. Since at least 1983, the

---

20. Peng Chong, (1987).
21. CCP Organization Department, *Chronology of Party Organization work, 1978–1988,* 267. The Party Group members were Wan Li, Xi Zhongxun, Peng Chong, Ye Fei, Liao Hansheng, Ni Zhifu, Chen Muhua, Wang Hanbin and Cao Zhi.
22. Among the Chairman, Vice-Chairpersons and Secretary General of the Eighth NPC Standing Committee, the CCP members, who presumably comprised the Party Group, were: Chairman Qiao Shi, Vice-Chairpersons Tian Jiyun, Wang Hanbin, Ni Zhifu, Chen Muhua, Qin Jiwei, Li Ximing, Lu Jiaxi, Bu He, Tomur Dawamat and Gan Ku, and Secretary General Cao Zhi.

quinquennial first session of a new National People's Congress has also been preceded by a full Central Committee Plenum which has approved the NPC agenda and personnel arrangements. Similar Party member meetings are held before at least some of the several Standing Committee meetings which are held each year. At these meetings, the Party General Secretary or other senior Party leaders are delegated to represent the Centre and discuss the NPC sessions's agenda, as well as the Centre's 'suggestions' and 'hopes' (*jianyi, xiwang*) for the forthcoming session. The leadership also suggests the tone the meeting should take: how open the debate should be, how much press coverage is planned and so on.[23] In March 1989, for example, Zhao Ziyang indicated to the NPC Party Members Group that the Centre wanted the Second Session of the Seventh NPC to adopt a more restrained tone than the wide-open March 1988 First Session.[24] Available sources indicate that Jiang Zemin made similar pleas for 'unity' and respect for Party leadership before the NPC meetings in 1990 and 1993.[25]

But a close look at these preparatory meetings underscores the most significant change in Party control over lawmaking since the mid-1980s: the great erosion of Party discipline among NPC delegates. Although the Centre still expresses its preference concerning the passage of a law, if a given Party-member NPC delegate absolutely opposes a law, he or she is now far more likely to abstain or even vote against the law without any clear expectation of suffering punishment as a result.[26] As Chapter 5 shows, moderate levels of dissenting votes are now quite common, far more common than the once ubiquitous unanimous votes. And dissenting votes occasionally reach high, even decisive levels, notwithstanding the Party Centre's prior approval 'in principle' of the draft legislation. Official press sources have reported that in 1990 the Standing Committee voted down a draft amendment to the Law on Organizing Village Committees. The amendment was formally put to a vote, but gained support from only sixty-five delegates—less than a quorum—and thus failed to pass.[27] Legal specialists who advise the NPC have reported even more dramatic levels of

23. Interviews 11-19-13-33/ADH, and 11-19-13-33/OKE, Beijing, 1989.
24. 'Speak No Evil. The Party Puts a Lid on Criticism', *The Far Eastern Economic Review*, 30 March 1989, 11.
25. A summary of Jiang's speech to the 1993 NPC Party members meeting was published in *Wen Hui Bao* (Hong Kong), 15 March 1993, 2, in FBIS-CHI, 15 March 1993, 13–15. Jiang's speech to the March 1990 session was issued as 'Guanyu Jianchi he Wanshan Renmin Daibiao Dahui Zhidu'.
26. This change in norms was noted by several interviewees, but most stressed by interest 26-17-13-33/TWS, Beijing, 1992.
27. At the March 1989 Second Session of the Seventh NPC, for example, 274 deletates vote 'no' and 805 abstained on Zhao Ziyang's proposal to grant the Shenzhen Special Economic Zone (SEZ) special legislative autonomy from Guangdong province, defying a strong request by Party leaders that they pass the measure. The increased tendency for NPC delegates to cast 'no' votes is discussed in greater detail in Chapter 5. For an interesting discussion of the 1988 vote and other examples of the new opposition in the NPC, see Zhang Sutang and He Ping (1993).

dissent, including two instances when the Standing Committee has actually submitted draft laws to a vote and then voted them down (again, see Chapter 5).

Even assuming these two reported negative votes are correct, there are still obvious, major limits to the delegates' autonomy and assertiveness. The actual voting down of legislation is still very rare, and, in fact, reported dissenting vote totals have exceeded the critical 40% level on fewer than five occasions. On the other hand, these numerical measures of formal legislative votes may not fully reflect the amount of dissent and therefore the degree of erosion of Party discipline. Most unpopular draft laws never make it to a formal vote. Instead, several mid-rank NPC sources have indicated to me that the preferred practice whenever a draft law appears destined for defeat or an embarassingly narrow passage is for the NPC leadership to withhold the draft from a vote and negotiate revisions with the organization which drafted it.[28] In addition, until the issuance of Central Document 8 [1991] on lawmaking, Party discipline did not permit the NPC to adopt any law which had not already been approved by the Centre. But these norms are still evolving away from tight Party control, and it is important to note that the post-Tiananmen persecution of Hu Jiwei and others has not stalled or set back this trend. Abstention and 'no' vote totals after 1989 quickly returned to and surpassed pre-Tiananmen levels, and the clear secular trend is that the willingness of Party-member NPC delegates to obey suggestions from the Party Centre has declined greatly since 1979.

Oversight of Lawmaking and the Party's Political-Legal (Zhengfa) System

In a striking contrast to Western notions of the separation of judicial, legislative and administrative functions, the Chinese Communist Party has a single 'political-legal system' (*zhengfa xitong*)[29] which subsumes not only lawmaking work but also the courts, prosecutors, police, intelligence-counterintelligence, prison/labour reform, civil affairs (such as firefighting, disaster relief) and many social affairs functions within one administrative system. At the top of this organizational system in Beijing is the Central Political-Legal Leading Group (*Zhongyang Zhengfa Lingdao*

---

28. Interviews 27-22-13-11-17/BNH; 27-13/15-16-32/BC; and 26-17-13-33/TWS, Beijing 1992.
29. English translations of the term *zhengfa* often reflect the problems Chinese and Westerners have in communicating the breadth of the concept. The official Chinese translation of 'political science and law' is an almost humorously benign translation for any organization which includes the secret police. 'Administration and Law' might be closer to the mark, but is still too vague. I will use the more standard translation 'Political-Legal'.

Xiaozu). Cadres who specialize in 'political-legal work' may, at various times in their career, shift back and forth between several or all of these tasks which may seem, to Westerners, widely disparate. Hence, in a deliciously ironic bureaucratic custom, many of the top leaders who have guided the development of the NPC, China's chief organ of socialist democracy, have spent the bulk of their careers in police and intelligence work.

In the past, many career political-legal cadres have been imbued with a conservative 'bureaucratic' view of law: a belief that while law should play a key role in ruling a modern Chinese state, it should principally be a tool of state control over citizens, not a weapon to protect individual political and economic liberties from arbitrary encroachment by the state.[30] While this represented a clear step forward from the legal nihilist view put forward during the Cultural Revolution, it is at odds with the legal relationship of state and society required for a transition to a market-oriented economy and a more liberal political system.[31] During the post-Mao era, however, this bureaucratic view of law has gradually been eroding within the NPC system.

The Central Political-Legal Leading Group: Organizational History and Evolving Role

In part because of this organizational connection between the legislature and the political-legal sector, Western analysts of Chinese lawmaking have long assumed that the Central Political-Legal Leading Group (CPLG), holds a unified leading role in lawmaking. This assumption remains a cornerstone of the traditional 'top-down' image of lawmaking in China, as has the notion that the CPLG and its leaders are the key sources of legislative proposals in the system. This controlling image of the CPLG is understandable. It has long been led by the CCP's 'tough guys' and 'enforcers'; the powerful, often brutal men who were responsible for protecting the Party from its enemies and imposing order in China's diverse society.[32]

There is, in fact, some evidence that in the very earliest days of the reform era, the CPLG under the leadership of Deputy Director Zhao Cangbi did play a much more comprehensive role in formulating Party legal policy, including legislative work. The CPLG convened a major meeting on legal work in October 1978 at which Group member Tao Xijin, who had headed Zhou Enlai's Legislation Bureau during the CCP's legal heydays of the 1950s, gave a major speech on laws which needed to be drafted.[33] Lacking detailed, reliable studies of the CPLG's role since that

---

30. Baum (1986).   31. See Paltiel, (1989).
32. Among the public security 'enforcers' who have previously served on the CPLG are Luo Ruiqing, Li Kenong, Peng Zhen, Kang Sheng, Xie Fuzhi, Peng Chong, Liu Fuzhi, and, more recently, Qiao Shi, Wang Fang and Tao Siju.
33. The meeting was reported in *Renmin Ribao*, 29 October 1978, 1–2; see also BXDS, 29 October 1978 in FBIS-CHI, 1 November 1978, 2. See also Foster (1982) for an analysis.

time, however, the assertion that it was and still is the key organization in the lawmaking process has always rested largely on presumption.

Whatever the CPLG's role may have been in the late 1970s, a variety of Chinese government, legislative and academic sources all independently confirm that its role in lawmaking has declined steadily since 1979, and is now almost negligible outside its narrow bailiwick of criminal law.[34] For a time during the mid-1980s, one source reports that liaison between the CPLG and legislative organs was maintained through former Leading Group Deputy Secretary General Gu Linfang, once a personal bodyguard to former NPC Secretary General Peng Chong. But Gu Linfang's lack of formal legal training limited the influence he could exercise over the details of legislative drafting. The CPLG's role, according to these sources, is also limited by its relatively small staff (none of the major legal scholars interviewed for this project, for instance, could think of any former student of theirs who now worked for the CPLG), and its general orientation toward police and social control issues. The expanding roles of the NPC Standing Committee staff and the State Council Legislation Bureau have largely obviated the need for direct CPLG involvement in lawmaking. By the late 1980s, it primarily concerned itself with resolving bureaucratic and personnel disputes between the major ministries and committees within its system (the Ministries of Public Security, Justice, Civil Affairs and Supervision, plus the Supreme People's Court and Supreme People's Procuratorate). As of the late 1980s, the CPLG's system did include the NPC Legislative Affairs Committee, according to one source, but their relationship did not concern lawmaking work and the CPLG system did not include the other NPC units.[35]

Former Party Chief and Premier Zhao Ziyang tried on at least two separate occasions to further diminish the role of the CPLG in the legal system, and weaken the influence of political conservatives on lawmaking. In 1984, Zhao established a Legislative Co-ordinating Group (*Lifa Xietiao Xiaozu*) directly under the Premier's office, and gave it the task of developing long-term legislative plans and resolving major bureaucratic disagreements between ministries. The Group was also dominated by proponents of relatively radical economic reform.[36]

Zhao's second attack came in the wake of the October 1987 Thirteenth Party Congress, when he tried to abolish the CPLG (at that time called a 'Committee' (*weiyuanhui*) altogether.[37] Gu Linfang was relieved of his

---

34. Interviews 11-19-13-33/OHK; 11-19-13-33/ADH; and 15-35-19/QXX (all Beijing, 1989); and interviews 26-17-13-33/TWS; 27-22-13-11-13-17/BNH, Beijing, 1992.
35. Interview 15-35-19/QXX, Beijing, 1989.
36. The Working Group members were An Zhiwen, Zhang Yanning, Gu Ming, Ma Hong, and Li Hao. See FBIS-CHI, 23 May 1985, K11.
37. In addition to the interview sources used in this study, see the following Hong Kong press sources: *Guangjiao Jing*, 16 January 1988, 1; *Wen Hui Bao*, 11 March 1988, 1.

CPLG post and transferred to Vice-Minister of Public Security. For a brief period around December 1987, the CPLG 'basically did not exist', according to one well-informed PRC legal scholar.[38] But Zhao's efforts failed in the face of resistance from several Party elders, led by the late former Politburo member Wang Zhen and reportedly including two former CPLG Chiefs, Peng Zhen and Chen Pixian, who feared the Political-Legal Committee's abolition might weaken Party control over the courts.[39] In the end, the Committee was merely downgraded to a Leading Group with diminished staff and responsibilities.

A high-ranking legislative source interviewed for this project indicated that as of 1992 there was no longer any single centralized office overseeing lawmaking within the Party's Secretariat.[40] Individual laws are reported to the Secretariat office or commission charged with overseeing the appropriate issue-area. Economic legislation, for example, is reviewed by the Secretariat's economic offices and the Financial and Economic Leading Group. Legislation on issues of Party or government personnel or organizational structure tends to go to the Central Organization Department, and so on. The CPLG apparently plays no role as a central reviewer of legislation, if indeed it ever did, beyond reviewing legislation narrowly related to criminal law and social control. Perhaps most significantly, the CPLG is not even mentioned in CCP Central Document 8, which gives detailed instructions on the prior approval of legislation by the Party Centre.

Prior Approval of Legislation

In the actual process of drafting a law, the single most important method for maintaining Party leadership is the power of veto. Until the issuance of Central Document 8 in 1991 (and perhaps, in practice, still), all draft laws to be passed by the NPC or its Standing Committee had to receive prior approval 'in principle' by the Party Centre. In practice, this usually meant the draft had to be approved by the Central Secretariat, the Politburo and 'other relevant senior leaders'.[41] But legislative officials and scholars report that until the issuance of Central Document 8, there were no documented procedures for this review, and such approval meetings, in any case, tended not to be very detailed, usually examining only the law's 'guiding princi-

38. This scholar and other sources believed Zhao enjoyed Deng Xiaoping's backing in trying to close down the Leading Group. Interview 15-35-19/QXX, Beijing, 1989.
39. Intriguingly, when asked, the source of this information indicated he had not heard of any evidence that Qiao Shi, at that time CPLG's Chairman, had opposed the abolition of the Group.   40. Interview 26-17-13-33/TWS, Beijing, 1992.
41. It is important not to put too fine an organizational edge on this picture of Party procedure, however. The relevant 'Party leadership' which must approve of a law can also include Party elders who, though not formally members of the Politburo, still have the personal power to involve themselves in policy-making on some issues.

The Erosion of Party Control over Lawmaking   65

ples', justification and most basic content. These sources indicate that these senior level officials tend to concern themselves only with whether or not the draft law's basic thrust fits in with the general direction (*fangzhen*) of current Party policy.[42]

Moreover, as the case studies in this volume make clear, the top Party leadership in practice often abdicates much of its power to control the content of legislation. This abdication of Party leadership tends to occur either by allowing the NPC to delay or amend significantly a draft law after it has been approved in principle by the Party Centre, or by failing to signal to the legislature any clear and unified intention concerning the handling of the law. There are generally three major reasons for this lack of clear Party leadership intent: the leadership is too deeply split over the issue to reach a decision solely within Party decision-making offices; some or all top leaders are simultaneously preoccupied with other issues and cannot give a law their attention; or the leadership simply lacks the expertise to understand the true meaning of the draft legislation under consideration.[43]

By the mid to late 1980s, the norms concerning the degree of insistence and level of detail the Party Centre exercised in reviewing draft legislation had already changed dramatically. Recent leadership suggestions to the NPC have often been much less specific, detailed or insistent than in past years. The Centre is apparently no longer able—or perhaps no longer feels the need—to prearrange a careful 'script' for all NPC sessions, with all the final wording of each piece of legislation worked out. Often the Centre cannot achieve consensus, and lacks a clear, strong preference concerning the content or passage of a draft law at the current session. If, later in the process, the Politburo is able to reach a consensus on the main features of a draft law, it will clearly express to the NPC Party members its 'hope' that the law will be finalized and passed at the current session.

An excellent example of this was the controversial 1986 Enterprise Bankruptcy Law, which is discussed in detail in Chapter 7. According to one Beijing legal scholar, before the Sixteenth and Seventeenth NPC Standing Committee sessions debated the draft, the leadership's instructions to NPC Party members, given by then-Premier Zhao Ziyang, were neither clear nor especially assertive, and tremendous debate and calls for extensive revision of the law ensued at the Standing Committee meeting. In October, prior to the Eighteenth Standing Committee meeting, NPC and State Council leaders extensively consulted local government, enterprise and labour union officials, and hammered out a compromise acceptable to almost all sides. Premier Zhao Ziyang reportedly gave a very strong speech to the preparatory session before the November Standing Committee meet-

42. Interviews 26-17-13-33/TWS, 27-13/34-19-28/XWQ and 27-22-13-11-13-17/BNH, all Beijing, 1992.
43. These three possibilities were discussed by Interviewee 11-19-13-33/ADH, Beijing, 1989 and 1992.

ing, indicating that the leadership expected final passage of the draft Bankruptcy Law at the current session. The session passed the law with just a handful of 'no' votes and abstentions.[44]

Central Document Number 8 [1991]: Towards an Institutionalized Party Review System

In early 1991, advocates of a stronger legislature scored a major victory with the issuance of Central Document Number 8, 'Several Opinions of the Central Committee on Strengthening Leadership over Lawmaking Work'. Central Document 8 is the first such document in the history of the People's Republic to spell out the principles and procedures of Party leadership over lawmaking.

There is an intriguing contradiction between Document 8's title and its contents. The title clearly suggests the intention of *tightening* Party control over lawmaking. Yet its contents, both the preamble and key operative provisions, clearly indicate that Party leadership over the NPC should henceforth be rather general and should not involve micromanagement. Chinese sources interviewed for this project indicate the drafting and circulation of the document were tightly restricted at a very high level,[45] and unfortunately they were unable to provide much information on the politics of drafting the document. One source did confirm what seems obvious, given the title/content contradiction, that considerable leadership disagreement attended the drafting. The document as originally commissioned was reportedly intended to tighten Party control, or at least give that impression. Apparently, however, the responsibility for drafting was turned over to a drafting committee controlled or influenced by advocates of greater legislative independence and decentralized Party control.

Leadership speeches from the period of the document's drafting (1990 to early 1991) suggest high-level disagreement over Party control of lawmaking between CCP General Secretary Jiang Zemin and NPC Standing Committee Chairman and Politburo Member Wan Li, disagreement which, according to one legal source, influenced the drafting of Central Document 8. In March 1990 both men, speaking only three days apart at the annual meeting of the NPC, addressed the issue of Party–legislature relations.[46] Wan Li, as he had done before, repeatedly and strongly stressed that if the CCP as a ruling party was to avoid major errors and prevent future

---

44. Interview 11-19-13-33/OKE, Beijing, 1989.
45. The document carries the designation *jimi* (roughly equivalent to 'secret' in the U.S. system). But the document also indicates that circulation is restricted to officials with rank equal to a State Council minister or higher, a far more restrictive circulation than 'secret' or even most 'top secret' documents get in the U.S. system.
46. The two speeches are Wan Li (1990) and Jiang Zemin (1990a).

The Erosion of Party Control over Lawmaking 67

1989-style uprisings, it must allow genuine democracy within the legislature, and heed the voice of the legislators. But Jiang Zemin, speaking three days later, stressed the need for unified Communist Party leadership over lawmaking, repeatedly castigating what he characterized as a tendency toward 'separation of powers'. Jiang omitted any mention of what the Party stood to learn from the voice of the people as communicated through the legislature. It is important to note that both men remained well within the official line on Party–legislative relations. But the difference in their emphases is striking. And since both men, by virtue of their positions, would certainly have played a role in drafting Central Document 8, it does not seem unreasonable to speculate that their disagreement may be the source of the glaring contradiction between its title and content.[47]

Turning to the document's content, the preamble suggests an effort to balance Party control with the evolving system of dispersed legislative power. The stated purposes for strengthening leadership over lawmaking strike a balance between four potentially contradictory goals: guaranteeing the legitimate authority of legislative organs (such as the NPC and State Council); better carrying out the Party line; speeding up lawmaking; and strengthening socialist modernization (economic development). The preamble notes that Party leadership over lawmaking is generally limited to 'leadership over the political line, direction, and policies', and may include 'reviewing and confirming' (*shending*) NPC-drafted legislative plans.

The document goes on to enumerate five basic dimensions or forms of the Party's leadership over lawmaking work, which may be summarized as follows:

(1) Establishing the nation's political line, general direction and major policies, which form the guiding principles for lawmaking.
(2) Examining and approving the NPC's annual and long-term legislative plans and guaranteeing that they are actually carried out.
(3) 'Suggesting' that the NPC and State Council codify into law those Party policies which have been proven effective in practice.
(4) Resolving and deciding any unclear or controversial points of Party policy which have been referred to the Party Centre by the NPC or its Standing Committee.
(5) Strengthening the role of law in society and guaranteeing that the Party obeys the law; co-ordinating and resolving intersectoral legislative disputes.

These five dimensions describe a picture of Party leadership which is solidly on the less interventionist side of actual current practice. They also show a willingness to stand behind the NPC in its efforts to exercise its powers.

---

47. Interviewee 11-19-13-33/AEDH (Beijing, 1995) confirms that a strong disagreement over Party–NPC relations does exist between Jiang Zemin and Wan Li.

Document 8 commits the Party Centre to 'support and guarantee' the power of legislative organs to carry out legislative plans.[48] These five points also show no desire to micromanage the NPC's lawmaking work, a point which the document asserts much more explicitly in its later discussion of review procedures.

The key operative sections of Document 8 are devoted to a relatively detailed discussion of the procedures for prior Central approval of legislation. Fascinatingly, this section does not assert that all laws which are to be debated and adopted by the NPC or its Standing Committee must undergo Central Party review. Instead, Document 8 divides draft laws into several issue-based categories; these categories apparently imply ranking of laws in terms of their importance or sensitivity. The document prescribes different review procedures for each of these categories, and explicitly exempts some categories of laws from required Central review.

The major categories named in Document 8 are: important laws and constitutional revisions[49]; political laws; important economic or administrative laws; and other laws outside the previous three categories. The term 'economic or administrative laws' is defined as 'laws which concern the development of the national people's economy or macroeconomic management, or draft administrative laws which concern the state management structure or which affect the rights and duties of citizens'. The vague-sounding category of 'political laws', however, is never defined, even implicitly. Party review procedures for the first three categories are discussed in separate sections of Document 8. The 'other laws' receive a brief but extremely important allusion at the end.

Constitutional revisions naturally receive the highest level of Party review. Document 8 requires that such revisions, whether they are submitted directly by the Politburo or through the Politburo by the NPC Standing Committee Party Group, must be discussed and approved by a Central Committee plenum. To the extent that the Central Committee plenum actually gets consulted on these revisions, this rule would represent a notable step towards intra-Party political democracy.

For political laws, the drafting ministry or unit must submit a report on the law's guiding thought and basic principles to the NPC Standing Com-

---

48. By comparison, the language 'support and guarantee' on its face seems to suggest an even stronger grant of NPC autonomy than the language used in 1988 to define the new, rather powerful position of state factory managers vis-à-vis enterprise Party committees, which were ordered to 'guarantee and supervise' the manager. See Chapter One, Article 8 of the State Owned Industrial Enterprises Law, which orders the Party committee to 'guarantee and supervise' (*baozhang jiandu*).

49. It is unclear what is intended by the term 'Important laws' (*Zhongyao Falu*), and the term is not revisited in the document. Perhaps this is a synonym for basic codes, such as the Criminal, Administrative and Civil Codes and their corresponding procedural codes; although, if that is the meaning, it is curious that the document did not use the well-established term *jiben falu*.

mittee or to its Party Group,[50] which would have the power to determine which questions in the law need to be referred to the Politburo for discussion and decision. After this point, Document 8 prescribes a procedure for both political laws and economic and administrative laws in which the wording is identical almost to a character. Before the draft laws are submitted to a plenary meeting of the NPC or its Standing Committee, they must be passed or agreed to by the Politburo or its Standing Committee. Among these, 'especially important' political, economic and administrative laws must also, like constitutional amendments, be submitted to a full Central Committee plenum. When the NPC Standing Committee or any other unit submits a draft law to the Politburo for approval, it must submit a brief report explaining the law, its purpose, major problems in it and how they have been dealt with, and a list of important issues regarding the law which the Party Centre must decide. Interestingly, the document does not specifically request that the unit submit the full current draft (*cao'an*) of the law. Only after the law has received Central approval may it be discussed and passed by the NPC.

Politburo review of these laws, according to Document 8, will be at a fairly general level, without micromanagement or individual review of legal clauses:

When the Party Centre discusses important laws, this will principally mean carrying out research on questions within the laws which touch upon important general directions and policies. There may be a few important legal clauses which require discussion. The majority of legal clauses need not be discussed.

Document 8 also grants the discretion to the NPC Standing Committee, not the Party Centre, to decide whether or not to ask the Party Centre to discuss or resolve other policy questions which affect lawmaking.

But in terms of the NPC's autonomy, the most remarkable clauses in Document 8 come at the end. The document closes with a reaffirmation of the lawmaking authority of the NPC and its Standing Committee, and pledges the Party Centre not to usurp the NPC's powers. Then it explicitly grants an unprecedented degree of autonomy to the NPC to carry on certain aspects of its lawmaking work without this formal Party review process:

Except for Constitutional revisions, political laws, and important economic and administrative laws, the NPC and its Standing Committee carry out the organization, drafting, and review of other laws, and normally do not report to the Party Centre. As for those few laws which need to be reported to the Party Centre for discussion, if the Party Centre has already expressed clear views or regulations, then these also need not be reported to the Party Centre again.

50. The inclusion of both the Standing Committee and its Party Group reflects standard protocol, which would require Party units to submit their reports directly to the NPC Party Group, and non-Party units to submit theirs to the NPC Standing Committee, which would in turn submit the reports to its Party Group.

Among law-making specialists familiar with the contents of Central Document Number 8, reaction has been mixed, but generally quite favourable. One official who had read the document expressed anger at its title, which clearly suggests stronger Party control over the legislature. This official noted, however, that in his experience, none of the actual Party review procedures set out in the document represented any toughening of long-standing unofficial practice.[51] Several scholars and NPC officials were pleased with the new grants of autonomy to the NPC and clearly hoped to expand them in the future. They also noted that the issuance of such a document represents an unprecedented level of Party respect for lawmaking work. Finally, one NPC official could scarcely contain his glee when noting that an official Party Central Document now required the Prime Minister and the State Council, long dismissive of the legislature, to submit key draft laws and plans through the NPC to the Party Centre.[52]

It goes without saying that these written regulations by themselves do not automatically prove there has been a major change in the realities of the Party's control over lawmaking. The gap between the real lawmaking process and the one ordained by Central Document 8 may be considerable, and further research on this highly secretive process is necessary.

At the same time, however, interview data on lawmaking suggest that the real process often comes much closer to the bottom-up policy-making model suggested in some parts of Document 8 than it does to a top-down model of the process. NPC sources report that it is often the NPC rather than the Party Centre which initiates consultations between the two. According to the document, if the NPC Standing Committee, in the course of deliberating a law, feels that current Party policy is insufficiently clear on some key point (a common occurrence), the Standing Committee, acting through its Party Group, may request instructions and ask the Party Centre to clarify, explain, decide or reconfirm a policy decision. In a 1992 interview, a long-standing high-ranking NPC official stated that when the Party leadership's indecisiveness on a major issue is delaying NPC efforts to draft a law, the NPC often uses a 'Request for Instructions' as a polite device to pressure the Party Centre to make up its mind and clarify policy.[53]

Institutionalizing Decentralization

Like many other authoritarian regimes, China has repeatedly been subject to cycles of policy decentralization and recentralization. Thus an important question when considering the impact of these changes on China's

---

51. Interview 27-22-13-11-13-17/BNH, Beijing, 1992.
52. Interview 27-13/34-19-28/XWQ, Beijing, 1992.
53. Interview 26-17-13-33/TWS, Beijing, August 1992.

The Erosion of Party Control over Lawmaking 71

prospects for a lasting transition to a more consultative system is: to what extent has the decentralization of Party control over lawmaking become institutionalized? The decentralized lawmaking arrangements established in the last nineteen years are now supported by changed attitudes and organizational forces which make it unlikely that power can be recentralized. Such attitudinal and organizational changes may also create pressure for further decentralization.

This topic will be discussed in detail in Chapter 10. But to anticipate that discussion somewhat, there is much evidence indicating that these decentralizing changes have survived even the post-1989 crackdown, and some have been pushed further. Changes in delegate selection norms and delegate behaviour, and the development of non-Party lawmaking organs continue to undermine centralized Party control. Moreover, the leadership during the post-Deng succession appears to lack the kind of internal unity necessary to take power back from these non-Party organs and return to the days when all major decisions could be taken exclusively within Party organs. Chapter 10 argues, however tentatively, that much of this decentralization has been institutionalized, and erosion of centralized Party control seems likely to continue in the future.

This chapter has stressed three important points. First, Party leadership over lawmaking is far less centralized and unified than has often been supposed by Western analysts. Secondly, that leadership has become even less centralized over the last nineteen years, notwithstanding any efforts to reassert general Party authority over society since 1989. Thirdly, this decentralization shows real signs of becoming institutionalized. Viewed from the 'commanding heights' of the legislative system, Party control over lawmaking and the legislature has devolved greatly to lower levels. How the legislature and the State Council have expanded their organizational powers to fill this emerging power gap is the subject of the next two chapters.

5

The Rise of The National People's Congress System

The Gradual Emergence of an NPC Power Base

Beginning with the Third Plenum's call for the National People's Congress to place lawmaking on its 'important agenda', the legislature and its leadership have carefully and gradually added to their powers. In the last fifteen years, the NPC has at last emerged not as a 'rubber stamp' forum, but as a key lawmaking arena; and the NPC Standing Committee and its permanent bureaucracy are now major organizational forces in lawmaking. It is important to reiterate that this subtle change has not involved any powerful open challenge to the concept of 'Party leadership' over lawmaking. The top NPC leaders continue to be, so far as can be ascertained, loyal CCP members. But just as State Council bureaucrats have, for decades, interpreted their duty to the Party as a mandate to accrue organizational influence and defend ministerial interests, the NPC leadership has expanded its organizational power and prerogatives within the rapidly eroding definitions of Party 'leadership' and 'discipline'. This chapter argues that there are three major sources of NPC's increased influence. While the first of these power sources represents a gradual, halting and uneven evolution in the Chinese *legal* tradition, the second and third represent classic reaffirmations of the Chinese *political* tradition.

First, NPC representatives are gradually developing new attitudes and norms concerning their proper role as people's representatives. Increasingly, delegates are willing to vote against or abstain on draft laws, decrees and even high level personnel appointments which Party and state bodies submit to the NPC for approval. Most importantly, this trend, which began in the late 1980s, quickly recovered after Tiananmen, and now exceeds pre-1989 levels.

Secondly, the NPC, like any other Chinese political organization, began to acquire greater influence because it has been led by powerful individual politicians who found it to be a useful conduit through which to exercise their power. Since 1978 the NPC Standing Committee, in particular, has become the home for dozens of 'retired' Party elders who retain great informal political influence but whose organization channels of influence have been focused increasingly through the NPC.

Quite naturally, these elders' presence on the NPC has facilitated the legislature's third and most important new power source: its rapid growth as a policy-making bureaucracy since 1979. Comparative legislative studies have long demonstrated that a well-developed permanent legislative bureaucracy and subcommittee system is one of the most important factors permitting a developing legislature to assume a significant policy-making role.[1] In 1979, a major cross-national survey of legislative subcommittee structures showed a near-perfect correlation between the power and organizational development of a given legislature's subcommittee system and that legislature's overall influence in the lawmaking process.[2] The ability of a legislature to develop an organizationally powerful subcommittee structure and permanent bureaucracy tends to enhance greatly its ability to force the executive bureaucracy to share power over policy-making. This organizational structure is also indispensible if the legislature is ever to develop a serious administrative oversight capacity. Legislative subcommittees and bureaucracies have been shown to be important power sources even in those political systems which lack many of the key 'contextual' factors which classically have a great impact upon a legislature's power, such as a multi-party system, low party cohesiveness, a Presidential rather than Parliamentary constitutional structure, and historically liberal-democratic cultural attitudes toward legislative and executive organs.[3]

When the NPC's organizational development, its emerging power base and the impact of the Party elders are considered, it quickly becomes apparent that the story is inseparable from that of one key Party leader, the late Peng Zhen (1902–97). Peng was the NPC's dominant leader throughout most of its existence. He served as Standing Committee Vice-Chairman from 1954 until his purge in 1966, a post from which he guided the NPC's initial bureaucratic growth. After his return to political life in early 1979, Peng effectively headed the NPC from 1979 to 1988, first as Chairman of the Legislative Affairs Commission (1979–81), and as Executive Vice-Chairman, then Chairman of the NPC Standing Committee (1983–88). Peng's personal authority derived in part from his seniority within the Party,[4] and also in part from his many years as mayor of Beijing (1949–66). Like so many other NPC leaders, he also retained much power from his past role as leader of the Party's 'political-legal' system. He led many of the suppression campaigns of the early 1950s which established CCP power in China, and through the late 1950s to mid-1960s he was one

---

1. See, for example, Lees and Shaw (1979). Several of Shaw's key conclusions are reprinted in 'Committees in Legislatures' in Norton (1990), 237–67; also Susan Webb Hammond, 'Legislative Staffs' in Loewenberg, Patterson and Jewell (1985), 273–321.
2. Lees and Shaw (1979), especially 383–91.   3. *Ibid.*
4. Peng Zhen was older than either of the two other dominant post-Mao leaders—Deng Xiaoping and economic doyen Chen Yun. Peng also ascended to Politburo rank before Deng Xiaoping. A former senior Chinese official who worked with all three men has indicated to me that, as a result of this seniority, Deng accorded both men unusual personal and policy deference, particularly in their respective policy spheres.

of the five top CCP leaders overseeing security affairs.[5] During the post-Mao years, Peng increasingly made the NPC his principal 'kingdom', in the process contributing enormously to its organizational institutionalization.

This chapter focuses on each of these new power sources, looking briefly at the new assertiveness of NPC delegates. The order of presentation—attitudinal changes, leadership and bureaucratic factors—is in inverse to my rough assessment of their relative importance to the long-range development of an NPC power base. Consequently, the great majority of the chapter is devoted to the NPC's internal organization and its bureaucratic development from 1954 to the present, including the role of the Party elders who joined the Standing Committee from 1979.

Changing Attitudes and Behaviour Among NPC Delegates

Although the Chinese Constitution declares that the approximately 2,800 delegates to the NPC Plenary Session constitute 'the highest organ of state authority', the plenary session has simply proved too cumbersome to establish any great ongoing political influence. Delegate numbers are too large, the plenary session meets once annually for about two weeks, its agenda is determined for it by the NPC leadership, and the leadership takes great pains to prevent extensive contacts among the various provincial and military delegations. Until 'rank and file' NPC plenum delegates develop freer means of organizing and co-ordinating their activism, their influence will probably remain relatively sporadic and diffuse. Real sustained influence within the NPC, as shown below, resides principally with the leadership of the NPC Standing Committee and the bureaucracy which it oversees.

These factors have not, however, prevented an impressive secular increase in delegate assertiveness since 1979 which is greatly reshaping the NPC's role in the system. In the initial years after 1979, as Dorothy Solinger and others have chronicled, a few relatively courageous delegates limited their assertiveness to making speeches critical of Party and state policy. But such speeches at first remained an irregular feature of the sessions,[6] and votes on draft laws and other decisions were still, overwhelmingly, unanimous, according to the available official reports.

But as the penalties for speaking out and disobeying central suggestions have greatly diminished, 'disobedience', assertiveness and criticism, even by Party-member NPC delegates has shown a marked increase. One recent survey among both national and local-level people's congress delegates documents their changing role perception, indicating that many increas-

---

5. See Leng Shao-chuan (1967), also Klein and Clarke (1971) and Potter (1986) on Peng's leading role in these campaigns.   6. Solinger (1982).

ingly behave as 'remonstrators' representing their perceived constituents before higher levels of government.[7] Many other sources indicate that since the mid to late 1980s, ordinary NPC delegates have gone further, increasingly rising up to embarass China's political leaders, and sometimes forcing important changes in major legislative decisions which had already received the approval of the Party Centre.[8] Gradually, beginning no later than 1986, delegate assertiveness started taking much stronger forms, as press reports began to indicate for the first time in the NPC's history that small but increasing numbers of delegates where either voting 'no' or abstaining on draft legislation, personnel decisions and other motions (see below).

Nor have the NPC's own bureaucratic leaders been immune from this new assertiveness—a point which underscores the inadequacy of analyses which attribute these delegate uprisings solely to the alleged backstage manipulations of an 'NPC faction' within the top Party leadership. Top NPC leaders must often face spontaneous rebellions from among their own delegates. In the late 1980s, for example, delegates successfully argued that the draft law on village-level government committees should be considered a 'basic law' and ought to be submitted to the full NPC for consideration. According to one NPC staffer, the NPC leadership had originally listed the law to be promulgated by the Standing Committee, without consideration by the plenary session.[9] In March 1988, a large number of delegates balked at NPC Secretary General Peng Chong's questionable manipulation of NPC rules in an effort to ensure the re-election of an aged and unpopular special committee chairman. In the end, Peng was able to force through both his interpretation of the rules and the nominee's re-election, but at the cost of considerable embarassment in both the official and foreign press.[10]

For analysts of the NPC two newly available and very useful statistical indicators allow a more systematic examination of whether or not these post-1979 trends in delegate assertiveness and dissent are becoming institutionalized. These are data on the number of 'motions' (*ti'an* or *yi'an*) delegates put forward at the annual plenary session and data on the number of dissenting votes they cost on draft laws, personnel nominations and other motions at plenary and Standing Committee meetings.

The hypothesis here is fairly straightforward. As tolerance for moderate dissent and assertiveness by NPC delegates becomes greater, delegates will be willing to put forward more motions and dissent from top leadership proposals more often. But if periods of increasing assertiveness and dissent are mere temporary cycles that can be shut down again with each Central crackdown on liberalism and dissent, then the increases do not necessarily

---

7. O'Brien (1994).
8. See, for example, Foreign Broadcast Information Service (FBIS) (1988).
9. Interview 12-32-17/34-19-28/ABE, Beijing 1989   10. FBIS (1988).

indicate an institutionalization of these trends. If, on the other hand, the NPC is growing out of its historical cycles of 'opening up–closing down' and assertiveness and moderate dissent really are becoming more 'normal' and institutionalized, there should be not only an increase in these indicators but also a certain stabilization in the upward trend. Specifically, delegate assertiveness and dissent should be more resistant to such antiliberal political 'shocks' which have crushed past periods of opening up, and should decline far less in the wake of such reversals. A stronger tendency for these indicators to remain stable or increase despite antiliberal crackdowns would strongly suggest that these trends are becoming 'tougher'—that is, institutionalized.

Before examining the trends in these new data, the strengths and weaknesses in each indicator should be addressed frankly. Annual delegate motions are a very valuable indicator of delegate assertiveness, though they are not without flaws. Motions are one of the principal ways delegates assert themselves in the legislative process, in addition to making speeches, talking in delegation meetings and casting votes. Once rare, these motions now number in the thousands each year and run the gamut of suggestions, assertions and criticisms. Many are fairly formal, detailed proposals by a number of delegates for the NPC or the State Council to draft important pieces of legislation. Some are calls for legislative investigations into government handling of a particular policy issue. The vast majority are procedurally less formal criticisms or praise for some aspect of the 'state of the nation' usually coupled with general suggestions for how the Party and state should cope with that issue, such as 'we must spend more money to strengthen education' or 'corruption in state government offices has become intolerable, and the Chief State Procurator should report back on special measures to deal with it'.

The impact and handling of these motions varies greatly. The NPC Standing Committee leadership either deals with these requests directly or, in most cases, forwards them to the appropriate NPC subcommittee or State Council ministry to deal with them. A number have become the original sources for important pieces of legislation or investigations, while many are simply ignored. Others end up being more or less 'bundled together' with similar cries from the heart about China's ills, and gradually contribute to the system-wide sense of urgency which motivates and shapes the policy agenda. The NPC does not publish the entire annual list of motions received, which delegates proposed them or how each was handled (thus making it impossible to assess their true content either as policy proposals or dissent). But each year during the annual session many of these motions are picked up by or leaked to official and foreign mass media, and press reports about certain high profile motions end up constituting a key part of the session's 'atmospherics'. They help influence the political agenda by becoming an annual source of some public controversy

The Rise of The National People's Congress System 77

and criticism of the Party and state leadership's policy performance, and a sort of semi-public referendum on the state of the nation. Delegate motions, therefore, have at least moderate political importance. As a whole, they are certainly far more than empty activity designed to make politically irrelevant actors feel meaningful.

At the same time, however, total delegate motions are not an appropriate measure of 'dissent', and even have flaws as a measure of 'assertiveness'. Until the NPC releases a detailed index of motions received there will be no way of knowing how many motions are critical of current leadership performance and how many are not. Nor are all motions equally controversial, important or well-considered. Some delegates who strongly support current leadership policies and performance submit motions of praise. For example, delegates have put forward motions which lauded anti-liberal attacks on 'spiritual pollution' and 'bourgeois liberalization' or praised the government's firm resolution in suppressing the 1989 Democracy Movement. Unquestionably, some unknown percentage of these motions represent the 'enthusiastic slavishness' of some delegates rather than genuine assertiveness.[11]

Norms of delegate behaviour have also changed so greatly since Mao's death that it is difficult to use mere statistics to compare the relative levels of assertiveness—and raw courage—represented by delegate motions during the Maoist and Reform eras. An increase in their overall number certainly does not represent anything like a standard interval increase in legislators' willingness to challenge the leadership. For example, given the stern punishments received by many delegates who spoke up during the 1957 Hundred Flowers Campaign, it almost certainly took far greater courage to put forward some of the mere forty-six motions made at the 1960 NPC Session than it did to make almost any of the 2,500-plus motions which were common at NPC sessions during the mid-1980s. On the other hand, such a difference in norms and expectations reveals exactly the type of institutionalized tolerance for assertiveness and moderate dissent which is the point of this analysis.

Procedurally, delegates' willingness to put forward motions can be affected by the NPC's specific procedures for accepting such motions, in particular the number of co-signers required. These procedures have changed more than once since 1954, and this represents another shortcoming in the data. Indeed, the NPC apparently even refused to permit motions at all during the first sessions of the 1975 Fourth NPC and the 1978 Fifth NPC. The rules for counting delegate motions have also changed at least once

---

11. I am grateful to Melanie Manion of the University of Rochester for this delightful characterization, and to Professor Manion and my Western Michigan University colleagues Neil Pinney and Kevin Corder for a good deal of trenchant and valuable methodological criticism of an early draft of this section. Remaining errors of method, fact, and interpretation are entirely my own.

since 1954. In 1983 the NPC Motions Committee responded to the post-Mao explosion in delegate motions by separating regular legislative 'motions' (*ti'an*—most of which were apparently suggestions for laws to be drafted) from the much larger category of 'suggestions, criticisms and viewpoints' (*jianyi, piping, yijian*). I have simply re-aggregated the post-1983 data using the pre-1983 rules, combining the two new categories into a single 'motions' statistic for each year after 1982. Still, one should not necessarily assume these pre- and post-1983 figures are perfectly comparable.

Even acknowledging these flaws, delegate motions have several advantages as a statistical indicator of NPC delegate assertiveness. Most significantly, the NPC Standing Committee's Research Office recently published the full time series of these motions for every NPC session from 1954 to the early 1990s, making them the only statistical indicator of assertiveness available to compare the Maoist and Reform eras.[12]

Tables 5.1 and 5.2 display and analyse the changing patterns in delegate motions from 1954 to 1996 and their responses in the face of major political reversals or campaigns. For historical comparison, the data are broken into Maoist and Post-Third Plenum periods, and each annual meeting is shown with the total number of motions made at that session (post-1982 data are also broken down by motion type) along with the magnitude of the change over the last session, either positive or negative, expressed in both raw percentages and standard deviation from mean number of motions for that period. The major liberal and anti-liberal political movements which occurred in the time between annual sessions are noted in order to permit examination of how much delegate assertiveness changed in their aftermath.

As argued above, if assertiveness is not merely increasing but also becoming 'institutionalized', as the NPC moves from the Maoist era through Reform to the present, it should be expected that the annual number of motions would not only increase, but the upward pattern should also 'stabilize'. Stabilization means fewer wild annual fluctuations and, in particular, fewer sharp declines in years after anti-liberal campaigns are launched. However, since there has been a massive increase in the average annual number of motions between Maoist-era and Reform-era sessions (from 116 per year to over 3,100), it would not be appropriate to assess changes in fluctuation (stabilization or institutionalization) by simply comparing year-to-year changes in the raw number of motions or by comparing

---

12. NPC Standing Committee General Office Research Office, *Zhonghua Renmin Gongheguo Renmin Daibiao Dahui Wenxian Ziliao Huibian 1949–1990* (Beijing: Zhongguo Minzhu Fazhi Chubanshe, 1990), 855–7. For many years now, these data on motions have also been reported in the annual NPC Standing Committee Work Report, delivered by the Secretary General at each annual session. I have used these reports to fill in the data for the years since 1990. The text of this annual report may be found in a number of places, including the CIA's FBIS translation service, and the annual *Zhongguo Falu Nianjian (Law Year Book of China)*, published by Falu Chubanshe in Beijing.

annual percentage changes. Focusing on fluctuations in raw numbers of motions would tend to exaggerate Reform-era instability, since a yearly change of, for example, 100 motions, which seems small today, would have appeared vast by the standards of the 1950s and 1960s. Conversely, focusing on annual percentage changes would exaggerate Maoist-era instability, when a change of a mere handful of motions translated into a huge change in percentage terms. To permit meaningful comparison between eras, Table 5.2 calculates the mean annual number of motions, standard deviations and coefficients of variation for both periods (and for selected sub-periods). The coefficient of variation (the standard deviation for the period shown as a proportion of the mean) enables more useful comparisons of fluctuation between time periods because it takes the measure of how 'spread out' the annual session data for each period are (the period's standard deviation) and then effectively 'deflates' the huge difference between the periods by showing how large that spread is in relation to the mean for the period. The two periods now become comparable. The smaller the coefficient of variation for the period, the less wildly the annual number of motions during that period tend to fluctuate.

A comparison of the Maoist-era data (1954–78) and post-Third Plenum or Reform-era data (1979–96) on Table 5.1 reveals both a dramatic increase in raw levels of delegate assertiveness and powerful evidence of its institutionalization against anti-liberal attacks. The most striking trend, noted above, is the tremendous increase in the mean number of motions in the Reform-era: about twenty-seven times the Maoist-era figure. Delegate motions which seldom exceeded 200 during the high point of the Hundred Flowers Campaign quickly exceeded 2,000 per year after 1979.

The second notable trend is the terrific stabilization in the upward trend during the Reform era. During the Maoist era annual total motions gyrated wildly in the face of alternating leadership moods of opening up and cracking down on dissent, and finally crashed to the ground entirely after 1965. Since 1979, the annual number of motions has been far more stable than before 1965, and has become more stable over time. The standard deviation for the Maoist period (81.71 motions) is huge compared to the rather small average number of motions per year (117), yielding a very large coefficient of variation (.70). From year to year delegate assertiveness moved up and down so severely that in terms of individual 'norms' of behaviour, a delegate preparing for an annual session had no idea in advance what kind of behaviour would be considered 'permissible' that year, and the previous year's standards would be of virtually no help. By contrast, the standard deviation for the entire period 1979 to 1996 (741 motions) is far smaller relative to the average annual number of motions (3,129), and produces of coefficient of variation of just .24. The clear trend during the era has been a gradual increase in the annual number of motions which have fluctuated within a much narrower range than during the

Maoist period. Moreover, if the Reform era is subdivided, it becomes clear that this stabilization trend has strengthened within the era. If the earliest ten years of the reform era (1979–88) are compared with the latest ten-year period (1987–96), year-to-year fluctuation for the recent period is far smaller than for the earlier period (coefficient of variation falls from .26 to .15) even though the average number of motions has increased by nearly 800. This last point is especially striking since the more recent decade includes the most dramatic attack on liberalism and dissent of the era—the crackdown after Tiananmen.

Finally, and most importantly, Reform-era delegates have been far less intimidated by leadership crackdowns on dissent than were their Maoist-era counterparts. The far right columns of Table 5.1 reveal how much the number of motions has risen or fallen off in years following major attacks on liberalism and dissent. The first column shows the change in motions since the previous session in percentage terms, the second column shows that year-to-year change in terms of the standard deviation for that overall period (Maoist/Reformist). Again, the Maoist-era sensitivity to political changes is dramatic. Delegate assertiveness rose sharply during the 'pro legal system' era of the mid-1950s and the openness of the Hundred Flowers Campaign, but plummeted just as violently with the crackdown of the Anti-Rightist Campaign and the subsequent Great Leap. Motions rose upwards again quickly during the recovery years of 1962–64, but disappeared entirely as the NPC was shut down during the Cultural Revolution.

But since 1979, the three great attacks on liberalism and dissent (the Campaigns against spiritual pollution (1983) and bourgeois liberalization (early 1987), and the 1989–90 post-Tiananmen suppression) have not produced nearly the same downturns in delegate activism seen before 1979. In the case of the 1983 Anti-Spiritual Pollution campaign, delegate activism actually went up modestly the following year. Both the early 1987 attack on bourgeois liberalism and the 1989 post-Tiananmen suppression produced modest drops over the preceding year (in both cases, less than 10% or one-half a standard deviation), and returned to original form the following year. Even these numbers may exaggerate the downturn, since in both cases it was measured against a preceding year which had witnessed a much higher than average number of motions. The failure of delegates to be intimated by 1989 is especially interesting, since it included the removal of NPC Standing Committee member Hu Jiwei for his democracy movement activities. In sum, the evidence seems to suggest very strongly that at least this form of NPC delegate activism is becoming far more institutionalized and far more immune to changes in the political wind than was the case in the Maoist era.

TABLE 5.1. *Delegate Motions at Annual NPC Plenary Sessions, 1954–1996 Maoist Period, 1954–78*

Year	Date Month	NPC number and session	Major political events since preceding sessions	NPC session motions Legislative motions	Viewpoints, criticisms, suggestions	Total motions	Change from prev. session in per cent	Change from prev. session in std. dev.
1954	Sep	1st NPC, 1st Sess.		39	n/a	39	n/a	n/a
1955	July	1st NPC, 2nd Sess.		214	n/a	214	448.72	2.14
1956	June	1st NPC, 3rd Sess.		176	n/a	176	−17.76	−0.47
1957	June–July	1st NPC, 4th Sess.	'100 Flowers' Liberalization	243	n/a	243	38.07	0.82
1958	Feb	1st NPC, 5th Sess.	Anti-Rightist Campaign	81	n/a	81	−66.67	−1.98
1959	April	2nd NPC, 1st Sess.	Great Leap Forward	80	n/a	80	−1.23	−0.01
1960	Mar–Apr	2nd NPC, 2nd Sess.	Peng Dehuai Purge, then Attack on 'Rightist Opportunists'	46	n/a	46	−42.50	−0.42
1961		(No Session)		0	n/a	0		−0.56
1962	Mar–Apr	2nd NPC, 3rd Sess.		163	n/a	163	254.35	1.99
1963	Nov–Dec	2nd NPC, 4th Sess.		172	n/a	172	5.52	0.11
1964	Dec–Jan	3rd NPC, 1st Sess.		188	n/a	188	9.30	0.20
1965		(No Session)		0	n/a	0	–	–
1966–74		(No Sessions)	Cultural Revolution	–	n/a	–	–	–
1975	Jan	4th NPC, 1st Sess.	Cultural Revolution	0	n/a	0	−100.00	−2.30
1976–77		(No Sessions)	Cultural Revolution		n/a			
1978	Feb–Mar	5th NPC, 1st Sess.		0	n/a	0	0.00	0.00

Post-Third Plenum Period, 1979–Present

1979	June–July	5th NPC, 2nd Sess.		1,890	n/a	1,890	N/A	N/A
1980	Aug–Sep	5th NPC, 3rd Sess.		2,300	n/a	2,300	21.69	0.55
1981	Nov–Dec	5th NPC, 4th Sess.		2,318	n/a	2,318	0.78	0.02
1982	Nov–Dec	5th NPC, 5th Sess.		2,102	n/a	2,102	−9.32	−0.29

TABLE 5.1. (continued)

Post-Third Plenum Period, 1979–Present (continued)

1983	June	6th NPC, 1st Sess.	61	2,331	**2,392**	13.80	0.39
1984	May	6th NPC, 2nd Sess.	114	2,697	**2,811**	17.52	0.57
1985	Mar–Apr	6th NPC, 3rd Sess. Attack on 'Spiritual Pollution'	128	2,832	**2,960**	5.30	0.20
1986	Mar–Apr	6th NPC, 4th Sess.	265	3,341	**3,606**	21.82	0.87
1987	Mar–Apr	6th NPC, 5th Sess. Attack on Bourgeois Liberalism	262	3,014	**3,276**	−9.15	−0.45
1988	Mar–Apr	7th NPC, 1st Sess.	488	3,847	**4,335**	32.33	1.43
1989	Mar–Apr	7th NPC, 2nd Sess.	411	3,778	**4,189**	−3.37	−0.20
1990	Mar–Apr	7th NPC, 3rd Sess. Tiananmen Crackdown	384	3,491	**3,875**	−7.50	−0.42
1991	Mar–Apr	7th NPc, 4th Sess.	471	3,909	**4,380**	13.03	0.68
1992	Mar–Apr	7th NPC, 5th Sess.	472	2,668	**3,140**	−28.31	−1.67
1993	March	8th NPC, 1st Sess.	611	2,325	**2,936**	−6.50	−0.28
1994	March	8th NPC, 2nd Sess.	723	2,401	**3,124**	6.40	0.25
1995	March	8th NPC, 3rd Sess.	732	2,930	**3,662**	17.22	0.73
1996	March	8th NPC, 4th Sess.	603	2,415	**3,018**	−17.59	−0.87

Source: 1954–90, *Zhonghua Renmin Gongheguo Renmin Daibiao Dahui Wenxian Ziliao Huibian 1949–90*, pp. 854–57. 1990-Present, NPC-SC Work Reports, in *Zhongguo Falu Nianjian*, (*Law Year Book of China*), (Beijing, Falu Chubanshe, annual ed.).

Delegate Motions: Conmparing Time Periods

Annual sessions	Mean motions per session	Standard deviation	Coefficient of variation (std. dev./mean)
1954–1978:	116.83	81.71	0.70
(1965–1978)	0	N/A	N/A
1979–1996:	3,128.56	741.25	0.24
(1979–1988)	2,799.00	722.65	0.26
(1987–1996)	3,593.50	538.27	0.15

Learning to Just Say 'No'

The study of dissenting legislative votes is a second and even more interesting new method for evaluating the NPC's assertiveness and its capacity to resist cyclical political shocks. As compared with the large number of undifferentiated motions studied above, dissenting vote totals are a much more powerful indicator of a potential change in the culture of the legislature. Since virtually all draft laws and motions which are submitted to a vote by the NPC or its Standing Committee must first receive approval in principle by the Party Centre, a dissenting vote is a much more unambiguous act of legislative assertiveness than a delegate motion. Indeed, before 1979 NPC delegates rarely if ever voted 'no' (information on abstentions and 'present, not voting' are unavailable). Thus the willingness of legislators actually to vote down a draft law or motion is one of the most dramatic indicators of the legislature's assertiveness and autonomy. When the NPC votes down a Politburo-approved draft law, or nearly half of the delegates vote 'no' or abstain, it becomes increasingly difficult to continue to maintain, as many journalists and some scholars do, that the Party still has a tightly unified control over the legislature.

Over the past decade, it has gradually become possible to assemble quite a large data set of NPC votes on various draft laws, motions, budgets and economic plans, work reports and nominations to high state office. Although the NPC certainly records such votes for itself, Chinese legislative scholars indicate that the NPC does not publish such cumulated voting data, even internally within the Chinese legal community. Thus, collecting such data requires assiduous culling of many official and non-official press sources in addition to a good deal of interviewing.[13] The 1995 publication of the legislative memoirs of Song Rufen, a former senior NPC official and long-term personal secretary to Peng Zhen, added significantly to this data collection.[14]

Table 5.2 displays voting data on about ninety draft laws and proposals considered by the NPC or its Standing Committee since 1979. Most date only from 1986 when the Standing Committee reportedly first began using secret electronic voting machines. These include vote totals on sixteen draft laws considered by the full NPC, thirty-two votes on draft laws considered by the NPC Standing Committee, and forty motions considered by the full NPC to approve budgets, economic, plans, work reports and Party nominations to state offices at or above the rank of minister.

These vote totals include votes in favour of a motion, opposed, abstaining and present but not voting. I have also tabulated from this a total and

---

13. I am grateful to WMU doctoral candidate Chen Ke for his remarkably dedicated and resourceful job of research assistance, helping to locate these voting data from a variety of sources.   14. Song Rufen (1995).

TABLE 5.2. *NPC and NPC Standing Committee Legislative Votes 1978–95*
Part 1: Votes by Full NPC

Year	Month	Law/motion	Votes for	Votes against	Abstained	Present, not voting	Total	Total dissenting (No + Abst + N/V)	Dissent as % of voting	Source
1979	July	Sino-Foreign Joint Ventures Law	2,610	34	55	14	2,713	103	3.80	SRF
1988	April	Sino-Foreign Co-operative Enterprises Law	2,836	1	2	0	2,839	3	0.11	SRF
1988	April	State-Owned Industrial Enterprises Law	2,826	2	11		2,839	13	0.46	BBC/SWB, SRF
1988	April	State Council Restructuring Plan	2,785	1	1		2,787	2	0.07	Kyodo
1989	April	Administrative Litigation Law	2,663	3	23	0	2,689	26	0.97	SRF
1989	April	Delegate Shenzhen Special Legislative Authority	1,609	274	805		2,688	1,079	40.14	BBC/SWB
1990	April	Administrative Litigation Law	2,662	3	23		2,688	26	0.97	BBC/SWB
1991	April	Hong Kong Basic Law	2,660	16	29	8	2,713	53	1.95	Pt,Dt
		Tax Law on Foreign-Invested and Wholly foreign Owned Enterprises								
1992	April	Three Gorges Project	2,313	118	163	16	2,610	297	11.38	SRF
1993	March	Govoernment Streamlining Plan	1,767	177	664	25	2,633	866	32.89	AFP
1993	April	Est. Hong Kong S.A.R. Preparatory Committee Working Group	2,274	210	292	40	2,816	542	19.25	SCMP
1993	March	Macao Basic Law	2,828	21	22	4	2,875	47	1.63	Reuters
1994	March	Budget Law	2,790	23	39	30	2,882	92	3.19	SCMP
1995	March	Central Banking Law	2,110	337	225	49	2,721	611	22.45	SRF
1995	March		1,821	n/a	n/a	n/a	2,678	857	32.00	(%est) Econ, AFP
1995	March	Education Law	1,989	359	300	30	2,678	689	25.73	Econ, UP1

TABLE 5.2. Part 2: *NPC Standing Committee Vote*

Year	Month	Law/motion	Votes for	Votes against	Abstained	Present, not voting	Total	Total dissenting (No + Abst + N/V)	Dissent as % of voting	Source
1986	Aug	Enterprise Bankruptcy Law (first vote—17th session)	54	—	—	—	110	56	50.91	SRF, intvws (EST)
1986	Dec	Enterprise Bankruptcy Law	101	9	0	0	110	9	8.18	Xinhua
1986	March	Mineral Resources Law	118	0	8	0	126	8	6.35	SRF
1986	Dec	Postal Administration Law	105	1	4	0	110	5	4.55	SRF
1987	Jan	Customs Law	107	0	3	0	110	3	2.73	SRF
1987	June	Technological Contracts Law	100	0	0	7	107	7	6.54	SRF
1988	Nov	Wildlife Protection Law	114	0	1	—	115	1	0.87	Xinhua/BBC/SWB
1988	Jan	Water Law	99	1	0	2	102	3	2.94	SRF
1988	Dec	Standardization Law	116	1	4	3	124	8	6.45	SRF
1989	Feb	Import-Export Goods Inspection Law	119	1	2	1	123	4	3.25	SRF
1989	Dec	City Planning Law	110	0	4	2	116	6	5.17	SRF
1989	July?	Public Demonstrations Law (First vote)	54	—	—	—	110	56	50.91	intvw (est)
1989	Oct	Public Demonstrations Law	103	—	—	—	103	0	0.00	BBC/SWB
1989	Dec	Environmental Protection Law	112	0	3	1	116	4	3.45	SRF
1990	Sept	Railway Law	94	7	9	2	112	18	16.07	SRF

TABLE 5.2. Part 2: (continued)

Year	Month	Law/motion	Votes for	Votes against	Abstained	Present, not voting	Total	Total dissenting (No + Abst + N/V)	Dissent as % of voting	Source
1990	Sept	Copyright Law	102	3	4	3	112	10	8.93	SRF
1991	Dec	Adoption Law	107	1	6	1	115	8	6.96	SRF
1991	June	Tobacco Monopoly Law	116	1	4	2	123	7	5.69	SRF
1991	June	Water and Soil Conservation Law	122	1	0	0	123	1	0.81	SRF
1992	Nov	Maritime Commerce Law	98	1	2	0	101	3	2.97	SRF
1992	Nov	Mine Safety Law	97	1	3	0	101	4	3.96	SRF
1992	Sept	Supp. Regs. for dealing with Tax Evasion and Resistance	98	0	3	3	104	6	5.77	SRF
1992	Sept	Tax Collection Administration Law	98	0	3	3	104	6	5.77	SRF
1992	Dec	Survey Law	96	0	3	3	102	6	5.88	SRF
1993	Feb	Trademark Law Revisions	102	0	2	2	106	4	3.77	SRF
1993	Feb	Supp. Regs. for dealing with Trademark Infringement	103	0	2	1	106	3	2.83	SRF
1993	Feb	Product Quality Law	100	0	4	2	106	6	5.66	SRF
1993	July	Agriculture Law	135	0	1	0	136	1	0.74	SRF
1993	Oct	Consumers' Interests Protection Law	127	0	0	0	127	0	0.00	SRF
1993	Dec	Corporations Law	124	9	2	1	136	12	8.82	SRF
1994	Aug	Arbitration Law	127	0	0	0	127	0	0.00	SRF
1994	Aug	Auditing Law	124	0	3	0	127	3	2.36	SRF

TABLE 5.2 Part 3: *Personnel and Work Report Votes, 1979–95*

Year	Month	Law/motion	Votes for	Votes against	Abstained	Present, not voting	Total	Total dissenting (No + Abst + NIV)	Dissent as % of voting	Source
1988	March	Approve Yang Shangkun as President	2,725	124	34	—	2,883	158	5.48	Kyodo
1988	March	Approve Yang Shangkun as State Military Commission Vice-Chair	2,739	121	23	—	2,883	144	4.99	Kyodo
1988	March	Approve Deng Xiaoping as State Military Commission Chair	2,850	25	8	—	2,883	33	1.14	Kyodo
1988	March	Approve Wang Zhen as Vice-President	2,594	212	77	—	2,883	289	10.02	Kyodo
1988	March	Approve Wan Li as NPC Standing Committee Chairman	2,808	64	11	—	2,883	75	2.60	Kyodo
1988	March	Approve Li Peng as Prime Minister	2,860	18	5	—	2,883	23	0.80	Kyodo
1988	March	Approve Zhao Ziyang as State Military Commission Vice-Chair	2,860	18	5	—	2,883	23	0.80	Kyodo
1988	March	Approve Li Guixian as People's Bank Director	2,439	404	16	—	2,859	420	14.69	JEN
1988	March	Approve Wang Bingqian as Minister of Finance	2,615	225	19	—	2,859	244	8.53	JEN
1988	March	Approve Zou Jiahua as Min. of Machine Bldg. & Elec. Ind.	2,811	42	6	—	2,859	48	1.68	JEN
1988	March	Approve Yao Yilin as Vice-Premier	2,811	43	5	—	2,859	48	1.68	JEN
1988	March	Approve Tian Jiyun as Vice-Premier	2,725	122	12	—	2,859	134	4.69	JEN
1988	March	Approve Wu Wueqian as Vice-Premier	2,723	123	13	—	2,859	136	4.76	JEN
1988	March	Approve Chen Muhua as NPC Stand. Comm. Vice-Chair	2,501	313	45	—	2,859	358	12.52	JEN
1988	March	Approve Song Jian as State Councillor	2,777	76	6	—	2,859	82	2.87	JEN
1993	March	Approve Government Work Report	2,838	20	19	—	2,877	39	1.36	SCMP
1993	March	Approve Supreme Procurator's Work Report	2,257	375	234	—	2,866	609	21.25	SCMP
1993	March	Approve Supreme Court Work Report	2,563	162	135	—	2,860	297	10.38	SCMP

TABLE 5.2 Part 3: continued

Year	Month	Law/motion	Votes for	Votes against	Abstained	Present, not voting	Total	Total dissenting (No + Abst + NIV)	Dissent as % of voting	Source
1993	March	Approve Li Peng as Prime Minister	2,566	210	120	—	2,896	330	11.40	LAT
1993	March	Approve Li Tieying as State Councillor	2,037	722	137	—	2,896	859	29.66	SCMP
1993	March	Approve Li Tieying as SCRES Chairman	2,032	655	169	—	2,856	824	28.85	SCMP
1993	March	Approve Qian Qichen as Foreign Minister	2,883	9	4	—	2,896	13	0.45	SCMP
1993	March	Approve Zhu Rongji as Vice-Premier	2,888	8	0	—	2,896	8	0.28	SCMP
1993	March	Approve Zhu Rongji as BPOC Director	2,459	358	79	—	2,896	437	15.09	SCMP
1993	March	Approve Li Guixian as State Councillor	2,487	323	86	—	2,896	409	14.12	SCMP
1993	March	Approve Ai Zhisheng as Minister	2,695	158	43	—	2,896	201	6.94	SCMP
1993	March	Approve Peng Peiyun as State Councillor	2,684	161	51	—	2,896	212	7.32	SCMP
1994	March	Approve Government Work Report	2,655	23	n/a	n/a	2,678	23	0.86	AFP, JEN
1994	March	Approve State Budget	2,110	337	425	49	2,921	811	27.76	AFP, JEN
1994	March	Elect Tsang Hin-chi to NPC Standing Committee	2,624	58	44	195	2,921	297	10.17	SCMP
1994	March	Elect Nie Li to NPC Standing Committee	2,608	78	40	195	2,921	313	10.72	SCMP
1995	March	Approve Wu Bangguo as Vice-Premier	2,366	210	161	15	2,752	386	14.03	SCMP
1995	March	Approve Jiang Chunyun as Vice-Premier	1,746	605	391	10	2,752	1,006	36.56	SCMP
1995	March	Approve Government Work Report	2,598	—	—	—	2,678	80	2.99	JEN (% est)
1995	March	Approve 1995 Economic Plan	2,571	—	—	—	2,678	107	4.00	JEN (% est)
1995	March	Approve 1995 State Budget	2,464	—	—	—	2,678	214	7.99	JEN (% est)
1995	March	Approve Supreme People's Procurator's Report	2,131	—	—	—	2,678	547	20.43	JEN, SCMP (est)
1995	March	Approve Supreme People's Court Report	2,215	—	—	—	2,678	463	17.29	JEN, SCMP (est)

TABLE 5.2. Part 4: Average or 'normal' vote

Full NPC: votes on draft laws
Average votes by year

	No. of laws	Average votes for	Avr. total delegates voting	Avr total dissenting votes	Average percentage dissenting
1979	1	2,610	2,713	103	3.80
1988	3	2,816	2,822	6	0.21
1989 (Before Tiananmen)	3	2,311	2,688	377	14.02
1989 (After Tiananmen)	0	n/a	–	–	–
1990	1	2,660	2,713	53	1.95
1991	1	2,313	2,610	297	11.38
1992	1	1,767	2,633	866	32.89
1993	3	2,631	2,858	227	7.94
1994	1	2,110	2,721	611	22.45
1995	2	1,905	2,678	773	28.86

NPC Standing Committee, draft laws
Average vote

	No. of laws	Average votes for	Avr. total delegates voting	Avr total dissenting votes	Average percentage dissenting
1986	4	95	114	20	17.11
1987	2	104	109	5	4.61
1988	3	110	114	4	3.25
1989 (Before Tiananmen)	1	119	123	4	3.25
1989 (After Tiananmen)	4	95	111	17	14.83
1990	2	98	112	14	12.50
1991	3	115	120	5	4.43
1992	5	97	102	5	4.88
1993	6	117	121	4	3.10
1994	2	126	127	2	1.18

FULL NPC: Personnel and work reports
Average votes: personnel work reports

	No. of motions	Votes for	Delegates voting	Dissenting votes	Percentage dissenting
1988 (all votes before May)	15	2,723	2,870	148	5.14
1993	12	2,532	2,88b	353	12.24
1994	4	2,499	2,860	361	12.62
1995	7	2,299	2,699	400	14.84

overall percentage of what are called 'dissenting votes', defined as the sum of all 'no' votes, abstentions and those present but not voting.[15] These totals and percentages are potentially an extremely important data source for monitoring the NPC's development in a far more reliable, far less impressionistic fashion than in the past. They permit analysts to go beyond the two major data sources of the past: press reports and a few interviewees' impressions about the general 'tone' of debate at an NPC session. As the voting data time series becomes longer and more complete, it will become increasingly valuable to efforts to chart the legislature's institutionalization and its potential contribution to deconcentrating and democratizing policy-making power in China. Unfortunately, the present set does not constitute any sort of known probability sample, nor is it complete enough to justify using any sort of advanced statistical techniques.

Still, the voting data reveal several very interesting points. Most obvious is that in general, the percentage of dissenting votes on most laws is still quite low by the standards of established democracies. On the other hand, the practice of unanimous voting, once the automatic outcome in the NPC, is quickly becoming rare to virtually non-existent. By itself this fact suggests important progress toward normalizing moderate levels of dissent.

Secondly, and most surprising, is that not all draft laws which are brought to a formal vote at the NPC actually pass. According to interview sources, there have been at least two occasions on which the NPC Standing Committee brought a draft law to a vote and actually voted it down, thus sending it back for extensive revision before resubmission. Although the official press has noted the Standing Committee's willingness to vote down draft amendments to laws, it has not, so far as I have been able to discover, reported a negative vote on any draft law. It will probably surprise few sinologists that one of the ill-fated drafts was the highly controversial 1986 Enterprise Bankruptcy Law, which was reportedly voted down during its second attempt at passage at the August 1986 Standing Committee session. The second negative vote, rather more surprisingly, occurred just a couple of months after the suppression of the 1989 student movement, when according to these sources the Standing Committee voted down a highly restrictive draft of the Law on Public Demonstrations drafted and sponsored by the Ministry of Public Security.[16] Coming during the post-Tiananmen crackdown, at the very time when Hu Jiwei was being driven

---

15. In the case of a couple of laws, actual numbers of delegates voting in each of these categories have not been reported, but observers at the session (usually foreign journalists) have reported the percentage voting 'yes' or 'voting no or abstaining'. For others, the number of delegates voting in favour of a law was calculated from the reported number of delegates present minus the number who voted 'no', abstained or did not vote.

16. For both of these laws, the sources could not report exact percentages. So in the chart, they are simply reported as 51% dissenting votes, the minimum possible estimate.

from the NPC for his late May efforts to convene the Standing Committee to overturn martial law, the vote obviously represented a bold assertion by the delegates.

Dramatic as these votes are, they are but two out of several dozen, and in both cases could be attributed to the emotionalism of the moment causing the negative vote totals to rise to very high levels. In assessing the institutionalization of legislative assertiveness, it is more important to get a sense of a 'normal' dissenting vote, and how the levels of normal dissenting votes have increased over time since the days when the 'normal dissenting vote' was invariably zero. In other words, on any given vote, how many delegates can be expected to vote 'no', abstain or simply refuse to vote 'yes'?

One simple means of ascertaining this 'normal' vote is a simple average percentage of dissenting votes for all motions considered in each year for which data are available (see Table 5.2, Part 4). In doing so, however, it must be stressed again that these data are not a known probability sample of all votes taken, so an average of them constitutes only the roughest indicator of 'normal' dissent. To give some sense of change over time, the data have been somewhat arbitrarily grouped together by calendar year. Since the total number of legislative votes taken in any year is still relatively small, the average figure from any sample is likely to be a somewhat unstable figure which is highly sensitive to the discovery of additional voting data for any of the laws not presently included. Examined over a longer period of time, however, the data do show some more stable trends.

The level and trends of normal dissenting vote percentages vary greatly between the NPC and its Standing Committee, and from type of motion to type of motion. The full 2,800-member NPC is, on average, more disagreeable than the approximately 125-member Standing Committee. But, it must be stressed, that is *on average*. When voting on work reports, economic plans and personnel appointments, the average annual dissenting vote has risen from 5.1% in 1988 into the 12% range by 1993, and by 1995 was nearly 15%. In the thirty-one known votes between 1989 and 1995, the dissenting vote total has exceeded one-fifth on twelve occasions—an increasingly common occurrence. On five occasions during that period, the top leadership has endured a dissenting vote which reached an embarrassing 32-40%. When voting on draft laws, the full NPC tends to be even bolder, with average annual dissenting votes in the past four available years running at 33%, 8%, 22% and 29%. And even though the addition of new data may drive these averages down, figures in the range of 20 to 30% are becoming quite common.

The Standing Committee shows a very different profile. These top NPC officials cast far fewer dissenting votes than the full NPC; on average only about 4% of these approximately 125 delegates refrain from voting 'yes' on any given vote. Moreover, while the dissenting votes have been on the increase in the full NPC, the percentage for the Standing Committee has stayed fairly stable over the past eight to nine years, with the exception of the surge in negative voting in the two years after Tiananmen.

Does this mean the standing Committee is more tightly controlled by the top Party leadership than the full NPC. This explanation is certainly quite plausible. Standing Committee members are, after all, on the *nomenklatura* list of the CCP Politburo, unlike members of the full NPC, most of whom are selected with far more provincial-level input. Nevertheless, as noted, it is the Standing Committee which has at times shown the greatest willingness to assert itself, twice actually voting draft laws down, and now quite commonly sending them back to their drafting ministries for revision without submitting them to a formal vote. It is conceivable that the Standing Committee is no less assertive than the full NPC but that the top NPC leadership may be better able to forecast the reaction to forthcoming drafts by these fewer, better-known and mostly Beijing-based Standing Committee members, and may therefore be able to forestall high-profile confrontations by sending drafts back for revision without a vote. Delegates to the annual sessions of the full NPC, however, often get the draft legislation to consider only a few weeks before the session, which would make their reactions more difficult for top NPC officials to forecast. It is also possible that since the Standing Committee meets several times a year but the full NPC meets only once, the leadership may feel it has less choice to delay a bill scheduled for passage by the plenary meeting, and chooses instead to suffer the higher negative vote totals. The Standing Committee's apparently higher need, or capacity, for consensus is an important and still unresolved riddle.

As with the data on legislative motions, what makes all three of these voting patterns most interesting is their resistance to political cycles and anti-liberal crackdowns. In the years following the 1987 Anti-Bourgeois Liberalism Campaign, and the Tiananmen massacre, dissenting votes in the full NPC continued to climb, quickly exceeding pre-crackdown levels. Fascinatingly, the usually more consensual Standing Committee became downright hostile in the two years following 1989, with average dissenting votes rising to 14%, far above the usual 4%. Even if the figure for the Public Demonstrations Law is removed from the annual average dissenting vote (which is estimated from interviews rather than taken from press reports), the figure is still an unusually high 12%. Very clearly, the anti-liberal crackdowns of 1987 and 1989 intimidated the legislators very little if at all, and far less than was the case in 1957 or the early to mid-1960s. Indeed, the 1989 crackdown may even have made the Standing Committee delegates unusually restive. If the military brutality of Tiananmen and the grim resolution of the pre-Revolutionary Party elders did not silence the NPC delegates, one wonders just how much direct coercion it would take the next time.

The Rise of The National People's Congress System 93

Properly sceptical readers will understandably point to the fact that only two laws appear to have been voted down. They may also stress that overall dissent totals remain relatively low, and the gap between the average dissenting vote totals and the percentage necessary to defeat a bill remains large—often between fifteen and thirty percentage points. This, it could be contended, is evidence that 'real' legislative resistance is still a long time off. Conceding these points, I would still argue that the actual defeat of even one draft law represents a crucial psychological barrier for the legislature to cross, one which makes future 'no' votes far less unthinkable. In the future, moreover, it should not be assumed that the rise in average dissenting votes will increase in a smooth, incremental, step-linear fashion. During a crisis, the increase could shoot up asymptotically to very high levels. If the anti-Leninist uprisings between 1989 and 1991 taught observers anything, it is that central control and societal norms in most Leninist systems may have been eroding gradually over a long period, but the collapse, when it occurred, came with the suddenness of a dam with a small hole in it. Thus, the nearly 2:1 or 3:1 ratios between the average negative vote counts and the level required to defeat laws do not necessarily mean that such defeats will not become more common in the near future.

Even with their many limitations, these data on legislative motions and vote totals raise some questions about the pessimism of many culturally-based forecasts of China's political future to which I will return in Chapter 10. Since 1979 new attitudes towards open policy debate and disagreement have been emerging among some of the NPC's current elite. These changes are showing signs of becoming institutionalized; they are far more able to endure and reassert themselves even in the face of a serious crackdown. The near disappearance of unanimous voting and its replacement with average dissenting vote percentages in the tens, twenties and thirties indicates that moderate levels of dissent and assertiveness by delegates are becoming 'normal' in the Chinese system. Any such normalization of regular, moderate dissent represents a very significant evolution in China's elite political norms, which have historically required that lower-level officials must show formal deference to a unified hierarchical leadership in public, whatever they may do in private. These data, therefore, strongly suggest that the NPC is making a genuine, serious contribution towards the openness and consultativeness of the system.

The NPC's Bureaucratic and Subcommittee Development

Early Development, 1954–1978

The NPC leadership made its first great effort to build a permanent legislative bureaucracy and a subcommittee system in the mid-1950s, as part of a brief high tide of interest in establishing a complete Soviet-style

94   The Politics of Lawmaking in Post-Mao China

legal system. CCP-member leaders of the NPC sought to build up the NPC as a moderately weighty bureaucratic organization while maintaining strict loyalty to the notion of Party leadership. But when, during the 1957 Hundred Flowers Campaign, some of the more liberal voices in the NPC and the Chinese People's Political Consultative Congress (CPPCC) began to advocate a full multi-party parliamentary democracy, the resulting Anti-Rightist backlash swamped even the mainstream Leninist debate over legislative development. The full-blown legal nihilism of the Cultural Revolution subsequently crushed the modest efforts to revive the NPC during the early 1960s.[17]

After the NPC's establishment in 1954, the Standing Committee moved quickly to establish a moderately large and rapidly expanding permanent bureaucracy, centred in the NPC's General Office (*bangongting*).[18] Standing Committee Vice-Chairman Peng Zhen's December 1954 report on NPC Standing Committee work organs provides the earliest extant plan for building the NPC bureaucracy.[19] Stressing China's increasing need to rely upon codified law in addition to 'educational campaigns' to carry out its policies, Peng argued the Standing Committee needed a greater capacity to master legal theory, carry out research and investigations, and look into contradictions among laws and between individual laws and the Constitution.[20] Peng's call for NPC organizational expansion also reflected his political frustration over the legislature's rather limited real influence. He was clearly stung by complaints that the Standing Committee's work was 'empty' or 'devoid of substance' (*kongkong dongdong*).

Peng argued for the establishment of several special offices under the NPC General Office. The most important of these were the Law Office (*falu shi*), charged with 'carrying out systematic legal research'; and the Research Office (*yanjiu shi*), charged with 'researching legal theory, China's "actual situation", and accumulating legal experience'. Notably, Peng stressed that these offices should search far and wide among other legal codes for models China could study. They need not limit their study to the Soviet Union and other communist states' codes, but should also consider China's own imperial codes and even the codes of 'some capitalist countries'.

17. Interview with a high-ranking NPC official, Beijing, August 1992.
18. Unless otherwise noted, all data on organizational development and staff size in this chapter are drawn from a report compiled by the Research Office under the NPC Standing Committee General Office, entitled 'Quanguo Renmin Daibiao Dahui ji qi Changwu Weiyuanhui Gongzuo Jigou de Lishi Yange' ('The Historical Evolution of Work Organs Under the National People's Congress and its Standing Committee') (Beijing, 1990) (hereafter, 'Historical Evolution of NPC Work Organs').
19. Peng Zhen, 'The Work Organs of the Standing Committee Must Serve Legislative Work' (29 December 1954), in Peng Zhen (1991).
20. Interestingly, there were limits to Peng's faith in legal codification, and he denounced efforts at abstract legal 'phrase-mongering' as a substitute for flexibly applying law in light of the concrete facts of a given case.

To aid in this research, Peng called on the General Office to establish a Translation and Compilation Office. He also argued for a Secretariat, an Administrative Office, a Nationalities Office, a Language Office (*yuyan shi*) and, in the future, an Advisors Office (*guwen shi*). This last was designed to help the NPC draw upon international, civil and criminal law experts from outside its own offices.[21]

Within a couple of months, the NPC had acted upon Peng's plan, establishing a Secretariat, a General Affairs Office and an Office for Receiving the People. The General Office took charge of most substantive lawmaking work, creating five subordinate offices: a Law Office, a Research Office, an Editorial and Translation Office, an Advisors Office, and a Nationalities Office. In 1956 the Advisors Office was closed and replaced with an International Legislatures Office.

Peng and the other NPC leaders initially showed some ambivalence concerning staff size. In keeping with then-current official Party campaigns which sought to streamline administration, Peng Zhen publicly argued that staff be limited to avoid overlap and duplication of work.[22] He lectured on the need for a work style of diligence, endurance, persistence and plainness, noting that 'one monk carries enough water to refill the empty bucket. But two monks will compete for the water. And with three, there will be no water left to drink.' Notwithstanding this, the NPC's personnel tripled during these first 'golden years' of the Chinese legal system, growing from a total staff of 120 in late 1954 to aproximately 360 by 1956.

While the NPC leadership moved quickly to build up its permanent bureaucracy between 1954 and 1957, efforts to establish a subcommittee system lagged far behind, mired in debate and dissent. Within the Soviet-oriented mainstream of the debate, the key question was how many committees to establish, and how closely to emulate the example of Moscow's Supreme Soviet. Some NPC officials felt the legislature ought to establish one legislative subcommittee for each department or ministry of the State Council, while others argued this would produce an impractically large number of committees. Another controversial issue was the proper power relationship between these legislative committees and their corresponding government departments: how much should the legislature be able to interfere with government work in the name of 'oversight'? Perhaps surprisingly, NPC sources report that Party Centre and State Council officials raised no significant opposition to establishing the subcommittees, despite the prospect that they might be construed as 'interfering' in the administrative offices' work.[23] Still, for three years no consensus emerged on the

21. Beyond what is noted here, Peng's report did not discuss these offices' proposed functions in any more detail.
22. On organizational campaigns of this period, see Harding (1981), especially 87–115, also 122–3.
23. Interview with a high-ranking NPC official, Beijing, August 1992.

number of committees or their role, and top NPC leaders like Peng Zhen and Dong Biwu were apparently unwilling to force a decision as they had done in the case of the permanent bureaucratic offices.

Their brief opportunity to build a powerful legislative organization was soon squandered. The Anti-Rightist backlash, sparked off in 1957, was later amplified by the Great Leap Forward policy style of 'campaigning' and strengthening the role of Party organizational control throughout society. For Peng Zhen personally this was a boon, as he was in 1958 placed in charge of a newly revived Central Committee Political-Legal Directorate (*kou*), in the process wresting much control over State Council legal organs away from Premier Zhou Enlai.[24] But for government and state organizations, staffed with large numbers of politically-suspect intellectuals, the new watchword was 'simplifying organization' at all levels. The fledgling NPC bureaucracy Peng Zhen had built up was decimated. In late 1958, the NPC General Office was forced to close its key lawmaking offices, including General Affairs, Research, Editorial and Translations, and International Legislative Relations. In July 1958, the total staff in the remaining four offices plummeted from 360 persons to a mere 59. The early 1960s saw some recovery: in 1961 total staff size was 97, and by 1965 the figure had crept up to 115. But never again during the Maoist era did the NPC bureaucracy even approach the level it had attained in 1956.

Amidst the legal nihilism of the Cultural Revolution, the NPC paid dearly for its traditional association with the Party's 'political-legal' sector. With the fall of Peng Zhen as the Party's political-legal chief in mid-1966, the NPC's Communist Party Committee was taken over by a newly created Leading Group in charge of NPC Party Committee Organs, headed by Peng's infamous successor as chief of political-legal work, Kang Sheng.[25] Under Kang's leadership, the remaining NPC staff offices were completely wiped out.[26] The several hundred staff of the Great Hall of the People Management Office were transferred to the CCP Central Committee General Office, as the opulent Great Hall became a regular site for Politburo and other Central Party meetings.[27] In June 1968, the Standing Committee professional bureaucracy was placed under military rule (*junguan*), which continued until March 1973.[28] In November 1969, all but about ten of the remaining NPC staff were 'sent down' for re-education in May Seventh Cadre Schools. These 'schools' were closed in June 1973. But the very small number of NPC staff

---

24. On the recreation of Party *kou* in the late 1950s, see Pang Song and Han Gang (1987).
25. Other members of the Leading Groups were Xu Bing, Liu Ningyi and Zhou Rongjin. NPC Standing Committee Research Office, 'Historical Evolution of NPC Work Organs'; also interview with a Senior NPC Cadre, Beijing, 1992.   26. *Ibid.*
27. Interview with a Senior NPC Cadre, Beijing, 1992.
28. NPC Standing Committee Research Office, 'Historical Evolution of NPC Work Organs'.

offices and personnel established for the Fourth NPC (1975) and the Fifth NPC (1978) show clearly that the overwhelming majority of the NPC staff hired in the 1950s and 1960s never returned to their old posts.[29]

Development Since 1978

Peng Zhen was rehabilitated in February 1979, nearly thirteen years after being purged, and placed in charge of the newly established NPC Legislative Affairs Committee. He quickly inaugurated a tremendous organizational build-up in the NPC which continued even after his dismissal as Standing Committee Chairman in 1988. Making effective use of the resources political fate dealt him, Peng ultimately worked out an organizational growth strategy which would have made any U.S. southern senator proud. His strategy, discernible in a September 1986 speech to the Standing Committee (see below), stressed that the effective development of an NPC power base lay in striking a balance: between the age, experience and bureaucratic power of the legislators on the Standing Committee and Special Committees; and the youth, education, energy and bureaucratic capacity of a rapidly expanded NPC bureaucracy. Deng Xiaoping's personnel policies of rejuvenation supplied the NPC with politicians of experience and power. Gradually, the NPC also built up a tripartite bureaucratic structure incorporating the staffs of the Legislative Affairs Committee, the NPC Standing Committee General Office and the permanent Special Committess under the Standing Committee.

Transforming the Standing Committee: Powerful Leaders Seeking Avenues of Power
During the early to mid 1980s, the NPC Standing Committee was widely attacked and denigrated as a 'dumping ground' for retired Party and government leaders. In his drive to rejuvenate the leadership, Deng Xiaoping had forced these elders to retire from key administrative posts in the central and provincial-level Party, government and military apparatus. But the Party still lacks an institutionalized, peaceful 'exit pattern' and appropriate tasks to occupy these restless revolutionaries.[30] Consequently many were relegated to posts in the NPC Standing Committee, the Party's Central Advisory Commission and other bodies which have traditionally been regarded as ceremonial posts or sinecures.

---

29. During the course of 1975, the Fourth NPC re-established a Secretariat Group (Mishu zu), plus a Foreign Affairs Group, a Political-Legal Group, a General Affairs Group, and later that year Policy Research Groups on Nationalities Affairs and on Religion. But the total staff for all these groups combined apparently only reached forty people. NPC Standing Committee Research Office, 'Historical Evolution of NPC Work Organs'.
30. On the 'exit pattern' in Chinese politics and its political importance, see Oksenberg (1976).

98 The Politics of Lawmaking in Post-Mao China

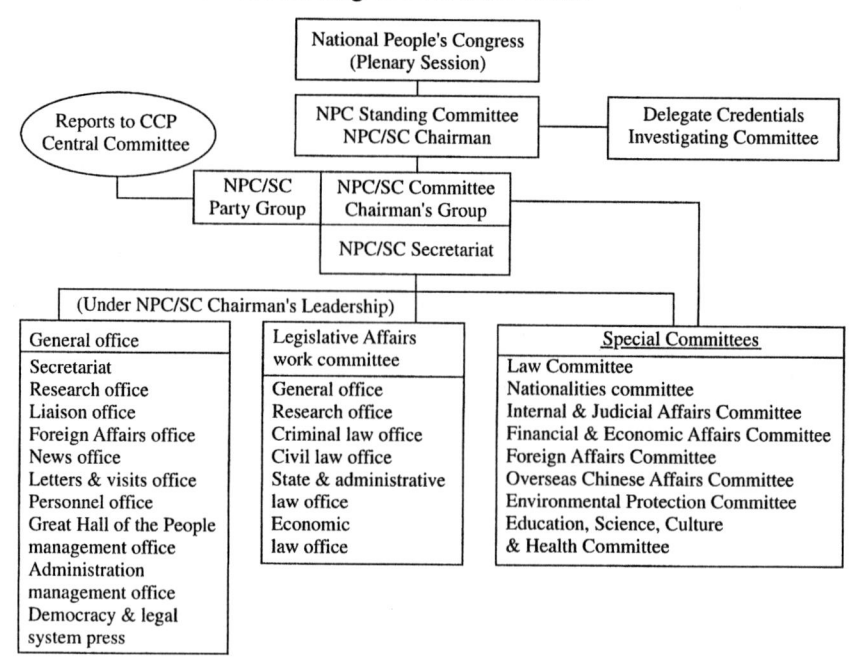

```
                         ┌─────────────────────────┐
                         │ National People's Congress│
                         │    (Plenary Session)    │
                         └─────────────────────────┘
  ┌──────────────┐       ┌─────────────────────────┐       ┌──────────────────────┐
  │ Reports to CCP│       │  NPC Standing Committee │       │ Delegate Credentials │
  │Central Committee│     │    NPC/SC Chairman      │       │Investigating Committee│
  └──────────────┘       └─────────────────────────┘       └──────────────────────┘
              ┌──────────────┬─────────────────────┐
              │   NPC/SC     │   NPC/SC Committee  │
              │ Party Group  │   Chairman's Group  │
              └──────────────┴─────────────────────┘
                         │    NPC/SC Secretariat   │
              ( Under NPC/SC Chairman's Leadership )
```

General office	Legislative Affairs work committee	Special Committees
Secretariat		Law Committee
Research office	General office	Nationalities committee
Liaison office	Research office	Internal & Judicial Affairs Committee
Foreign Affairs office	Criminal law office	Financial & Economic Affairs Committee
News office	Civil law office	Foreign Affairs Committee
Letters & visits office	State & administrative	Overseas Chinese Affairs Committee
Personnel office	law office	Environmental Protection Committee
Great Hall of the People management office	Economic law office	Education, Science, Culture & Health Committee
Administration management office		
Democracy & legal system press		

FIG 5.1. *NPC organization structure*

But in China, power has always tended to inhere in individuals rather than in their formal positions, and many of the elders have been extremely powerful. As a result, their presence on the Standing Committee has without question become a key source of the NPC's gradually expanding power. A biographical analysis of the elders' backgrounds gives some flavour of their impressive influence. Among those serving on the Sixth and Seventh NPC Standing Committees were seven current and former Politburo members who had played key roles in rebuilding the post-Mao leadership—Peng Zhen, Peng Chong, Chen Pixian, Geng Biao, Wei Guoqing, Chen Muhua and Ni Zhifu—in addition to several high-ranking career policy specialists, and a large number of cadres who had held the rank of vice-minister, provincial deputy Party secretary or above.[31] Indeed, in a 1986 speech Peng Zhen noted that over half of the 155 members of the Sixth NPC Standing Committee had previously held rank at least equal to

---

31. These would include former State Agriculture Commission Chairman Wang Renzhong, former Minister of Foreign Affairs Huang Hua, former Vice-Minister of Foreign Affairs Liao Hansheng, and Ye Fei, former Chief of the PLA Navy.

a State Council minister, vice-minister, provincial governor or vice governor (or mayor/vice mayor).[32] This represented a major change in NPC recruitment practice in two respects. First, previous Standing Committees had allocated more slots to 'model workers', 'democratic personages', national minority leaders and other non-political luminaries. Secondly, and more importantly, in the past, senior Party leaders who held top NPC spots usually held concurrent official posts within the Party and government which were their true conduits of power.[33] For most of the members of the post-1978 Standing Committees, the NPC is now their principal organizational conduit of power.

Uncomfortable with retirement, many have been searching for a new political role to play, and have found it by insisting on a more literal interpretation of one tenet of 'socialist democracy' which previously was only honoured in the breach: that the NPC have some say in drafting state documents. The elders' sense of displacement has made the NPC a legislature looking for some place to assert itself. The inevitable result has been a dramatic increase in the NPC's organizational assertiveness, especially vis-à-vis the State Council, which is unaccustomed to such a legislative rival. The elders' defiance is particularly great whenever they have felt themselves cast in the role of the faithful defenders of socialism and the working class against the alleged incursions and insensitivities of economic and political reformers.[34]

In June and September 1986, during a pair of remarkably frank internal speeches to Standing Committee members, Peng Zhen discussed this change in the character of the NPC leadership and its effect on the power of the institution. In the June address, Peng began by noting that 'today's NPC is in many respects different from those of the past'. In the past, 'relatively few [Standing Committee members] had a lot of real work experience' in government administration. But now the character and rank of the Standing Committee members had increased greatly, 'and many comrades who have previously served as provincial Party secretaries, provincial governors, or ministers of state have come to the NPC Standing Committee to work'. In terms of their political resources, Peng placed particular emphasis on their policy expertise ('they are relatively familiar

---

32. Peng Zhen, 'Jiaqiang Minzhu yu Fazhi Jianshe', Jiaqiang Renda Changweihui Gongzuo' ('Strengthen Construction of Democracy and the Legal System. Strengthen the Work of the NPC Standing Committee'), speech at an NPC Standing Committee delegates' work meeting, 27 June 1986, in Peng Zhen (1989), 324-31.

33. For excellent discussions of these forced retirements, see Mills (1983) and Manion (1993).

34. In addition to legislative matter, the NPC Standing Committee has also become increasingly assertive on other matters. In July 1988, for example, the Standing Committee for the first time in PRC history vetoed a State Council personnel appointment, a Ministry of Foreign Affairs nominee. BXE, 1 July 1988, FBIS translation, personal copy, unpublished.

100   The Politics of Lawmaking in Post-Mao China

with practical work'), and their personal connections or *guanxi* ('they know people relatively well'). Such a group of leaders, Peng concluded, could greatly expand the NPC's power:

> With so many comrades who have so much experience, so much ability, who have personal understanding of the 'Cultural Revolution', and who are in relatively good health, we have the foundation from which we can do the NPC Standing Committee's work well, and we have excellent conditions.[35]

Peng also repeatedly noted that these new NPC delegates were far more assertive than their predecessors. Speaking at the height of the Standing Committee's rancourous battle over the State Council's Enterprise Bankruptcy Law, he even took a thinly veiled swipe at the Cabinet and others who were unhappy at this assertiveness:

> There were those who used to say that the NPC is a 'rubber stamp'. But that is no longer a problem. It has even reached the point that some people would like the NPC *to be more of a rubber stamp*. That is their affair, that's fine. . . . [36]

Peng's talks also captured perfectly the NPC Standing Committee's sense of 'searching', painting a picture of a legislature full of powerful, impatient, anxious officials, hunting for issues on which to assert themselves:

> Those comrades who used to do party and government work, and who now have switched to doing NPC work, have a problem of changing work habits and work style. In the past when they did party or government work, they had many daily tasks to take care of, and were very busy.
>
> Now that they have changed to doing NPC Standing Committee work, the situation is not the same. They must take part in researching and deciding major state policies, major situations. . . . But there is not as much daily work, and there is time to read, do research and investigations, and there is time to ponder major problems.[37]

It is clear from this and other of Peng's speeches that he felt he was having trouble getting many of the new Standing Committee members to focus their energies on lawmaking work. Many clearly preferred to devote their time to their 'oversight' responsibilities, inspecting and intervening in ministerial and government affairs (probably in their former bureaucratic units). At this time, Peng consistently drew a line against the excessive involvement in oversight, arguing in both speeches that Standing Committee officials should focus their time on the work of legislating, and not try to use oversight as an excuse for usurping State Council responsibilities. He closed his June address by asking, rhetorically, 'in doing oversight work, if

---

35. The two speeches are Peng Zhen, 'Strengthen Construction of Democracy and the Legal System', and 'Guanyu Quanguo Renda Changweihui de Gongzuo' ('On the Work of the NPC Standing Committee'), speech dated 6 September 1986, in Peng Zhen (1991), 560–71.
36. Peng Zhen, 'Strengthen Construction of Democracy and the Legal System'.
37. *Ibid.*

NPC Standing Committee delegates constantly surpervise this ministry or that ministry... what will the ministers have to do?'

Clearly, if Deng Xiaoping's intention in retiring these Party elders to the NPC Standing Committee was to ease them out of political life, his plan backfired. Not only have the elders used the NPC as a conduit to continue their political influence, their presence on the Standing Committee has plugged that organization more firmly into key personal (*guanxi*) networks within the Party and government, and has infused it with a dose of bureaucratic expertise and experience. The end result is that the NPC Standing Committee now has much more of what has long been the traditional stuff of power in China. To give these elders bureaucratic 'legs', the NPC quickly revived and expanded its pre-1966 staff offices, beginning in 1979 with the Legislative Affairs Committee.

The Legislative Affairs Committee

In analysing the Legislative Affairs Committee (LAC), it is important to remember that from its establishment until the end of the Fifth NPC's tenure (1983) it functioned both as a permanent legislative subcommittee and as a key part of the NPC's expanding permanent bureaucracy. As a subcommittee, the LAC had only mixed results. It made the NPC more of a 'going concern' which could meet to debate draft legislation when the full NPC and the Standing Committee were not in session. In the early days after the Third Plenum, the LAC lent great prestige to the NPC's deliberations, bringing together such powerful recently rehabilitated officials as Peng Zhen and Hu Qiaomu. These elders' prestige also strengthened the NPC's claim on staff and resources to rebuild its permanent bureaucracy.

But as a working legislative subcommittee, the LAC was flawed, according to LAC officials who served at this time. First, it was not a true standing committee, for it could only meet very irregularly. Secondly, it was too large (fourteen vice-chairpersons and over seventy members) to permit efficient, focused discussions or allow a meaningful division of labour among its members. Ironically, though, as the NPC's only lawmaking subcommittee, the LAC's policy writ was also too broad. Consequently, it could not even begin to develop the kind of area expertise it would need to rival the State Council ministries as a lawmaking organ, especially given the explosion of new legislation at that time. Finally, all but a few of its members were far too old for sustained legislative work, even though several nevertheless continued to hold concurrent posts elsewhere in the Party and government which siphoned off what little time they had. There were exceptions, of course. Former Justice Minister Shi Liang, for example, threw herself into the committee's research and deliberations, and LAC officials fondly recall her activism even after age and illness had confined her to a wheelchair. Between 1979 and 1983 several committee members,

TABLE 5.3. *Legislative Affairs Committee*

Year	LAC staff size
1979 (year end)	54
1980	75
1981	102
1982	120
1983	121
1984	138
1985	155
1986	168
1987	182
1990 (June)	173
1992 (August)	c. 180

including Shi Liang died, and fewer and fewer members were even able to attend meetings, let alone draft new legislation or carry out research and investigations.[38]

Like the NPC organization of the 1950s, however, the LAC was far more successful as a permanent bureaucratic organ than as a subcommittee. Under Peng Zhen's leadership, it soon established itself as the organizational heart of the NPC and its chief drafting organ, playing the key role in drafting, or organizing drafting work, on many of the most important pieces of legislation passed by the NPC. Of all the NPC professional organs, the LAC has by far the largest staff; between a quarter and one-fifth of all professional NPC staff work for it.[39] Table 5.3 indicates that staff size has increased steadily from 1979 to the present, with only a modest dip between 1987 and 1989.[40]

The staff qualifications of the LAC are also the best in the NPC bureaucracy. Staffers from other NPC offices stress that the LAC has over 100 legal/technical specialists (*zhuanye jishu renyuan*), by far the largest number of any NPC department.[41] Because of this enormous and well-trained staff, the Law Committee (the Special Committee which is responsible for reviewing all laws considered by the other NPC Special Committees), jointly uses the LAC's staff and offices.

The LAC is divided into six permanent offices, four of which specialize in substantive areas of law:

38. Interview with a high-ranking NPC official, Beijing, August 1992.
39. By 'professional staff', I am excluding those staff who work for the Great Hall of the People Management Bureau.
40. Figures are from NPC Standing Committee Research Office, 'Historical Evolution of NPC Work Organs'. The August 1992 figure comes from an interview with a high-ranking Legislative Affairs Work Commission official.
41. By comparison, the General Offices of the seven special committees each have approximately ten specialists and no other subordinate staff offices.

(1) The State and Administrative Law Office (*Guojia yu Xingzhengfa Shi*)
(2) The Civil Law Office (*Minfa Shi*)[42]
(3) The Economic Law Office (*Jingjifa Shi*)
(4) Criminal Law Office (*Xingfa Shi*)
(5) General Office (*bangong shi*)
(6) Research Office (*Yanjiu shi*)

One of the LAC's most important functions is helping the Committee Chairmen's Group summarize and interpret Standing Committee discussions. After each Standing Committee meeting, the Committee Chairmen's Group convenes a meeting with LAC staff to consider the various (often inchoate) comments of the deputies on draft legislation. The Committee Chairmen's Group tells the LAC which of the delegates' comments and suggestions deserve to be drafted into formal amendments, and the LAC staff is responsible for translating Standing Committee members' vague suggestions into concrete language.

By 1983, the NPC leadership recognized that, while the LAC was functioning well as a bureaucracy, it was inadequate as a subcommittee. With the selection of the Sixth NPC in 1983, the LAC ceased to function as a subcommittee, though it continued as a 'work committee'—part of the permanent bureaucracy—and its name was changed to the Legislative Affairs Work Committee ('LAWC' *Fazhi gongzuo weiyuanhui*).

The NPC General Office Bureaucracy

The Legislative Affairs Work Committee, though it is the largest, is not the only lawmaking branch of the NPC permanent bureaucracy. Indeed, during the early post-Mao years, much of the NPC's bureaucratic build-up was focused on its General Office, which took on an increasingly diverse array of responsibilities for research, liaison with other people's congresses, and the day-to-day management of the NPC as a *danwei* and of the Great Hall of the People. Its burgeoning workload once prompted Peng Zhen to label it the NPC's 'coolie'.

After 1979 the General Office gradually re-established and extended many of its pre-1958 staff offices. In 1980, its Secretarial, Foreign Affairs, Political-Legal and General Affairs 'Groups' (*zu*) were promoted to the rank of permanent offices (*shi*). The following year, the Research Office was re-established, though initially with a meagre staff of three. These changes raised the General Office staff to over 100 from 30 just a couple of years earlier. With the establishment of the Sixth NPC in 1983, these five offices were again promoted in bureaucratic rank, this time to the equivalent of ministerial bureaus (*ju*). In 1985, the Research Office further expanded, with the approval of the CCP Secretariat, adding office-rank groups in charge of Comprehensive Affairs, Economics, Political-Legal/Educational/ Cultural Affairs, and International Affairs. By 1989 additional offices had been added, and in 1991 the Research Office boasted a total staff of 78, apparently second in size only to the LAWC.

The Research Office is the NPC General Office's most important unit in lawmaking and long-term legislative planning. It is responsible to the NPC Committee Chairmen's Group and the Secretary General's Office, and does most of its research for them. Research Office staffers contrast their work to that of the LAWC, saying that their research relates to broader issues of building the legal system, not just lawmaking. They also research issues of legislative oversight, building up the legal system, elections, the NPC's organizational development, questions of legal theory and other macro-level issues.[43] The LAWC, by contrast, is the NPC's principal drafting office, and hence its research tends to be more short-term, narrowly and concretely related to drafting particular pieces of legislation. It also tends to work on tighter schedules, as its work involves organizing seminars on draft laws and interministerial discussions.

The Special Committess

It was 1983—not 1979—which turned out to be the real turning point in the NPC's effort to develop a serious subcommittee system, as the Sixth NPC Standing Committee established six (now eight) permanent special committees (*zhuanmen weiyuanhui*).[44] Although they are formally elected by and subordinate to the full NPC, these subcommittees in reality report to the Committee Chairmen's Group of the NPC Standing Committee, and their staffs are subordinate to the Secretary General's Office (*mishuchu*). The chairpersons of these subcommittees, accordingly, sit as members on the Committee Chairmen's Group, which, as shown in Chapter 4, had essentially the same membership as the NPC Standing Committee Party Group (except for the non-Party member chairs of special committees). Consequently, they can exercise a great deal of influence over NPC work and the NPC agenda. The eight special committees are:

(1) Law Committee (*Falu Weiyuanwei*)
(2) Nationalities Committee (*Minzu Weiyuanhui*)
(3) Financial and Economic Affairs Committee (*Caizheng Jingji Weiyuanhui*)

---

43. One Research Office official I spoke to, for example, was focusing on the development of the Oversight Law, the Two-Year Legislative Plan, and longer term issues of whether the NPC should continue to rely upon 'experience-based lawmaking'.
44. Much of the information on special committees in this seciton comes from Guo Daohui's (1988) excellent discussion of the NPC internal structure, at 47–55.

(4) Foreign Affairs Committee (*Waishi Weiyuanhui*)
(5) Overseas Chinese Affairs Committee (*Huaqiao Weiyuanhui*)
(6) Education, Science, Culture and Public Health Committee (*Jiaoyu Kexue Wenhua Weisheng Weiyuanhui*)
(7) Internal and Judicial Affairs Committee (*Neiwu Sifa Weiyuanhui*) (added in 1988)
(8) The Environmental Protection Committee (*Huanjing Baohu Weiyuanhui*) (added in 1993)

In recent years, the special committees have been most influential in investigating (*shenyi*) and deliberating draft legislation at the request of the NPC Committee Chairmen's Group (or the Presidium of the NPC plenum). One 1989 article suggested that they provide the NPC with political bridges which improve NPC access to, and influence in, the ministerial drafting process:

The majority of draft laws are drafted by the State Council. The NPC Special Committees strengthen relations (*jiaqiang guanxi*) with the concerned ministries of the State Council. [This allows the NPC] to know in a timely fashion the situation and problems which exist in drafting, and to put forward all sorts of views and suggestions. With regard to those laws which the committees are themselves helping to draft, the committees are able to fully use social power (*shehui liliang*), and organize specialists, scientific research, and educational units to take part in this work.[45]

The Law Committee, by far the most important of the eight, is charged with carrying out 'unified investigation' (*tongyi shenyi*) of all draft laws which are to be considered by either the NPC or its Standing Committee. As such, it acts as a contact point for the other seven committees, farming out investigative assignments to those most directly concerned with a given law. As noted, the Law Committee, working with the Legislative Affairs Commission, is also responsible for working out the NPC's long-term legislative plan.[46]

The Law Committee also has a great deal of influence over the flow of information and opinions within the NPC. After a debate session, it works with the Committee Chairmen's Group to summarize the NPC delegates' rather general comments and transform them into legal wording for amendments. Afterwards, the Law Committee discusses the delegates' comments with the law's drafting group and sponsoring ministry, suggesting possible amendments. This is also, as noted, in tandem with the Legislative Affairs Commission. The Law Commission has had three chair-

---

45. 'Zhuanmen Weiyuanhui Gongzuo You Qi Se', *Fazhi Ribao*, 22 March 1989, 3.
46. The Committee's planning functions are similar to those of the State Council's Legislation Bureau, though how the two co-ordinate their work is unclear to me. See BXE, 30 July 1988, in FBIS, 3 August 1988, 13.

men since 1983, former Politburo member Peng Chong (1983–88), Wang Hanbin (1988–93) and Xue Ju (1993–present).[47]

As part of the NPC's oversight function, the special committees also examine cases in which State Council administrative regulations appear to violate the Constitution or other laws approved by the NPC. Since 1987, the special committees have tried to expand this function, periodically inviting State Council officials to come and give explanations to them.[48]

The members of the special committees—two-thirds of whom are concurrently NPC Standing Committee members—are quite naturally chosen largely for their political connections and functional expertise, as well as their ability to devote a great deal of time to NPC work.[49] Most of the committee members are recent retirees from high-ranking Party and government posts which dealt with the very same issues as their respective special committees. Their selection greatly reinforces NPC access to the expertise and influence on the State Council ministries, while at the same time giving the NPC more in-house experts with long backgrounds in major policy issues.

The Internal and Judicial Affairs Committee (IJAC), established in March 1988, by the First Session of the Seventh NPC, provides an impressive example of these ministerial and personal connections. It is 'charged with drafting, proposing, and approving bills and other legal motions' for 'political-legal system' institutions, including the Supreme People's Court, the Supreme People's Procuratorate, and the six ministries of Justice, Public Security, State Security, Supervision, Civil Affairs, and Labour and Personnel.[50] The first IJAC Chairman, Xi Zhongxun, spent many years dealing with issues of personnel, intelligence, and secure document handling in the State Council General Office, and later served briefly as Chairman of the NPC Legislative Affairs Commission. IJAC Vice-Chairman Zou Yu and Advisor Yu Shutong formerly served as Minister and Vice-Minister of Justice, respectively. Other members included: a former Supreme People's Court Justice, a Vice-Minister of Civil Affairs, a Vice-Minister of Labour and Personnel, several People's Liberation

---

47. Indeed, Western analyses often confuse the two committees, in part because of their similar English and Chinese names (Falu Weiyuanhui and Fazhi Gongzuo Weiyuanhui). While there is some personnel overlap between the Law Committee and the Legislative Affairs Commission, the majority of members do not hold dual appointments.

48. See, for example, '*Zhuanmen Weiyuanhui Gongzuo You Qi Se*'; also '*Zhuajin Lifa Gongzuo, Jiaqiang Falu Jiandu*', ('Firmly Grasp Legislative Work, Strengthen Legal Supervision') *Fazhi Ribao*, 22 March 1989, 3.

49. Guo Daohui (1988), 47–8, notes that in order to facilitate regular committee meetings, the vast majority of special committee members are permanent Beijing residents.

50. BXE, 1 August 1988, in FBIS, 3 August 1988, 14. On an unrelated point, the inclusion of the Ministry of Labour and Personnel is frankly puzzling, since within the CCP, personnel matters are historically considered 'organization work' and not 'political-legal work'.

Army Officers who served in sensitive regions and posts, the widow of Procurator General (and PLA Marshal) Luo Ronghuan, and a longstanding subordinate of former Public Security Minister Wang Fang.[51] Virtually every organization which the IJAC oversees appears to have at least one 'alumnus' or representative on the committee.

Relations between legislative subcommittees and government ministries are a key force helping to determine how influential a developing legislature can become in making laws and exercising oversight of government implementation of law. Such close personnel ties between the subcommittees and the ministries suggest intriguing questions about the relations between the two. How close are subcommittee–ministry relations? What is the flow of information and influence? Do the long-powerful State Council ministries see these new legislative subcommittees fundamentally as policy allies or as critics?

At least two equally plausible possibilities, both rooted in organizational politics theories, suggest themselves. The first is a mutually supportive relationship, more or less suggestive of what students of American politics refer to as 'iron triangles'—three-sided self-reinforcing policy alliances between congressional subcommittees, the cabinet departments they ostensibly oversee and their 'client' interest groups in society.[52] Recent Western studies which highlight the enduring power of Chinese government ministries and their organizational ideologies would probably suggest such an 'iron triangles' relationship, with the ministries placing ministerial 'alumni' on the committees as 'agents' whom they attempt to manoeuvre to support ministerial interests. The result of such a ministerial–subcommittee relationship might be a far less assertive National People's Congress in which legislative work was unofficially segmented along the same lines of organizational 'directorates' (*kou*) and 'systems' (*xitong*) that Barnett and others have found in the Party and state bureaucracies.[53] It would, at a minimum, represent a setback to efforts to reform and oversee the massive state bureaucracy. On the other hand, the former ministry officials' preferential access to ministerial policy information and decision-making could give them greater entrée at the early stages of policy-making.

A second hypothesis might posit that the new members of the legislative subcommittees, despite their past organizational associations, begin to develop their own new corporate sense as legislators. The legislators, by attaching increasing value to concepts of law, legal procedure, consultation

---

51. This biographical information was culled from Bartke (1987).
52. The origin of the term 'iron triangles' is actually rather obscure, though it is usually ascribed to Prof. J. Leiper Freeman. In any event, the concept is described in Heclo (1978).
53. Barnett (1967), 3–10. Lieberthal and Oksenberg elaborate on the concept: (1988), 141–2; see also Lieberthal (1995), 192–208.

or even rights, and their role as overseers of government activity (or perhaps 'censors' in the classical Chinese sense), might begin to use their unique organizational experience and access to restrict or block excessive power-seizing by ministries. The result would be a far more adversarial subcommittee–ministerial relationship, and a far more assertive NPC. This hypothesis is also inspired by organizational theories, except that in this view, the legislators attach a stronger commitment to their current organizational assignment, the subcommittee, than they do to their historic organizations, the ministries. This might be labelled a 'professional legislator' model.

The case studies do not, unfortunately, provide any systematic evidence for either hypothesis. Other interview data suggest a complex reality in which both hypotheses are sometimes true. One State Council source enthusiastically argued that the legislative subcommittees gain great access and informal influence by incorporating so many former State Council Ministers and Vice-Ministers. Special committee members 'quite regularly' (*jingchang*) get policy-related research and data from their former ministries. This source believed that ministries sometimes attempt to use their alumni who are special committee members as their agents or representatives to support their views, producing some fascinating and complex influence strategies. For example, the State Council may adopt a policy proposal X, supported by Ministry A but opposed by Ministry B. Ignoring Ministry B's objections, the State Council may then submit policy proposal X, in the form of draft law X, to the NPC Standing Committee for review. This source indicates that Ministry B, in a last ditch effort, will sometimes ask its former minister—now a member of the NPC special committee charged with investigating draft law X—to raise objections to the law (*ti yijian*) when it comes before the NPC. Unfortunately, this and other interviews did not shed light on how common this gambit is.[54]

There is, however, a good deal of evidence that many of these Special Committee members' behaviour seems to be far closer to the 'professional legislator' model than the 'iron triangles' model. Another, more experienced former NPC official (now a legal scholar) emphatically argued that the Party elders who have joined the NPC special committees have been something of a surprise, and have often preferred to use their influence as an organizational check on excessive institutional power seizing by the government, including their own former ministries.[55] Most subcommittee members, according to this and other NPC sources and legal scholars, tend to undergo a major change in their orientation towards law and the power

---

54. Interview 15-35-19/CSW, March 1989.
55. Interview 26-17-13-33/TWS, Beijing, August 1992.

of administrative agencies. The official described the subcommittee members' attitude change in interesting detail:

When they [the subcommittee members] are serving as government ministers, they are in favour of 'managing', 'controlling' things (*guan, kong*). But once they leave, they become just like your country's 'opposition party'. . . . They stand in a detached position from the government, and their thinking becomes more 'open' (*kaifang*). . . . But since they previously served as ministers of these concerned ministries, they have a far better understanding of these ministries' internal political situations. So they can better help the NPC counter the tendencies of these ministries. They 'turn over' (*fanguolai*). They say [to the ministries] 'I understand you. I understand your internal political stituation. And I understand your interests'.[56]

The source summed up the elders' political metamorphosis with the words 'if you no longer sit in a person's chair, you no longer concern yourself with his plans' (*bu zai qi wei, bu mou qi zheng*)—a phrase strikingly reminiscent of Graham Allison's famous bureaucratic axiom 'where you stand depends on where you sit'.

Asked for concrete evidence of the elders' change, these sources provided several interesting examples of former ministry officials using their new NPC positions to fight power grabs by their former units. One case involved some early 1990s draft legislation on China's seaports put forward by the Ministry of Transportation. The draft would have greatly expanded the ministry's control over all Chinese seaports, and correspondingly weakened port access by other ministries, including the Ministry of Agriculture, Animal Husbandry and Fisheries. A former Minister of Transportation, then an NPC subcommittee member, recognized the bill's potential impact on the inter-ministerial balance of power. He attacked his former ministry's draft, reportedly saying, 'I know that you don't want to open these ports to other ministries'. In another, more dramatic case (discussed below), China's former Justice Minister and other political-legal sector officials used their positions on the Internal and Judicial Affairs Committee to resist the Ministry of Public Security's post-Tiananmen efforts to prevent any future public demonstrations.[57]

The issue of whether the 'professional legislator' or the 'iron triangles' model better describes NPC subcommittee behaviour is important and certainly merits more detailed, systematic research than was possible in this study. If these sources are correct, and the subcommittee members are undergoing this sort of change in attitude, then there is reason to be optimistic about the NPC's prospects for developing a stronger corporate sense as a legislature. In either case, both models underscore the important ways in which the addition of a 'legislative arena' to the

56. *Ibid.*   57. Interview 26-17-13-33/TWS, Beijing, August 1992.

lawmaking system can change the politics of the process and the content of the laws it produces.

Problems and Efforts at Bureaucratic Self-strengthening

By the summer of 1986, the NPC leadership was in a stock-taking mood, examining its organizational shortcomings. Many of these were still the result of staff limitations. Peng Zhen, in his major September 1986 address, continued to press for a permanent bureaucracy which was larger, younger, better equipped and better educated, especially in legal theory.[58] NPC staff needed to be 'in the prime of life', not only so that they could shoulder more complex tasks, but also so that, by serving longer, they could add organizational continuity (*lianxuxing*) to the NPC's work. The current staff, in Peng's view, was clearly a major bottleneck preventing the NPC from expanding its organizational mission and had to change. 'In the area of organizational structure, we must not decide our tasks on the basis of our personnel; rather, we must let our work needs determine our organizational structure'. It is certainly true that by late 1986, the NPC, in comparison with its State Council and Party counterparts, could hardly be said to suffer from an embarrassment of organizational riches.

Nevertheless, Peng's speech and other leadership comments indicated that by 1986, after seven years of relatively successful organization building, the problems from which the NPC was suffering were increasingly those of a large, well-developed and complex bureaucracy, not a small, skeletal one. Foremost among these were unclear or overlapping lines of authority, weak communications and turf wars. In particular, the NPC's three major substantive lawmaking bureaucracies—the General Office, the Legislative Affairs Work Committee and the special committee staffs—had grown up in relative isolation from each other. Until 1988, as noted in Chapter 4, these three sets of organizations even had separate Communist Party Groups with no clear authority lines between them.

At a Committee Chairmen's Group meeting on the eve of the September speech, Peng Zhen ordered then-Standing Committee Vice-Chairman Peng Chong to undertake a full-scale investigation on how to solve the bureaucratic problems in the NPC work organs and staff. This highly detailed study, which took almost a year to complete, included separate studies of the Special Committees and of the permanent bureaucracies under the General Office and the Legislative Affairs Commission.[59] The findings, summarized in Peng Chong's July 1987 report 'On Improving the

---

58. The text of Peng Zhen's speech, 'Guanyu Quanguo Renda Changweihui de Gongzuo', ('On the Work of the NPC Standing Committee') is in Peng Zhen (1991), 560–71.

59. The investigation reportedly included more than twenty-eight discussion meetings of NPC cadres, and issued two major reports and twenty-five minor reports in the nine months leading up to May 1987.

The Rise of The National People's Congress System 111

Performance and Organization of the NPC's Work Organs', provide a frank and highly detailed look at NPC bureaucratic weaknesses. The report also set out numerous suggestions for rectifying these shortcomings.[60]

Peng Chong began with a blunt attack on bureaucratic infighting and turf wars among the three major bureaucratic staffs; an attack which I would argue added up to a substantial indictment of the NPC's bureaucratic administration under the leadership of Secretary General Wang Hanbin. Time and again in the first few paragraphs, Peng Chong pointedly reminded NPC Committee members and staff that they were on the same team; the various NPC internal organs were merely constituent parts (*zucheng bufen*) of a unified whole (*tongyi de zhengti*). In Peng Chong's view, these turf wars were exacerbated by unclear administrative relationships and divisions of labour. The NPC internal organs were too loosely organized (*songsan*), and lacked an effective co-ordinative mechanism.[61]

At present, the NPC's work units suffer from such problems as relatively loose structure, lack of potent co-ordinating mechanisms, bureaucratism in routine internal work, sluggish information flows between top and bottom, overlapping responsibility and disparity of workload.

Peng Chong insisted that the three major lawmaking offices (the General Office, Legislative Affairs Work Commission, and the special committee staffs) cease duplicating effort, clearly delineate their respective responsibilities and co-operate (*fengong xiezuo*), and make their relations more 'reasonable and smooth' (*lishun*).

To accomplish these tasks, Peng Chong's report called for the establishment of a Secretary General's Office (*mishuchu*) under the Committee Chairmen's Group which could centralize and unify leadership (*jizhong tongyi lingdao*) over all three of these lawmaking bureaucracies. The new Secretariat, headed by the Standing Committee Secretary General (a post which, not surprisingly, Peng Chong was to take over just eight months later), would take charge of leading the daily work of all NPC internal organs (including the special committees) and would co-ordinate their inter-agency relations.[62] In the case of bureaucratic disagreements, the Secretary General would have the power to convene inter-departmental meetings which could resolve these disputes.

Peng Chong's report also had strong words for the special committees. According to Peng, strong, expert, well-developed NPC special committees

---

60. Peng Chong (1987).   61. 'bumen zhijian quefa youli de xietiao jizhi', *ibid.*, paragraph 3.
62. *Ibid.*, paragraphs 1–5. According to the report, the new Secretariat would be headed by the NPC Secretary General, the post Peng Chong acceded to less than a year later, replacing Wang Hanbin.

were a linchpin of NPC power in lawmaking, oversight, personnel appointment and policy-making. But numerous bureaucratic shortcomings were preventing the committees from fulfilling their legal potential. The report urged the committees to make their work more regular and substantive. It also called on more Standing Committee members to take part in the special committees' work, noting that at that time, only 63% of NPC Standing Committee members were involved with these committees. Peng also criticized committee members who spent too much time working in other units, arguing that they should be full-time (*zhuanzhi*) members, and should rearrange their 'outside' activities so that they could spend more time on the committees' work. For those members who were not already members of the NPC Standing Committee, Peng suggested they begin sitting in on Standing Committee sessions.

The report also called for the expansion and development of the Special Committees' permanent staffs. The committees lacked permanent subordinate offices and were badly understaffed. Peng argued that this shorthandedness and 'organizational deficiency' greatly weakened them. Certainly, given the subcommittees' terrifically rich political contacts within the bureaucracy, the lack of permanent staffs hampered their ability to, as the Chinese say, 'give full play' to their potentially substantial political influence.

Organizational Response to Peng Chong's Report

Over the next year and a half, the NPC made several organizational changes based on Peng Chong's report, aimed at streamlining control over the NPC bureaucracy while expanding its organizational capacity. One major change, which I have already discussed in Chapter 2, was that the NPC received permission from the CCP Central Committee to centralize and streamline its Party Group (*dangzu*) structure. This important step toward organizational unity was undertaken as part of the transition to the Seventh NPC, and announced in April 1988. Since this change also ccincided with the near elimination of the only Central Party office which had ever historically exercised any unified control over lawmaking, the Central Political-Legal Commission, the overall effect was almost certainly more solidly to establish the NPC's organizational coherence and self-government within the Party organizational system.

Perhaps most important, by the spring of 1988 the NPC established a new Secretary General's Office under the Committee Chairmen's Group, which oversaw the General Office, the LAWC and the special committees. Peng Chong, as architect of these changes, was named Secretary General, succeeding Wang Hanbin.

The bulk of the organizational changes based on Peng Chong's report were focused in the NPC General Office and the Special Committees. In

1987, the General Office added a News Bureau and a Personnel Bureau. Two years later, in February 1989, the General Office established the NPC's first major open publishing organ, the China Democracy and the Legal System Press. Overall NPC staffing increased steadily, with the number of cadres rising by the end of 1987. Of these, 332 worked for the General Office, 150 for the LAWC, and 109 were divided among the various special committees.

Many of the organizational changes designed to beef up the special committees were also timed to coincide with the selection of the Seventh NPC in the spring of 1988. The addition of the Internal and Judicial Affairs Committee underscored the NPC's desire to play a more powerful role in this highly sensitive area of policy. As noted above, it also brought into the NPC system several experienced former leaders of the government and Party's political-legal sector. At the same time, all the special committees established their own General Offices, with rank equivalent to a ministerial bureau. They also established other permanent offices, based on their particular demands. The new IJAC, for example, set up two offices, one each on Internal (Civil) Affairs and Judicial Affairs. The Nationalities Affairs Committee increased its legislative capacity, establishing a Legal Motions Office (*fa'an shi*) and an Investigation and Research Office. The Special Committee on Education, Science, Culture, and Public Health established four separate Research Offices—one each for Population/Public Health, Educational, Scientific and Cultural Affairs.

The NPC Organization Since Tiananmen: Toward Institutionalization

One of the principal goals of the NPC's bureaucratic development has been to institutionalize the legislature and protect it from again falling prey to the wild swings which have characterized modern Chinese politics. The NPC's pre-1979 record in this respect was bleak, as this chapter has shown. Major political setbacks to legal development, such as the Anti-Rightist Campaign and the Cultural Revolution, produced devastating organizational attacks upon the NPC, and eventually the complete closure of the NPC bureaucracy for over a decade. After the Hu Jiwei case, one would certainly have expected similar attacks on the NPC in the wake of Tiananmen. And indeed, a number of provincial and local Party secretaries did try to weaken the position of the people's congresses in their areas, as Secretary General Peng Chong noted in his April 1991 Report on the Work of the Standing Committee.[63]

But remarkably, the NPC's organization development after 1989 did not suffer any major setback, and indeed continued to expand both its organizational capacity and its real influence over lawmaking. NPC and

63. The text of Peng's report may be found in *Renmin Ribao*, 13 April 1991, translated in BBC Summary of World Broadcasts, 24 April 1991, on NEXIS-LEXIS.

TABLE 5.4. Number of National People's Congress staff

Office	July 1987	June 1990
General Office	322	376
LAWC	150	173
Special committees	109	136
Other 'logistical' staff	189	1,185
Total Staff	770	1,870

non-NPC legislative sources interviewed before and during the 1989 Beijing Spring, and again in the summer of 1992 and 1995, were unanimous in arguing that the NPC permanent bureacracy had expanded in both size and quality since 1989. No major NPC office had been closed or significantly cut back in size since 1989, according to a high-ranking NPC cadre and to official NPC internal reports. One scholar noted, for example, that a number of key 'backbone positions' in the NPC bureaucracy (for example, upper middle management at the Office Chief and Deputy Office Chief levels) which were still waiting to be filled in 1989 had since been filled with quality officials well-trained in government and law. The most reliable available indicator is the size of the permanent NPC staff, which increased across every major department between July 1987 (the last date before 1989 for which there are comprehensive figures) and June 1990, as shown in Table 5.4.[64]

In addition to staff build-up, the NPC has continued to redefine its organizational relationship with the CCP Central Committee, as discussed in Chapter 2. Central Document Number 8 [1991], the first Party Central Document to define the Party–legislature lawmaking relationship, delimited and decreased the concrete involvement of the CCP Secretariat and Politburo in lawmaking work. This, coupled with the continued erosion of Party organizational control over lawmaking, has further expanded the organizational autonomy of the NPC bureaucracy, subcommittees and all other parts of the legislature.

Standing Committee and subcommittee members have also shown no decrease in their willingness to criticize and amend draft legislation during the post-Tiananmen period; a strong indication that their new conception of their role as lawmakers has also become institutionalized. One of the

---

64. The source for this data is NPC Standing Committee Research Office, 'Historical Evolution of NPC Work Organs'. The astounding increase in the figure for the logistical staff is the result of a major bureaucratic victory which the NPC won in 1988, when more than 1,000 personnel of the Great Hall of the People Management Office, which Kang Sheng had taken away from the NPC during the Cultural Revolution, were transferred out of the CCP Central Committee General Office back to the NPC General Office.

most dramatic examples of this continued assertiveness came during the late 1989 discussions over the Public Demonstrations Law when some subcommittee members resisted the legislative designs of some of their former State Council bureaucratic allies. The draft law had been debated during several NPC sessions prior to the Democracy Movement. In the wake of Tiananmen, however, the Ministry of Public Security seized the moment and attempted to force through a highly restrictive version of the law which would criminalize virtually all future demonstrations. But when the NPC Internal and Judicial Affairs Committee reviewed the law, the attack on the draft was led by Committee Vice-Chairman Zou Yu, who, as former Minister of Justice, was once China's top jail-keeper. Zou Yu, Xi Zhongxun and other committee members argued that the draft defined the right to demonstrate far too narrowly and attempted to place too many restraints on it. Since the right to demonstrate is enshrined in China's Constitution, they argued, the law must treat that right more 'positively' (*jijide*), granting it greater protection and encouragement. Ultimately, according to these sources, the draft was submitted to a vote by the Standing Committee, rejected and sent back for major revision. Although the final draft was more restrictive than the pre-Tiananmen version, the subcommittee and the full Standing Committee did succeed in forcing the Ministry of Public Security to revise it extensively and loosen several of its restrictions.[65]

Since Tiananmen, the NPC Standing Committee has also asserted greater influence over China's long-term legislative agenda, which has long been under the control of the State Council's legislative offices (see the next chapter). In these efforts, the dividends paid by the NPC's bureaucratic and subcommittee development have been especially clear, and the NPC now has a far greater influence than ever before over which laws are drafting priorities and which organizations will draft key bills, as well as the timing and content of annual and longer-term legislative plans. The bulk of this planning still apears to be done by the State Council, but the NPC no longer accepts the State Council's legislative agenda as passively as it did before the late 1980s. Indeed, in the last few years, the NPC has made bold efforts to influence the State Council's legislative agenda. The NPC bureaucracy now also takes charge of the major NPC-State Council meetings which staff out (*luoshi*) the legislative plan for all laws which are likely to be considered by the NPC. This includes deciding which departments will lead the drafting work on these laws, and fixing relatively firm target dates by which the drafts are due to be turned over to the State Council and the NPC.

---

65. Interview 26-17-13-33/TWS and 11-19-13-33/ADH, Beijing, August 1992 and July–August 1995.

In the summer of 1991, the NPC drafted a two-year legislative plan to cover the remaining period until the NPC and State Council terms ended in 1993. The process of developing the plan appears to have been as follows.[66] Its general policy lines came from CCP Secretariat directives. These directives called for rapid legislative work on drafting those laws which are necessary to establish reform-oriented macro-economic legal controls over the economy. The staffs of the NPC Legislative Affairs Work Committee and the Research Office then fleshed out the directives, producing a plan which included a list of specific new laws which needed to be drafted, and others which needed to be revised (such as the Copyright, Trademark and Patent Laws). The plan also included brief descriptions of these laws' principal contents and policy direction, and specified both the organizations responsible for drafting them and the approximate dates by which the NPC expected them to be submitted to the NPC Standing Committee for review, revision and approval.

The plan included a number of laws which, if enacted, would certainly undercut the bureaucratic interests of several key State Council economic planning ministries. These included the Banking Law, the Economic Planning Law, the Price Law, the Agricultural Investment Law, the Auditing Law, the Electrical Power Law, the Budgeting Law, the Social Insurance Law, the Law on Market Regulation, the Commerce Law and more than two dozen others. The plan took effect in October 1991 and originally covered the period until March 1993, when the new NPC was to be seated.

In the summer of 1992, the NPC General Office convened a major Legislative Work Conference with the concerned State Council departments in order to further staff out the plan and review progress in drafting the laws. At Wan Li's behest, Secretary General Peng Chong used the occasion to reprimand State Council administrative departments which were holding up the two-year plan and not pushing ahead with drafting major pieces of economic reform legislation in their policy areas. The ministries were delaying the drafting work on pieces of legislation which were intended to transform the tools of state economic management from administrative to market and legal ones, and which were therefore inimical to the ministries' interests. 'Economic legislation' Peng argued, 'still lags behind economic construction', and the ministries still had not drafted several key laws which 'are badly needed in real economic life'. Peng went on, implicitly attacking specific ministries by naming specific draft laws which were being held up:

As examples: there are now numerous companies, and even though repeated efforts have been made to curtail their establishment, another high tide of setting up new

---

66. I have recosntructed this from excerpts of an untitled NPC/Secretariat internal document and from interviews with legislative experts and staffers, including some who were involved in developing the plan and presenting it to the State Council.

companies has appeared—and yet we still do not have a corporation law . . .

all kinds of stocks and securities are on the market, but we have yet to have a law governing negotiable instruments and securities . . .

and while the number of maritime cases has multiplied and our courts are handling them, we still do not have a maritime law . . .

In nearly every year since 1985, we have been calling for making important laws about planning, banking operations, investing in fixed assets, working, banning improper competition, and promoting scientific and technological development. . . .

The NPC Standing Committee has stressed the need to draw up these laws, but no matter how many times we have said it, these laws have yet to be enacted.[67]

Peng insisted that the legislative plans drawn up by the NPC Standing Committee 'must be fully—and not partially—fulfilled', and went on at the meeting to assign personal responsibility for drafting the laws with the heads of the various departments.

Then, in a section of the speech which was not published, Peng drew upon the NPC bureaucracy to threaten the State Council ministries. He indicated to the ministries that if they continued dragging their feet on drafting these laws, the NPC Standing Committee would 'organize its own forces' (*zuzhi zijide liliang*) and draft the laws for itself. Using its own staff, plus outside help from think-tanks, academics, local people's congresses and other concerned State Council departments, the NPC bureaucracy would take over leadership of the drafting work. Peng implied, but left unspoken, the real threat: that if the NPC had to take over drafting these key laws on planning, banking, companies and so on, the ministries would like the final contents of the laws far less than if they stopped delaying and drafted the laws themselves. That an NPC Secretary General would even dare to threaten the representatives of the State Planning Commission and other major ministries with taking over responsibility for drafting such major laws represents a major shift in the NPC's role in the policy-making system. NPC staff members, moreover, were perfectly confident that they had the staff resources and high-level Party leadership backing to carry out Peng Chong's threat, if necessary.

Conclusions

The evidence in this chapter underscores that in China, as in many other systems, a legislature can begin to develop its institutional and policy-making power long before the political system as a whole becomes democratic. Three forces—changes in delegate attitudes, the addition of assertive, powerful Party elders to the NPC Standing Committee, and

---

67. FBIS-CHI, 22 June 1992, 38–9.

the organizational development of the NPC's subcommittee system and permanent bureaucracy—have all had a tremendous impact upon the NPC's lawmaking influence. The NPC, especially its permanent bureaucracy, now has far greater influence over the legislative agenda, the organization of drafting groups, and the drafting and revision of major legislation. The NPC plenary session and Standing Committee sessions are by no means a 'rubber stamp' forum, but are now a significant adjunct arena of political warfare for legal policy issues where the contents of key laws regularly undergo significant revision.

Nevertheless, the Chinese lawmaking system still in many ways reflects the influence of its East Asian and Stalinist traditions, with the legislature subject to 'Party leadership', and the lion's share of legislative initiative and drafting work—not to mention the actual implementation of laws—still the responsibility of the administrative organs of the State Council. The NPC leaders are keenly aware of this point, and since late 1987 have focused their efforts on building up the NPC's oversight capacity. Even recognizing these limitations, the NPC Standing Committee and its bureaucracy have carved out, apparently permanently, a significant sphere of real operational autonomy from the Party Centre. In 1991–92, under Wan Li and Peng Chong, the organization also took advantage of a reformist revival to make a significant challenge to State Council control over China's legislative agenda. The power relationship between these two state lawmaking organizations is now, at a minimum, far less clear-cut and hierarchical than at any time in the past. The political muscle which made this once-absurd dream worth attempting comes in large measure from the NPC's subcommittee and bureaucratic development over the past fourteen years.

As this book shifts from issues of policy process to issues of system transition, a final cautionary note is in order. To argue, as I have, that the institution of the Chinese legislature is organizationally and politically much stronger and more 'relevant' than in the past does not necessarily imply that China has made a great stride forward toward a more representative, consultative or even democratic system. Indeed, a good deal of research on the development of legislatures suggests that the opposite is frequently true. Kenneth Shepsle, writing some years ago about early U.S. Congressional development, even posited that in order to become politically relevant, a legislature may be forced to professionalize in a number of ways which strengthen the role of certain specialist legislators at the expense of representation by average legislators. The process of developing a role in 'governance' can place the legislative leadership under heavy pressure to become less representative and more aloof from the masses of its constituents.[68] The key question, then, is how does this expanding group of legislative professionals interact with the general public? How

---

68. Shepsle (1988), 461–84.

'permeable' or 'open' is the NPC becoming? Is there evidence, for example, that the elite are emulating the pattern seen in many democratizing systems by reaching down to mobilize the 'social power' of interests or groups in society to assist them in their legislative battles, and thereby opening up the system? Are NPC delegates and officials developing new conceptions of who their constituencies are and how they should best represent them? My own very limited research on this point, and that of other scholars, suggests such changes are going on. I will return to these questions in the final chapter.

6

The State Council Lawmaking System

State Council Lawmaking Organs

From the standpoint of the prospects for democratization, the power and policy relationships between the Communist Party Central Committee offices and the NPC surely seem more interesting than the bureaucratic details of State Council policy-making. But to look at where real lawmaking power lies, one must return to the State Council. For in China, as in most parliamentary systems, the bulk of legislative drafting is performed by the cabinet and its ministries. In this case, that means the State Council and its subordinate committees, ministries and bureaus. The majority of all 'laws and regulations' promulgated at the national level are promulgated by the State Council without NPC consideration. Even focusing, as this study does, primarily on those laws promulgated by the NPC or its Standing Committee, the majority of these laws' original drafters are still ministries of the State Council.

Moreover, the battle for a transition toward a more consultative Chinese political system by no means ends with the Party–NPC relationship. Even if Marxism-Leninism disappeared from China tomorrow, China would still be a developing country, with a Confucian-influenced political culture and a state system which is basically parliamentary in structure. Even a cursory comparison with other similar states in the region indicates that each of these factors is highly conducive to strong government administrative systems, weak electoral and legislative systems, and substantial government resistance to democratization. The calls by many Chinese reformist advocates of 'neo-authoritarianism' for a strong reformist state, a weak legislature, and the sequencing of market and democratic reforms underscores the importance of understanding the State Council's power over lawmaking.[1]

The Battle Against 'Departmentalism' in Lawmaking

For China's Premiers—from Zhou Enlai to Li Peng—the principal legislative headache has always been 'departmentalism' (*benwei zhuyi*) and the lack of inter-ministerial co-ordination in drafting legislative and other

---

1. An excellent summary of the schools of thought and the debates over 'neo-authoritarianism' is Sautman (1992).

policy proposals. One Chinese legislative scholar has listed four common manifestations of this phenomenon, which he labels 'borrowing the law to expand one's power' (*jie fa kuo quan*):

(1) Using the law to expand a department's rights beyond its own sphere.
(2) Using law to push one department's duties onto another department.
(3) Using law to force resolution of larger problems a department cannot solve in its daily work.
(4) Drafting laws which are either illegal or unconstitutional.[2]

A related problem is the lack of delineated authority to resolve these disputes at lower levels. Because ministries generally lack the bureaucratic authority to issue binding orders to other ministerial units of comparable rank (and because China as a whole is just beginning to build a system of administrative law to help bear the burden of delineating proper ministerial authority), even relatively trivial inter-ministerial disputes are often kicked upstairs to the State Council Standing Committee for resolution. The result is a hopelessly overcrowded State Council agenda and a policy-making bottleneck.[3] And despite their apparently varying attitudes towards law, Premiers Zhou Enlai, Zhao Ziyang and Li Peng have all responded by building up special State Council legal bureaus whose principal duty has been to try to resolve interministerial disputes before they reach the Standing Committee.

The State Council Legislation Bureau and the Economic Legislation Research Centre

The earliest incarnation of the current State Council Legislation Bureau was the Legal System Committee (*Fazhi Weiyuanwei*) established in 1950 under the State Council's precursor, the Government Affairs Council. In 1954 Zhou Enlai established a Legislation Bureau (*Fazhi Ju*), reporting directly to the State Council, with Tao Xijin as its head. The Bureau had about half a dozen subordinate offices which were overwhelmingly devoted to economic issues. Among the Bureau's chief responsibilities were overseeing implementation of the State Council's legislative plan, examining draft decrees from State Council ministries, assisting these organs in drafting legislation, and personally drafting specialized items of legislation for State Council promulgation. The Bureau thus stood at the hub of a fully articulated network of legal bureaus (*falu shi*) in each of the State Council

2. Guo Daohui (1988), 85–6.
3. Lieberthal and Oksenberg (1988) provide an especially good discussion of the State Council's difficulties in trying to resolve interministerial disputes below the level of the State Council Standing Committee.

committees and ministries, co-ordinating inter-agency activity. Unfortunately, the Bureau's precise powers to resolve inter-agency disputes during this period are unclear from the available sources.

During its short-lived (five-year) first incarnation, the Legislation Bureau was a driving force behind the effort to strengthen and regularize the role of law in China. Like many other legal reformers, the Bureau (as well as the Ministry of Justice) came under attack during the 1957 Anti-Rightist and 1959 Anti-Right-Deviationist Campaigns, when the power of the Communist Party Central apparat and of local Party officials were asserted at the expense of state organs and enacted laws. During this period, many legal policy co-ordinating functions were removed from the State Council and transferred back to the newly re-established Party Political-Legal Directorate, headed by Peng Zhen. In 1959, the Legislation Bureau was formally closed, and Tao Xijin was purged and transferred to an obscure local post in Guizhou. Most of the ministerial legal bureaus were also closed during this period; the few that remained fell prey to the Cultural Revolution seven years later.

For the next twenty-two years the State Council lacked any legal policy co-ordinating office similar to the Legislation Bureau, until Zhao Ziyang established the Economic Legislation Research Centre (ELRC) in 1981.[4] Between 1977 and 1980, only about four ministries and committees had legal and treaty offices, and these appear to have played a prominent role in drafting key pieces of post-Mao legislation.[5] After the 1978 CCP Third Plenum, ministerial legislative drafting work accelerated, but in the absence of a central State Council legislative co-ordinating office.[6] The predictable result was increased 'departmentalism', manifested not so much in delays, but rather in redundant or contradictory legislation issued by rival ministries. One pair of authors, writing in 1981 in *People's Daily*, attacked some ministries for simply refusing to engage in even basic co-ordination of law drafting work. As a solution, they called for the re-establishment of a

---

4. This lack of a single central State Council co-ordinating mechanism is confirmed by the comments of former Central Political-Legal Committee Secretary General Jin Mosheng (1978). See also Wu Daying *et al.* (1984), 106; and Yang Hong and Wang Jinzhong (1981). This last article, which calls for the re-establishment of such an office, preceded by only weeks the establishment of the ELRC.

5. According to Wu Daying *et al.* (1984), the following had legal and treaty offices during this period: the State Planning Committee, the State Economic Committee, the Ministry of Finance, and the Ministry of Foreign Economic Relations and Trade (MOFERT). There may be some confusion on this last, since MOFERT was not actually established until some years later. Wu may mean MOFERT's precursors, the Ministry of Foreign Trade and the State Foreign Investment Control Committee.

6. In a 6 December 1978 *Renmin Ribao* commentary, Jin Mosheng—a leading member of the State Political-Legal Committee during the early 1950s—criticized the State Council's legislative work under Hua Guofeng. Jin noted the important role played by the former Legislation Bureau, and argued for its re-establishment, noting that 'the State Council does not now have an organ for concrete legislative work'.

central legislative co-ordinating office and the development of a comprehensive legislative plan.[7]

The Economic Legislation Research Centre

The ELRC was established in July 1981 under the leadership of Gu Ming, an extremely well-connected and capable industrial planning bureaucrat who had once been a personal secretary to Zhou Enlai. In its first years, however, the Centre apparently did not yet function as a broker or a strong co-ordinator of legislative drafting work. Its efforts were restricted to helping re-establish legislative bureaus within ministries, convening national legislative conferences, and re-establishing the State Council's central archives and compiling the first comprehensive compendium of economic laws, regulations and interpretations in the post-Mao period.[8]

Within two years, however, the ELRC had very high-level access and was playing a major role in legal policy-making on economic issues. In a key move, Gu Ming had successfully argued that China needed to develop both annual and long-range legislative plans (called the *lifa jihua* and *lifa guihua*). Such plans, argued the former State Planning Commission (SPC) Vice-Chairman, would help establish drafting priorities for the State Council and the NPC, and would co-ordinate the development of the new economic-legal reforms with the SPC's annual and five-year Economic Plan. Sources close to Gu Ming's office report that his suggestion for legislative planning was strongly opposed by a number of senior legal officials and scholars, including former Legislation Bureau Director Tao Xijin, who saw these plans as a continuation of the Stalinist features of the Chinese administrative system, rather than a move toward greater 'rule of law'. Yet, by early 1983, the ELRC was responsible for developing these plans. A 1986 ELRC report indicates that at about the same time, it also controlled the important task of soliciting opinions from the top Politburo members on which key laws should be included in the two plans.[9] In addition it had secured a hands-on role organizing legislative drafting groups for economic laws, which gave it the authority to determine which

---

7. Yang Hong and Wang Jinzhong (1981).
8. On the clerical disruption of the period and the ELRC's efforts to restore order, see Wu Daying *et al.* (1984), 59–74; and the 'Opinion' of the ELRC in *Zhongguo Fazhi Bao*, 4 December 1981, 2.
9. 'Guanyu Guowuyuan Jingji Fagui Yanjiu Zhongxin Chengli Yilai Gongzuo Qingkuang de Huibao' ('A Report on the Work Situation of the State Council Economic Legislation Research Center Since its Establishment'), report to Premier Zhao Ziyang dated January 1986, reprinted with Zhao's comments in *Jingji Fazhi* (Beijing), No. 3 (1988), 22–25. See also '1982–1986 Nian Jingji Lifa Guihua (Cao'an)' ('1982–1986 Economic Legislative Plan [Draft]'), in the ELRC internal journal *Jingji Fagui Yanjiu Ziliao* (issue number and date unavailable: approximate date, spring 1983).

government and Party organizations sat on the drafting group and which were excluded. By 1983–84, ELRC Chairman Gu Ming was personally leading work on several key projects, including the laws on Economic Contracts and Bankruptcy.

Resurrection of the Legislation Bureau

In 1982, Premier Zhao Ziyang re-established the Legislation Bureau under the State Council General Office.[10] Before this time, legislative work in the State Council was overseen on an ad hoc basis by the ELRC and by State Council Secretary General's Office, headed in turn by Tian Jiyun and Chen Junsheng. The Legislation Bureau, like the ELRC, was one of several consultative advisory groups Zhao established to help organize and funnel advice to Zhao on issues of economic and political reform policy.

From its original 1950s incarnation down to the present, one of the Legislation Bureau's major responsibilities has been lightening the enormous work load of the State Council Standing Committee by resolving inter-ministerial disputes over document drafting before they can clog up the Standing Committee's agenda. Nevertheless, because the Bureau only held rank equal to a ministerial bureau at the time of its re-establishment, it often lacked the authority to carry out this key mission effectively.[11]

In 1986, Zhao Ziyang undertook a major reorganization of the State Council legislative organs, and simultaneously increased the Legislation Bureau's power. Its director was promoted from the rank of a bureau chief to a rank just above a vice-minister and just below a minister. This confusing-sounding shift was nevertheless crucial, for the Bureau now outranked the ministerial legislative bureaus with which it regularly dealt, even though it was still inferior to the ministries themselves. The Bureau was also taken out from under the State Council General Office and placed directly under the State Council Standing Committee.[12]

The Bureau's personnel limit (*bianzhi*), also grew with its influence. At its establishment in 1982, it had only forty staff. By 1986, this had grown to over 100. That year, the Bureau merged with the Economic Legislation Research Centre, and the new Bureau's combined staff exceeded 140. In 1988, the State Council ministries were reorganized, and most departments

---

10. Much of the following information on the State Council Legislation Bureau, its history, structure, and functions, relies on the following three interviews: 15-35-19/QXX, March 1989, 15-35-19/CSW, March 1989 and 15-35-19/DBJ, June 1989.

11. Hence, the Bureau Director's rank was equal to that of any other ministerial bureau chief. Since most of the ministry legal offices also hold bureau rank, the Legislation Bureau chief met his main counterparts only as a bureaucratic equal, not a superior.

12. Interview 15-35-19/QXE, March 1989. According to the source, apart from the Legislation Bureau, the powerful State Statistical Bureau is the only other bureau directly under the State Council Standing Committee with an equally high rank.

were required to accept draconian manpower cuts. But the Legislation Bureau again expanded, with its staff numbers gradually growing to over 260 by the beginning of 1989.[13]

The Bureau's increasing influence was also reflected in the quality of its hiring standards. By 1986 staff standards had become very high, and almost all recruits were required to have at least five to ten years experience at the central level before they could test (*kaohe*) for the Bureau. Later, however, when the Bureau's ever-accelerating manpower expansion showed these levels to be unrealistically high, it began recruiting some students from major Chinese university law departments, but it still demanded that the students' departments personally recommend and guarantee their performance (*tuijian baozheng*).[14]

But the major change affecting the Legislation Bureau at this time concerned legislative drafting procedures. Beginning in 1986, it became responsible for leading the drafting work for all laws and regulations to be promulgated by the State Council. According to State Council sources speaking in 1989, this change meant that, in a departure from past practice, the drafting group leader for all such documents would hereafter be a Legislation Bureau staff member rather than a staff member of the principal drafting ministry. Moreover, before the principal drafting ministry could start any such work, it had to receive formal approval from the Legislation Bureau. This change in formal procedure has, according to these sources, helped somewhat to restrain the competition among ministries to present their cases before the State Council Standing Committee, and has helped shift this competition to a lower level of the system. Nevertheless, this competition remains intense, as shown below.[15]

Legislation Bureau Internal Structure and Lawmaking Role

The current internal structure of the Legislation Bureau is described in Figure 6.1.[16] The bulk of its activity is spent on three aspects of the legislative process: compiling annual and long-range legislative plans; resolving bureaucratic quarrels over legislative content and presenting draft laws before the State Council Standing Committee; and drafting implementing regulations for laws which have already been adopted by the State Council and the NPC.

---

13. Interview 15-35-19/QXE, March 1989.   14. *Ibid.*
15. The Byzantine politics of receiving such approval will be discussed below. Interviews 15-35-19/QXE, March 1989 and 15-35-19/DBJ, June 1989.
16. The data on the Legislation Bureau internal structure was provided by interviews 15-35-19/QXE, March 1989 and 15-35-19/DBJ, June 1989. Both sources independently gave identical breakdowns of the names and responsibilities of these internal bureaus and offices.

126 The Politics of Lawmaking in Post-Mao China

Bureau Chief 局长	
Deputy Bureau Chief 副局长	

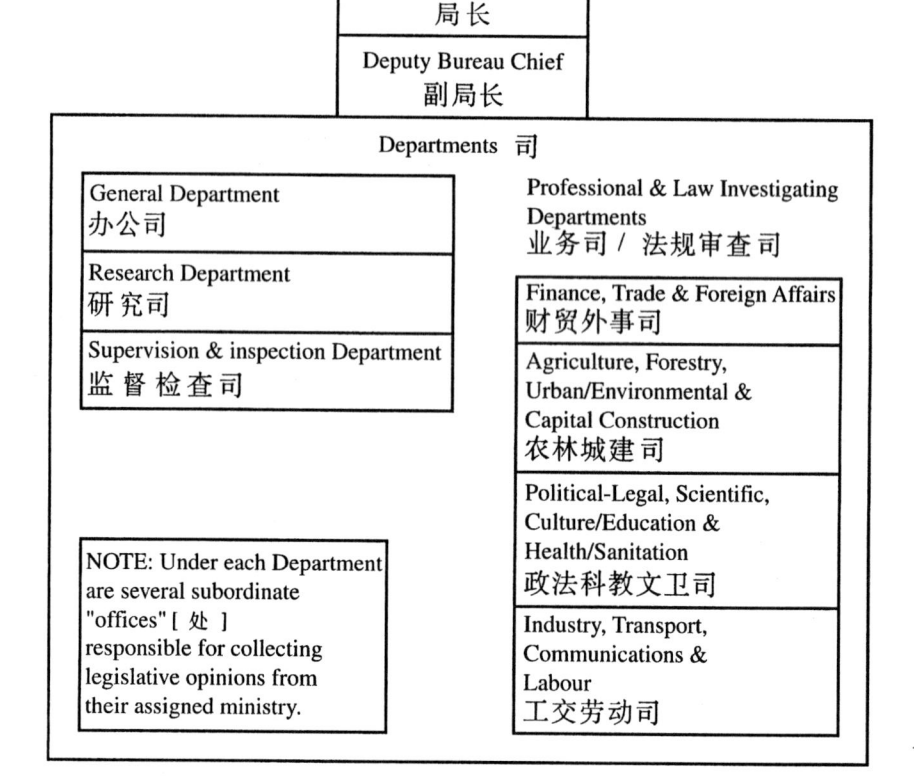

Departments 司

General Department 办公司	Professional & Law Investigating Departments 业务司 / 法规审查司
Research Department 研究司	Finance, Trade & Foreign Affairs 财贸外事司
Supervision & inspection Department 监督检查司	Agriculture, Forestry, Urban/Environmental & Capital Construction 农林城建司
NOTE: Under each Department are several subordinate "offices" [处] responsible for collecting legislative opinions from their assigned ministry.	Political-Legal, Scientific, Culture/Education & Health/Sanitation 政法科教文卫司
	Industry, Transport, Communications & Labour 工交劳动司

Fig 6.1. *State Council Legislation Bureau* [法制局] *internal organization*

Legislative Planning

The Legislation Bureau compiles two legislative plans, annual and five-year. The five-year plan can be enormous—over 1,000 pieces of legislation—and its contents are strongly influenced by the contents of the concurrent five-year economic plan. Most of my sources, however, indicated that getting a law on the five-year plan is relatively easy. The plan is not followed very closely and inclusion of a law is no guarantee that it will, in fact, be drafted.

The annual plan, on the other hand, is much smaller, typically consisting of from seven to nine laws to be promulgated by the NPC or its Standing Committee, and up to seventy laws and regulations to be promulgated by the State Council. This plan is followed quite closely by the Bureau. A law which wins a place on the annual plan also has a strong claim on the attention of State Council departments, and is very likely to be finalized and promulgated by the end of that year.

The State Council Lawmaking System 127

Ministries (and, sometimes, localities) employ various tactics to get their preferred laws on the Bureau's annual legislative plan. The process typically begins in a relatively formal, civil fashion. Legislative proposals come to the Bureau primarily—though not exclusively—from the ministries. Formally, the ministry must establish a liaison with the Legislation Bureau through the ministry's own Bureau of Laws and Regulations (called the *Fagui ju* in most ministries and provinces). One Legislation Bureau cadre described the politics of the process this way:

Usually, a ministry will send the chief of its own Legal Bureau over to the Legislation Bureau to try to convince us of the vital nature of their ministry's work. They will also argue that if they are not permitted to pass 'their' laws this year, social activity in that particular area will be ungovernable (*wufa keguan*[17]). If this doesn't work, ministries frequently go to see a 'central leading comrade'—usually either a member of the Politburo or the State Council Standing Committee—to get them to write a commentary (*pishi*) for drafting the law now.[18]

As an example, this source cited a set of regulations on private enterprise passed by the State Council in early 1989. As of late 1988, no office under the State Council had taken any initiative at all toward drafting such regulations. But the Wuhan City Communist Party Committee, which had taken the lead in a variety of market-oriented reforms, was extremely anxious that some such regulations on private enterprise be adopted, to help them carry out their reforms. So in late 1988, the Wuhan Party Committee planted a story in one of the limited circulation newspapers published for the senior leadership. The story detailed the difficulties of administering reforms in private enterprise in the absence of a comprehensive set of regulations. Zhao Ziyang saw the story, and immediately wrote a note to the Legislation Bureau ordering that it do something about drafting the law as soon as possible. The law was drafted by the Bureau and passed by the State Council Standing Committee all within the space of four months.[19]

The Legislation Bureau and Interministerial Bargaining

If a ministry is successful in winning a place on the annual plan for its draft law, the ministry and the Legislation Bureau will establish a drafting group for the law (*qicao xiaozu*). In a change from the pre-1986 practice reflected in the two case studies in this book, the leader of the drafting group is now a Legislation Bureau official who works with the appointed representatives of the principal drafting ministry and representatives of other concerned

---

17. The Chinese term here provides an interesting ambiguity. *Wufa keguan* could be translated as 'lacking any way/method (*fa*) to govern it' (i.e. 'ungovernable'), or, alternatively, as 'lacking laws (*fa*) with which to govern it'.   18. Interview 15-35-19/QXE, March 1989.
19. *Ibid.*

departments to produce an 'opinion-solicitation draft' (*zhengqiu yijian gao*).

Two points deserve special attention. First, Legislation Bureau sources quite frankly concede that they usually do not have an enormous amount of influence over the precise content (*zixi neirong*) of the draft, since the principal drafting ministry usually has a relatively well-developed basic draft in hand long before the draft law is placed on the annual plan. The Bureau does, however, have a good deal of influence over the resolution of inter-ministerial disputes on content, and over which other departments will have a spot on the drafting group.

When the first opinion-soliciting draft is finished,[20] the Legislation Bureau is responsible for circulating the draft to all provincial governments and to all concerned departments.[21] The provinces and ministries have a set time within which they are asked to respond with comments and suggested revisions. These revisions, in turn, are forwarded to the Bureau through the appropriate office (*chu*) which is assigned to deal with a given ministry or province. Each office then forwards these comments up the ladder to the appropriate department (*si*) which oversees the drafting of laws in that particular issue area. The department compiles and reviews these comments, and then the Legislation Bureau and the drafting group use them as the basis for revising the draft law or regulation. This process may be repeated several times before the Legislation Bureau finally decides the law is ready to be submitted to the State Council Standing Committee for discussion and a vote.

Another source of power for the Legislation Bureau is its role as chief presenter of all draft legislation before the State Council Standing Committee. Both China's most recent Prime Ministers—Zhao Ziyang and later Li Peng—have assigned the Legislation Bureau this role as summarizer, presenter and arbiter of draft laws and regulations precisely in order to ease the press of ministries wanting to plead their cases before the State Council. According to Bureau sources, when a draft law is presented to the State Council, only three individuals who are not members of the State Council are permitted to take part in the discussion: the drafting group leader from the Legislation Bureau, usually accompanied by the Bureau's Director, and the designated representative of the principal drafting department, almost always an official of at least vice-minister rank, and usually the Minister-in-charge of the department.

These three officials present a minimum of four documents at the

---

20. My research indicates that several, perhaps even dozens, of such 'opinion-soliciting' drafts are produced in the course of drafting a law.

21. Again, the Bureau appears to have a good deal of power over which departments will be allowed to comment on a draft. At the same time, however, Bureau sources indicate that they try to be fairly liberal in their determination of which departments have a legitimate interest in seeing a given draft.

Standing Committee meeting. The first, of course, is the draft law (*cao'an*). Secondly, the representative of the principal drafting department must give a brief explanation of the law (*shuoming*)—typically about three pages in length—spelling out the purpose of drafting the law and its major provisions. Thirdly, the Legislation Bureau presents a relatively detailed investigation report (*shencha baogao*) on the law, which contains several parts: the results of the Bureau's investigations of other department's opinion on the law; a brief but frank summary of differing ministerial opinions on the contents of the draft; and the Legislation Bureau's forecast of potential problems which might be encountered if the law is adopted and implemented. Finally, the Legislation Bureau gets the last word, presenting its own final recommendation (*yijian*) on how the Standing Committee ought to dispose of disputed clauses and mitigate the effects of potential problems in the law. Legislation Bureau sources stress that this last recommendation is viewed as very important by both the Bureau and the Standing Committee, because 'if anything goes wrong after the law is implemented, the Legislation Bureau will be held responsible'.[22]

Drafting Implementing Regulations

Recent empirical studies of the Chinese policy process have demolished any lingering impression created by the old 'totalitarian model' that Central Party decrees and laws might be self-implementing. The organizations with responsibility for implementing a policy can often cause its substance to differ radically from the intentions of its drafters.[23] NPC promulgation of a law does not mark the end of the lawmaking game, only the mid-point. Hence, to understand the politics of lawmaking, one must understand something about how the laws are implemented in China.

Because historically, China has lacked an independent judiciary or a tradition of judicial review, laws are primarily implemented through administrative (such as ministerial and local government) organs. Moreover, laws in China are often drafted in general, hortatory language with few precise clauses which could aid even the best-intentioned local official in interpreting Beijing's purpose. Implementing regulations (*shishi tiaoli*), drafted after a law is passed, are intended to provide more precise instructions to lower levels. As a result, whether and how any law promulgated by the NPC or its Standing Committee gets implemented depends in large measure on the substance of these implementing regulations. Put another way, the officials who draft the implementing regulations for a law can potentially use these regulations to subvert the intentions of the original law's drafters.

22. Principal source, interview 15-35-19/QXE, March 1989.
23. See Lampton (1987); also Lieberthal and Oksenberg (1987).

Several sources indicated the Legislation Bureau and the State Council ministries are usually the key players in drafting the implementing regulations for laws passed by the NPC.[24] Since most laws are originally drafted by State Council ministries, the Legislation Bureau usually works with that ministry to draft the implementing regulations. Normally, the Legislation Bureau convenes a series of symposia to solicit the opinions of the principal drafting ministry as well as other concerned ministries, Party organs and representatives of the NPC Standing Committee staff (usually the Legislative Affairs Committee). Based on these meetings, the principal drafting ministry and the Legislation Bureau draft the implementing regulations, which must then go through the same sort of State Council inter-agency review (often prolonged) as the original law did.

Sources diverge on the all-important issues of how much influence the Legislation Bureau has over the content of these implementing regulations, and whether or not the Bureau uses its influence to promote its own policy agenda. Bureau sources indicate that the principal drafting ministry usually contributes the main content of the implementing regulations. These sources emphatically assert that the Bureau's role is normally that of a technician and a watchdog: to ensure proper legal language is employed, to guard against 'excessive' deviations between the original law and the implementing regulations, and to resolve inter-agency disagreements over the language of the implementing regulations. They deny any effort on the Bureau's part to promote its own policy views through its influence over implementing regulations.[25]

But the case studies in this book point to a different interpretation. During the last phase of the March–April 1988 NPC debates over the State-Owned Industrial Enterprises Law, Legislation Bureau Director Sun Wanzhong spoke to delegates on the principles his office would follow in implementing the law. Sun seemingly ignored successful efforts by NPC delegates to delete or water down some of the most radical industrial reform-oriented clauses in the draft (such as those strengthening factory managers or encouraging experiments with ownership reform), and declared, before the NPC vote, that his Bureau would draft implementing regulations and companion legislation which would strengthen many of the very same reforms which NPC delegates had found so odious. The relatively clear conclusion is that the Legislation Bureau does have a policy agenda of its own, and it is not above using its power over implementation to promote it.[26]

Legislation Bureau sources speaking in 1989 and 1992 indicate that staffers from the NPC do not customarily play a major role in discussing and drafting implementing regulations. As one source noted, the NPC special temporary offices established for drafting major legislation are often closed after the NPC passes their particular law, and do not see

---

24. Interview 15-39-19/CSW, March 1989.   25. *Ibid.*   26. See Chapter 6.

The State Council Lawmaking System   131

the law through the drafting of the implementing regulations.[27] For example, three months after the NPC passed the State Enterprise Law, the Legislation Bureau began the implementing process by convening a series of meetings on drafting implementing regulations and 'companion' legislation for the law. Legislation Bureau sources, speaking in the spring of 1989, indicated this process was just getting started, and they did not anticipate that the NPC LAWC would be heavily involved. The source indicated merely that the Legislation Bureau 'might listen to their opinions' as part of the consultative process, but that was all.[28]

In recent years, however, the NPC has shown increased irritation with the State Council's power over the implementation of laws, and has tried to expand its influence in this area. At the 1989 Second Plenary Session of the Seventh NPC, both delegates and NPC leaders argued that the NPC should shift its focus to expanding its powers over implementation and oversight.[29] Sometimes, NPC delegates have tried to take the responsibility for drafting implementing regulations away from the State Council and give it to other authorities whom they believe will cleave closer to the intent of the law as promulgated. According to sources in the Supreme People's Court, for example, the power to draft these implementing regulations became a key sticking point when the NPC debated the 1989 Administrative Procedures Law. The battle lines were drawn between Li Peng's State Council on the one hand, and the NPC and the Supreme People's Court on the other. The State Council wanted its Legislation Bureau to draft the implementing regulations. It also wanted the law to stipulate that whenever courts adjudicate lawsuits against a given ministry, the courts must make reference to the internal administrative and personnel regulations of that ministry; in effect, elevating these internal regulations to the level of the Administrative Procedures Law. The Supreme People's Court and the NPC leadership, however, wanted the court to draft the implementing regulations. Further, they wanted to give the courts the right to ignore internal ministry regulations if they chose to do so.[30]

Conclusion: From 'United Leadership' to an 'Ambiguous' Law-Making System

Clearly, the central theme which emerges from the discussion of China's lawmaking organs in Chapters 3 to 6 is that they constitute, in the language

---

27. Interview 15-39-19/CSW, March 1989. My sources did not shed any light on the reason for this. It is possible that NPC Standing Committee staff are limited, and thus unable to focus on drafting implementing regulations. It may also be that the NPC regards this work as more appropriately the province of the State Council and its ministries.
28. 'Women keneng yao tingqu tamende yijian.'   29. See Chapter 5.
30. Interview 39-31-0-41/EEZ, April 1989.

of the Garbage Can model, an increasingly 'ambiguous decision-making technology', in which authority relationships have blurred and power has become ever more decentralized over the last fifteen years. Despite constitutional reforms since 1978, both the constitutional and the informal 'rules' of lawmaking which might define the relationship between Party, government and NPC organs have remained unclear, even to the system's experts and practitioners. Organizational power trends during this period have reinforced this trend towards decentralized power and authority. A gradual but persistent erosion of the Party Centre's organizational control over lawmaking has been mirrored by tremendous bureaucratic development and political assertiveness by the State Council and the NPC Standing Committee. In part, as noted in Chapter 4, this reflects Deng Xiaoping's very conscious decision to decentralize policy-making power, and in part it reflects Deng's apparently backfired strategy to ease aging rivals away from more traditional avenues of influence. As a result, power within the lawmaking system, just as in other sectors of the Chinese policy-making system, is fragmented among numerous individuals and organizations. The various lawmaking organizations have and continue to evolve their own unique packages of power resources which allow them to influence lawmaking in differing degrees, at different stages of the process. The result is a lawmaking 'system' which daily looks less like any 'system' worthy of that name, in which any law must pass through multiple decision-making arenas and endure prolonged, shifting political struggles.

Advocates of a top-down model of lawmaking might object that the Politburo could, if it so chose, end much of this confusion, since it does have the power of prior approval over laws. But as noted in Chapter 4, the top Party leaders frequently fail to exercise their influence fully, either for lack of consensus, or because they lack the training or the interest to concern themselves with the details of a draft bill. Government ministries, on the other hand, have enormous influence over the detailed content of legislation and its implementation, but are often forced into important compromises, either with other ministries, or local authorities, or, increasingly, with the NPC and its Standing Committee. In such a system, political actors who are dissatisfied with the current consensus on a draft law will unavoidably be drawn to resume the battle in another, more sympathetic arena.

PART III
Case Studies in Lawmaking

7

The Case of The Enterprise Bankruptcy Law

The long process of drafting the 1986 Enterprise Bankruptcy Law can be broken down into four stages. The initial stage, that of getting the law on to the government's agenda, is a dramatic example of policy enterpreneurship which says much about the potential importance of individual intellectuals in the Chinese system, at least during Zhao Ziyang's tenure as Prime Minister. The politics of this stage closely approximate the politics of the Garbage Can model, with its fluid interplay of problem streams, proposed policy solutions, political moods and an entrepreneur labouring to bring these together. In stark contrast, the second stage, that of inter-agency consensus-building, illustrates the potential for leaden immobilism in the policy-making bureaucracy and the periodic necessity for high-level intervention to kick-start the process. It is the Organizational Politics model at its best—and worst. Stage three, top leadership decision-making, unfortunately remains unclear owing to the lack of reliable source material; the available evidence does indicate, however, that the Bankruptcy Law's content changed little during this stage. Stage four, that of NPC review and debate, shows vividly the legislature's new potential for influence in the post-Mao lawmaking process. Like the agenda-setting stage, the legislative debate also shows some of the wide-open entrepreneurship of the Garbage Can model.

Stage One: Getting a Socialist Heresy on the Agenda

For thirty years before 1983, the very topic of bankruptcy was absolutely forbidden in the Chinese study of economics. Its sudden emergence on the policy agenda defies any conception of policy-making 'incrementalism'. To understand how such a dramatic socialist heresy could win a place on the agenda, it is first necessary to look at the dogged self-styled entrepreneur who authored the law: Cao Siyuan.

Born in Jiangxi province in January 1946, Cao resembles nothing so much as a smaller Chinese version of Luciano Pavarotti, complete with the great tenor's disarming gregariousness, overwhelming self-confidence and incredible energy level. Cao shatters many Western stereotypes of Chinese intellectuals. He is a free-wheeling 'ideas man' and unabashed self-promoter, and is ready at a moment's notice with sweeping radical new solutions to any major social problem one cares to bring up.[1] He has led a peripatetic career, in contrast to the classic careerist Chinese bureaucrat whose fate is inextricably bound up with one unit.[2]

Like his American policy entrepreneur counterparts, Cao's persistence has made him something of a 'snake-oil salesman'—constantly and deftly repackaging his pet policy proposals and marketing them as a cure-all for whatever problems currently hold the centre of the political stage. The repeated metamorphoses of his bankruptcy proposal, especially over the first five years, make fascinating reading for the policy analyst. When one compares Cao's job history with his list of publications, it is immediately clear that no matter where he has worked since 1983, he repeatedly succeeded in turning these organizations into the chief bureaucratic sponsors of his proposals, and not vice versa, as the Organizational Politics model would suggest.

Cao's first publication suggesting a bankruptcy system appeared in a late 1980 issue of the Chinese Academy of Social Sciences (CASS) internal economic journal *Caimao Jingji*. Cao, however, had got the idea for a bankruptcy law three years earlier, in 1977, while still a graduate student at CASS. Cao has described these first years after Mao's death as a 'lively time of thought' when a variety of new ideas were being put forward. At that time, however, he had not yet begun to think of bankruptcy as a method of spurring enterprises to use new technology—the justification which ultimately won it the support of its first organizational backer, the State Council's Technical Economic Research Center (TERC). Rather, Cao thought of bankruptcy in general terms of improving managerial efficiency, and ending enterprise losses caused by the practice of 'everyone eating out of the same pot'. Almost incredibly, Cao had not yet begun to consider the political sensitivity of proposing bankruptcy in a socialist system.[3]

In October 1980, facing enormous state enterprise deficits, the State Council, with Zhao Ziyang as the new Premier, issued 'Temporary Regulations on Maintaining and Developing Competitiveness in Society'. The document was among the first even to allude to bankruptcy, arguing that it was 'inevitable' that during competition, some backward enterprises would 'fall by the wayside' (*taotai*). From this important policy shift, Cao con-

---

1. Foreigners who met Cao during his Stone Corporation days (late 1980s) were hastened into his office by a member of his staff (indeed, 'entourage' or 'groupies' might be better terms), and instantly handed xerox copies of articles about Cao meticulously clipped from major Western, Chinese and Hong Kong newspapers, on which staffers have written titles such as 'Cao Siyuan, Father of the Chinese Bankruptcy Law, Meets Famous American Judges'. Other materials proffered include Cao's 'résumé'—a glossy 24-page booklet with inch-high characters on the front—which lists Cao's major achievements, publications, and press interviews.
2. In the seven years since Cao left graduate school he worked for three different offices of the State Council before establishing himself as the Director of Social Development Research Institute of the now famous Stone Corporation in October 1988.
3. Interview 28-29-16-28/XHB, March 1989.

cluded that 'it was thus necessary to begin researching and drafting methods for closing and dealing with bankruptcy enterprises'.[4]

Cao's first of over eighty pro-bankruptcy articles—unprovocatively entitled 'How to give full play to the role of insurance companies in the course of competition'—was not a call for a 'winding-up' style bankruptcy law intended to threaten ill-managed enterprises.[5] Still less was it a detailed American-style plan to protect and balance the rights of debtors and creditors. Rather, it was a relatively benign and diplomatic proposal for using insurance companies to save chronic money-losing enterprises. Cao argued that by regularly paying a percentage of their wage bill to insurance companies, enterprises could build up a fund which could be used to support staff and workers in the event the firm ever had to shut down. Unemployment funds for workers in closed factories had traditionally come either from state treasury subsidies or from state bank loans which were seldom repaid (which amounts to the same thing). Cao's twin goals were to ease pressures on the state treasury while encouraging insurance firms and enterprises to work together 'in a socialist fashion' to cut factory losses. He went to great lengths to leave the threat of bankruptcy implicit. The article never used the word 'bankruptcy' (*pochan*), preferring more mild terms implying going out of business (*taotai, daobi*). Cao barely even alluded to the possibility of workers being unemployed. The article nevertheless encountered considerable scholarly criticism for even accepting the premise that socialist enterprises could go bankrupt.[6]

During the next two years the indefatigable Cao hawked his plans for business insurance and a bankruptcy system from one end of the Beijing bureaucracy to the other. He first took his idea directly to the state insurance companies, trying to persuade them to sponsor a bankruptcy law as a way of expanding their own social role. But the companies rebuffed Cao and his scheme, calling it 'uncustomary' for Chinese insurance firms. Cao repackaged his proposal and next presented it to the People's Bank of China (PBOC), arguing that as China's largest creditor, the bank would obviously benefit from a bankruptcy system. But the PBOC also declined to support the controversial plan, expressing a fear that if enterprises could be declared 'bankrupt', it would reveal to the world that the PBOC had 'unsound lending practices'. Even Cao's *alma mater*, the CASS Economics Research Institute, was not interested in sponsoring the law. None of these institutions denied the importance of the enterprise problem, but none was interested in Cao's controversial solution.[7]

The turning point for Cao came in early 1983, when he was employed as a researcher for the State Council's Technical Economic Research Centre (TERC), an economic reform think-tank which was headed by one of Zhao

---

4. Cao Siyuan (1988b), 52.   5. Cao Siyuan (1980).
6. Interview 28-29-16-28/XHB, March 1989.   7. *Ibid.*

Ziyang's closest advisors, the famed economist Ma Hong.[8] In the spring of 1983 TERC researchers completed a major internal study of technology absorption in Chinese industry which revealed several depressing truths. Five years after China had inaugurated its open-door economic policy–principally aimed at gaining access to advanced Western technology–most major enterprises' technological levels were still the same as they had been in the 1950s and 1960s. Labour productivity, the report argued, lagged 'twenty to thirty years' (sic) behind advanced industrial countries. Furthermore, the study noted, advanced countries' industries were devoting 60–70% of fixed capital investment to technological and equipment modernization, as compared with 30% in China. New technology was not being put to work quickly enough, resulting in a slow transition to the manufacture of new product lines. Even in the wide-open coastal areas, new product lines were only 3% of production.[9]

The TERC researchers argued that the blame for slow technology absorption lay in a lack of competition. There was no threat which forced enterprises to innovate, and enterprises whose productivity lagged could rely on the state to bail them out. In Cao's colourful idiom, they could 'rest peacefully in the wind-sheltered harbour of the state, never forced to sail into the full wind and waves of economic competition'.[10]

Early 1983–1984: Mood Shifts

The TERC report, which landed on Zhao Ziyang's desk in early 1983, was just one sign of a rising mood of concern within the top leadership about the backward state of Chinese industry and the losses the treasury was incurring underwriting its deficits. In the ensuing twelve months, the mood gradually turned from concern to deep frustration over the failure of traditional techniques, and open searching for innovative solutions. On 6 June 1983, Premier Zhao Ziyang revealed the leadership's frustration, searching and willingness to consider strong action in his annual Government Work Report at the Fifth Session of the Sixth National People's Congress:

In 1982, the combined deficit of industrial enterprises that ran at a loss came to 4.2 billion *yuan*. . . . Unless this situation is changed soon, it is bound to seriously affect our construction and production. . . . All enterprises that run at a loss due to poor operation must reverse this trend within a given time limit. Otherwise, they must be ordered to shut down, suspend operations, amalgamate with others or switch to the manufacture of other products.[11]

From the perspective of the Garbage Can model, it is interesting that the leadership's anger over this problem was being fanned not so much by

---
8. On Ma Hong and the TERC, see Nina Halpern (1986).
9. Cao Siyuan (1988b), 52–53, and interview 28-29-16-28/XHB, March 1989.
10. Cao Siyuan (1988b), 53, and interview 28-29-16-28/XHB, March 1989.
11. *Beijing Review*, 4 July 1983, XI.

advocates of the bankruptcy 'solution' as by other leaders and bureaucracies, each coincidentally pursuing their own independent agendas. In particular, the powerful State Economic Commission (SEC), China's main agency tasked with trying to improve enterprise efficiency and management, was pushing hard to heighten attention to the problem, and was ultimately both the principal recipient of this high-level pressure and the major beneficiary of leadership concern. Throughout 1983 and early 1984, the SEC's top leaders, in a series of documents, speeches and meetings, stressed that recent administrative efforts to improve enterprise efficiency had failed to bring about a major turnaround in enterprise performance, and they vaguely hinted that unspecified stronger measures might be necessary. SEC Chief Minister Lu Dong has noted that in August 1983 the SEC received a directive from 'the leading Comrades of the State Council [that] ... the State Economic Commission must grasp in an all-round manner and conscientiously shoulder the responsibility for the issue of raising economic results in our industrial production'.[12] But interviews and documents reveal that the SEC's principal policy goal at this point was not to promote a bankruptcy law. Rather, the SEC was chiefly interested in building support for its own pet proposal, the Factory Manager Responsibility System, which was enshrined in the forthcoming State-Owned Industrial Enterprises Law (see Chapter 8). In the process, however, the SEC, apparently inadvertently, fanned the mood of frustration and searching which prepared the ground for the TERC's forthcoming bankruptcy proposal.

Despite great administrative pressure on the state enterprises by the SEC and other agencies, the results were disappointing. After nearly a year of heavy Central emphasis on improving economic performance, new SEC Minister-in-Charge Zhang Jingfu noted in his speech to the SEC's February 1984 National Economic Work Conference that there had been 'no fundamental change for the better in improving the economic performance of enterprises'.[13] In a January 1984 article, the SEC's grand old man of enterprise management, Vice-Minister Yuan Baohua, threatened inefficient plant managers that they might be fired without reassignment, and numerous chronic money-losing enterprises might find their subsidies cut off and their operations closed down.[14]

Cao's Breakthrough

Amidst this brewing political mood of late spring 1983, TERC chief Ma Hong commissioned an internal study for Premier Zhao on how China could spur enterprise competition and hasten technology absorption. Ma's

12. Remarks of Lu Dong in *Jingji Ribao*, 2 March 1984, 1–3 in JPRS-CEA-84-025, 4 April 1984, 1–26.
13. Zhang Jingfu in BXE, 6 March 1984, in JPRS-CEA-84-021, 26 March 1984, 1–2.
14. *Jingji Guanli*, No. 1 (5 January 1984), 3–5, in JPRS-CEA-84-022, 2–4.

chief assistant entrusted the job to his deputy, who was also Cao Siyuan's boss. But when Cao's boss handed in a draft which was 'uninnovative and unsatisfactory', the task of rewriting the report fell to Cao.[15] What happened next could be ascribed to bureaucratic good luck, but given Cao's persistent, unabashed promotion of his own radical proposals, his bosses must have had some inkling of what to expect.

The resulting TERC report, entitled 'Suggestions on Several Problems Concerning the Struggle for Technological Progress to Spur Economic Development', argued that 'unless those who are backward are allowed to fall by the wayside, there is no such thing as competition' (*bu taotai luohou, jiu wu suowei jingzheng*). In Section Seven of the report, Cao argued that unless enterprises began to feel a 'sense of crisis' (*weiji gan*), they would never begin to compete. If the non-policy-based losses of an enterprise reached a certain point (unspecified in this report), then the state banks should stop giving the enterprise loans to pay wages, and the enterprise should be declared 'bankrupt' (*pochan*). Cao closed this section by proposing that the State Economic Commission (SEC) be invited to draft an Enterprise Bankruptcy Consolidation Law.[16]

Before being circulated to other departments, Cao's report went first through internal agency review. The bankruptcy proposal was, predictably, the focus of his superiors' concern. Before putting forward such a radical new proposal, Cao's bosses were anxious to find a proper ideological basis (*yiju*) to justify it, such as a quote from Marx or from a Central Leading Comrade. But when Cao's bosses asked him to cite his basis for suggesting bankruptcy, Cao half-jokingly cited his own 1980 *Caimao Jingji* article.[17]

Fortunately for Cao, his bosses were still willing to back the suggestion, and Ma Hong made no unfavourable comment when he saw the bankruptcy proposal. Ma took the report to Zhao Ziyang, who also did not veto the proposal, but apparently suggested Ma begin preliminary inter-agency co-ordination of it. During the summer, in around August, the TERC convened a preliminary meeting of all concerned departments of the State Council to discuss the bankruptcy law proposal. The concerned departments included the State Economic Commission and the Ministry of Labour and Personnel, in addition to other ministries.[18] Many at the

15. Interview 28-29-16-28/XHB, April 1989.
16. State Council Technical Economic Research Centre, 'Suggestions on Several Problems Concerning the Struggle for Technological Progress to Spur Economic Development', 1983. While the report is still not in open circulation, the author has seen it and compared the wording of section 7 with the description in Cao Siyuan (1988b), 53 and found them identical, except that the latter refers to 'the concerned department' (*youguan bumen*) rather than naming the SEC. According to Chang Ta-Kuang, the text of the report is also available in the journal *Gongye Jingji Guanli* (*Industrial Economic Management*), No. 3, 1984. This appears to be an internal circulation journal, and I have thus far been unable to locate this source.
17. Interview 28-29-16-28/XHB, April 1989.
18. *Ibid.* The source notes that the NPC Standing Committee permanent bureaucracy was not represented at these meetings.

The Case of The Enterprise Bankruptcy Law 141

meeting strongly supported Cao's proposal. Even more interestingly, no one opposed the proposal at this initial meeting.[19] The State Economic Commission, perhaps recognizing how controversial bankruptcy would be, voiced strong support for the measure, but declined to be the principal drafter of the law. All present agreed the proposal needed revision and fleshing out, and suggested the TERC draft a tentative proposal (*shexiang*) for the law.[20] Having received the go-ahead from the preliminary meeting, Cao and his colleagues at TERC began to draft a tentative proposal entitled 'Implement a Bankruptcy Law, Struggle to Heighten Efficiency'.[21]

Stylistically, the tentative proposal was much closer to an essay than a draft law, lacking the clauses and precision of a legal document.[22] The document began by justifying the need for the law and then sketching out its proposed basic contents. These included the law's effective scope, the conditions for declaring bankruptcy, the procedures for bankruptcy consolidation, the sources and management of the bankruptcy aid fund, and the question of trial implementation of the law. The justification stressed the importance of competition to improving enterprise performance, calling competition the 'voiceless command' (*wusheng zhi ming*), a phrase stunningly evocative of Adam Smith's 'invisible hand'.[23] Many factories, the report argued, are in fact already 'bankrupt', lacking any way to cover their losses. These factories actually survived only by siphoning off subsidies from profitable enterprises, based on the false principle that state-owned factories could not go bankrupt. The proposal argued the law should apply to all non-private enterprises, except for those which were 'important to the Plan and to the people's livelihood', a category which included railways, airlines, electrical plants, post offices, and very large scale state and city enterprises. Any such factory which had lost money for two consecutive years, or whose debts reached 50–80% of fixed assets, could be considered for bankruptcy consolidation. Cao insisted that the law specify such a percentage of fixed assets as a cut-off point, but he also recognized that during the legislative process, this percentage would probably be changed, or might vary from industry to industry. Most factories would undergo a year of consolidation rather than immediate bankruptcy. The tentative proposal prescribed tough measures to motivate workers in money-losing enterprises to work harder to save the factory during this year's grace period. For example, the staff and workers would continue to receive a basic maintenance wage, but this should in principle be high

---

19. Interview 28-29-16-28/HXB, March 1989. See also Cao Siyuan (1988b), 53.
20. The precise date of the meeting is unclear. One interview source believes it was in November, but the dates of documents drafted subsequent to the meeting (see n. 21) indicate it must have been held before September 1983.   21. Cao Siyuan (1983).
22. *Ibid.*
23. Cao's choice of phrasing must have confirmed the worst suspicions of bankruptcy critics who believed the law was a 'capitalist measure'.

enough only to maintain their livelihood, and low enough to spur them to 'save themselves' and the factory. During this period, none of the workers could be transferred out of the enterprise. If the enterprise was ultimately declared bankrupt, the workers would receive a declining percentage of their original wages, decreasing over six months from 85 to 55%. The proposal called for the creation of a labour insurance system funded by a contribution from all enterprises of about 5% of their wage bills. Finally, and most ominously, it advocated establishing 'labour service companies'—apparently unemployment agencies—and the gradual development of what it called 'flexible . . . pools of labour'.

A comparison of Cao's tentative proposal with his previous articles on bankruptcy reveals a key entrepreneurial tactic. Throughout this process, Cao, like policy entrepreneurs in the United States, tried to broaden his support coalition by skilfully altering his justification for the bankruptcy system to suit his many different audiences. He tried to sell his bankruptcy 'solution' by arguing it was the best answer to a dizzyingly broad array of problems. When writing for Ma Hong and the TERC, he narrowly stressed bankruptcy's value as a spur to technological innovation. But in the later tentative proposal, which circulated among at least a dozen ministries, he greatly broadened his justification. Among the 'ills' the bankruptcy medicine could cure, Cao claimed it could promote competition, increase sales, raise state revenue, improve factory mangement and prevent losing enterprises robbing from profitable ones. Only on the last page of the twelve-page tentative proposal did Cao allude briefly to bankruptcy's ability to promote technology absorption, previously the central justification which had originally won it the TERC's sponsorship.[24]

The law's justification was further tailored to suit the audience when it was first formally proposed to the NPC in May 1984. NPC Standing Committee Member Wen Yuankai's cover proposal insistently argued that a bankruptcy law would stengthen the development of the legal system by adding teeth to several pieces of legislation which the NPC had already passed. In a politically astute bit of salesmanship, Wen's proposal singled out the Economic Contracts Law—the drafting of which had been a pet project of Chairman Peng Zhen—as a key law whose implementation bankruptcy would strengthen.[25]

And so, by the spring of 1984, Cao and his TERC associates had been able to place the bankruptcy law proposal squarely on the State Council's policy agenda. In doing so, they had skilfully nagvigated a rising tide of attention and frustration over the intractable problems of enterprise inefficiency and slow technology absorption. Yet this heightened recognition of the problem was less a result of Cao's own efforts than of the unrelated entrepreneurial efforts of the State Economic Commission to promote

24. Cao Siyuan (1983).   25. *Ibid.*

The Case of The Enterprise Bankruptcy Law   143

interest in managerial autonomy (about which I will have more to say in the next chapter). Cao, as has been shown, searched persistently for years for just such a high profile problem for which his bankruptcy law could be seen as the solution. His real skill lay in his persistence and his thoughtful repackaging of the proposal until he was able to bring the streams of perceived problems and policy proposals together.

Elated as they were that their proposal had won a place on the State Council's agenda for inter-agency review, the TERC researchers were still well aware that such a controversial plan could easily be bottled up as it moved into the more bureaucratic review process. Indeed, as the tentative proposal circulated within the government, the TERC researchers were tipped off that it was likely to be opposed by a high-ranking State Council lawmaking official during inter-agency review. The TERC researchers' greatest fear was that this senior official's opposition might restrain the proposal, and thus make later publication over his objections difficult. And so, before the formal inter-agency review group was formed to convene further meetings on the tentative proposal, the TERC researchers moved to place the proposal before the public by publishing it in the 27 February 1984 issue of *Liaowang* magazine, at that time China's most prominent reformist journal.[26] This bold move initiated the public phase of the bankruptcy debate, diffusing the idea and allowing lower-level support to build naturally. Such prominent publication, in turn, greatly diminished the likelihood that the bankruptcy law could be buried quietly within the State Council bureaucracy.[27] The tactic also seems to have had the desired effect of mobilizing a local constituency for the law, most notably among local banks and other creditors who were anxious to improve their leverage for recovering bad loans. Local courts also wanted clearer regulations for dealing with non-repayment cases. Cao Siyuan, in his *Bankruptcy Primer*, notes that other local government officials also endorsed the law:

Many local leaders were very worried over the situation of year after year trying to get control over losses and raise profits, but ending up paying subsidies to a few badly managed long-term money losing enterprises.... After the 'Tentative Plan'

26. Interview 28-29-16-28/XHB, April 1989.
27. This was only the first of several articles authored by Cao advocating the law. Cao's résumé lists some 84 published articles and interviews between 1980 and 1986. For some of the more notable, see the following journals: *Liaowang*, No. 9 (27 February 1984), 18–19; *Jingji Ribao* 7 July 1984, 1, 2; *Jingji Ribao* 16 November 1985, 2, in FBIS-CHI, 10 December 1985, K18–21; *Jingji Ribao*, 14 June 1986, 3, in FBIS-CHI, 24 June 1986, K13–15; *Jingji Ribao*, 16 May 1986. By far his most sophisticated treatment is in *Jingji Fazhan yu Tizhi Gaige* (*Economic Development and Structural Reform*), No. 5 (1986), 32-40 (Beijing, Chinese Economic Structural Reform Research Institute & Beijing Young Economists Study Society Joint Publication), personal copy; 'Pochanfa yu jingji tizhi gaige', in *Zhong Qingnian Jingji Luntan* (*Young Chinese Economists Discussions*) (Tianjin), No. 1 (1985), 16–17; 'Zengjia qiye huoli de falu cuoshi', *Minzhu yu Fazhi* (*Democracy and the Legal System*), No. 11 (1984).

was published in the magazines and papers, several regions and departments immediately indicated their welcome for the plan, and some even actively and spontaneously began testpoint work.[28]

Stage Two: State Council Inter-agency Review

The internal State Council review was personally chaired by Gu Ming, the influential Director of the Economic Legislation Research Centre. On 24 May, Gu invited a group of concerned ministries to convene the first Bankruptcy Law drafting symposium. This symposium met six times between May and October. Its principal functions were to exchange reactions to the proposal, revise and flesh it out, try to iron out disagreements, and, ultimately, determine if there was sufficient consensus on the proposal to merit drafting it as a law.

State Council sources report that Gu Ming and the ELRC had a fairly free hand in determining which ministries would be invited to attend this symposium, based on the ELRC's assessment of how much the bankruptcy proposal was likely to affect each of the various ministries' daily work.[29] The ELRC chose to invite the following nine organizations:

The ELRC (Chair)
The TERC
The State Economic Commission
The Ministry of Labour and Personnel (MLP)
The People's Bank of China
The Ministry of Finance
The General Administration of Industry and Commerce
The Ministry of Foreign Economic Relations and Trade (MOFERT)
The Ministry of Light Industry
The Supreme People's Court[30]

If this list is considered in light of the potential impact of a bankruptcy law, a number of surprising omissions are apparent. Despite the obvious potential for bankruptcy-induced unemployment, the All-China Federation of Trade Unions (ACFTU) was not invited. Nor were any CCP Central Committee or National People's Congress Standing Committee offices included. And notwithstanding the potential impact of the law on China's state-run enterprises, neither the State Planning Commission nor any of the State Council's industrial line ministries took part in these early meetings which played such a key role in shaping the content of the law. The

---

28. Cao Siyuan (1988b), 56.   29. Interview 15-39-19/QXX, March 1989.
30. The Supreme People's Court was not among the original participants in the symposium, but was invited later when the discussion began to focus on bankruptcy procedure. Interview 28-29-16-28/XHB, April 1989.

The Case of The Enterprise Bankruptcy Law 145

potential power of the ELRC as chair and chief organizer of the early drafting symposium is thus quite clear.

Some of these sources spoke about why certain organizations were excluded. According to trade union legal experts, the ACFTU is often excluded from State Council internal legislative discussions, a practice they strongly resent.[31] The CCP Secretariat and the Political-Legal Committee have a limited staff to handle legal affairs, according to several academic and government sources. As a general rule, they only become involved in drafting 'basic laws' (*jiben fa*) which have a very broad impact on society. According to a variety of sources, the Bankruptcy Law was simply not regarded as important enough to merit Secretariat involvement—a statement which says much about the limits on Party micromanagement of lawmaking.[32]

This internal review saw the first significant opposition to the bankruptcy proposal, and the law temporarily became stalled. Some ministries which in late 1983 had in principal supported the idea of drafting a bankruptcy law now began voicing objections to the specifics of TERC's tentative proposal.[33] Disagreement at the symposia centred on two issues. The first was whether or not a socialist country like China should even have bankruptcy. The Ministry of Labour and Personnel strongly opposed drafting any form of bankruptcy, labelling it anti-socialist and anti-worker. While sources at the meeting have described the Ministry's opposition as 'quite fierce', the MLP was apparently alone in its view. All the other participants were willing to support some form of bankruptcy system. For these ministries, the principal dispute was over the law's applicable scope; specifically, whether or not it should apply to state-owned enterprises. The original TERC proposal, as mentioned earlier, called for a single, all-inclusive law for all non-private enterprises, including state-owned, collective, wholly foreign-owned, and Sino-foreign joint ventures and co-operative ventures. Four of the ministries, however, opposed including state-owned enterprises. As a counter-proposal, these ministries

---

31. Interview 27-22-13-33/TSE, April 1989. We might ask if the trade union viewpoint is represented within the State Council by other organizations, such as the Ministry of Labour and Personnel (MLP). But despite the fact that, in this case, the MLP's viewpoint on bankruptcy was similar to the trade union's, the ACFTU clearly regards the MLP as representing a 'government' rather than a 'trade union' point of view.

32. At the same time as the ELRC bankruptcy symposium (early/mid-1984), the Secretariat was heavily involved in discussions of enterprise management which led to the October 1984 CCP Decision on urban economic structural reform and the 1988 State-Owned Industrial Enterprise Law. See Chapter 6.

33. Cao Siyuan's written account alludes to these interministerial disputes, but only in general ideological terms: 'The question of bankruptcy had for 30 years been a "forbidden zone" in our nation. [Also] the notion that socialist enterprises cannot go bankrupt had become deeply rooted in many people's minds. Accordingly, on the question of drafting a bankruptcy law, this stage of "internal fermentation" (*neibu yunniang*) had no sooner begun than a "bitter debate" (*jilie zhenglun*) began.' Cao Siyuan (1988b), 53.

suggested drafting two different documents. One would be a bankruptcy law applicable to all non-state-owned enterprises. The second would be a set of State Council internal regulations or measures (*banfa*) for handling cases of state-owned enterprises which incurred excessive losses. These measures would in essence resemble the existing system of 'stopping, closing, reorganizing and reopening' which had been in use for decades. Enterprises would not face final closure, their assets would not be sold off and the case would not end up in court. These measures were based on traditional Chinese practice, and it is probable that they would also have preserved ministerial control over the enterprises in their system by not allowing creditors to go outside the system and appeal to courts for recovery of assets. The four proponents of this 'two laws' counter-proposal were the Ministries of Finance, Light Industry, and Foreign Economic Relations and Trade, plus the People's Bank of China. The attitude of the ELRC at this point was unclear. It was sympathetic to the 'two laws' proposal at this early stage, but over time it gradually became convinced that a strong, inclusive bankruptcy law was necessary, and all Chinese sources indicate that the support of ELRC Chief Gu Ming was pivotal in getting the law passed.[34]

Since both MOFERT and the Ministry of Light Industry controlled a number of state enterprises which might be threatened by a state-enterprise bankruptcy system, their support for the 'two laws' counter-proposal is understandable. But at first glance it might seem puzzling that the PBOC and the Ministry of Finance—the nation's leading creditors—would not favour a strong, inclusive bankruptcy law which might strengthen the position of creditors. In fact, the PBOC was only lukewarm in its support for the entire bankruptcy proposal, according to a non-PBOC source close to the meeting. This source reported that despite the fact that the PBOC in theory stood to gain greatly from legal measures which would allow it to recover some of its bad loans, it was concerned that a bankruptcy law might lead to tremendous embarrassment for the bank. The public spectacle of bankrupting and closing a number of enterprises would spotlight the unsoundness of the PBOC's lending practices.[35]

The TERC was unwilling to accept the 'two laws' proposal, however. Originally, the powerful State Economic Commission and the General Administration of Industry and Commerce supported the TERC's stand. They were later joined in their support for a single, inclusive law when the Supreme People's Court was belatedly added to the discussions.[36]

The symposium remained stalemated throughout the summer and autumn of 1984, as MLP officials remained implacably opposed to any bankruptcy law, and the other organizations were split four-to-four

34. Interview 28-29-16-28/XHB, April 1989.   35. *Ibid.*   36. *Ibid.*

over whether or not to apply the law to state-owned enterprises. The ELRC as chair did not yet support the 'one law' view strongly enough to move the proposal on to the next stage. The impasse continued until the October 1984 Central Committee plenum intervened and broke the stalemate.

Although still stalemated, the May–October symposium did make some important progress in fleshing out TERC's original tentative proposal into a preliminary 'suggested text' (*jianyi gao*). In fact, less than one month after the last meeting of the symposium, TERC researchers were able for the first time to publish the suggested text (in China's best-known popular legal journal *Democracy and the Legal System*) which was a far more specific and carefully drafted document than the earlier tentative proposal. Another sign of progress during the meetings was TERC's decision, taken around June 1984, to begin work on the next-stage document: a request to the State Council formally to organize a Bankruptcy Law Drafting Group.[37]

But while the proposal languished at the Centre, interest outside Beijing was building. As Cao and the TERC researchers had hoped, their February 1984 *Liaowang* article had let the genie out of the bottle by indicating that bankruptcy was finally a legitimate policy issue. Scholars and local officials began debating how such a law might improve enterprise performance. In August, for example, *Liaowang* published a response to Cao's article by a Gansu Province Justice Department official who endorsed drafting a 'bankruptcy law with Chinese characteristics' which did not 'mechanically copy' the laws of other countries. The author, Li Quande, advocated a weaker, more paternalistic law which would 'take conciliation as the main factor while making bankruptcy subsidiary'.[38] Li showed greater faith than TERC that financial assistance and reorganization could turn around most enterprises before bankruptcy was necessary. Li also argued that an enterprise's debts should exceed its fixed assets before bankruptcy could be declared, a higher cut-off standard than TERC's proposed 50–80%.

But as the debate went on in the press, local officials began to move. The city of Shenyang, under the leadership of an ambitious new reformist mayor, Li Changchun, was the first to seize the opportunity Cao's article presented. In June 1984, the Shenyang CCP Committee decided it would declare bankrupt several badly-managed, long-term money-losing industries, and tasked the city Industry and Commerce Department to draft a bankruptcy law for collective enterprises. The city government issued the new regulations on 3 February 1985, and followed them with several months of vigorous propaganda work. The first bankruptcy warnings

37. Cao Siyuan (1988b), 53–4, and interview 28-29-16-28/XHB, March 1989.
38. Li Quande (1984).

were issued in August 1985 amidst great local publicity, which, according to an official source, was very consciously orchestrated to shame the factory management and staff into improving their performance.[39]

The city of Wuhan was the next to move, issuing a set of experimental regulations which differed significantly from those of Shenyang. Most importantly, they applied to large, state-owned enterprises in addition to collectively-owned firms. Wuhan issued its first bankruptcy warning to the Wuhan Radio Plant in June 1985.[40] The political impact of these local experiments on the national debate was apparently quite significant. Interviews and published sources repeatedly note that the apparent success of these local bankruptcy experiments helped ease the fears of Beijing officials about the possible impact of the bankruptcy innovation. Time and again during the next two years, a major push to get the law passed in Beijing was anticipated by encouraging reports on local bankruptcy experiments.[41]

October 1984: Breakthrough at the Third Plenum

The Third Plenum of the Twelfth CCP Central Committee turned out to be a major turning point in breaking the bureaucratic impasse over the Bankruptcy Law. The 'Decision of the Central Committee on the Restructuring of the Economic System' (hereafter the 'Decision') represented a major political and theoretical breakthrough for advocates of market-oriented reform. Interview data vividly confirm how such major meetings and policy documents can radically change the political mood in the system and send messages to lower level officials, forcing them to alter their viewpoints and actions on certain issues, even when those issues have not specifically been addressed by the top leadership. The question of whether or not to adopt a bankruptcy law was never actually discussed during the plenum or the

---

39. On the manipulation of publicity as a form of pressure, see the report prepared for the SCRES by Chen Yongjie and Sun Tao (1985). On the Shenyang Bankruptcy Regulations and their genesis, see also Lin Songgen (1986); also BXE, 3 August 1985, in FBIS-CHI, 6 August 1985, S 1; BXE 1 August 1985, in FBIS-CHI, 9 August 1985, S 1; BXE, 10 November 1985; BXDS, 9 November 1986; *South China Morning Post*, 12 December 1986, 1.

40. The Wuhan Regulations were discussed by BXE, 10 November 1985; BXDS, 9 November 1986; also *South China Morning Post*, 12 December 1986, 1.

41. The available evidence suggests that the localities had a good deal of autonomy in implementing the experiments. For example, the SCRES investigative report cited above (Chen Yongjie and Song Tao, 1985), makes no mention of the central authorities having authorized the Shenyang experiment, nor does it note that any central department was managing the experiment. On the other hand, it is possible that the central departments advocating passage of the law were promoting these experiments as a way of undercutting the opposition or presenting them with a fait accompli. In this connection, we should note that the Wuhan and Shenyang experiments were overseen by local administrative offices whose Beijing counterparts were strong advocates of bankruptcy: the State Committee for Reforming the Economic System (SCRES) and the General Administration for Industry and Commerce (GAIC).

informal discussions which preceded it, according to one source.[42] Nevertheless, the Decision very clearly reaffirmed two theoretical propositions which finally provided the bankruptcy proposal with the necessary political 'basis' (*yiju*). These were the economic principles of 'socialist competition', and 'allowing the excellent to win and discarding the inferior' (*yousheng lietai*).[43] Cao Siyuan's written account hints at this effect of the Decision on the process, saying that it '. . . quickly unified the thought and recognition of the departments concerned about drafting the Bankruptcy Law'.[44] The ministries participating in the ELRC bankruptcy symposium interpreted the strong language of the Decision as a signal that the new Central leadership consensus would now be receptive to a strong bankruptcy law. If that were so, these ministries apparently did not want to be perceived by upper levels as obstructionists. After the plenum, the four ministries which had stalled the law suddenly dropped their resistance to its passage. The suggestion to split the tentative proposal into a non-state enterprise bankruptcy law and a set of state enterprise consolidation measures was also dropped.[45]

Seizing this opportunity, the TERC researchers, drawing upon suggestions made by the inter-agency symposium, took the bold move of publishing a 'suggested text' of the law in the November issue of *Democracy and the Legal System* (*Minzhu yu Fazhi*).[46] Internal copies of draft laws actually circulate quite widely within the Chinese legal community before their adoption. But the publication of such an early draft in the popular press was then, so far as I can determine, completely without precedent.

The scope of the law still encompassed 'all enterprises which are responsible for their own profits and losses'—including state-managed, collective, private, Sino-foreign joint-venture and co-operative, foreign wholly-owned and a variety of other enterprises.[47] The draft still had an explicit cut-off point for declaring bankruptcy: when 'accumulated debts'—which were more precisely defined in article 4—could not be met on time and/or exceeded 60% of the enterprise's total 'productive capital' (*shengchan zijin*). The suggested text contained little to reassure workers accustomed to lifelong jobs and a high level of social security. In order to spur employees to save an endangered enterprise, wages in firms in danger of bankruptcy would be cut back, first to 90% and later to 75% of regular levels. The draft

---

42. Interview 28-29-16-28/XHB, April 1989. According to this source and an ELRC staffer involved in drafting the law, the Party Centre did not send down any documents endorsing bankruptcy at this time, nor was the bankruptcy proposal discussed in any of the post-Plenum Party meetings convened to explain the Decision and its implications.
43. See *Decision of the Central Committee of the Chinese Communist Party on the Reform of the Economic System*.   44. Cao Siyuan (1988b), 56.
45. Interview 28-29-16-28/XHB, April 1989.
46. *Minzhu yu Fazhi*, November 1984, 7.
47. *Minzhu yu Fazhi*, November 1984, article 2.

did little to commit the state to support workers in the event that the enterprise actually did go bankrupt. It called for state labour and personnel and financial offices to estabilish labour insurance companies to support unemployed workers, and all enterprises would pay 5% of their total wage bill to the fund as a hedge against bankruptcy. Unemployed workers would receive 60% of their previous wages from this fund. Workers were to receive job training (though it is unclear who would be responsible for this) and were to be encouraged to seek employment through other channels, including through private enterprise. No provision was made for the state to pick up health care, disability, pension or other benefits previously provided by the enterprise, though families in particularly bad straits could apply to local Civil Affairs Bureaus for assistance.[48]

Immediately after the October plenum, two more events coincided which further improved the political climate for the Bankruptcy Law's passage. A late 1984 series of discussions between Party, State Council and NPC leaders affirmed the need for the NPC to focus its legislative work on economic reform and simultaneously strengthen the State Council's autonomous legislative powers in this respect.[49] On the economic front, end-of-year data dramatically underscored the need for radical new measures to deal with the problem of enterprise losses. The government noted that 20–30% of all state-owned industrial enterprises were now running a deficit every year. Total 1983 state enterprise losses had been equal to 18% of the national government's revenues.[50]

Whether by design or by luck, Cao and the other TERC chose this moment to give the law its next major push. On 26 December 1984, the TERC researchers handed a Report Requesting Instructions Concerning Drafting a Bankruptcy Law to the State Council Standing Committee, specifically seeking permission to establish formally a Bankruptcy Law Drafting Group. Three days later, the 'leading comrade(s)' of the State Council approved the establishment of the Drafting Group, with the ELRC's Gu Ming as official leader, and including 'other concerned departments'.[51] After its formal establishment in January 1985, the Drafting Group set up a smaller, subordinate Working Group headed by Cao Siyuan

---

48. *Minzhu yu Fazhi*, November 1984, articles 11 and 12.
49. These discussions were alluded to by Peng Zhen in an NPC seminar on economic law in January 1985. The original text is in *Renmin Ribao*, 24 January 1985. A translation appears in FBIS-CHI, 24 January 1985, K13–15.　　　　　　　　　50. *China Daily*, 8 January 1985, 4.
51. Cao Siyuan (1988b), 56. Given the available evidence, we can only infer which 'leading comrades' of the State Council might have seen the report. Unfortunately, we have no access to the comments they might have made. Zhao Ziyang would certainly have seen so sensitive a proposal. Also likely to have seen the proposal would be those Vice-Premiers and State Councillors who were influential in industrial affairs (Yao Yilin, Gu Mu and Zhang Jingfu), legal affairs, especially economic legislation (Wan Li and Gu Mu), or those whose ministries were involved in the inter-ministerial symposium (Finance Minister Wang Bingqian, MOFERT Minister Chen Muhua, and former SEC Minister Zhang Jingfu).

which 'concretely took responsibility for the investigation, research, and drafting'.[52]

It appears that between early 1985 and July of that year, drafting and co-ordination work once again became bogged down in inter-ministerial disputes. By May 1985, the Drafting Group had produced an Enterprise Bankruptcy Law Outline (*gangyao*). Over the next few months, the Group continued to consult the concerned State Council department. It also separately took the Outline to five cities—Chongqing, Chengdu, Wuhan, Tianjin and Qingdao—all of which were experimenting with enterprise reform, to do further research and investigations, and to solicit local officials' opinions. But by July, Zhao Ziyang and the State Council again had to intervene to speed up the drafting. One source notes that 'on 30 July 1985 the 78th meeting of the State Council Standing Committee, chaired by Zhao Ziyang, discussed and directed that "The Enterprise Bankruptcy Law" should be drafted as quickly as possible'.[53] The State Council's intervention had the desired effect. The drafting group was able to iron out a major new revision by September.[54]

Late 1985: 'Soliciting Opinions' and Spin Control

In September, the Drafting Group further broadened the consensus-seeking process, sending the newly-completed Opinion Solicitation Draft (*zhengqiu yijian gao*) to every department of the State Council and every provincial level unit. Opinion-solicitation meetings, however, became the object of a 'spin control' battle between Bankruptcy Law advocates, who wanted to use the meetings largely to promote the law, and opponents, who tried to use the meetings to mobilize and publicize popular criticism of the proposal. Hence, over the next five months, both supporters and critics of

---

52. Interview with a Chinese Scholar, April 1987; see also Lin Songgen (1986), 3; also Cao Siyuan (1988b), 54; Gu Ming's leadership of the drafting group is noted in *Liaowang* (Overseas Edition), No. 50 (12 December 1986), 6.

53. Lin Songgen (1986), 3. The period from early 1985 to January 1986 is the least clear in the history of the laws drafting. Lin's is the only account which discusses the internal politics of process at this time.

54. There is an alternate explanation for the State Council move. In late 1984, early 1985, Zhao, Deng and other economic reformers came under attack from conservative leaders (most notably Deng Liqun and Hu Qiaomu) because the economy was overheated, enterprises engaged in trade were wasting too much foreign exchange, and because the opening to the West was accompanied by increased corruption and crime in society. In late spring 1985 the State Council put the brakes on the money supply—especially foreign exchange—causing many enterprises—especially collectives—to go under. Perhaps the failure of so many enterprises persuaded the State Council of the need for a 'winding up law' to deal with failing enterprises. The late July State Council meeting would also have coincided with the reformers counterattack, most notably the sacking of Deng Liqun as CCP Propaganda Chief in August. Zhao may have felt that this was also a politically appropriate time to proceed with a reform which was appropriate to both a 'market-oriented' and 'tight money' economy. On the politics of this period, see Fewsmith (1986), 78–85.

the law circulated throughout the localities soliciting data and opinion to buttress their respective cases, with all sides seizing on this key procedure of 'socialist democracy' in an effort to colour the Central leadership's view of the potential gains and risks of adopting the law.[55]

An interesting new twist to these forums was the use of extensive and detailed opinion polling of participants. The propaganda function of the poll was clear. Nearly 1,000 economic, judicial and management cadres, workers and educators were shown a summarized version of the Bankruptcy Law. Before being asked their opinions, however, the respondents were also shown an article entitled 'Economic reforms badly need an Enterprise Bankruptcy Law'.[56] Such survey methodology shortcomings notwithstanding, the poll and the meetings still revealed substantial popular wariness and opposition to the law.[57] Bankruptcy advocates' efforts to promote the law at these meetings were overcome by local union leaders and workers, who seized on the meetings as their first real chance publicly to counter-attack the law. Although the official press makes little mention of worker views at these meetings, a January 1986 internal ELRC report notes that during the solicitation of views, the main problem on most people's minds was the unresolved issue of how to make arrangements for the unemployed workers in a bankrupted factory.[58]

Questions posed at the seminar revealed the workers' extremely sophisticated understanding of the new risks the Bankruptcy Law might force them to bear. Who would help the workers search for new jobs? What kind of new job training, if any, would be supplied, and who would pay for it? If and when the workers found new jobs, would they keep their old wages and seniority? If a factory were declared bankrupt, who would guarantee the pension payments for long-retired workers, their widows and orphans, who could hardly be held justly responsible for the factory's present insolvency? How would the work of the factory Communist Party Committee be handled in bankrupt factories and at the workers' new jobs?[59] Cao Siyuan and the Drafting Group, who, as shown above, had side-stepped many of these touchy issues in the past, were apparently ill-equipped to respond to this onslaught of questions. Cao himself notes that on the basis of these discussions, the law was revised over twenty times between September and December.[60]

But in the battle of 'spin control', the cards were clearly stacked against the official unions and worker groups. Zhao's State Council had shown clearly in July 1985 that it was interested in passing a bankruptcy law. Moreover, the

---

55. Cao Siyuan (1988b), 54; See also Li Si in *Jingji Ribao* 16 November 1985, in FBIS-CHI, 10 December 1985, K 21; and also Cao Siyuan in *Jingji Ribao*, 14 June 1986, 3, in FBIS-CHI, 24 June 1986, K13–15. Unfortunately, in this article, Cao does not reveal precisely when these meetings were.
56. *Jingji Ribao*, 14 June 1986, 3, in FBIS-CHI, 24 June 1986, K13–15.
57. See 'Liaowang Explains Draft Bankruptcy Law', FBIS-CHI, 13 February 1986, K21–5.
58. Liu Xiuping (1986), 24.   59. *Ibid.*   60. Cao Siyuan (1988b), 54.

organizations which most closely advised Zhao on enterprise policy—the TERC, SEC, State Commission for Restructuring the Economic System (SCRES) and General Administration of Industry and Commerce—all firmly supported the proposal. Several had been working behind the scenes to mobilize both local Chinese and foreign opinion to support the law.

In September 1985, for example, the SCRES sent two young economists, Chen Yongjie and Sun Tao, to investigate the Shenyang bankruptcy experiment and report back to Beijing on the preliminary effects. Drawing upon Shenyang's experience, Chen and Sun were also to make recommendations which could be used in drafting the central-level Bankruptcy Law.[61] The SCRES report, which circulated internally in late 1985, provided powerful ammunition for advocates of a tough bankruptcy code with high, explicit targets for performance. The report lauded the Shenyang experiment and said it should be made a national model. Chen and Sun's specific suggestions included developing similar regulations for *state-owned* enterprises, and toughening the standards a 'warned' factory must meet in order to be considered to have 'turned around'. They also endorsed the Shenyang law's use of an explicit standard for defining bankruptcy, which was a total debt/fixed asset ratio exceeding 80%. Most importantly, the SCRES report played down political concerns over workers, and sharply contrasted with the union and worker criticisms launched at the local opinion-solicitation meetings. On the contrary, the report argued that the embarrassment of the public bankruptcy warning helped save the factories by shocking the workers into greater efforts. At the same time, the authors asserted that with 'good propaganda work', any negative reaction among the employees could be kept within manageable limits.[62]

*Stage Three: Top Leadership Decision-making January 1986—
The State Council Approves a Compromise*

The Enterprise Bankruptcy Law and the Enterprise Bankruptcy Relief Methods (see below) were approved in principle by the 99th Session of the State Council Standing Committee on 31 January 1986 with only minor changes in language (*wenzi xiuding*). Unfortunately, almost no information is available to Western scholars about the Standing Committee's debates over this draft, or concerning which State Councillors, if any, may have opposed the law.[63]

61. Chen Yongjie and Sun Tao (1985).   62. *Ibid.*, 7–8.
63. Every source interviewed for this study either asserted or implied that Zhao Ziyang strongly favoured the law, even though he never publicly endorsed it. The only State Councillors who publicly endorsed the law either before or shortly after the State Council approved it were Gu Mu, who hosted a foreign experts symposium on the law in late 1985, and long-standing central planning expert Yao Yilin, who stated in a 3 April 1985 press conference that 'China needs a bankruptcy law'. See FBIS-CHI, 3 April 1986, K1, and 4 April 1986, K1, W1.

A content analysis of the draft Bankruptcy Law which the State Council approved shows that the almost two-year-long inter-agency review process resulted in a wealth of small and medium concessions to an array of ministerial and other social actors, but still preserved the core of a forceful bankruptcy proposal.[64] It is clear that the other State Council ministries and the unions had forced the drafting group to make a number of changes concerning the applicability of the law, as well as giving ground on some labour issues. But advocates of a strong bankruptcy law apparently made no concessions on the cut-off limits for declaring bankruptcy (the debt/ fixed asset ratio). And despite the open solicitation of views towards the end of the inter-agency review process, many of the key provisions of the law which would later prove so obnoxious to the NPC Standing Committee had changed little from the proposals Cao Siyuan first put forward in his 1984 articles.

On the key issue of applicability, the State Council-approved draft still applied to state-owned, Sino-foreign joint ventures and foreign companies, although no final decision had been made on Cao's original proposal that the law also apply to collective enterprises. As Cao had long argued, the law also continued to exempt firms which were 'important to the State Plan and to the people's livelihood', and this was now explicitly extended to exempt military, 'third line' and Public Security-related production facilities.[65] The explicit debt/fixed asset ratio for warning an enterprise was preserved, though this ratio appears to have been loosened from 50–80% to 80–90%, and 'policy-based' or intentional losses were exempted.[66]

On the issue of bankruptcy relief and retraining for unemployed workers, however, both policy and process were murkier than ever. The State Council-approved draft did not firmly commit the state to provide workers with either new jobs or support, but this issue was still wide open for discussion.[67] The trade unions and the Ministry of Labour and Personnel had re-established some control over policy-making on this question through the formation of a special office to study worker relief issues. Most importantly, although the Bankruptcy Law would be forwarded to the National People's Congress for consideration, the issue of worker relief would not be. The State Council decided to divide the law into two documents, submitting an Enterprise Bankruptcy Law to the NPC, but retaining control over the Enterprise Bankruptcy Relief Methods (*Qiye Pochan Jiuji*

---

64. The sources being compared here are the earlier drafts of the law, the contents of which are in Cao Siyuan (1983); and Cao Siyuan (1984b). The sources on the State Council-approved draft of the law are Liu Xiuping (1986); also Cao Siyuan's article in *Jingji Ribao*, 14 June 1986, 3, in FBIS-CHI, 24 June 1986, K13–15, and Sun Yaming's article in *Liaowang* (Overseas Edition), No. 4 (27 January 1986), 10. 65. Liu Xiuping (1986), 18.
66. *Ibid.*, 23. See also Sun Yaming (1986).
67. *Liaowang* (Overseas Edition), No. 4 (27 January 1986), 10.

Banfa) which would be drafted and promulgated separately within the State Council system, presumably under the State Council's newly-acquired authority to issue reform-related 'temporary regulations' without immediate NPC approval.[68] In a fascinating procedural manoeuvre, the legislature would get to debate the questions of the definition, applicable scope, cut-off level and legal procedures for bankruptcy. But the crucial issues of worker relief would remain under the control of the State Council, albeit in the hands of the law's most virulent critic, the Ministry of Labour and Personnel.[69] These regulations were ultimately drafted by the Ministry of Labour and Personnel and issued on 13 July 1986 as Provisional Regulations for Government Unemployment Insurance for State-owned Enterprises.[70] Ultimately, however, the NPC did not allow this arrangement to remain entirely unaltered, and found a way of reinjecting itself into this key part of the debate.

This analysis of the State Council-approved draft seems to confirm that the stage of inter-agency review is characterized by multiple rounds of opinion-solicitation, negotiation and compromise. The organizations and personnel involved in this process are expanded gradually, first incorporating only those state agencies most directly concerned, and spreading concentrically outwards to involve localities and mass organizations. As predicted by the Organizational Politics model, both the process and the policy outcomes are slow, incremental and highly susceptible to stalemate. Also, despite the formal emphasis on broad consultation and consensus-building at this stage, the views of some groups faired far better than others. Certain organizations, such as the military and public security apparatuses, won near complete exemptions from the law's effects with little or no discernible lobbying activity. Bankruptcy advocates, such as Cao, the SEC and the SCRES, won many victories, but still had to endure watching the scope of the law being gradually whittled away despite the clear support they received from the Premier's office (though not publicly from the Premier). Worker and union representatives, even though some were intimately involved in the process from start to finish, fared worst of all, and ended this stage of the process assuming the bulk of the risks involved in the bankruptcy experiment.

Stage Four: NPC Review and Debate

In early 1986, as the Bankruptcy Law was about to face NPC review, Zhao Ziyang shifted his strategy to focus on the 'darker side' of market-oriented economic reform. Zhao stepped up the pressure on unproductive enter-

---

68. Liu Xiuping (1986), 24.   69. Cao Siyuan (1988b), 54.
70. *Ibid.*, 54; also Klein (1987).

prises to improve their performance, a shift he noted in his March Report to the NPC on the Seventh Five-Year Plan:

> Enterprises that have shown poor management over a protracted period should be reorganized or ordered to shut down, suspend operations, merge with others, or switch to the manufacture of other products in accordance with the principal of survival of the fittest.[71] . . . As the new economic mechanism becomes operational, the survival and development of enterprises, and the improvement in the material interests of their workers and staff will be determined more and more by their managerial ability and the results of their operations. . . . In the past we did not sufficiently stress this point. As a result, some people laboured under the misconception that reform is just giving enterprises greater power and letting them retain more profits.[72]

By the first few months of 1986, it was clear that more radical reformers such as Zhao, Tian Jiyun and Hu Qili were restless to move forward on a wide range of enterprise reforms during 1986.[73] Since the draft Bankruptcy Law was ready by the end of January, it could be turned into a notable policy victory for reformers. Thus the law began to receive a burst of publicity on the eve of the NPC Standing Committee's Sixteenth Session in June. The decision to try to finalize and pass the law by the end of the year was noted on 14 May, when the economic legislation plan for the year was announced.[74] The publicity push culminated in June in a highly publicized National Bankruptcy Law Meeting in Shenyang which was attended by over 200 national experts.[75]

It was only at this time that the top leadership began publicly to associate itself with the controversial proposal which had already been under serious debate for over three years. Vice-Premier Yao Yilin, one of China's top-ranking economic planners, was the first Politburo member publicly to endorse the law. Yao noted at a 3 April press conference for foreigners that 'China needs a bankruptcy law'. NPC Standing Committee Vice-Chairman Chen Pixian followed with a less enthusiastic statement on 20 April which

---

71. Zhao Ziyang (1986). The quote is from page K17.   72. *Ibid.*, K21.
73. For examples of this restlessness, see Zhao's Five-Year Plan Report (n. 64 above); Hu Qili's address to the Central Party School in *Beijing Lilun Yuekan* No. 2, 25 February 1986; and especially Tian Jiyun's speech to the '8,000 Cadres Conference' on 6 January 1986, in FBIS-CHI, 13 January 1986, K5–20.
74. BXE, 14 May 1986, in FBIS-CHI, 16 May 1986, K18. The announcement divided the legislation into two groups: those 65 laws (including *tiaoli*) which would definitely be passed by the end of the year, as well as others which would be passed that year 'if conditions permitted'. The Bankruptcy Law was one of nine laws individually promised for passage by the end of the year.
75. The meeting was covered in BXE, 20 June 1986, in FBIS-CHI, 24 June 1986, K13. One of the minor mysteries of the NPC debate over bankruptcy is why the drafting group would choose to hold a meeting of over 200 of the nation's leading experts on bankruptcy (and presumably, most of its most ardent supporters) in Shenyang on the very same day that the law was being debated before the NPC in Beijing. Compare FBIS-CHI, 17 June 1986, K2.

refrained from endorsing the law and simply noted that the law was being readied for NPC consideration.[76]

In the spring, the NPC Legislative Affairs Work Committee had begun independently soliciting opinions on the draft law in order to prepare reference materials for the NPC Standing Committee's Sixteenth Session in June. In doing so, the LAWC, under Wang Hanbin's leadership, dispatched its own investigation teams to talk to officials in Shenyang, Tianjin, Chongqing and Shanghai—the same cities in which the ELRC had carried out investigations the preceding autumn.[77]

One former high-ranking NPC official has indicated that NPC officials did not initially object to the law, or to having the law placed on the NPC's annual legislative plan. But as the investigations progressed, it became apparent to NPC staffers that an enormous amount of additional legal infrastructure would be necessary before a bankruptcy system could be made either effective or fair. The content of the reference materials the NPC LAWC staff prepared for the Standing Committee members is not known, nor can any biases in those materials be estimated. But interview evidence and the members' reactions at the June meeting all suggest very strongly that the reports reflected the reservations which many local officials and union leaders had concerning the law. Nevertheless, NPC officials and staffers indicate that Zhao's State Council was insistent about pushing the Bankruptcy Law through to NPC ratification as soon as possible.[78]

Shortly before the NPC Standing Committee session—probably in late May or early June—a CCP Politburo meeting considered the agenda for the NPC session, in particular the legislation to be passed. According to well-informed Chinese legal scholars, the Politburo meeting saw serious disagreement on whether to pass the Bankruptcy Law at the current session. The Politburo approved the law 'in principle' and sent it on to the NPC Standing Committee for discussion. But lacking a consensus, the Politburo was unable to make a clear, forceful recommendation to the Standing Committee concerning the disposition of the law when the NPC Standing Committee Party Members Group convened their preparatory meeting on the eve of the session. The NPC would debate the law, but the Politburo would not insist upon its passage at that time.[79]

The NPC Standing Committee Sixteenth Session saw the first public signs of serious trouble. On behalf of Premier Zhao, Vice-Minister Zhang Yanning of the SEC read out a summary of the draft law to the assembled

---

76. Yao's comments came in a highly publicized joint press conference for Western reporters with then Vice-Premier Li Peng. For a 'text' and other reports, see FBIS-CHI, 3 April 1986, K1, and 4 April 1986, K1, W1. Chen Pixian's remarks are in BXDS, 20 April 1986, in FBIS-CHI, 25 April 1986, K1.   77. Guo Daohui (1988), 89.
78. Interviews 12-32-17/34-19-28 ABE, May 1989, and 26-17-13-33/TWS, August 1992.
79. Interview 11-19-13-33/OKE, February 1989.

158   The Politics of Lawmaking in Post-Mao China

delegates. Opposition to the law was rather acrimonious. In a now-familiar parliamentary tactic, many Standing Committee members affirmed the necessity of passing a bankruptcy law, but argued that 'conditions were not yet ripe to pass and implement the law'. Delegates tried to stall the law by insisting that the State Council and NPC first complete work on a long list of other 'reform' legislation, much of which would guarantee the state's commitment to workers. Specifically, they called for prior passage of the long-stalled State-Owned Industrial Enterprises Law, laws on labour service companies and the State Council regulations on social insurance (which had been split off from the Bankruptcy Law).

Delegates also put forward a variety of other demands. Some thought the NPC should first complete work on laws on Sino-foreign joint ventures and collective enterprises. Others feared that factory workers and staff would end up bearing the consequences of losses which were beyond their control. They insisted on an amendment guaranteeing that local government and department officials whose policies had caused bankruptcy would be punished under criminal laws. Faced with this reaction, the Committee Chairmen's Group (headed by Peng Zhen) apparently decided to 'do more investigations' of the law and returned the draft to the State Council for 'cautious consideration'.[80]

In the wake of the surprisingly bitter debates at the NPC Standing Committee session, the process temporarily returned to the politics of the preceding autumn and winter, with all sides soliciting information on local bankruptcy experiments and convening meetings to solicit opinions and promote the law. In July, Wang Hanbin's Legislative Affairs Work Committee began a continuous series of meetings to hear the views of Beijing city and Central officials on how the law should be revised.[81]

Meanwhile, a variety of local bankruptcy experiments were beginning to show great promise. The cities of Chongqing, Taiyuan and Wuhan had all issued bankruptcy warnings to a number of troubled local factories in the late spring. According to published sources, by July and August many of the threatened enterprises were beginning to show signs of tremendous progress. In contrast to the attacks levelled at the NPC Standing Committee session, these encouraging reports probably provided advocates of the law in Beijing with additional ammunition to argue that the law should be implemented now.[82]

The most dramatic of these occurred on 3 August when, with considerable publicity, the Shenyang Explosion-Proof Apparatus Factory became

---

80. Information of the 16th session come from interviews 11-19-13-33/OKE, February 1989, and 12-32-17/34-19-28/ABE, May 1989; and from the following printed sources: *Beijing Review*, 7 July 1986, 7–9; BXE, 24 June 1986, in FBIS-CHI, 25 June 1986, K 4; BXE, 4 September 1986, in FBIS-CHI, 5 September 1986, K3–4; Guo Yuanfa in *Liaowang*, 1 December 1986, 5; and Guo Daohui (1988), 89.   81. Guo Daohui (1988), 89.
82. Cao Siyuan (1988b), 56–8.

The Case of The Enterprise Bankruptcy Law   159

the first communist-era Chinese enterprise ever officially declared bankrupt.[83] The Shenyang City Industry and Commerce Department confiscated the factory's licence and took charge of the sell-off of property. The City Civil Affairs Bureau, in co-operation with local labour service companies, was put in charge of reassigning workers.[84] Moving with impressive dispatch, the assets of the factory were auctioned off on 25 September.[85] During the autumn and early winter, the Central press was full of a steady stream of reports on how well the workers in the bankrupted factory were doing in their new careers.[86]

In early August, against this backdrop, bankruptcy advocates stepped up their pressure for immediate passage of the law just as the NPC Standing Committee was preparing to hold its Seventeenth Session. On 2 August, Yuan Mu, in his capacity as Deputy Secretary General of the CCP Central Financial and Economic Leading Group (chaired by Zhao Ziyang) published a strongly worded endorsement of the law on page one of the Leading Group's official paper, *Jingji Ribao*.[87] Yuan attacked the NPC's delaying tactics, arguing that the preconditions for a bankruptcy law were sufficient already, and if the NPC delayed until all conditions were ripe, no law would ever be passed. Six days later, in an apparent effort to be a 'good soldier' for the State Council, the respected veteran Finance Minister Wang Bingqian reversed his Ministry's previous position and publicly endorsed the Bankruptcy Law at the National Financial Work Conference.[88] The State Economic Commission also continued to push hard for passage of the law.[89]

Such was the public pressure the NPC leadership faced in the run-up to the late August Standing Committee sessions. Both the NPC Financial and Economic Committee and the Law Committee held discussion meetings on how to revise the law, based upon the views presented at the still-ongoing LAWC meetings.[90] A variety of sources indicate that several moderately important compromise amendments were incorporated into the law's text at this time. First, a clause guaranteeing the minimum standard of living for workers in bankrupt enterprises was added. Secondly, in an effort to make higher level officials think twice before declaring a factory bankrupt, the law now contained a clause endorsing disciplinary actions for superior

83. BXE, 3 August 1986, in FBIS-CHI, 6 August 1986, S 1.   84. *Ibid.*
85. It is interesting to note that the assets of the Shenyang Explosion-proof Apparatus Factory were sold by the City to the Engineering Section of the City Gas Supply Company. We should keep open the possibility that the factory assets in this case were simply resold to the previous owner. BXE, 10 November 1985.
86. See, for example, BXE, 13 October 1986; BXE, 24 November 1986; BXE, 5 December 1986; BXDS, 8 August 1986, in FBIS-CHI, 12 August 1986, K1.
87. *Jingji Ribao*, 2 August 1986, 1.
88. BXDS, 6 August 1986, in FBIS-CHI, 7 August 1986, K12–14. My interpretation of Wang Bingqian's action is based upon an interview with a Chinese scholar, April 1987.
89. See BXDS, 8 August 1986, in FBIS-CHI, 12 August 1986, K1.
90. Song Rufen (1994), Vol. One, 130–4; also Guo Daohui (1988), 89.

officials whose actions and policy decisions could be shown to have caused the bankruptcy.[91] The most important revision involved drastically narrowing the scope of the law. In deference to the wishes of local Party officials, collective enterprises were once and for all dropped from it. Sino-foreign and foreign enterprises, which had still been included in January, had also been dropped from the law by this time.[92]

It appears that it was this revised draft which was then resubmitted to the Politburo for consideration before the NPC Standing Committee session in late August. Once again, the Politburo was reportedly deeply split over whether or not the law should be passed in its current form, but still approved it 'in principle' and allowed it to be listed on the Standing Committee's Seventeenth Session agenda. In a repeat of June's performance, the NPC Standing Committee Party Member's Group heard only a lukewarm Politburo endorsement of the law during their preparatory meetings.[93]

But despite the reported ambivalence within the Politburo, the official Party press was sending out a different, much more strongly pro-bankruptcy message. On 28 August, the eve of the Standing Committee session, *Renmin Ribao* published an unsigned page-one commentator's article which strongly endorsed immediate passage of the draft Bankruptcy Law, even if numerous 'needed' social insurance regulations were not yet in place.[94] It is difficult to interpret this divergence between the Party paper and the reportedly weak Politburo consensus, but it probably indicates that Zhao and other bankruptcy advocates were getting a powerful and well-timed boost from Party Chief Hu Yaobang.

But despite the numerous compromises in the new draft and the high-profile Central pressure for the NPC Standing Committee to pass the law, the NPC Standing Committee remained unmoved. The Seventeenth Session witnessed some of the bitterest and most tenacious debate of any NPC meeting in PRC history. Meetings of the LAWC, the Law Committee and the Financial and Economic Committee discussed the draft on the eve of the session. At the LAWC meetings, State Economic Commission Vice-Ministers who wanted immediate passage of the law battled with a number of NPC Standing Committee members who opposed passage, at least

91. AFP, 28 August 1986, in FBIS-CHI, 28 August 1986, K3.
92. AFP, 28 August 1986, in FBIS-CHI, 28 August 1986, K3; Song Rufen (1994), Vol. One, 130–4; Also, Gu Ming had noted the need to drop Joint Ventures from the law in a later article, see *Jingji Ribao*, 11 November 1986, 3.
93. Interview 11-19-13-33/OKE, February 1989, Beijing.
94. *Renmin Ribao*, 2 August 1986, 1. The placement of the article, page one, suggests its obvious importance to the *Renmin Ribao* editorial staff. The choice of authorship format, an unsigned 'Commentator' article, is of course a less authoritative endorsement than an editorial of the paper (*shelun*), but the choice of an anonymous rather than an individually signed commentator article does suggest a higher level of organizational approval by the paper. Hence, this article constitutes a *fairly strong* endorsement of the law, if not the *most* authoritative.

The Case of The Enterprise Bankruptcy Law 161

under current conditions. LAWC Vice-Chairman Song Rufen, who, like LAWC Chairman Wang Hanbin was also a long-standing personal aide to Peng Zhen, was most prominent in arguing that conditions were not yet ripe to pass the law.[95] But in his recently published memoir of his legislative work, Song Rufen states that his viewpoint enjoyed majority support among the other top NPC Standing Committee officials at these meetings. 'Of the eleven NPC Financial and Economic Committee Members who took part in the meeting, there were nine who did not agree with promulgating the law at that time. A majority of the members of the Law Committee [also] did not agree with promulgating the law at that time.'[96]

When the full Standing Committee convened, the battles continued unabated. Legal scholar and NPC advisor Guo Daohui has described the Seventeenth Session thus:

> There were further debates about the Bankruptcy Law, with the key point still being whether or not the law could be carried out (*kexingxing*). Many delegates spoke. Some delegates wanted the law passed then. Some did not want it passed then. Some did not agree with the way it had been revised. Among those who disagreed with passing the law, many pointed out that much of the legislation which would have to accompany the law (e.g. the State-Owned Industrial Enterprises Law and the Labour Insurance Law) had not yet been drafted.[97]

Attacks on the law continued throughout the session, as delegates made it increasingly clear that they were willing to embarrass the State Council by voting against the law in large numbers. Journalist Tao Guofeng, writing after the law's passage in *Jingji Ribao*, reports that of the roughly 150 Standing Committee members at that time, forty-two spoke on the law at the Seventeenth Session. Of those forty-two, only seventeen favoured full passage at that time. Four delegates advocated further experimentation with bankruptcy before passing it nation-wide. Twenty-one opposed the law.[98]

Then, it appears, the unprecedented occurred. According to two legal advisors to the NPC, the NPC leadership submitted the draft Bankruptcy Law to a formal vote, and the Standing Committee rejected it.[99] It was,

---

95. See the comments Song and the SEC Vice-Ministers made at one meeting, cited in BXE, 4 September 1986, in FBIS-CHI, 5 September 1986, K3–4.
96. Song Rufen (1994), Vol. One, 131–2.   97. Guo Daohui (1988), 89.
98. Tao Guofeng in *Jingji Ribao*, 3 December 1986, 1.
99. Interviews 26-17-13-33/TWS, Beijing, August 1995, and 11-19-13-33/ADH, Beijing, July 1995. Recognizing that this information will be controversial, I want to be as frank as possible about the strengths and limitations of how it was obtained. The two NPC legal advisors who provided it are highly credible sources with excellent access to information who have reported reliably and accurately on a number of other issues related to lawmaking. They spoke independently of each other. As part of a general discussion of the NPC voting data (presented in Chapter 5), each was responding to a direct inquiry of whether or not the NPC or its Standing Committee had ever actually voted down a draft law placed before it. Both independently and without prompting identified the Bankruptcy Law and the Public Demonstrations Law. I wish to stress, however, that I have discovered no documentary evidence which

according to all the sources consulted for this study, the first time in its history that the NPC had voted down a draft law. Neither of these two interview sources knew the precise percentage of delegates who had voted for and against the draft (in the statistical tables for this study I have chosen to list the 'dissenting votes' as a bare 51%). One interviewee attributed the defeat to a miscalculation; the vote was one of the first times that the Standing Committee had used an electronic push-button voting system which permitted anonymity, and when the NPC leaders put the draft to a vote, they had no idea how many delegates would take advantage of the opportunity to vote 'no'. Obviously, less generous interpretations of the NPC leadership's actions in putting the unpopular draft to a formal vote are possible. In any case, Peng Zhen and the Committee Chairmen's Group decided to return the draft to the Legislative Affairs Work Committee for further revisions.[100]

After the debacle at the Seventeenth Session, the work to get the Bankruptcy Law passed proceeded on two tracks. On the first, the State Council made an apparent concession to delegates' objections and finalized a large block of supporting economic legislation. This package included four major provisional regulations on labour system reform, trade union legislation and regulations on the plant director responsibility system. The most important of these were the former Enterprise Bankruptcy Relief Methods which had been adopted in principle by the State Council in January. The Provisional Regulations on Unemployment Insurance for State Enterprises were announced on 27 September, and took effect on 1 October. The Regulations were designed to guarantee basic living expenses for unemployed state workers and promote labour mobility. Funds for unemploy-

---

either confirms or contradicts that either of these two drafts was actually put to a formal vote at the reported NPC Standing Committee sessions, or that they failed to pass. The credibility of their reports is somewhat enhanced, however, by a good deal of independent evidence which suggests that a majority or close to a majority of the Standing Committee opposed the draft Bankruptcy law at the 17th session, and hence that the law might well have failed if it had been put to a vote. Journalist Tao Guofeng's *Jingji Ribao* description of the numbers of speakers for and against the draft at the session (discussed above) suggests this possibility of majority opposition, although only about a third of the delegates chose to reveal their views by speaking on the issue. Song Rufen's account of the meeting (1994, 130) is somewhat more helpful, since he attempts to assess the mood of *all* the delegates at the session, though he merely suggests a deadlock, rather than stating that the opposition held *more* than 50% ('Those who approved promulgating the Bankruptcy Law then and those who did not approve promulgating the law then each occupied about one-half [of the support]'). But Song does not say flatly whether or not the draft law was put to a vote. Guo Daohui's published description of the session, quoted above, is non-committal on actual numbers, simply stating that 'some delegates wanted the law passed then. Some did not want it passed then'). Based on the great overall reliability of the two interviewees, the independent conditions of their reports, and this rather general reporting of the mood of the session, I have chosen to believe their reports on the Bankruptcy and Public Demonstrations Law, in the absence of other hard corroborating evidence.

100. Guo Daohui (1988), 89; also *Liaowang* (Overseas Edition), No. 50 (12 December 1986), 1.

The Case of The Enterprise Bankruptcy Law   163

ment relief were to come from a 1% contribution from enterprise payroll, and from unspecified 'local treasuries'. Unemployed workers would receive 60–75% of their base pay for one year after becoming unemployed. Workers with over five years seniority would be eligible for an additional year's support at 50% of base pay.[101]

Available sources have been unable to confirm whether or not the State Council deliberately accelerated drafting the Provisional Regulations, or altered their content, in order to speed passage of the law, though this appears to be the case.[102] At a minimum, however, it can be said that by committing the state to support workers unemployed as a result of bankruptcy, the State Concil was able to lessen—but not eliminate—opposition to the Bankruptcy Law. As one source has noted:

> To a certain extent, they [the regulations] provided back-up legal conditions for the Bankruptcy Law. Therefore, some members who previously did not agree with the adoption of the Bankruptcy Law changed their opinion.[103]

Chinese sources make it very clear that the SEC deliberately dusted off the long-stalled State-Owned Industrial Enterprises Law in order to get passage of the Bankruptcy Law. At the Eighteenth Session the former was reconsidered by the NPC Standing Committee for the first time since January 1985.[104]

On a second front, Peng Zhen and Chen Pixian took personal charge of trying to broker a deal for passage of the law. In September and October, Peng and Chen led a group of Standing Committee members to Shanxi, Wuhan, Beijing and Tianjin to carry out further investigations and solicit local views. The Legislative Affairs Work Committee in co-operation with the ELRC did the same, convening meetings with a number of local People's Congresses. Several other NPC Standing Committee Vice-Chairmen convened Bankruptcy Law forums in about a dozen major cities.[105]

---

101. *China Daily*, 27 September 1986, 1; also Klein (1987).

102. There is some evidence for this interpretation. In mid-May 1986, when the Ministry of Labour (MOL) held its National Labour Conference about the same time that the Annual Economic Legislative Plan was announced, neither the MOL nor the ELRC announced plans for finalizing any labour legislation quite this ambitious before the end of the year. See BXE, 7 May 1986, in FBIS/CHI, 16 May 1986, K18–19.

103. Guo Daohui (1988), 90; see also *Liaowang* (Overseas Edition), No. 50 (12 December 1986), 1.

104. One State Economic Committee source indicates that the pace of drafting the Enterprise Law was altered as a result of the NPC Standing Committee's manoeuvre: 'Because the 18th Meeting of the Sixth NPC Standing Committee made implementation of the Bankruptcy Law contingent upon the passage of the State Enterprise Law, this raised the problem of when to promulgate that law. So the State Enterprises Law was brought up a second time by the NPC.' Lian He (1988), 5–10. See also Yuan Baohua's explanation of the State-Owned Industrial Enterprises Law in *Renmin Ribao*, 16 November 1986, 1.

105. According to *Liaowang* (Overseas Edition), No. 50 (12 December 1986), 1, forums were held in Beijing, Tianjin, Shanxi, Gunagdong, Sichuan, Shanghai, Ningbo, Shenyang and Wuhan. See also Guo Daohui (1988), 89.

164   The Politics of Lawmaking in Post-Mao China

Peng Zhen and the NPC staff helped work out the final compromises in late October–early November. The NPC's local meetings culminated at this time with an eight-day (from 25 October to 1 November) conference jointly sponsored by the Legislative Affairs Work Committee and the NPC Financial and Economic Committee. Approximately 75–100 bankruptcy law leaders from the NPC, the central government departments and the provinces attended the Conference. Afterwards, the Legislative Affairs Work Committee again circulated a revised draft to all provinces and concerned central units for their opinions. Peng Zhen's report, apparently based on the results of the eight-day conference, formed the basis for the final revised draft of the law.[106]

For a third time, the Politburo considered the draft before submitting it to the Eighteenth Standing Committee session. This time they were able to reach a consensus on the deal which had been worked out, and again approved the law 'in principle'. According to one well-informed legal scholar, Zhao Ziyang delivered a very strong address at the Standing Committee Party Member's preparatory meeting, making it clear that the Politburo was united behind the law and expected its passage at the current session.[107]

The State Council had made a number of important concessions since the Seventeenth Session. First, conditions for the law were 'riper' as a result of State Council's recent package of economic and social security legislation. In addition to this legislation, the text of the new draft now also contained a clause committing the state to help unemployed workers find new jobs. The State Council also ended its stalling and resubmitted the State-Owned Industrial Enterprises Law for Standing Committee consideration at the Eighteenth Session.[108]

Peng Zhen set out the substance of the final deal in his address to the Standing Committee session. He announced that the law would be applicable only to state-owned enterprises, and that these enterprises would only bear limited civil liability for their losses in the case of bankruptcy, thereby effectively limiting the potential costs to the state treasury.[109] Peng's speech embraced the views of the 'pragmatic opposition', which professed to support the law in principal, but argued that a variety of preconditions be met before it could be passed:

106. Guo Daohui (1988), 90; also *Liaowang* (Overseas Edition) No. 50 (15 December 1986), 6; *Liaowang* (Overseas Edition), No. 48 (1 December 1986), 5; and *Ta Kung Pao* (Hong Kong), 20–6 November 1986, 1; also BXE, 18 November 1986.
107. Interview 11-19-13-33/OKE, February 1989.
108. BXE, 15 November 1986; BXE, 26 November 1986; BXDS, 26 November 1986; and Gu Ming's comments in *Jingji Ribao*, 11 November 1986, 3.
109. Peng Zhen, 'Peng Zhen Weiyuanzhang Zai Renda Changweihui De Shiba Ci Huiyi Lianzu Huiyi Shang de Jianghua Yaodian' ('Main Points of Chairman Peng Zhen's Address to the Joint Group Meeting at the 18th Session of the NPC Standing Committee'), 29 November 1986. This is a personal copy from an unidentified internal journal (apparently an NPC publication). Peng's speech was also summarized by BXDS on 29 November, although the contents of these two summaries vary slightly.

The Case of The Enterprise Bankruptcy Law 165

> The State-Owned Industrial Enterprises Law has not yet been formulated, so we have problems formulating an Enterprise Bankruptcy Law. The crux is that enterprises have yet to acquire greater powers of self-decision in operations and management; and workers have yet to exercise their right to democratic management within the enterprises. Hence, enterprises are not yet ready to bear the responsibility of bankruptcy. . . . We still lack experience in handling bankruptcy. Many comrades have said we are not yet equipped with the conditions for formulating this law, although the need is widely recognized. . . . [110]

Then Peng noted the pragmatic opposition's greatest victory:

> As a result of consultations, we agreed to pass the Enterprise Bankruptcy Law as a law for trial use, and test it out a bit after its passage; after promulgation of the State-Owned Enterprise Law, test it out some more, sum up our experience, and revise it again.[111]

In other words, the law would be passed at the current session, but it would not be carried out nation-wide until three months after the State-Owned Industrial Enterprise Law had been passed. Even then, it would only be implemented for 'trial use', a vague term which left unclear whether the law would ever be implemented nation-wide. The opposition had succeeded in deferring the battle to the indefinite future.

The Enterprise Bankruptcy Law (for Trial Use) of the People's Republic of China was passed by the Eighteenth Session of the Sixth NPC Standing Committee and was officially signed into law by President Li Xiannian on 2 December 1986. The actual vote reflected the change in norms for Party members serving in the NPC. Despite the Politburo's consensus and Zhao's insistent call for passage of the law at this session, a number of delegates, many of them Party members, according to several sources, remained implacably opposed to passing any bankruptcy law and cast abstaining votes. The final total was 101 votes for, zero opposed, and nine abstentions.[112]

This is not, however, the end of the story. It took the NPC three sessions and over a year and a half to complete consideration of the State-Owned Industrial Enterprises Law. The law was repeatedly tabled by the NPC leadership, which again argued that 'conditions were not yet ripe' for its passage. The NPC's highly successful 'salami tactics' continued until Peng Zhen was removed as a Politburo member in October 1987, and later as Chairman of the NPC Standing Committee in April 1988.[113] Local bankruptcy experiments continued in Shenyang during 1987, but the national law remained stalled.[114]

Unsuccessful efforts were made in late 1988 by the SEC—especially

---

110. *Ibid.*   111. *Ibid.*   112. Delfs, (1987), 46.
113. The politics of Peng's removal are discussed in somewhat greater depth in the case study on the State-Owned Industrial Enterprises Law.
114. Cao Siyuan (1988b), 59.

Vice-Minister Zhang Yanning—to resurrect the Bankruptcy Law three months after the State Enterprise Law went into effect. The State Council Legislation Bureau began preliminary work on drafting implementing regulations for the law. According to one source close to the Bureau, research on implementing the law had begun, but there would be no push actually to draft these regulations until 'political conditions were appropriate'. The source, asked to elaborate, indicated that they meant there was no push coming from the leadership to implement the law, and so it was not a major priority with the Bureau.

Any hope of actually implementing the law seemed to slip away for a long time after hardliners crushed the 1989 Democracy Movement. Zhao Ziyang was deposed as Communist Party General Secretary and placed under house arrest. Chief drafter Cao Siyuan—who never stopped pushing for implementation of the law through his post at the 'Bankruptcy Information Office' under the now-famous Stone Corporation—was arrested for supporting the Democracy Movement. He remained in custody for a year until his release in May 1990. But not even prison would dampen the spirit of this quintessential entrepreneur. Cao almost immediately resumed his research and lobbying activities, establishing his own consultancy office to assist troubled enterprises and gather data on bankruptcies nationwide. By the mid-1990s, when intractable state enterprise losses were once again front and centre on the leadership's agenda, Cao and his ideas re-emerged. Supported by the State Economic and Trade Office (the organizational successor to his old ally, the SEC), he was once again pushing for the NPC to revise, clarify and toughen the Bankruptcy Law. Thanks in large measure to Cao's tenacity, the tale of the Bankruptcy Law continues.

8

The Case Of The State-owned Industrial Enterprises Law

Background

In contrast to the Bankruptcy Law, which addressed an entirely new issue in PRC politics, the 1988 State-Owned Industrial Enterprises Law had deep roots. Power relations within state enterprises have been among the hardiest recurring issues in PRC history, and China's goals of promoting rapid industrialization while trying to maintain Party control over society and the economy ensure that these dilemmas will remain on the leaders' agenda for some time to come. In this sense, the 1988 'State Enterprises Law' was but the most recent of several major policy documents which have addressed this issue since 1949. But all the law's documentary ancestors were drafted either as CCP Central Documents or as State Council administrative documents, with little or no public debate and scrutiny.[1] This time, however, the CCP leadership chose to address these issues via a different documentary rubric and hence a very different process: drafting the new regulations in the form of a 'basic law' submitted to the publicity of the lawmaking process. That choice of process ultimately had important implications for the content of the policy document which was finally promulgated.

The drafting process for some of these earlier documents—most notably the 1975 'Twenty Articles on Industry'—had been motivated far more by factional struggle than by any desire for coherent economic policy-making. The Twenty Articles were, on the surface, an effort to quell the industrial chaos which had led to sharp declines in factory productivity during the early to mid 1970s. But both the proponents and opponents of the Twenty Articles clearly seemed to have recognized the more immediate political purposes of the document: as a vehicle for Deng Xiaoping and his followers to undermine the policy position of his chief political adversaries, in particular the 'Gang of Four'.[2]

---

1. On enterprise policy more generally, see Andors (1977), Azrael (1970), Chamberlain (1987), Donnithorne (1967), Lee Lai To (1986), Schurmann (1968), Solinger (1984 and 1986) and Walder (1987).
2. The politics of drafting the 'Twenty Articles' is discussed in Lieberthal *et al.* (1978). Lieberthal's case studies—which describe the highly closed process of drafting of CCP 'Central Documents'—provide an excellent contrast with the far more open access in the lawmaking process.

168 The Politics of Lawmaking in Post-Mao China

Getting the Law on the Agenda

At the outset, the drafting process for the State Enterprise Law was also shaped more by the dictates of leadership struggle than by the needs of industrial policy or lawmaking. Deng Xiaoping's now famous report at the November 1978 Central Work Conference—the first document which called for drafting a 'Factory Law'[3]—was more a tool of political struggle than a carefully considered policy document.[4] Lawmaking was literally an afterthought. When the leaders assembled at that acrimonious session heard Deng argue that China should move away from a system of 'wise leaders' and 'rule by man' (*renzhi*) towards a system of 'socialist democracy' and 'rule by law', those present recognized that he was in fact attacking those Party leaders whose legitimacy as office holders rested upon Mao's deathbed benediction, rather than upon law, democracy or any established Party succession procedure, most notably Party Chairman Hua Guofeng, Wang Dongxing and Ji Dengkui.

> To insure people's democracy, we must strengthen our legal system . . . so as to make sure that institutions and laws do not change whenever the leadership changes, or whenever the leaders change their views or shift the focus of their attention. . . . . The trouble is . . . very often, what leaders say is taken as the law and anyone who disagrees is called a law breaker. That kind of law changes whenever a leader's views change.[5]

But Deng—importantly for this story—did not stop at this thinly veiled attack on Hua and his programmes. He went on to argue that China urgently needed to draft many key pieces of legislation and then listed several major laws whose drafting he felt was particularly pressing:

> . . . So we must concentrate on enacting criminal and civil codes, procedural laws and other necessary laws concerning *factories*, people's communes, forests, grasslands and environmental protection, as well as labour laws and a law on investment by foreigners . . .[6] (emphasis added)

---

3. The law actually went through two name changes. It was originally called the State-Managed Factory Law (*Guoying Gongchang Fa*), later the State-Managed Industrial Enterprise Law (*Guoying Gongye Qiye Fa*) and finally the State-Owned Industrial Enterprises Law (*Quanmin Suoyouzhi Gongye Qiye Fa*). Both these name changes were politically significant and will be explained in the text. Nevertheless, for the sake of simplicity and to avoid confusing the reader, I will customarily refer to the law by the shorthand name the Enterprise Law or the State Enterprise Law. The reader should also note that in the interest of brevity, all three versions of the law's name which I have listed above omit the law's formal preface, which is 'The People's Republic of China' (*Zhonghua Renmin Gongheguo*).
4. Deng Xiaoping, 'Emancipate the Mind, Seek Truth From Facts and Unite as One in Looking to the Future', speech delivered 13 December 1978, at the closing session of the November–December Central Work Conference, in Deng Xiaoping (1984), 157–8.
5. *Ibid.*, 157.
6. *Ibid.*, 158. Deng did not further discuss the law *per se*. But in a separate section of the speech, he laid out a factory policy which hinted as to the content he might prefer in such a

Obviously, the key question of agenda-setting is why these particular laws got into the report. Why were innumerable other potential legislative proposals omitted? Who actually led the drafting of the report?

According to one high-ranking source, the text of Deng's report was drafted in great haste, with far less inter-agency co-ordination than might be expected for such a major document, and with little or no input from the Party's top legal policy organ, the Central Political-Legal Group. Deng Xiaoping's published speech was drawn up after the fact, based upon his scattered comments at the Work Conference.[7] Deng originally gave Party ideologist Hu Qiaomu the task of drafting the speech, but found Hu's original draft wanting. Deng next turned the job over to his younger ally Hu Yaobang, who organized a three-man drafting group composed of aides from Deng's State Council Research Office. Owing to the urgency of the moment, the first draft was written up in one or two days. In their original work conference comments, however, neither Deng nor any other senior leader had singled out any particular laws which they felt needed to be drafted. Reportedly, the three-man drafting group—none of whom had any legal training—did not have time to consult other sources on which laws to include, not even the staff and members of the Political-Legal Group, who in any case were under the organizational control of Deng's adversaries Wang Dongxing and Ji Dengkui. The three-man group simply came up with the specific laws—such as the Factory Law, the Labour Law, the Commune Law—by brainstorming amongst themselves. Over the next couple of days, Hu Yaobang, Deng Xiaoping, Deng Liqun, Hu Qiaomu and other top leaders reviewed the draft, suggesting additions and corrections before it was officially presented. But the short-list of laws presented in the original draft, according to this source, remained essentially unchanged.

But even if Deng Xiaoping understood very little about the *legal* significance of the laws he endorsed that day, all the sources consulted for this study, both interview and documentary, are nevertheless quite unanimous about the *political* significance of Deng's endorsement. His address put the Factory Law on the government's agenda, where it remained for ten years. He settled once and for all the issue of whether or not a major enterprise law of some sort would be passed.[8] From that

---

law. Deng suggested some reforms in what was then the current system of factory management, that of 'the factory manager assuming overall responsibility under the leadership of the Party committee'. Deng called for an expansion of authority and responsibility for all managerial personnel, including factory directors, accountants and technical experts. See *ibid.*, 161–3.

7. The source is a former Chinese offical who personally took part in drafting the Third Plenum Report.

8. It is notable that of the laws Deng mentioned in his 1978 speech, all but one–the commune law—have since been passed. The commune system was scrapped soon after this

170 The Politics of Lawmaking in Post-Mao China

day on, the only issues remaining were the timing and content of that enterprise law.[9]

First Attempts at Drafting, 1979–1982

The story of the Enterprise Law also features a prominent 'policy entrepreneur', though the story lacks the personal heroics of Cao Siyuan's obsessive, high-profile lobbying. In stark contrast to Cao, State Economic Commission (SEC) Vice-Minister Yuan Baohua was China's classic Stalinist industrial bureaucrat. Yuan's career spans almost forty years at the upper reaches of the industrial planning apparatus.[10] Interviews with officials who have worked with Yuan, in addition to his own speeches and writings, make it evident that he saw his mission in terms of rationalizing China's enterprises by improving the quality of their management. Studying Yuan, one gets a sense that he believes the salvation of China's managers may be found in the Trinity of increased technological investment, improved management education and enhanced managerial authority. Throughout the 1980s, Yuan consistently favoured strengthening the position of managers, often at the expense of enterprise Party committees. Yuan also devoted much energy to improved education of managers, heading numerous national management education groups. Towards these ends, Yuan made a long-term personal commitment to promoting the Enterprise Law, as one Chinese source noted with some humour:

The State Economic Commission . . . felt that the state and enterprises urgently needed the formulation of an enterprise law. Yuan Baohua, Vice-Minister in Charge of the SEC, whose hair is now all white, found it a bounden duty to accept this task,

report. At time of writing, the Labour Law is still on the government agenda, and is being revised by the All-China Federation of Trade Unions (ACFTU). In early 1989, ACFTU officials expressed certainty that the law would ultimately be adopted, in part because Deng endorsed it back in 1978.

9. In analysing how the speech was drafted, it would of course be wrong to place excessive reliance upon any one source, no matter how good. For example, a second source with good access (but nevertheless inferior to that of the first source) indicates that Deng's speech was drafted by a larger group of specialists. Within that larger group, a smaller contingent of legal experts from several organizations and ministries—including, for example, the ACFTU—contributed to the list of laws in the speech. The truth probably lies somewhere in between the two stories, though closer to the first source's version.

10. In the 1950s and early 1960s, Yuan successively served as a Vice-Minister of Metallurgical Industry, Vice-Minister of the original State Economic Committee, and Minister of Materials allocation. During the early 1970s, Yuan served as Vice-Minister of the State Planning Committee under Yu Qiuli, until August 1978, when he was transferred back to the newly resurrected SEC and in charge of the SEC's Comprehensive Department, which oversaw enterprises and their management. During the 1980s, Yuan headed a large number of national societies concerned with enterprise management. For more on his career, see Bartke (1987); also Klein and Clark (1971, Vol. II).

and organized a force to begin work in 1979, and drafted an 'article to solicit opinions' on the Factory Law in October 1979.[11]

Although Yuan personally advocated greatly increased managerial authority, the 'article' he circulated within the bureaucracy was more cautious, and stuck close to the policy framework suggested by Deng's December 1978 remarks. Yuan proposed that China, for the time being, continue the system of enterprise Communist Party Committee control or 'leadership' over the factory manager, though apparently with some enhanced authority for the manager.[12] Among those who saw the article, however, many were already calling for a more radical devolution of power designed to strengthen managers, and they recommended giving them 'overall responsibility' while weakening the Party committees' role from leadership to an ill-defined one of 'guaranteeing and supervising' the manager's performance. But with views on this issue still badly split, Yuan's proposal for the law apparently remained stalemated for another year.[13]

In August 1980, Deng again intervened, repeating his call for reform of the management system and implementation of a system of greater responsibility for managers.[14] In the same month, at an enlarged Politburo meeting, Deng again underscored the need for clearer systems of responsibility in all Party, government and institutional offices. In particular, he endorsed still greater authority for managers, and called for eventually introducing an ill-defined system of 'workers' and staff members' congresses' in all factories which would have the right to discuss and decide on major factory decisions, and could call upon higher levels to dismiss incompetent administrators.[15] Deng's reassertion of the need for enterprise reform, coupled with a concurrent major shake-up in the Party leadership, temporarily galvanized the system to move ahead with drafting the Enterprise Law.[16]

Available details are sketchy, and suggest there was a complex organizational response to Deng's initiative amongst the various lawmaking institutions, with overlapping structures and confused lines of authority. Some time in August 1980, newly appointed Premier Zhao Ziyang and NPC Legislative Affairs Committee Director Peng Zhen began organizing their forces, jointly it seems, to draft the 'State-Managed Factory Law'.[17] Zhao Ziyang instructed the 'relevant departments' to begin research and drafting

11. Lu Mu (1988) 4.
12. The formal name of this system is 'managerial responsibility under the leadership of the Party committee' (*dangwei lingdao xia de changzhang fuzezhi*). 13. *Ibid.*
14. Lian He (1988), 5.
15. 'On the Reform of the System of Party and State Leadership', Deng Xiaoping (19?4), 302–25, especially 323.
16. *Ibid.*; also Lian He (1988), 5. Deng also announced in his August 1980 speech that Hua Guofeng was resigning as Premier and that he would be replaced by the key economic reform leader Zhao Ziyang.
17. The formal title at this time was *Guoying Gongchang Fa*.

172 The Politics of Lawmaking in Post-Mao China

on the law, with Yuan Baohua's State Economic Commission heading the actual Drafting Group (*qicao xiaozu*).[18] Another source suggests, however, that despite these appointments from Zhao's State Council, this Drafting Group was formally subordinate to Peng's NPC Legislative Affairs Committee rather than the State Council.[19] That same month, the Legislative Affairs Committee established a Factory Law Investigation Group (*Gongchang Fa Diaocha Zu*), apparently much larger than the Drafting Group, and charged it with carrying out local investigations and gathering data to be used in drafting the law.[20] Peng Zhen, it appears, was able to make the case that a law of such far-reaching importance should be regarded as a 'basic law' requiring NPC approval.

One consultant to the Drafting Group reports that from the very beginning, the Party Centre felt that the law should represent a negotiated balance between the three major power centres within state-managed enterprises: the factory administration; the enterprise Party committee; and the workers, as represented by the official trade unions.[21] As a result, throughout almost all of the nine-year drafting process, these three groups' interests were officially represented on the Drafting Group. The Drafting Group chair—the SEC—was chosen to represent the interests of administration (*xingzheng*) which in this case, meant both managers and the state bureaucracy.[22] The Communist Party's Organization Department represented the interests of the Party (*dang*), which meant the enterprise Party committees and secretaries. And the All-China Federation of Trade Unions (ACFTU) was chosen to represent the interests of labour (*laodong, gongren*), which meant workers and their official unions.[23]

Two months after the drafting group was formed, in October 1980, the group produced its first draft, called the Outline of the State-Run Factory Law (*Guoying Gongchang Fa Dagang*). This Outline—based on Yuan Baohua's 1979 'Article to solicit views'—is unfortunately unavailable. It is known, however, that it advocated a major change in enterprise power relations, replacing the twenty-three-year-old system of 'Manager Responsibility under Party Committee Leadership' with a new system of 'the

---

18. Zhang Sutang and He Ping (1988).   19. Lu Mu (1988), 4.
20. Lian He (1988), 5.
21. Interview 27–22–13–33/TSE, Beijing, 29 March 1989. Unfortunately, this source refused to be drawn out on precisely whom he meant by the vague term 'Party Centre' (*dang zhongyang*).
22. This particular organizational selection—grouping managers with the state administration—represents the state of the ideological debate at the time. By 1984, Zhao Ziyang and others (whom I shall label 'radical reformers') began arguing that the rights of management and ownership needed to be separated within state-owned factories—increasingly freeing managers from industrial bureau interferance. In late 1987, as shown below, this radical reformist viewpoint gained a seat at the Enterprise Law drafting table, when Zhao's newly formed State Committee for Restructuring the Economic System (SCRES) became a key player in debate over the law.
23. Interview 27–22–13–33/TSE, 29 March 1989, Beijing.

Factory Manager Assuming Full Responsibility Under the Leadership of the Staff and Workers Congress'.[24]

At Peng Zhen's suggestion, Zhao Ziyang and other Central leaders temporarily seconded personnel from fifty-nine ministries, committees and other offices, apparently to the NPC Legislative Affairs Committee's Factory Law Investigation Group, to assist in the massive process of soliticing ministerial and local responses to the Outline. During late 1980, the Group divided up and took the Outline to sixteen provinces, municipalities and autonomous regions to solicit opinions.[25] The Outline spawned tremendous disagreement, focused on the proper allocation of duties, rights and power in the factory leadership system.[26] According to one source, 'some comrades' concurred with its suggestion of a system of 'Manager Responsibility under Worker and Staff Congress Leadership'. Others disagreed, and argued for a system of full managerial responsibility with a Management Committee (*dongshi hui*) assuming formal leadership. But apparently the largest number of those consulted preferred continuing the existing system of Party committee leadership.[27]

The State Council Standing Committee discussed these controversial new management proposals some time between April and September 1981, but could not resolve the dispute. Unable to achieve a national consensus on the draft law's key features, the State Council temporarily suspended drafting work, claiming that 'drafting conditions were not yet ripe' for a factory law.[28]

Zhao, Yuan and the SEC were still quite anxious to reform the factory management system and strengthen the hand of factory managers. But Zhao and the State Council leadership also needed some new regulations—reformist or otherwise—by which to govern intra-factory relations until consensus on the reforms could be achieved among the numerous concerned parties. They apparently chose what might be called a 'log-rolling' strategy, splitting the difference between the contending organizations.

24. Lu Mu (1988), 4.
25. *Ibid.*, 4. Note: this source incorrectly identifies Peng Zhen as Chairman of the NPC Standing Committee, a post he did not occupy until June 1982.
26. Gu Ming (198?), 1; also Lu Mu (1988), 4.
27. Lu Mu (1988), 4. This source is rather vague on how many officials supported each of the plans. It notes that 'some comrades' supported each of the first two plans, but that 'a fairly large number of comrades' supported Party Committee Leadership. I interpret this to mean that the third option was the most popular. This source also indicates that there was some regional and historical basis for these views. The system of full manager responsibility—and the even more centralized Soviet system of one-man management—was popular in North and Northeast China during the early 1950s. Although the Eighth CCP Congress in 1956 attacked this system as giving too much power to the manager, the article suggests it was still popular among those who had served in those areas. Schurmann (1968, 220–308) has also discussed the role of the Northeast in promoting the Soviet-oriented system of one-man management', arguing that this system may have been discredited because of its association with the purged Northeast Regional Party Secretary Gao Gang.
28. Lian He (1988), 5; Gu Ming (1987), 1; Zhang Sutang and He Ping (1988), 17.

Between April 1981 and April 1983, the State Council and Party Central Committee drafted and promulgated four separate sets of temporary regulations (*zhanxing tiaoli*) on various aspects of factory management. These regulations governed, respectively, the rights and duties of: the enterprise congress of workers and staff (adopted in July 1981); the factory manager (January 1982); the basic-level enterprise Party committees (June 1982); and state-managed industrial enterprises.[29] Each of the three main bureaucratic combatants—the SEC, the Organization Department and the trade unions—took the lead in drafting the regulations pertaining to 'their' corresponding enterprise organization. All three organizations reviewed and commented on each of the documents, but the basic solution to the stalemate was to allow each one to write the regulations for 'its' sector of the factory.

To the student of bureaucratic politics, the results of this process were absolutely predictable. While certain core principles were maintained in all three documents, the regulations were nevertheless highly contradictory and sent unclear and inconsistent messages about the balance of power to the factory floor. They also did not represent a major step forward for reform. Nowhere is the vagueness of these regulations clearer than in the sections dealing with managerial powers. All three sets endorsed the current system of management responsibility with Party committee leadership. But thereafter, the similarities ended.

The SEC's regulations on managers, while reaffirming Party committee leadership, stressed the manager's operational authority. According to the regulations, the manager exercised 'unified leadership . . . over production and operational activities' (article 14) and the manager had control over the deployment of the enterprise's 'personnel, funds and physical capital', so long as the manager operated within the vaguely defined parameters of 'state regulations' (article 15). Most important, perhaps, was an emergency escape clause which granted the manager the power to make virtually any decision in administrative or production matters required 'in urgent circumstances', even if that decision was well outside the manager's normal authority. The only requirement placed on the manager was that he 'report' the decision to the appropriate decision-making authority after the fact (article 19).

---

29. Lian He (1988), 5; Gu Ming (198?), 1. The full texts of all four documents are conveniently published in the appendix to Yang Zixuan (1986). Single and translated copies may be found in the following sources: 'Provisional Regulations for the Workers Congresses in State-Owned Industrial Enterprises', BXE, 19 July 1981, in FBIS-CHI, 23 July 1981, K3–7. Unlike the other three, the Party committee regulations were not published in the State Council Bulletin, though a detailed commentary did appear in *Ban Yue Tan*, No. 13 (10 July 1982), 6–8; in FBIS-CHI, 22 July 1982, K7–9. See also 'State Council Provisional Rules for Further Expansion of Decision-making Power of State-Run Industrial Enterprises', *State Council Bulletin*, No. 10 (30 May 1984), 323–5; in JPRS-CPS-84-087, 13 December 1984, 7–10.

The Organization Department's Regulations on Party Committees, issued six months later, also called generally for the Party committee not to interfere directly in 'production' decisions. But these regulations stressed that a variety of managerial decisions should be made by the manager submitting a suggestion to the Party committee, which would in turn make the final decision (article 11). This list included so many key factory decisions that they added up to a framework of tight Party committee control over the manager's production-related decisions.[30]

These overlaps and contradictions notwithstanding, the decision to draft four separate sets of regulations had two major political effects. First, although the State Council got what it needed immediately—a set of factory management regulations—it did so at the cost of a highly fragile, unsustainable compromise over factory policy. Many reformers attacked the regulations, claiming they simply reaffirmed and codified excessive Party committee control over management. The regulations also failed to strengthen managerial authority and loosen the grip of state industrial bureaus over the enterprise.[31] Advocates of further reforms—Zhao Ziyang, his followers, the ELRC and the SEC—had no choice but to bide their time until a chance arose to move beyond the confusing compromises of 1981–82. The second political effect of drafting temporary regulations rather than a law was to end for a time the involvement of Peng Zhen and the NPC in the enterprise policy debate.[32] This absence of NPC involvement was underscored in the State Council's 1982 annual economic legislative plan, drawn up in late 1981 by the Economic Legislation Research Centre.[33] The 1982 plan did not indicate that the NPC or its Standing Committee would consider any policy document on state-run enterprises that year.[34] Instead, the Temporary Regulations on State-Managed Industrial Enterprises, primarily drafted by the SEC and based on the Factory Law Outline, were issued by the State Council in April 1983.[35]

---

30. The decision areas governed by this decision-making system included: (1) 'Managerial policy decisions' (*jingying juece*); (2) Long-range and annual plans; (3) Major technological renovation plans; (4) Plans for staff training; (5) Wage adjustment policies (*gongzi tiaozheng fangan*); (6) Mechanical transformations; (7) Establishment, revision and abrogation of factory constitutions.

31. Later sources strongly suggest that the Economic Legislation Research Centre and the State Economic Committee levelled precisely such criticisms at the regulations and the system of Party committee leadership. See Lian He (1988), 5; Gu Ming (1987?), 1. As noted, Lian He at this time worked for the SEC Bureau of Law and Regulations, while Gu Ming was Director of the Economic Legislation Research Centre.

32. None of my sources indicated that the NPC undertook any activity on the Enterprise Law from 1981 until Peng Zhen began leading the reformed Investigation Group in 1984.

33. The ELRC's short-list of laws for drafting and promulgation by the State Council in 1982 included a set of Temporary Regulations on State-Run Industrial Enterprises.

34. On the meeting and the 1982 annual plan, see 'The ELRC Directorate Meeting Studies and Arranges This Year's Work' ('Jingji Fagui Yanjiu Zhongxin Changwu Ganshi Yanjiu Bushu Jinian Gongzuo'), *Jingji Fagui Yanjiu Ziliao* (approximate date, March 1982), 38–40.

35. The text is in Yang Zixuan (1986).

Late 1983: Resurrecting the Law

Amidst a rising sea of state enterprise deficits, the State Enterprise Law re-emerged on the leadership agenda some time in late 1983 or early 1984. An October 1983 Central Committee seminar 'solemnly pointed out' that a turnaround in the economic situation was impossible until something was done about chronic state enterprise losses.[36] As a result, in early 1984, 'The Centre repeatedly (*zaici*) demanded that the Factory Law be drafted as quickly as possible'.[37]

As drafting work started up again, the law underwent an apparently semantic change which actually had important implications. At the request of the ACFTU, the draft law's name was changed from the State-Managed Factory Law (*Guoying Gongchang Fa*) to the State-Managed Enterprise Law (*Guoying Qiye Fa*). The trade unions successfully contended that in most countries which have a factory law, that law governs labour relations and is used to control workers. China's Enterprise Law, they argued, was intended more to govern enterprise–state relations and management issues.[38] Behind these arguments lay the ACFTU's desire to protect its autonomy in developing policy towards workers. It had been working on its own Labour Law since the 1978 Third Plenum and wanted to preclude the SEC's Factory Law from usurping its authority.[39]

The Enterprise Law once again emerged on the agenda because several actors with very different bureaucratic interests and policy proposals all simultaneously wanted to reopen the debate over the balance of power in factories. Hoping to benefit from the increased leadership attention, the State Economic Commission worked hard to heighten leadership anxiety over state enterprise losses and focus interest on its agenda. In late 1983 and early 1984, the SEC convened a series of national meetings in which it promoted a mood of increased concern about the problem of enterprise deficits. SEC officials also resumed their fight for a clearer enterprise management policy, one which strengthened the role of managers.[40]

---

36. See Yuan Baohua's speech in *Jingji Guanli*, No. 1 (5 January 1984), 3–5, translated in Joint Publications Research Service, China Economic and Agricultural Report (JPRS-CEA), 84–022, 27 March 1984.

37 Lian He (1988), 5. Another source corroborates this information, noting that the Central Authorities decided in February 1984 once again to start the preparatory work for drafting the law. *Shijie Jingji Daobao* (Shanghai), 21 December 1987, 13, in FBIS-CHI, 21 January 1988, 18.   38. Interview 27–22–13–33/TSE, Beijing, 29 March 1989.

39. *Ibid*.

40. This series of SEC-organized meetings is discussed in detail in the Bankruptcy Law case study, Chapter 6.

The Case Of The State-owned Industrial Enterprises Law 177

Peng Zhen and the NPC Get Back in the Game

This SEC offensive coincided with efforts by NPC leaders—principally Peng Zhen—to re-insert themselves into the enterprise policy debate. Peng Zhen, unlike such experienced industrial planners as Bo Yibo, Chen Yun and Yao Yilin, has never been a major player in the CCP's industrial policy-making apparatus. Hence, the only legitimate way for Peng to insert himself into the enterprise debate was to redefine enterprise policy to fit his bailiwick, political-legal affairs. Because the Enterprise Law is both enterprise policy and a law, it fell legitimately into Peng Zhen's policy sector in a way that no other enterprise policy issue could.[41]

As a first step in re-inserting itself into the issue, the NPC resurrected the Enterprise Law Investigation Group, moribund since the initial 1980 investigations.[42] Personally led on many occasions by Peng Zhen, the Investigation Group once again toured several provinces soliciting opinions on the law, drawing on these views to formulate a new draft.[43] Press sources stress the tremendous size, speed and scope of the local investigations which the Investigation Group undertook. Between February and October 1984, it made four major tours, visiting several hundred large and medium-sized state enterprises in ten different provinces.[44]

Peng Zhen's forceful participation in these investigations re-secured his place in the enterprise policy debate. Leaving Beijing in early 1984, Peng led investigations in East and North China, accompanied by Yuan Baohua and ELRC Chief Gu Ming, among others. For Peng, these large meetings with managers, Party secretaries and workers became both his classroom and his soapbox. Under the rubric of 'legislative work', Peng seized the

---

41. This interpretation of Peng's behaviour, while admittedly speculative, nevertheless accords with his previous behaviour. Roderick MacFarquhar, for example, argues that as Beijing Mayor, Peng tried to establish himself as a nation-wide leader in industrial policy during the 1955–56 'socialist transformation' of industry by deliberately exceeding the prescribed speed for nationalizing industry. See MacFarquhar (1974). In late 1983–early 1984, Peng was also one of several 'conservative' Party elders simultaneously reasserting himself on a variety of policy issues by deliberately broadening the scope of debate over curbing 'spiritual pollution'. See Gold (1984).

42. It is notable that Peng's focus during these trips was clearly on issues of enterprise policy, and not on more narrow issues of lawmaking. In none of the available reports on Peng's investigation trips did he even touch on more narrowly 'legislative' concerns, such as the format of the law, number of articles, legal language, interpretation, enforceability or potential conflicts with other regulations. Peng's speeches were strictly on enterprise policy. Yet, by defining the enterprise issue as 'lawmaking work', Peng and the NPC leaders were able to insert themselves into aspects of the debate which were beyond their normal personal provenance as Party leaders.

43. Lu Mu (1988), 4; Zhang Sutang and He Ping (1988), 17; Gu Ming (198?), 1; Lian He (1988), 5; see also Yuan Baohua's NPC speech in FBIS-CHI 17 January 1985, 7–8.; also the report on Peng Zhen, Yuan Baohua and Gu Ming's joint trip to Hangzhou in February in FBIS-CHI, 22 February 1984, K17.

44. Lu Mu (1988), 4; Zhang Sutang and He Ping (1988), 17. These provinces included Zhejiang, Shanghai and Liaoning.

opportunity to develop his expertise on enterprise issues, flesh out his own policy views and expound several favourite themes on enterprise policy.[45] In 1987, Peng publicly stated that these meetings made him a supporter of the system of full managerial responsibility as early as 1984, and persuaded him of the need for a clearer delineation of managerial powers within the factory. Upon his return to Beijing, he proposed adopting the system during a 1984 Politburo Standing Committee meeting.[46]

Peng's 23 March 1984 address to the Investigation Group and a meeting of 'local' enterprise officials and union chairmen provides the most complete available summary of his views on enterprise policy at this time, and suggests these were less emphatic or clear than he later portrayed them. Peng immediately separated himself from the Organization Department/ACFTU view by attacking the current system of Party committee leadership, arguing that under this system enterprise Party committees had become too heavily involved in the daily management of production. But he attacked as equally flawed the organizational ancestor of the system of full factory manager responsibility, the 1950s Soviet-style system of 'one-man management'. He argued that this system had given far too much power to the factory director.[47]

Peng stated that the Party Centre had given great thought to this issue, and that the 'current tendency at the Centre' was towards adopting the system of full managerial responsibility. On this occasion, Peng did not explicitly associate himself with this 'tendency'. Indeed, he even noted that some comrades disagreed with the system or had concerns. But he did endorse the system in other speeches given at that time.[48]

But Peng also parted company with more radical reformers, arguing that enterprise policy must make clear that the manager cannot dispense with or weaken the Party's leadership (though, as he had noted, this need not mean wide-ranging, direct operational leadership). He stressed the need for many important factory decisions to be made collectively among the manager, Party and trade union. Peng's conception of the appropriate duties for the Party committee was also much broader than the one which was eventually incorporated into the enterprise law—the vague provision

---

45. On Peng's involvement in these meetings, see Peng Zhen's speech at one such conference among Shanghai and Zhejiang cadres on 23 March 1984. 'Guanyu Caoni Guoying Gongchang Fa de Wenti' ('On Problems of Drafting the State-Managed Factory Law'), in Peng Zhen (1989), 225–30; also his speech in Shenyang, BXDS, 24 July 1984, in FBIS-CHI, 26 July 1984, K19–20.

46. Peng's claim may be found in 'Peng Zhen Meets Hong Kong, Macao Reporters', Beijing Television Service, 8 April 1987, in FBIS-CHI, 9 April 1987, K1–16, especially K11. Given Peng Zhen's generally conservative outlook and well-documented capacity for public prevarication, it is tempting to note the circumstances of his claims and discount their veracity. In this case, a good deal of independent evidence corroborates the bulk of Peng's claims. Most important are statements by Lian He (1988), 5; Gu Ming (1987), 1; see also Peng's own speeches in the previous footnote.   47. Peng Zhen (1989), 225–30.

48. BXDS, 24 July 1984, in FBIS-CHI, 26 July 1984, K19–20.

of 'guaranteeing that production and management don't leave the Party line' which proved such anathema to Yuan Baohua and the SEC. Peng closed his speech with a *cri de coeur* attacking the failure of enterprise Party committees since the 1950s in educating workers in basic knowledge of Marxism–Leninism, the basic nature of capitalism and the superiority of socialism. This, Peng argued, was something the Party committees must stress as they remove themselves from the day-to-day administration of enterprises.[49]

It is not known what recommendations, if any, Peng made to the Politburo after these investigations. But he returned convinced that: enterprise Party committees were excessively involved in management; these committees needed to concentrate more on Party ideology and organizational matters; managerial authority needed to be more clearly delineated; and this was best done via some form of 'full managerial responsibility system'. It is also clear, however, that Peng's notion of such a system fell far short of the powers many reformers wanted to grant to managers. Moreover, he was apparently unclear in his own mind just how Party leadership over factories should be reconciled with full managerial responsibility, or what mechanisms should be employed to ensure appropriate collective decision-making among the manager, Party committee and union. Peng also failed to specify which types of decisions should be made collectively. He clearly wanted the Party and union to have greater influence than, for example, Zhao Ziyang and Hu Yaobang were arguing for at that same time, but less influence than the CCP Organization Department and the ACFTU were arguing for (which included continued Party committee leadership over the manager).

The NPC Investigation Group returned to Beijing in April, and shortly thereafter came up with a new draft of the law. The draft was distributed to an unspecified list of units in May to solicit their opinions.[50] During April, the Investigation Group was invited to present their reports to Hu Yaobang's Secretariat, which was just then beginning a series of meetings to discuss enterprise reform policy issues.

April 1984–January 1985: The Secretariat Takes Charge

Just as Peng Zhen and the NPC had succeeded in re-inserting themselves into the enterprise policy debate, the Party Centre—specifically General Secretary Hu Yaobang and the Secretariat—moved to re-assert control over

---

49. Peng Zhen (1989), 229–30.
50. Yuan Baohua reports that the draft law underwent six major revisions between May and January 1985, when the law was first debated by the NPC Standing Committee. See Yuan's speech in FBIS-CHI, 22 January 1985, K4.

the pace and direction of the debate.[51] For at least the next eight months (from April 1984 until January 1985), Hu's Secretariat tried to set the broad parameters of debate over enterprise policy and control the pace of that discussion.[52]

The available reporting suggests strongly that the spring Secretariat meetings saw considerable disagreement. One source notes that at this time, 'many high-level personages held that the time for making the "enterprise law" was immature'.[53] As before, the chief problems concerned the appropriate role for workers' congresses and Party committees, and how to control the interference of industrial bureaus in managerial decision-making.[54] But Hu Yaobang, Zhao Ziyang and their allies on the CCP Secretariat were clearly impatient at the long list of obstacles to implementing full managerial responsibility.[55] The Secretariat meeting officially pointed out that 'the time is long overdue when we should carry out the reform of the factory leadership structure and implement the factory manager responsibility system in production and management work'.[56]

Faced with so many objections and obstacles, however, reformers on the Secretariat compromised and decided to press ahead with the reform simultaneously on two tracks. Drafting work on the Enterprise Law went forward, with the NPC-led Investigation Group continuing its work of soliciting opinions, promoting the reform and revising the draft law.[57] In May, the Central Committee General Office and the State Council General Office jointly issued the draft Enterprise Law to provinces and ministries to solicit their opinions.[58] In the meantime, the Secretariat decided that the State Council should revise and update the 1983 Temporary Regulations on State-Managed Enterprises, and only implement the full managerial responsibility system in selected testpoint areas, rather than immediately attempting to implement them nation-wide. As a result, in late April 1984, the Central Committee and the State Council jointly issued Central Document Number 15, under

---

51. The Secretariat was able to mould enterprise reform policy through its control over drafting the key policy document of this period, the Central Committee's October 1984 Decision on Reform of the Economic System (see below).

52. The Secretariat's involvement is discussed in Wang Baoshu (1988). See also Lian He (1988), 5. Wang Baoshu's article (at 6) also cites some obviously valuable, apparently internal, reference materials on the Secretariat meetings which I was unable to secure: *Changzhang Fuzezhi Cankao Ziliao* (*Reference Materials on the Factory Manager Responsibility System*) (Beijing, Zhongguo Jinghi Chubanshe, 1985). 53. Wang Baoshu (1988), 6.

54. *Ibid.*, 6–7.

55. Zhao, though Premier and not a member of the Party Secretariat, sat in on such meetings *ex officio*, and gave a major speech on enterprise reform policy, the text of which is cited in *ibid.*, 6, which I was unable to obtain. That speech is in *Changzhang Fuzezhi Cankao Ziliao*. 56. *Ibid.*, 6.

57. Lian He (1988), 5–6. 58. Gu Ming (1987), 1.

which factories in selected cities would experiment with full managerial responsibility.[59]

Apparently dissatisfied with the pace of enterprise reform, Zhao Ziyang wasted no time in stepping up the pressure for more radical reforms. On 4 May, Zhao took a little publicized but more radical step to advance the enterprise reform. While listening to a progress report on the expansion of enterprise authority, he became the first top leader to argue that more radical surgery would be necessary to end ministerial micro-control of state enterprises. He called for separating the manager's 'right of management' and the state and the ministries' 'right of ownership' in state-owned factories.[60]

The goal of 'separating the two rights' was to find a way of maintaining formal state ownership of major enterprises while diminishing industrial bureaus' direct interference in production and management. This ideological formulation was later used as a justification for experiments with leasing out state-owned factories, selling enterprise stocks and even bankruptcy.

Zhao and the SCRES's proposal for 'separating the two rights' was not immediately adopted, and the October 1984 Central Committee reform Decision only hinted that such a proposal was under consideration.[61] But in 1988 the SCRES leaders seized on the Enterprise Law as an opportunity to enshrine this radically anti-Stalinist new economic proposal in law.

On 15 May, Zhao followed this radical proposal by using the occasion of his annual Government Work Report to argue that 'it is necessary to gradually adopt the system of the plant director assuming full responsibility in the state enterprises so that the plant director, who is entrusted by the state, can have full power in management and operation, and production'. This was, to date, the most prominent public endorsement of the full managerial responsibility system.[62] During the summer, the system was first tried experimentally in 207 state-owned enterprises in the five designated cities. On paper, at least, the policy permitted factory managers to have the final say in all matters of technical and operational management. They were also allowed to appoint their own deputy directors, and they enjoyed greater freedom to pay bonuses to stimulate production.[63]

59. The testpoint cities were Beijing, Tianjin, Shanghai, Dalian, Shenyang and Changzhou. A separate document selecting the specific enterprises to participate in the experiment was apparently issued by the CCP General Office and the State Council in May. The number of enterprises taking part, though small at first, quickly expanded. *Shijie Jingji Daobao* (Shanghai), 21 December 1987, 13, in FBIS-CHI, 21 January 1987.
60. Lu Mu (1988), 4.
61. 'Decision of the Central Committee of the Communist Party of China on Reform of the Economic Structure', 20 October 1984, in *Beijing Review*, No. 44 (29 October 1984), I–XVI (hereafter Decision). The Decision only notes that 'As Marxist theory and the practise of socialism have shown, ownership can be duly separated from the power of operation', at VI.
62. The political significance of Zhao's speech is noted in Zhang Sutang, 17.
63. *China Daily* (Beijing), 8 August 1984, 1.

182 The Politics of Lawmaking in Post-Mao China

To the delight of the State Economic Commission and other management reform advocates, the responsibility system experiments were initially extremely successful in raising productivity in the participating factories, according to a variety of sources. As a result, the number of factories taking part expanded rapidly. By the end of the summer, State Council Deputy Secretary General Gu Ming felt emboldened to announce that the system would be expanded nation-wide during 1985. By January 1985 more than 2,900 state-owned enterprises were reportedly experimenting with the system.[64]

The spring and summer of 1984 continued to be good to enterprise reform advocates. During July 1984, Peng Zhen, who had resumed his tours with the Investigation Group, was arguing that 'it is necessary to institute the system of directors assuming the responsibility for the plant . . .'. He still, however, continued to indicate his suspicion of granting too much power to managers at the expense of Party committees and trade union groups.[65]

October 1984: The Third Plenum

The October 1984 Third Plenum Decision on economic structural reform was a major victory for advocates of greater managerial power in enterprises. The Decision called for relaxed administrative controls over enterprises, stating that 'from now on, government departments at various levels will, in principle, not manage or operate enterprises directly'. The Decision flatly called for implementing the system of full managerial responsibility within the factory, arguing that 'modern enterprises' required a 'unified, authoritative and highly efficient' management system.[66]

The Decision generally diminished the role and powers of the enterprise Party committees and trade unions, though some clauses remained ambiguous. Party committees were admonished to '*actively support directors* in

---

64. Lu Mu (1988), 4 notes the political significance of this initial success. See also Yuan Baohua, cited in FBIS-CHI, 17 January 1985, K8. On expansion of the system, see Gu Ming's remarks in *China Daily* (Beijing), 8 August 1984, 1.

65. For example, Peng showed scepticism of excessive managerial authority in one speech, arguing that 'It is necessary to harness the enthusiasm of the plant director, Party Committee and the Trade Union at the same time in order to jointly fulfill the production task . . . *a director must follow the mass line*, coming from the masses and going to the masses. . . . Without the support of the masses and the Party Committee, it will be difficult for the manager to perform his duty. Therefore, *harnessing the enthusiasm of the director alone is not enough*; it is also necessary to fire the enthusiasm of the plant director, the Party Committee and the Trade Union at the same time . . . the Party Committee exercises power to ensure the fulfillment of state tasks and ensures and checks implementation of the Party's principles and policies in an enterprise. *The powers that embody the Party's leading role must never be overlooked.*' BXDS, 24 July 1984, in FBIS-CHI, 26 July 1984, K19–20.

66. Decision, at X.

exercising their authoritiy' over management. At the same time, however, the committees were given the ambiguous charge of guaranteeing and supervising 'the implementation of the principles and policies of the Party and the state'—wording which clearly could be twisted to justify substantial Party interference in management.[67]

On 29 October, Hu Yaobang and the Secretariat met the Enterprise Law Investigation Group in order to put their own spin on the ambiguous Decision. The Secretariat issued detailed instructions (*zhishi*) which affirmed the managers' powers more emphatically than had the Decision. The Secretariat further insisted that Party committees' chief responsibility was actively to support the manager's powers—in the process dealing a solid blow to the interests of the Organization Department.[68] Emboldened by this meeting and their Third Plenum victory, the SEC and the more radical reformers pushed ahead with the Enterprise Law in the last months of 1984, revising the law for a sixth time, with an apparent view towards getting it passed in 1985.[69]

But an October–November NPC Standing Committee symposium showed clear signs of dissent. Convened right on the heels of the Secretariat meeting, the symposium was called to discuss the Decision and its implications for legislative work. Standing Committee member and noted reform economist Xue Muqiao argued that all NPC work should focus on drafting economic legislation which would support and institutionalize the urban reforms.[70] Peng Zhen, however, was not ready to fall into step and enshrine the Decision in law. In his summation on the last day of the conference, Peng pointedly reasserted the NPC's constitutional right to make up its own mind, in its own time. He stressed that even though the document constituted a decision of the Central Committee, it was not yet law, and only those things which are 'proved right by experience' and 'drafted through legal procedures' had the authority of law.[71]

There was also considerable disagreement within the Drafting Group, especially over the issue of whether or not to include any clause defining the

---

67. *Ibid.*, at XI. As for trade unions, the Decision vaguely called for enterprises to 'give play to the authority and role of the trade union organizations and workers and staff members' deputies. . . .'

68. According to one source, 'The CCP Secretariat . . . clearly pointed out that after the implementation of the factory manager responsibility system, the *enterprise Party committee must not interfere in production and management*, and must firmly establish the authority of the factory manager. The Party organization's *chief responsibility is to actively support the manager* in carrying out his powers of unified leadership of production and management activities, guaranteeing and supervising that all Party and state policies are thoroughly carried out, and strengthening the Party group's own organization.' Lian He (1988), 6. See also Wang Baoshu (1988), 48, which provides the date and confirms the basic content of this Secretariat meeting.

69. FBIS-CHI, 22 January 1985, K4.

70. The NPC symposia were discussed in *Renmin Ribao* on two separate days. See *Renmin Ribao*, 16 November 1984, 1 and 18 November 1984, 1.

71. *Renmin Ribao*, 18 November 1984, 1.

Party committees' role and powers. The SEC was uncertain, but remained concerned lest any such clause be used as a pretext for interference by Party committees in production decisions. The Organization Department and the ACFTU both flatly favoured including such a clause. The Drafting Group invited two groups of legal scholars from several universities and research institutes to discuss the issue. Although some took the view of the Organization Department and the ACFTU, the majority argued that the Party committees' role should be defined in the CCP Constitution, not in state law. The Organization Department and the ACFTU countered that since the role of the Party was already defined in the Preamble to the PRC Constitution there was no reason to exclude such a clause from the Factory Law.[72] But the SEC—the leader of the Drafting Group—was more persuaded by the lawyers' argument, and decided to omit any clause on the Party. In the wake of the Third Plenum Decision's call to separate the Party from government, the Organization Department and the ACFTU decided not to challenge the SEC's decision.[73]

In January, the CCP Secretariat convened a third time to hear from the Investigation Group's report on the revised draft law. For reasons that are unclear, the Secretariat decided that the 'time was not yet ripe' for the NPC to promulgate the Enterprise Law, notwithstanding the emphatic endorsement the Secretariat had given to the enterprise reforms just three months earlier. But the Secretariat also decided—in a move which underscored the distinct role the NPC had begun to play in the Chinese system—that even though the draft was not yet ready for final passage, it should nevertheless be submitted to the NPC Standing Committee for investigation and discussion (*shenyi*). At the same time, the Secretariat decided instead to move reform ahead on the State Council 'track' by further expanding the number of reform testpoint cities.[74]

On 15 January, therefore, the State Council formally submitted the Enterprise Law to the NPC Standing Committee for the first of what would ultimately be an unprecedented four NPC debates on the law.[75] Yuan Baohua gave a detailed explanation of the draft law's contents at the Standing Committee session.[76] Some of the main points are summarized below:

---

72. The 1983 PRC Constitution endorses Deng's famous 'four basic principles', which include the 'leading role of the Communist Party'.
73. Interview 27–22–13–33/TSE, Beijing, 29 March 1989. This source stressed that the legal scholars' ability to hold their own against the CCP Organization Department was an important victory in their effort to expand their influence as policy advisors.
74. Lian He (1988), 6.   75. Zhang Sutang and He Ping (1988), 17–18.
76. This information on the content of the draft law is from my interviews with Chinese officials who participated in drafting the law, and from two press reports which describe Yuan Baohua's address to the NPC. See BXDS, 15 January 1985, in FBIS-CHI, 22 January 1985, K4–6, and ZGXWS, 15 January 1985, in FBIS-CHI, 17 January 1985, K7–8.

Management: Enterprises were to adopt the system of *full management responsibility*. The *manager would exercise unified leadership* and assume full responsibility for directing production and management. The draft indicated that the factory could choose to establish a management committee 'or adopt other forms' of management bodies to assist the factory director in decision-making. The manager had 'a responsibility of reporting his work to the Party organization and the workers' congress, listening to their views, and accepting their supervision'.

The Party Committee: The draft contained no clause pertaining to the position, role and duties of the Party committee. Yuan Baohua publicly noted the SEC's argument that it was 'not advisable [to define the Party's powers] in state laws'.[77]

Democratic Management: The General Principles of the draft noted that in order to foster the initiative and enthusiasm of workers, the state 'guarantees the master status of the workers in the enterprises'. This status was to be exercised through the workers' congress in the factory. The law did not, however, require the manager to follow any of the decisions of the congress, merely to report his work to the congress, listen to its views, and 'accept its supervision'.[78]

Trade Union: The draft apparently did not affirm the trade union committee's right to lead the work of the workers' congress.

Before the Standing Committee session, NPC staff assembled and distributed to all 150-plus Standing Committee members detailed Investigation Committee reports which were generally quite positive in their assessment of the management reforms, noting that the reforms had speeded up development in testpoint areas.[79] But to the surprise of the Standing Committee staff, the draft law faced considerable criticism during the mid-January Standing Committee debate. For many delegates, the most controversial aspect was the omission of a clause codifying the position of the Party committee, which they regarded as an attack upon the Party's leading role not only in the factory but in society as a whole.[80] Critics of the draft were unimpressed by the rudimentary legal argument that since the

---

77. Yuan did note informally his own conception of the Party organization's role, saying that it could discuss major production and management decisions with the manager, express its views and make suggestions. But it could no longer make decisions, and its role had changed from one of exercising unified leadership to one of providing guarantees and supervision.

78. Yuan's speech noted that the draft contained additional provisions spelling out the precise powers of the workers' congress, but Yuan did not discuss those in detail.

79. Interview 12–32–17/34–19–28/ABE, Beijing, April 1989. The generally positive tone of the Investigation Group reports is noted in a BXE report, translated in FBIS-CHI, 22 January 1985, K4. See also Lian He (1988), 6. These NPC investigation reports reportedly even went so far as to endorse an experiment in Wuhan—then quite prominent in the press—whereby a diesel engine factory had hired a German manager to run the factory.

80. Interview 27–22–13–33/TSE, Beijing, 29 March 1989; also Zhang Sutang and He Ping (1993), 17; Lian He (1988), 6.

leading role of the Communist Party was enshrined in China's Constitution, which legally superceded the Enterprise Law, there was no need to rewrite the Party's leading role into each separate law.[81] These critics wanted clauses added which precisely defined the Party committee's powers in the enterprise.[82] Other delegates, clearly unhappy with the Third Plenum Decision on reform, attacked the new manager responsibility system, charging it would give excessive power to managers. But more militantly reformist delegates countered that the law, if anything, did not make the manager's powers clear enough.[83]

After surveying the opposition to the current draft, the Standing Committee Chairmen's Group decided to table the draft. It returned it to Peng Chong's Law Committee and Wang Renzhong's Financial and Economic Committee and charged them with revising the draft based on the delegates' comments.[84] The Standing Committee's unexpected opposition to the law was a modest political victory to the CCP Organization Department and the ACFTU, and a blow to the SEC. In the months after the NPC session, the trade unions and the Organization Department soon resumed pressuring the SEC to include a clause on the Party committees' role. Their efforts did not pay off until almost three years later, when further NPC attacks forced a final compromise which assigned Party committees the vaguely defined power of 'guaranteeing and supervising' that the manager follow Party and state policies.[85]

Critics of the law also received new ammunition at this time, as many local experiments with the management responsibility system began to go awry. During the Lunar New Year, managers in many enterprises abused their new autonomy to give out excessive bonuses. Later that year, newspapers were full of reports of managers who made poor decisions or abused their new power over hiring and firing, or who angered Party organizations. Politically, however, the most sensitive reports concerned managers who went so far as to discharge factory trade union chairmen from their posts. Chinese chroniclers of the draft law's history note the effect these incidents had on the political mood, heightening criticisms of both the law and the responsibility system.[86]

---

81. Interview 12-32-17/34-19-28/ABE, Beijing, April 1989.

82. One NPC staffer attributed these arguments to the relatively low level of education—especially legal education—among most of the delegates. Many simply didn't understand the fundamental legal principal of the Constitution taking precedence over other laws, and were unwilling to support the Enterprise Law unless it also contained a clause reaffirming the Party's fundamental right of leadership. Interview 12-32-17/34-19-28/ABE, Beijing, April 1989. 83. Lian He (1988), 6.

84. BXDS, 21 January 1985, in FBIS-CHI, 22 January 1985, K13.

85. Interview 27-22-13-33/TSE, Beijing, 29 March 1989.

86. Lu Mu, for example, notes that 'some people . . . [attributed these problems to] the excessively great powers of the factory managers'. Indeed, at the State Economic Committee's spring 1986 National Economic Work Conference, the SEC faced a revolt in its own backyard, as a number of delegates raised objections to the manager's personnel power, and called for a return to the policy of allowing the Party to manage enterprise cadres. Lu Mu (1988), 4.

The Case Of The State-owned Industrial Enterprises Law 187

These management excesses also forced ACFTU leaders to reconsider their original desire that the Enterprise Law say as little about trade unions as possible. As more and more managers began encroaching on the extensive property belonging to trade union committees—such as hospitals, retirement homes, shops, small factories, exercise facilities, offices—the ACFTU decided to sacrifice its legislative autonomy in order to protect its property. It now felt that unless the Enterprise Law contained at least a few clauses protecting the unions and their property, such predations would continue and increase.[87]

Faced with these objections, State Council reform advocates apparently decided to take a low profile on drafting the law for more than a year. Very little public legislative activity on the law took place during late 1985 and most of 1986, and even Yuan Baohua seems to have fallen silent on its passage during this period.[88] Using its newly won authority to implement provisional economic reform legislation, the State Council simply continued carrying out the managerial responsibility system without resubmitting the Enterprise Law to the NPC.[89] The Secretariat and State Council instead began revising and strengthening the three sets of temporary regulations on factory managers, Party committees, and workers and staff congresses.[90] When the Legislation Bureau listed its annual plan for laws to be completed and passed by the end of 1986, the Enterprise Law was not among them.

It took a clever piece of legislative 'hostage taking' by the NPC Standing Committee to force the Enterprise Law's return to the legislative agenda and to open debate. As the debate over the Enterprise Bankruptcy Law raged during the summer and autumn of 1986, increasing numbers of NPC Standing Committee delegates insisted that a series of supporting legislation must first be passed to provide the 'appropriate conditions' for bankruptcy.[91] At the top of this list stood the State Enterprises Law. Hence, a key part of the final deal which won the Bankruptcy Law's passage was a clause stating that it would only take effect three months after final passage of the State Enterprise Law.[92] In November 1986, faced with no choice,

---

87. Interview 27-22-13-33/TSE, Beijing, 29 March 1989.
88. One Finance Ministry source familiar with the law has speculated that the State Council was tired of seeing its policy assaulted in the NPC Standing Committee.
89. Interview with former Finance Ministry Staff Member, Detroit, January 1987.
90. *Shijie Jingji Daobao*, 21 December 1987, 3, in FBIS-CHI, 21 January 1988, 18.
91. I have labelled this group of anti-bankruptcy delegates the 'pragmatic opposition'.
92. Lian He, an SEC official, insinuates that before the NPC placed these conditions on the Bankruptcy Law, little thought was being given to moving the Enterprise Law towards passage in the near future. 'Because the Eighteenth Meeting of the Sixth NPC Standing Committee made implementation of the Bankruptcy Law contingent upon the passage of the Enterprise Law, this raised the problem of when to pass the Enterprise Law'. See Lian He (1988), 6. If this interpretation is correct, then it strongly suggests that the NPC Standing Committee successfully used legislative hostage-taking to force the State Council (and, perhaps, the Secretariat) to alter their agendas with respect to the Enterprise Law.

Yuan Baohua and the SEC finalized the current draft and re-submitted it to the Eighteenth Session of the Standing Committee for its first NPC debate in twenty-two months.[93]

Yuan Baohua's explanation of the law before the Standing Committee made clear that despite twelve major revisions, the draft's key points had changed little since the January 1985 session.[94] The manager responsibility system still formed the core of the draft, which still contained no clause on the role of the Party committee. This did not prevent Yuan from arguing, in an *obiter dictum*, that enterprise Party committees should follow the Central Committee's 1984 Decision, which meant confining themselves to supporting the manager in carrying out his powers, 'guaranteeing and supervising' the manager's work, and giving ideological and political leadership while strengthening leadership over the trade union and the communist youth league group in the factory.[95] Debate over the law at this Standing Committee session was limited, but criticisms were quite predictable, given that the draft had changed so little. Delegates again attacked the lack of a Party committee clause, and many called for the law more clearly to define the limits on the factory manager's powers.[96]

After the November 1986 session, NPC officials stepped up investigations and local opinion-soliciting trips concerning the Enterprise Law. Several NPC Vice-Chairmen and Standing Committee members carried out on-the-spot inspections of state-owned enterprises experimenting with the new management system. At the same time, views on the draft were sought from numerous Party and government departments and several state-owned enterprises.[97] But just as these investigations were getting under way, leadership politics forcefully intervened once again. Not only did Hu Yaobang's January 1987 ouster as Party General Secretary deprive the enterprise reformers of a key ally, the subsequent campaign against bourgeois liberalization gave Enterprise Law critics a golden opportunity to attack the reform. As Lu Mu, one of the law's chief chroniclers, has noted: 'When the ideological trend of bourgeois liberalization emerged in

---

93. *Renmin Ribao*, 16 November 1986, 1. The fact that this was the twelfth draft is noted by Zhang Sutang and He Ping (1988), 17–18.

94. The one significant change was the law's name, which had been changed again, from The State-Managed Enterprise Law (*Guoying Qiye Fa*) to the State-Owned Industrial Enterprise Law (*Quanmin Suoyouzhi Qiye Fa*). Yuan Baohua indicated that the new name was chosen because of the new relationship between enterprises and the government after economic reform. *Renmin Ribao*, 16 November 1986, 1. Although none of my sources commented on this, the title clearly seems to reflect the influence of Zhao Ziyang's advisors at SCRES, who argue that the right of factory ownership, which remained with the state, needed to be separated from the right to manage the factory. SCRES officials apparently hoped that they could leave open a window for greater management reforms by redefining the factories as 'state-owned' rather than 'state-managed'. 95. *Renmin Ribao*, 16 November 1986, 1.

96. Zhang Sutang and He Ping (1988), 18.

97. Zhang Sutang and He Ping (1988), 18; Lian He (1988), 6.

society, some people regarded the system of the factory manager assuming full responsibility as a specific expression of that liberalization'.[98]

It was amidst this radically changed political atmosphere that the NPC Standing Committee convened again in March.[99] NPC staffers report that the emotions of Enterprise Law critics were stoked by the campaign, and their attacks were more vocal than ever. Returning to an old theme, delegate Song Chengzhi argued that the law must endorse the Party committee's guiding role in ideology and Party affairs. Others went even further, attacking the current draft for failing to guarantee the socialist orientation of the enterprise. They wanted the law to stipulate that the Party committee should uphold the four cardinal principles, strengthen ideological and political work in the factory, and ensure the factory's socialist orientation. Indeed, based on the admittedly scanty public record of the debates, this session appeared to mark the high point of calls for strong, specific clauses defining the Party's role in factories.

An NPC staffer present at the meeting reports that the State Council, in particular the SEC, fought this proposal vigorously, and was not without allies on the Standing Committee.[100] Delegates Zhang Zhizhai and Wu Juetian countered that many Party secretaries had hamstrung implementation of the responsibility system, and codifying the Party committees' role in law would only make this worse. Other delegates argued that real Party leadership over enterprises lay in the Party's overall leadership of society, and should not be confused with Party committee leadership on the shop floor. The committee's leadership, they argued, was made clear enough in the 1984 Central Committee Decision. Between two-fifths and three-fifths of the Standing Committee members present favoured adding some clause defining the role and function of the Party committee, according to this same staffer.[101] Many simply refused to believe that either the 1984 Decision or the Constitution's endorsement of the four cardinal principles was sufficient to protect the Party's role in factories.

On the second major point of contention—the role and powers of the manager—Delegate Peng Qingyuan was one of several who argued that the manager should not be the ultimate decision-maker in the factory. These delegates favoured creation of a collective enterprise committee (*qiye*

---

98. Lu Mu (1988), 4.
99. The following discussion of the Twentieth Meeting of the Sixth NPC Standing Committee is based upon the following sources: Interview 12–32–17/34–19–28/ABE, Beijing, April 1989; Press Conference by NPC Spokesman Zeng Tao, BXDS, 24 March 1988, in FBIS-CHI, 24 March 1988, 16–18; NPC Press Conference, Beijing Television Service, in FBIS-CHI, 8 April 1987, K1–5; Zhang Sutang and He Ping (19??), 17–18; BXE, 5 February 1988, citing 'current issue' of *Liaowang* magazine (FBIS translation, personal copy); BXE, 13 March 1987, in FBIS-CHI, 17 March 1987, K19; 'Peng Zhen meets with Hong Kong, Macao Reporters', Beijing Television Service, 8 April 1987, in FBIS-CHI, 9 April 1987, K1–15.
100. Interview 12–32–17/34–19–28/ABE, May–June 1989.
101. Interview 12–32–17/34–19–28/ABE, Beijing, April 1989.

weiyuanhui) to make major decisions. But delegate Gu Gengyu and others disagreed, arguing that giving the manager overall responsibility was beneficial to the factory. Gu believed that enterprise committees, if they were established at all, should be limited simply to reviewing and discussing major decisions.

Prior to the session, NPC Law Committee Vice-Chairman Song Rufen canvassed numerous delegates and other officials to summarize the debate over managerial authority. After polling a large number of enterprise managers, Party committee secretaries and trade union leaders, Song and his staff distilled the debate into two alternative clauses, which he circulated before the session. The first stated: 'The director exercises unified leadership over enterprise management and operations, and carries out unified direction in production according to law. He should assume full responsibilities'. The second was more general, and allowed management far greater potential authority: 'The director is in the central position of the enterprise and assumes full responsibilities'.[102]

Not surprisingly, most of the managers preferred the second version of the law. Echoing the 1950s' advocates of one-man management, they argued that nothing could be accomplished if the factory had multiple centres of power. Party committee secretaries and trade union delegates, on the other hand, overwhelmingly preferred the first, more restrictive version. They argued that this adequately spelled out the essence of the responsibility system and gave the manager ample powers to run the factory. They feared the second formulation would give managers a pretext for expanding their powers well beyond production-oriented decisions. Some delegates flatly stated their fear that managers would abuse the law and try to take over leadership of the Party committee, the trade union and the communist youth league. In an adroit bit of argument, some Party secretaries and trade union officials turned the reformers' argument on its head, claiming that the second version would set back the reformers' goal of 'separating the Party from management' by giving managers too much power over the Party. Such managerial involvement in Party affairs would, they argued, dissipate the manager's energy which he would need to run the factory.[103]

Faced with a deeply divided Standing Committee, and sentiment running strongly against the current draft law, Peng Zhen opted for a procedural delay, which dealt the State Council and the SEC a serious setback. At Peng's suggestion, the NPC Committee Chairmen's Group decided not to submit the current draft to the forthcoming NPC Plenary Session for discussion and a vote. In discussing this decision, Vice-Chairman Chen

---

102. Zhang Sutang and He Ping (1988), 18. The major viewpoints on the law are also discussed in detail in Song Rufen (1994), Vol. 2, 47–51.
103. Zhang Sutang and He Ping (1988), 18; Song Rufen (1994), Vol. 2, 48–9.

The Case Of The State-owned Industrial Enterprises Law 191

Pixian noted, rather disingenuously, that after three years of reform experimentation, there was 'universal agreement' on the need for implementing the factory manager responsibility system. Nevertheless, Chen argued, many important questions needed to be worked out, and the views of more sides needed to be heard.[104]

Peng discussed the delay, and the politics behind it, during a wide-ranging televised NPC press conference. He was brimming with self-confidence and this press conference presented the high point in his promotion of himself and the role of the NPC.[105] At the same time, he carefully refuted press charges that he personally was behind the attack on the law:

Now there are people saying that the current NPC session has frozen the Enterprise Law and that the NPC is conservative. In addition, they consider me among the leaders of the conservatives. As a matter of fact, I consulted with Premier Zhao on this matter. Before the Chairmen's Office[106] decided on the matter, we had discussed it with Premier Zhao over the telephone. I told him that there were still many different points of view on the Enterprise Law, that there were only a few days left, and that it would be difficult to achieve a consensus on it. We cannot adopt a major law like this if we do not have a consensus of views. Our discussion concluded that the law should not be brought up at the current session. However, the NPC Standing Committee had decided to institute the system of plant directors assuming full responsibilities ... Regarding the law, we have agreed on a majority of the provisions. We decided to take up the few provisions on which there are differing views later, Isn't that what we stated in our news release? That was the view of our NPC Standing Committee.[107]

NPC Legislative Affairs Committee Vice-Chairman Wu Fuzhao added to the State Council's loss of face, announcing at another nationally televised NPC news conference that before the NPC could adopt the Enterprise Law, the management responsibility system would have to be carried out nation-wide, not just in local experiments.

But Zhao Ziyang, now the Party's Acting General Secretary after Hu Yaobang's dismissal, was not about to be deterred from his reform goals, even if the NPC would not acquiesce in passing the Enterprise Law. Faced

---

104. Zhang Sutang and He Ping (1988), 18.
105. 'Confident' is perhaps an understatement. In a performance which must have galled other senior leaders like Deng Xiaoping and Chen Yun, Peng frankly asserted that he had been offered a spot on the Politburo Standing Committee in 1982, but had turned it down because of his age. Indeed, less than a minute after noting that Deng and Chen were only two and three years younger than he (85), Peng stated that even if a spot on the Politburo Standing Committee were offered him, he would decline it. Peng asked rhetorically 'What can a man in his 80s do? Why not choose someone younger?' It seems probable that Peng's grandstanding performance contributed to his downfall only eight months later; a downfall which helped clear the way for the Enterprise Law. See the transcript of Peng's televised press conference, in FBIS-CHI, 9 April 1987, K12.
106. 'The Chairmen's Office'—that is, the NPC Committee Chairmen's Group.
107. FBIS-CHI, 9 April 1987, K12.

with ongoing conservative efforts to turn the anti-bourgeois liberalization campaign against the economic reform, Zhao apparently decided—as he had in 1981 and 1985—that the best way to promote his reforms was to retreat temporarily to his home court, which was now the CCP Secretariat. Between March and August, Zhao used the occasion of the forthcoming Thirteenth CCP Congress, scheduled for that autumn, as an opportunity to secure and promote a wide range of economic and political reforms, including management reforms. Echoing Hu Yaobang's 1984 strategy, Zhao temporarily ignored the NPC track, concentrating instead on enshrining his proposals in the Party Congress' Work Report, which he was in charge of drafting.

In April, Zhao's Secretariat organized a drafting group of nineteen advisors, including several reformist economists and officials of the State Committee for Restructuring the Economic System.[108] The report went through seven drafts in six months. According to an official account, Zhao took great care, throughout the process, to submit all major aspects of the report to Deng Xiaoping for his explicit prior approval. In particular, Deng and Zhao agreed in advance that despite the recent attacks on bourgeois liberalism, the report's main theme should be accelerated economic reform. Later, Zhao and his aides convened a series of meetings with other senior central and local leaders and intellectuals, all in an effort to build consensus behind the report.[109]

The Thirteenth Party Congress gave a major political boost to advocates of an aggressively reformist Enterprise Law.[110] Ten years later, Zhao's report still stands as one of the most radical visions of economic and political reform ever enshrined in a major CCP document, and it laid the ideological foundations for a wide-open, albeit short-lived, new round of reforms. According to Zhao's central thesis—that China was now in the 'initial stage of socialist development'—virtually any measures which added to social production could be considered ideologically acceptable.[111] The report called for immediate nation-wide implementation of the manager responsibility system, and, in a clear victory for the SCRES, endorsed separating the rights of ownership and the operation.[112] But perhaps the most radical of Zhao's proposals was a call for further weakening the role

---

108. For a surprisingly detailed official account of the drafting of the Thirteenth Party Congress report, see the report by ZGXWS, 4 November 1987, in FBIS-CHI, 6 November 1987, 11–14.   109. *Ibid.*

110. Lu Mu (1988), 4.   111. Zhao Ziyang (1987).

112. In the months leading up to the Congress, An Zhiwen—Zhao's chief deputy on the SCRES and a chief drafter of the Congress Report—vocally supported accelerated enterprise reform, separation of 'the two rights', and stringent limits on the impact of the anti-bourgeois liberalization campaign upon the economic reform. In fact, it is likely An was in part speaking for Zhao Ziyang in these matters. See, for example, An's article in the SCRES journal *Zhongguo Jingji Tizhi Gaige*, No. 8 (23 August 1987), 4–6, in FBIS-CHI, 9 September 1987, 17–20.

of Party committees over day-to-day work in factories and other institutions. Zhao even suggested that Party committees gradually be transferred out of some economic units entirely.[113]

A number of key personnel decisions announced at the Congress also eased the law's passage. Most importantly, Peng Zhen and several other senior leaders were not re-elected to their Politburo posts, and pre-Congress leadership meetings in the seaside resort of Beidaihe also decided that Peng should step down as NPC Standing Committee Chairman at the following spring's session.[114]

Shortly after the conclusion of the Congress, an important bureaucratic manoeuvre made it clear that Zhao and his allies had decided to seek quick passage of the Enterprise Law. A new, more reform-oriented three-man committee was established to work out a final compromise draft.[115] As before, Yuan Baohua headed the group. But now Yuan was joined by An Zhiwen, an advisor to Zhao's SCRES, and by NPC LAWC Vice-Chairman Song Rufen, Peng Zhen's long-standing personal aide. The new three-man group controlled which organizations, groups and individuals would be consulted in revising the law, and which views would be incorporated in the draft. But the Organization Department and the ACFTU, original members of the drafting group and the key critics of strengthening managers, were no longer drafting committee members, though they were still consulted.[116] ACFTU leaders were deeply disappointed by the blatant departure from the balanced triangle of forces which had worked on the law for eight years. Pressed on the point, one trade union source was unable to name any member of the new drafting group whom the ACFTU regarded as representing the interests of labour, not even Song Rufen, who in any case was politically weakened in the wake of the Party Congress.[117]

---

113. Zhao Ziyang (1987), 38.

114. Peng was forced to step down in particular disgrace. Unlike almost all of the other senior leaders who resigned at the Thirteenth Party Congress, Peng was not even rewarded with a sinecure post on the Party's Central Advisory Committee. Thus, with his resignation as NPC chief, Peng Zhen no longer held any official position in either the state or Party hierarchy for the first time since 1979, a humiliating blow to one of the CCP's three most senior leaders. We do not know the politics behind Peng's sudden removal so soon after he had publicly flirted with the idea of his possible membership on the Politburo Standing Committee. It is possible that Peng's manipulation (or at least tacit consent) of the NPC to attack reforms during the anti-bourgeois liberalization campaign, coupled with his blatant self promotion at the spring NPC session, had offended Deng and many other senior Party leaders, and put Peng beyond the pale. Hong Kong's *Chengming* magazine laid out one possible scenario, reporting that during the Beidaihe conferences, Deng and Zhao had made a deal with Chen Yun and other elders to remove the conservative Peng as NPC Chief, replacing him with the more radically reformist Wan Li. In return for assenting to Peng's ousting, Chen Yun allegedly insisted that conservative Party elder Wang Zhen be named State Vice-President. *Chengming*, No. 127 (1 May 1988), 6–9.

115. Lu Mu (1988), 4. The content of this report was largely confirmed and elaborated upon by interview 27–22–13–33/TSE, April 1989.   116. *Ibid.*

117. Interview 27–22–13–33/TSE, Beijing, 29 March 1989. The source did note ELRC Chief Gu Ming's personal participation in the three-man group's activities, in a manner which

By early January, the three-man committee had met with representatives of concerned agencies and groups and produced a new draft which was presented to the 9 January Plenary Meeting of the new Politburo for dicussion and a vote.[118] The new draft contained several victories for reformers. Over the objections of the ACFTU, the Organization Department and the majority of NPC Standing Committee members, the draft adopted the more pro-management of the two formulations on the managerial responsibility system which Song Rufen had put forward the previous January.[119] It also clearly subjugated the workers' right to participate in 'democratic management' to the authority of the manager,[120] and did not spell out clearly what 'democratic management' would mean in practice. The powers of both the trade union committee and the workers' and staff congress were mostly limited to making 'suggestions', and even for those few issues they were empowered to decide, such as disbursement of welfare funds and housing assignments, the draft did not clearly order managers to respect these decisions.[121]

The trade unions and the Organization Department did win one major victory, however, as a clause defining the role of the Party committee was reinserted for the first time since December 1984. It was brief, vague and double-edged, however, and left the Party committee with as many obligations as powers.[122] Nevertheless, the clause contained far stronger

strongly suggested that the unions at least regarded Gu as reasonable. Even if Song Rufen wished to use his position on the three-man group to slow or block some of the reforms, he nevertheless came to the table with a very weak political hand. The Thirteenth Party Congress Report had placed the Party stamp of approval on many of the ideas advocated by the SEC and SCRES, and the Congress had also decided to remove Song's patron from all of his posts. Song, as we have seen, had played a prominent role in dismantling the State Council's Bankruptcy Law draft just one year before. Moreover, between the November Party Congress and next NPC plenary session—scheduled for March 1988—the senior leaders were debating amongst themselves the other half of the personnel appointments announced at the Thirteenth Congress—the leading NPC and State Council personnel appointments which would be announced at the NPC plenum. Thus, as Song took part in the three-man group's deliberations, he could not help being keenly aware that his own reappointment to the NPC LAWC Vice-Chairmanship hung in the balance.

118. 'Law of the People's Republic of China on Enterprises Owned by the Whole People (Draft)', BXDS, 11 January 1988, in FBIS-CHI, 20 January 1988, 27–32, article 43.

119. According to article 43 of the draft: 'An enterprise shall institute a production and managerial system headed by the plant director. The plant director *shall assume the central role* in the enterprise, and he is legally responsible for the enterprise's operations in all areas.' *Ibid.*

120. Article 49 states that 'Workers' congresses and trade unions shall support the plant director in exercising his functions and powers . . . [and] . . . educate workers to work as owners of the enterprise, obey labour discipline and regulations, and fulfill production quotas or other assignments without fail.' *Ibid.*   121. *Ibid.*, article 48 and article 43, paragraph 5.

122. Article 7 states 'The basic organization of the Communist Party of China in an enterprise *guarantees and supervises* the implementation and specific policies of the Party

The Case Of The State-owned Industrial Enterprises Law 195

language than the SEC and the SCRES had been willing to support in the past.[123]

The Politburo approved the draft in principle at the January meeting.[124] It then took two unprecedented moves, one designed to underscore the democratic aspects of the legislative process and one which clearly undermined that democratic process. First, the Politburo decided that the NPC Standing Committee should publish the draft law in the open press, so that it could be debated throughout the country. Accordingly, the full text of the draft Enterprise Law was published in the 12 January issue of *Renmin Ribao* and several other major papers.[125] Secondly, the Politburo stepped up the pressure on the NPC leadership by publicizing—in advance of the NPC session—its decision to approve the law in principle. The tone of the press announcement was diplomatic and constitutionally correct. The Politburo noted its approval, and then 'suggested' that the State Council 'invite' the NPC Standing Committee to examine the draft. But the effect was clearly to signal to the NPC and to the public that this time, after one last brief round of debate in the NPC, the Enterprise Law would be voted on and passed.[126] Two days later, the NPC Committee Chairmen's Group 'decided' that the draft Enterprise Law should be published nationally for discussion.[127]

and state in that enterprise. *It supports the director in discharging his authority* according to law' (emphasis added). *Ibid.*, article 7. For the sake of consistency within this case study, I have changed the FBIS-CHI translation of the Chinese *baozheng jiandu* from 'ensures and oversees' to 'guarantees and supervises', which is more common in the other Chinese translations I have seen.

123. Interview 27-22-13-33/TSE, Beijing, 29 March 1989.

124. The actions of one senior leader before the 9 January meeting suggests that the law's passage was a foregone conclusion. Qiao Shi, a newly promoted Politburo Standing Committee member, and Chairman of the Political-Legal Leading Group, publicly anticipated the law's passage on the eve of the Politburo meeting, in an 8 January interview. Qiao endorsed the Enterprise Law, noting that 'it will free enterprises from impracticable, confused directions from administrative departments . . . it will surely be beneficial to deepening the reform inside enterprises'. BXE, 8 January 1988, in FBIS-CHI, 11 January 1988, 30; see also *Renmin Ribao*, 9 January 1988, 1. Yuan Baohua, speaking two days before the Politburo meeting at a 7 January management seminar also noted that the Enterprise Law would 'soon' be submitted to the NPC Standing Committee for approval. BXE, 7 January 1988, FBIS translation, personal copy, unpublished.

125. While draft laws circulate rather freely in Chinese legal circles as low-level internal (*neibu*) documents, a draft law had never before been published so widely for public perusal and debate. See the report in *Renmin Ribao*, 10 January 1988, 1; also Zhang Sutang, 7.

126. It is well known in Chinese legal circles that the Politburo must approve in principle the drafts of all basic laws before they may be passed by the NPC. But, in deference to the NPC's constitutional stature as the highest organ of state authority, the CCP Politburo has never previously given this level of publicity to its prior endorsement of a draft law. The effect was clearly to signal to the NPC and to the public that this time, after one last brief period of debate and revision, the Enterprise Law would be passed by the NPC. *Renmin Ribao*, 10 January 1988, 1.

127. An accompanying circular encouraged all provincial level people's governments and people's congresses to hold meetings to solicit the views of workers, managers, government department, academics and others on the draft law. *Renmin Ribao*, 12 January 1988, 1; Zhang Sutang, 7.

But when the NPC Standing Committee met a day later, many delegates were as firm as ever in their opposition to the 'excessive' managerial powers in the draft, notwithstanding the Politburo's approval and the acquiescence of the Committee Chairmen's Group. One Xinjiang delegate wanted the law to limit the manager's term of office. Also, in an apparent backdoor move to strengthen the Party committees, the same delegate called for a clause requiring enterprises to abide by the state Constitution, which affirms the Party's leading role in society. Other delegates suggested a clause explicitly stressing that fulfilling state-planned tasks was the enterprise's 'principal responsibility'.[128] Zhang Ruiying, one of the most influential trade union delegates on the NPC Standing Committee, criticized the draft's relatively weak role for unions, arguing that the union's role as the employees' representative needed to be clearer.[129]

But the draft was going forward despite these delegates' criticisms, and the session ultimately approved an agenda for the first Plenary Session of the Seventh NPC which called for discussion and debate on the law—another strong signal that the law would be voted on and passed.[130] Advocates of a pro-management Enterprise Law were apparently grateful for this pressure on the NPC, and tried to put a democratic face on this Standing Committee meeting, calling the session a 'major breakthrough in the delegates' understanding of reform and the law', despite the obvious high level pressure and overwhelming evidence from delegates' statements that many Standing Committee members continued to oppose the Politburo-approved draft.[131]

When the announcement of a public debate over the law made it clear that a major enterprise policy decision was imminent, policy advocates of every stripe, not just unions and managers, tried to seize on the law as a convenient vehicle to promote their views.[132] The Enterprise Law's extreme prominence and enormous potential scope as a policy document made it an irresistible political target. The response was enormous. Between January and April, advocates and critics of the law convened dozens of conferences and symposia, published scores of articles and speeches, all trying to get in on one of the best political games in town.

One late January symposium of managers and 'entrepreneurs', convened by the Chinese Academy of Social Sciences, called for major revisions to

---

128. Lu Mu (1988), 1; Zhang Sutang and He Ping (1988), 17–18.
129. *Renmin Ribao*, 15 January 1988, 2, and 16 January 1988, 2.
130. *Renmin Ribao*, 22 January 1988, 1.
131. For example, one State Economic Committee expert described the meeting this way: 'Unlike the three previous times, at the beginning of [1988], the Twenty-fourth Meeting of the NPC Standing Committee . . . brought up the bill for the fourth time made a fundamental conceptual breakthrough, it solved the problems at dispute, and deeply embodied the brand new spirit of reform'. Lian He (1988), 6; see a similar statement by Gu Ming (1988), 1.
132. In the language of the Garbage Can model, this imminent decision could be called a 'choice opportunity'.

The Case Of The State-owned Industrial Enterprises Law 197

strengthen radically managerial authority which would have rivalled even the Stalinist 'one-man management' system. Participants wanted to limit or even destroy the power of industrial bureaus, Party secretaries, trade unions and workers' congresses to intervene in factory affairs.[133] Some opposed the clause in the law that permitted the establishment of any collective decision-making structure which might dilute or rival the manager's power. Others wanted the workers' power of 'democratic management' divorced from the manager's power of 'decision-making'. Most wanted article 7 which called for Party committees to 'support' the manager's authority, taken out entirely, noting bitterly that the law provided no punishment for Party committees which failed to 'support' the manager. Likewise, they called for removing clauses which called on factories to promote 'socialist spiritual civilization', and revising others so that the enterprise's sole 'fundamental task' was 'making profits', rather than 'accumulating capital'. Finally, they called for guarantees of the factory's right to engage freely in foreign trade.

But while these managers saw the forthcoming decision on the law as an opportunity to promote further change, other groups with a stake in the current system saw the law's imminent passage as a serious threat. The ACFTU in particular bitterly attacked the Politburo-approved draft. Trade union officials indicated that despite being consulted on the new draft by the three-man group, their views were not respected, and they found the resulting draft completely unacceptable. ACFTU Senior Legal Advisor Guan Huai immediately labelled the draft a 'factory manager's law', and called for major revisions.[134] From that point, the ACFTU began lobbying quite publicly to revise the law, seeking help from their allies in the NPC.[135]

Ironically, many radical reformers, including some of the ACFTU's strongest political adversaries, were also unhappy with the draft. Many SCRES officials, whose proposed reforms still lay well outside the reform 'mainstream' of that time, worried that swift passage of such a major enterprise policy document, especially one with the purported stability of a law, might freeze reforms at their current state and preclude future change. They preferred, for the foreseeable future, that enterprise issues be addressed by a more 'fluid' process, which would permit greater flexibility to adopt more far-reaching reforms. SCRES Vice-Minister Gao Shangquan wanted the draft to spell out more clearly the separation of ownership and management rights, make further cuts in state industrial bureaus' powers, and expand further enterprises' powers to control and

---

133. *Guangming Ribao*, 11 February 1988, 3.
134. Guan Huai's views and position are noted in Guan Huai (1988). The ACFTU's reaction is discussed in *Beijing Review*, 13–26 February 1989, 31; also interview 27–22–13–33/TSE, Beijing, 29 March 1989.
135. Interview 27–22–13–33/TSE, Beijing, 29 March 1989.

dispose of their own funds and properties without state interference.[136] Participants at a mid-December 1987 Enterprise Law conference in Beijing neatly summarized the radical reformers dilemma between reform and legal codification:

> The current reforms have touched a series of problems of more penetrating proportions, such as how the governments and administrative organs will separate ownership from the power to readjust and control, and administrative powers from property rights... An Enterprise Law must not necessarily be completely identical with reality. What counts in this regard is to see whether it lags behind or anticipates the times.[137]

Finally, in a classic case of Garbage Can model politics, many other groups whose broader agendas were less directly or even tangentially related to enterprise management issues nevertheless tried to take advantage of the public debate to promote their views. The All-China Women's Federation, representing huge numbers of female factory workers, wanted the law revised to support these workers' rights. They noted instances in which factories seeking higher profits had restricted female workers' pay, and infringed upon their maternity, health care and vacation rights.[138] Minority nationality officials wanted the law to contain articles which would ensure the rights of minority peoples and give these regions protection and preference in establishing and running state enterprises.[139]

To sort out this cacophony of public debate and determine which views would receive a hearing, the three-man draft revision group and the organizations they represented (the SEC, the SCRES and the NPC LAWC) convened a series of six meetings. The format was textbook corporatism. Selected representatives of the key groups and organizations whose interests were affected by the law were invited to take part. Within the norms of consensus-building politics, the three chairing organizations had the power to choose which interests would be consulted and who would represent them.[140] At one meeting, the three-man group heard the views of ten prominent legal specialists. At another, ten economists gave their reactions. The other meetings included the managers of about a dozen of China's most important state-owned factories, specialists from the major concerned industrial ministries, several leading factory Party committee

---

136. See Gao's comments in *China Daily*, 11 March 1988, 4. See also the remarks by SCRES official Yin Guanghua at an Enterprise Law forum, in *Renmin Ribao*, 9 February 1988, 2, in FBIS-CHI, 25 February 1988, 25–9.

137. *Shijie Jingji Daobao*, 27 December 1987, 13, in FBIS-CHI, 21 January 1988, 17–20. Participants at the conference included representatives from the Legislation Bureau, the NPC Legislative Affairs Committee, CASS, the Beijing University of Foreign Economic Relations and Trade, Peking University and 'several factories'.

138. BXE, 28 January 1988, in FBIS-CHI, 29 January 1988, 26.

139. Lu Mu (1988), 1.

140. The fit between this particular stage of the policy-making process and classic definitions of corporatism is particularly striking. See Schmitter (1974).

secretaries (selected by the CCP Organization Department) and trade union representatives (selected by the ACFTU).[141] The Legislative Affairs Work Committee assembled suggested revisions from these sessions and other sources (such as the CASS 'entrepreneurs' meeting described earlier) and drafted proposed revisions to the law.[142] During this two-month period of public debate, the NPC LAWC reportedly received over 1,800 suggestions, and the law went through ten additional drafts.[143]

In late March, the CCP convened the Second Plenum of the Thirteenth Central Committee in preparation for the Seventh NPC, and officially concluded the personnel battles over the new state leadership which began the previous summer.[144] As expected, Peng Zhen, Chen Pixian and several other senior NPC leaders lost their posts. Hong Kong press sources indicate that Peng Zhen was particularly angry at losing his NPC Standing Committee Chairman's job to Wan Li, and vowed to hold on to his power up to the end.[145]

The Second Plenum sent very mixed signals to Party-member NPC delegates concerning the tone and policy direction the Politburo wanted to see at the NPC. On the one hand, the leadership encouraged a wide-open highly 'democratic' session. For the first time ever, the Party leadership approved a list of candidates for the NPC Standing Committee election in which the number of candidates (145) exceeded the number of seats on the committee (136). Zhao Ziyang's report to the plenum, moreover, invited open debate and press coverage at the NPC meeting, and called for accelerated economic and political reforms.[146]

On the other hand, the Party leadership tried to place some stringent limits on this democracy. While the Politburo permitted multiple candidates for the Standing Committee election, it permitted no choice in elections for the core of the NPC leadership, the members of the Committee Chairmen's Group (including the Standing Committee Chairman, Vice-Chairman and Secretary General). Also, while Zhao's publicized address to

141. Interview 27-22-13-33/TSE, Beijing, 29 March 1989. The meetings were also alluded to in BXDS, 5 March 1988, in FBIS-CHI, 7 March 1988, 55. My sources did not provide me with a complete list of the factory managers or Party secretaries invited to the meeting (in itself a fascinating question of access and representation), but did note that the managers of the Anshan, Baoshan, and Shoudu Iron and Steel Works were all invited.
142. *Renmin Ribao*, 6 March 1988, 1, in FBIS-CHI, 7 March 1988, 55–6.
143. See the article by Marlowe Hood in the *South China Morning Post* 25 March 1988, 7.
144. The Congress session also announced other significant, though lower level personnel changes, including the selection of economist Jiang Ping as a new Vice-Chairman of the key NPC Law Committee. Jiang strongly advocated a wide variety of enterprise reforms, including the full management responsibility system, separation of management and ownership rights, as well as complementary reforms in China's political structure and its pricing, planning, monetary and investment systems, plus the implementation of the Bankruptcy Law. On the NPC Standing Committee Meetings, see *Wen Wei Po* (Hong Kong), 8 March 1988, 2, in FBIS-CHI, 9 March 1988, 16; also BXE, 8 March 1988, in FBIS-CHI, 9 March 1988, 14–15.
145. *Chengming* (Hong Kong), 1 April 1988, 6–9, in FBIS-CHI, 1 April 1988, 42.
146. See Zhao's report to the plenum reported in *Renmin Ribao*, 21 March 1988, 1.

200 The Politics of Lawmaking in Post-Mao China

the plenum had encouraged open debate and press coverage, privately, he reportedly directed Party-member NPC delegates, about 66% of all delegates, to adhere to Party discipline in casting their votes.[147] Finally, merely by choosing to deliver publicly an economic policy *tour d'horizon* at a Party plenum so soon before the NPC, Zhao inevitably upstaged the NPC somewhat, and undermined his own calls for 'separating the Party and the government'.

But the NPC delegates seem to have heard only the first half of Zhao's message, and the Seventh NPC produced perhaps the most open debate and the toughest criticisms in that body's history, certainly tougher than any Party leader, reformist or conservative, appears to have anticipated or desired.[148] Delegates attacked conservative obstruction of reforms, but also turned their ire on several of Zhao's most cherished economic reforms, in particular price reform. Ultimately they forced removal or watering down of several proposals in Acting Premier Li Peng's Government Work Report. Many representatives criticized NPC Secretary General Peng Chong from the floor, charging him with undemocratic constitutional and procedural irregularities.[149] Delegates also attacked one conservative, 89-year-old NPC Vice-Chairman—whom the Politburo nominated for yet another five-year term—arguing that someone younger should be chosen for the post to allow the elder Vice-Chairman 'a good rest'.[150]

Amidst this mood of mild uprising, general debate on the Enterprise Law began at the 31 March session, with outgoing SEC Chairman Lu Dong formally summarizing the law to the delegates. Lu stressed three strong points of the draft, but avoided discussion of management responsibility:

- First, the draft explicitly endorsed separating the right of enterprise ownership and management, and allowed experimentation with enterprise contracting and leasing.

147. According to Hong Kong press sources, Zhao's Second Plenum instructions were: 'The Party-member people's deputies must keep in line with the principles of the Party. There must not be any discrepancy between the votes they cast and the decisions of the Party.' *Ching Pao (The Mirror)* (Hong Kong), No. 129 (10 April 1988), 34–8, in FBIS-CHI, 19 April 1988, 39–44.

148. The presence of several brutally frank NPC delegates from Hong Kong and even Taiwan, as well as an unprecedentedly large Chinese and foreign press contingent certainly encouraged delegates to be more outspoken in their criticisms. Two excellent reports on the atmospherics of the NPC session are China News Analysis (Hong Kong), No. 1360 (15 May 1988); and U.S. Foreign Broadcast Information Service, 'China's National People's Congress Session: Reform Amid Controversy', Analysis Report No. FB 88-10007, 10 June 1988, 2–4, 23–9.

149. Peng arrogated powers of the NPC Plenary Session to the NPC Standing Committee. He also refused to allow delegates to vote separately on each of the nominees for the NPC special committees, insisting instead that delegates cast one vote only—either up or down—for an entire list of candidates for each of the committees.

150. The besieged Vice-Chairman was Zhou Gucheng, who chaired the NPC Standing Committee's Committee on Education, Science, Culture, and Health. See Foreign Broadcast Information Service, 'Analysis Report: China's National People's Congress Session: Reform Amid Controversy', Report FB 88-10007, 10 June 1988, 2–6.

- Secondly, Lu argued that the draft made very strong provision for democratic management by allowing the establishment of 'enterprise management committees' on which staff and workers congress representatives would sit.
- Thirdly, the law made state control less direct by separating the government from the enterprise.[151]

But when the floor opened to debate, the draft again came under considerable attack for allegedly granting excessive power to managers. Also, a wide variety of interests—regional, sectoral and professional—continued using the debate to promote their separate agendas, or to seek special favours and exemptions from the law's provisions.

Both management and labour representatives attacked the draft, trying to wring out additional concessions. At a meeting of the Sichuan provincial delegation, for example, one state enterprise manager attacked the law as too restrictive, calling it a 'leash' on managers. Several worker delegates shot back, however, that the law did not sufficiently recognize the status of workers as 'masters' of the factory, or spell out workers' rights of 'democratic management'. A jurist on the delegation tried to pour oil on the troubled waters, pointing out that since the Enterprise Law was a broad, 'basic law', it could not contain everything, nor spell out all matters in minute detail.[152]

On 2 April, the reformist mayors of the Shenzhen, Zhuhai and Shantou Special Economic Zones (SEZs) held a press conference in which they asked that their zones receive special treatment while implementing the Enterprise Law. The mayors considered the current draft too conservative, and worried that it might restrict ongoing reforms in their SEZs. In particular, they wanted to protect from possible prosecution risk-taking entrepreneurs whose enterprises lost money. The mayors also wanted the rewards for successful managers to be spelled out just as clearly as the punishments for unsuccessful managers. Finally, they wanted the NPC to resolve an ambiguity between clauses 30 and 37 in the law, which left unclear whether the factory or 'state law' would govern the amounts of wages and bonuses managers could hand out.[153]

National minority delegations also sought special dispensations. A group of Tibetan delegates, for example, wanted the law amended so that minority regions could implement it in line with their specific local conditions. They argued, in particular, that state-owned enterprises in their area should be freer to hire, fire, sign contracts and import and export products than enterprises in the rest of China.[154]

151. *Renmin Ribao*, 1 April 1988, 2.
152. BXDS, 2 April 1988, in FBIS-CHI, 6 April 1988, 22.
153. BXE, 2 April 1988, in FBIS-CHI, 4 April 1988, 35–6.
154. BXE, 4 April 1988, in FBIS-CHI, 5 April 1988, 13.

At the 3 April plenary session, Law Committee Vice-Chairman and reform economist Jiang Ping tried to rebut these cricitisms. Jiang also endorsed 'separating the two rights' of enterprise ownership and management, and stressed the importance of protecting the enterprise's independent operation as well as its responsibility for profit and loss.[155]

At this point, the doors closed and the law disappeared into a fortnight of murky high-level deliberation. On 4 and 5 April, Wang Hanbin and the Law Committee met to compile and summarize the proposals for amending the law, which generally ran against many of the key reforms. This meeting crafted a revised draft and turned it over for discussion and debate by executive members of the NPC Presidium (that is, the members of the Committee Chairmen's Group).[156] About a week later, Wan Li, Peng Zhen's successor as NPC Standing Committee Chairman, chaired a meeting of principal NPC leaders and several of the law's key proponents and critics.[157] At this meeting, advocates of a strongly reformist Enterprise Law, facing continued stiff opposition within the NPC and anxious to avoid further loss of face, apparently decided to cut their losses by accepting a considerable weakening of the law. These concessions secured, the meeting ironed out the final language of the draft, and decided to submit it to the 13 April closing plenary session for a vote, without any additional debate.

A comparison of the final draft and the 11 January draft reveals dramatically that the ACFTU and the Organization Department, backed up by stiff resistance from within the NPC Standing Committee, won several major victories.[158] First, with respect to Party committees, the key compromise clause, which made the Party committee responsible for 'guaranteeing and supervising the implementation of Party and state policies' (article 7), survived intact despite continued opposition by the SEC, SCRES and several powerful state factory managers. Moreover, the second half of article 7, which obliged the Party committee to 'support the director in discharging his legal authority', was removed from the final draft.

The new law still preserved many important new managerial powers. But the factory balance of power was considerably confused by several other new amendments which granted a variety of new, ill-defined or nominal

---

155. BXE, 4 April 1988, in FBIS-CHI, 5 April 1988, 13.
156. BXDS, 9 April 1988, in FBIS-CHI, 12 April 1988, 28–9.
157. Unfortunately, my source on these deliberations provided few details, and could not name the participants at this meeting nor indicate how many people took part, other than to suggest that the meeting was not large. The source also did not believe the law was formally resubmitted to the Politburo, but refused to rule out the possibility that individual Party leaders—apart from Wan Li—were consulted on the final compromise draft.
158. The 9 January draft is translated in FBIS-CHI, 11 January 1988, 27–32. The final draft was translated in FBIS-CHI, 23 April 1988, 26.

powers to the trade unions and workers. The law also granted workers a good deal more protection from potential predations by factory managers.

- A new clause obliged the state to 'ensure that the staff and workers enjoy the status of the masters, and the lawful rights and interests of staff and workers shall be protected by law' (article 9).
- Another new clause, required the manager to 'rely on the staff and workers' and 'support the work' of their congress in fulfilling enterprise obligations. Most important, the law now required managers to 'implement the legal decisions of the staff and workers' congress' (article 46).
- The final draft dropped a clause from the January draft—offensive to workers' congresses and trade unions—requiring that these organs 'shall *support the plant director in exercising his functions and powers*' (article 49). In its place, the new law stressed that 'staff and workers . . . shall have the right to participate in its democratic management' (article 49).
- Another new clause also required that even in those factories where government organs appointed the manager, 'the opinions of staff and workers shall be solicited' (article 44).
- In a key organizational victory for the ACFTU, the revised law greatly solidified the official trade union's power over workers and the staff and worker's congress: 'The trade union . . . shall represent and safeguard the interests of the staff and workers and conduct its work independently according to law. The trade union in the enterprise shall organize the staff and workers for participation in democratic management and democratic supervision' (article 11).' The trade union committee of the enterprise shall be responsible for the daily work of the staff and workers' congress' (article 51).

Moreover, while the draft law gave managers the right to 'reward and punish workers in accordance with law', it still did not explicitly guarantee managers the right to sack workers if their work was not satisfactory.

The NPC Presidium's decision to issue the final draft suddenly on the last morning of the Congress and move it to an almost immediate vote surprised and angered delegates, who up to this point had revelled in the Congress' openness. One delegate appealed for more time to examine the law, complaining that he had only seen the final changes on the morning of the vote. When his request fell on deaf ears, the delegate complained to Western reporters that the government was 'bulldozing' the law through the NPC. Nevertheless, the vast majority of delegates chose to go along with the NPC leadership. The State-Owned Industrial Enterprises Law was adopted the same afternoon, with only eleven abstentions and two 'no' votes, one of which was cast by a Hong Kong trade unionist.[159]

159. *South China Morning Post* (Hong Kong), 14 April 1988, 7.

From Passage to Explication

The next battle, over the explication of the law, would help determine just what it would mean as practical policy, or indeed, whether it would ever even transcend 'symbolic politics' and become practical policy. *People's Daily* made the first effort at 'spin control', in a 16 April 'commentator' article which tried almost desperately to put a good face on the defeats at the NPC session.[160] The paper sought to undercut critics of the earlier 9 January draft by selectively interpreting the law, emphasizing those aspects of it which strengthened factory managers and limited state intervention in the enterprise.[161] The article closed by suggesting that the fight would continue, and calling upon government offices to formulate implementing regulations and auxiliary laws quickly to ensure the law's 'successful' implementation.

In truth, the State Council Legislation Bureau had fired the first shot in the implementation battle long before the law was even adopted. During one plenary session, Bureau Director Sun Wanzhong bluntly underscored his office's responsibility for drafting the implementing regulations, noting that over a dozen sets of regulations for implementing the law would be drafted during the next year. Some, indeed, were being drafted even before the law was finalized.

Sun's remarks revealed clearly the Bureau's own strongly reformist agenda and its preferred interpretation of the law, which would further strengthen managers at the expense of industrial bureaus and Party committees. The implementing regulations would, according to Sun, stress several more radical reform experiments, including enterprise shareholding, contracting and leasing. They would also promote full managerial responsibility, and ban 'superior units' . . . extortion' against enterprises. Sun argued that the January draft had already given 'enough care . . . to the Party committee's role', implying his opposition to further legal protection for the Party committee's power. Indeed, Sun bluntly stated his belief that Party leadership over the manager simply would not work. The

---

160. Commentator, 'Conscientiously Implement the "Enterprise Law",' *Renmin Ribao*, 16 April 1988, 1, in FBIS-CHI, 19 April 1988, 51–2. Such *People's Daily* articles merit close attention because they are routinely issued to lower levels along with new laws as 'reference materials'.

161. 'The soul of the Enterprise Law lies in . . . "separating the two kinds of rights" . . . namely, proprietary rights and management rights . . . competent departments must no longer excessively stress proprietary rights for the purpose of flagrantly interfering in enterprise affairs . . . "Within . . . the enterprise, it is imperative to separate the functions of the Party from those of the government, for the purpose of ensuring that the enterprise director holds a central position and plays a key role . . ." Having the staff members and workers participate in democratic management of enterprises will *primarily provide strong support for enterprise directors* and will *secondarily enable staff and workers to play a supervisory role* as well as a role in imposing restrictions' (emphasis added). *Renmin Ribao*, 16 April 1988, 1, in FBIS-CHI, 19 April 1988, 51–2.

Bureau Director, in short, made it quite clear that the battle over the Enterprise Law's content would not end with NPC passage, and he hoped his bureau would have the last word on the law's meaning as practical policy.[162]

The Legislation Bureau immediately began organizing to draft implementing regulations and companion laws, convening a multi-day conference in June and inviting representatives of the State Council's various economic ministries. The NPC LAWC also attended, but principally as discussants and observers, not drafters. But the meeting quickly bogged down. A published report indicates 'there was disagreement among conference delegates on how to separate management and ownership functions'.[163] The key issue, according to my interviews, was how and how much to restrain industrial ministries from interfering in enterprise affairs. Many departments were quite protective of their powers over their factories, and were not enthusiastic to take part in drafting implementing regulations. One Legislation Bureau source involved in the meeting lamented that he did not believe further progress was possible without stronger intervention by the central leadership to implement the law.[164] The slow cycle of drafting the Enterprise Law had apparently started all over again.

162. Information on this meeting comes from two major sources: State Council Legislation Bureau Research Office, 'Yiding Yao Jianli Juyou Zhongguo Tese de Qiye Zhidu' ('We Must Definitely Establish an Enterprise System with Chinese Characteristics'), *Fazhi Ribao*, 11 July 1988, 2; also interview 15–35–19/CSW, 19 March 1989, Beijing.   163. *Ibid.*
164. Interview 15–35–19/DBJ, June 1989.

PART IV
Conclusions

9

Stages And Processes In Chinese Lawmaking[1]

A Serious, Multi-stage, Multi-arena Process

The institutional analyses and case studies in this book make it very clear that over the last nineteen years, China's lawmaking system has developed into a serious, politically sophisticated process which can no longer be thought of as a unified, top-down policy-making system. By any comparative standard it is still a 'weak legislature' system. A great deal of the contents of a law are hammered out in processes led by the State Council. Still, the major changes in content which the laws studied here underwent at the hands of the NPC make it quite clear that the phrase 'rubber stamp' is no longer defensible as a description either of lawmaking in China or the NPC. The NPC has developed an impressive array of resources and strategies for influencing lawmaking.

Lawmaking is now better thought of as a 'multi-stage, multi-arena' process. The process of drafting a law actually comprises five relatively distinct stages: agenda setting, inter-agency review, top leadership decision-making, NPC debate and explication/implementation.[2] Recalling the policy-process models discussed in Chapter 2, the case study data make clear that no one of these models adequately describes all stages of the process. Instead, as a law progresses through these stages, it moves among China's three major 'arenas' of lawmaking institutions: the State Council, the Party Central Apparatus and the NPC (the expanding influence of the Supreme People's Court, as noted, also requires much more research). Each stage appears to be characterized by its own typical set of organizational and individual actors, its own typical process style, and its own characteristic 'biases' which can affect the content of policy. Policy-making at each stage corresponds quite closely to one particular model of the process, or to some characteristic mixture of these models. During the stage of inter-agency review, for example, the key actors are ministries

---

1. I am deeply indebted to the participants in the May 1994 *China Quarterly* conference on Law in China for their comments on earlier versions of this chapter, in particular Pitman B. Potter and the conference organizer, David Shambaugh.
2. As I noted in the first chapter, a detailed review of the actual implementation of law as policy is an extremely important issue. To discuss this stage of the process with care would require an enormous amount of on-the-ground research which is beyond the modest scope of this study. My lack of data on this stage, together with the lack of detailed data on top-level decision-making constitute two of the most serious shortcomings in this study.

and other bureaucracies pursuing some vision of their organizational 'mission', and the pattern of the process closely matches the Organizational Politics model with its bias towards slow, incremental policy change. The politics of this stage are centred overwhelmingly within the State Council system.

At the same time, one should not put too fine an edge on these stages. They merge into each other, with one stage beginning before the previous one has ended. For example, the case studies indicate that the politics of agenda-setting often correspond to the fluid image evoked by the Garbage Can model. And yet, the end of this stage is strongly flavoured by the politics of the following stage—the highly bureaucratic process of inter-agency consensus-building. Thus, a key process in the latter part of the agenda-setting stage is the 'marrying' of policy proposals to specific strong bureaucratic patrons, if they lack such a patron already. These organizational patrons have the staying power and political weight to see the proposal through the long inter-agency review. In the latter stages of inter-agency review, in turn, the process opens to a wider array of actors as 'opinion solicitation drafts' are submitted for more public discussion before the law goes on to the NPC.

Unfortunately, the data in these case studies do not provide enough solid information to support much discussion of the top leadership's internal decision-making processes beyond those conclusions already presented in the individual case studies. Accordingly, this chapter does not discuss this stage in great detail. The data do no more than sketch out an image of top-level decision-making: an image of sporadic intervention and vague, heavily staff-assisted involvement by most Party Central leaders. Those Central leaders who have been responsible for lawmaking in general (such as Peng Zhen, Qiao Shi, Wan Li, Chen Pixian, Peng Chong, Wang Hanbin and Tian Jiyun) and those policy specialists who are responsible for the particular issue area under discussion, will occasionally intervene strongly in the process.[3] The case studies do suggest that there is a good deal less control or micromanagement of lawmaking by the top leadership than has often been assumed in studies of the Chinese legal system. Still, the lack of a clearer understanding of leadership decision-making processes is clearly a major, if unavoidable, weakness of this study.

With that disclaimer, this chapter now turns to a discussion of the politics and policy-making processes which characterized each of the four remaining stages of the lawmaking process as reflected in the case studies.

---

3. For example, during the drafting of the laws in the case studies, Zhao Ziyang, Yao Yilin and Gu Mu were among the major policy specialists in industrial economics who intervened in drafting these two laws.

Agenda-setting

In defining China's active legislative agenda at any given time, it is important to distinguish between the hundreds of available legislative proposals ('policy solutions') swirling through the system, and the few dozen draft laws which are actually receiving serious consideration from top legislative officials. In general, a legislative proposal has clearly found a spot on the lawmaking agenda when the State Council Legislation Bureau[4] or the NPC Legislative Affairs Work Committee are giving it their sustained attention. A higher stage on the agenda is reached when the State Council or the NPC Standing Committee officially approves a drafting group for the law. When the law is included on the Legislation Bureau's or the LAWC's annual legislative plan, it has probably reached the most active stage, and inclusion suggests a serious effort is under way to finalize and promulgate the law within the next twelve to eighteen months.

Since 1978, the processes by which legislative proposals break out of the pack to win a place on this overcrowded agenda have been opened to a far greater variety of political actors. For even though some actors' policy proposals are undeniably far 'more equal than others', it is now the case that new ideas can sometimes emerge from anywhere: top leaders, career organizational bureaucrats, think-tanks and even individual entrepreneurs. That no one type of actor has a monopoly over the generation of new ideas in the legislative 'stream' is underscored by the recent passage of draft laws championed by such radically unequal actors as the self-styled policy entrepreneur Cao Siyuan, the conscientious Stalinist administrator Yuan Baohua and China's pre-eminent leader Deng Xiaoping.

Some internal data on Chinese legislative planning during the early reform era provide a rare glimpse into which types of actors tend to fare best in getting their proposals on the legislative agenda. Table 9.1 reports data from the (now defunct) State Council Economic Legislation Research Centre's 1982–86 Five-Year Economic Legislative Plan (published internally in 1983).[5] The plan contained 146 laws to be drafted and promulgated over the ensuing five years, approximately half by the NPC or its Standing Committee, and half by the State Council. For each law, the plan listed the organization or actor which formally put forward the drafting proposal to the NPC or State Council.

Naturally, these data must be read with great caution. Clearly, since they are internal, they have the advantage of being much franker on some key issues of influence (for example, they note that several laws were put

---

4. Or, in the past, the Economic Legislation Research Centre.
5. '1982–1986 Nian Jingji Lifa Guihua (Cao'an)' ('1982–86 Economic Legislation Plan [Draft]'), in State Council Economic Legislation Research Centre, *Jingji Fagui Yanjiu Ziliao* (*Research Materials on Economic Legislation*), approximate date early 1983, 3–16.

forward by Central Party leaders, a fact which is rarely noted in open-source data). On the other hand, they are still rather formal and constitutionally precise. According to Chinese constitutional law, for example, only certain state organs and groups of legislators may officially propose legislation (*ti'an*). And so, these data generally indicate only the organization which officially sponsored these laws, not any original, informal sources, such as provincial governments, think-tanks, trade unions and other mass organizations, teams of specialists, or individual entrepreneurs. For example, if the Bankruptcy Law had been available for the legislative agenda at the time this plan was drawn up, it would have been listed on this plan as having been officially put forward by either the TERC or by Wen Yuankai and several NPC Standing Committee delegates, not by its true promoter, Cao Siyuan. Consequently, the data probably overstate the agenda-setting influence of high-ranking leaders and Central Party and state organs. Moreover, since the mid-1980s, greater access has been extended to other lower level actors. Still, even with these important caveats, these data provide a fascinating look into the process.

Unquestionably, the most striking finding in the data is the very small percentage of legislative proposals which are put forward by Central Leading Comrades, less than 11% by the most generous count. In fact, however, this concurs with information from interviews with Chinese officials, who indicate that top CCP and government leaders are more of a background presence at this stage. The political jockeying and personal manoeuvring among the most senior leaders, who are motivated as much by political concerns as by any notion of problem solving, does indeed do much to define politically which key problems are ripe for attention at any given time. Leadership moods and balances of power, moreover, constantly define and redefine the limits of acceptable policy proposals, as well as the system's general receptivity to radical new policy departures. But clearly, policy-related thinking at this rarified level of the system is often extremely vague, and all available evidence indicates that top level leaders do not, as has often been supposed, directly initiate or dictate many legislative proposals.

Instead, data on lawmaking seem to confirm recent findings by other scholars that agenda-setting is characterized by a good deal of 'competitive persuasion' by the senior policy advisors to top leaders.[6] Top leaders appear to depend heavily upon their key advisors and their advisors' subordinates to generate and screen policy options for them, and to feed them other policy-relevant information such as feasibility studies, results from local 'testpoint' policy experiments and the views voiced at 'opinion-solicitation meetings'. The top leaders may only very vaguely understand the policy options which are presented to them.

6. The phrase 'competitive persuasion' is Nina P. Halpern's. See Halpern (1992), 126.

Stages And Processes In Chinese Lawmaking 213

TABLE 9.1 The legislative agenda

Source of legislative proposals as formally put forward in Five-Year Economic Legislative Plan (1982–86), by type of actor	Number of laws (plan total: 146)	Percentage of total
'Central Leading Comrade'	2	1.37
'Central Leading Comrade', State Council Ministry and NPC Delegate	1	0.68
'Central Leading Comrade' and State Council Ministry	2	1.37
'Central Leading Comrade' and NPC Delegate(s)	8	5.48
The State Council	17	11.64
'State Council Leading Comrade'	2	1.37
State Council Ministry (one or more, includes PBOC).	80	54.79
(of which, Ministry of Finance = 16 laws, or 10.46%)		
State Council Ministry and State Corporation	1	0.68
NPC Delegate(s)	22	15.07
NPC Delegate(s) and State Council Ministry(-ies)	6	4.11
NPC Standing Committee and State Council Ministry	1	0.68
Chinese People's Political Consultative Congress	4	2.74
Total	146	100.00

Relative involvement by State Council, NPC, and central actors

All categories involving State Council/State Council Ministry	108	73.97
All categories involving NPC Standing Committee or Delegates	38	26.03
All categories involving 'Central (or State Council) Leading Comrade'	15	10.27

Promulgating bodies

State Council	76	52.05
NPC Plenary Session	17	11.64
NPC Standing Committee	53	36.30

Occasionally, in fact, legislative proposals can almost literally be 'slipped in' by key advisors, and the top leaders may lend their powerful public endorsements to them without fully appreciating the import of the proposals initiated in their names. The State-Owned Industrial Enterprise Law provides a startling example. As noted in Chapter 8, the law first found its place on the agenda when Deng Xiaoping called for the drafting of a 'factory law' in his 1978 Third Plenum speech. Following Deng's endorsement, Yuan Baohua and the State Enterprise Commission began an unrelenting ten-year struggle to draft and pass the law. But how did Deng, untrained in law, come by the idea? According to a former high-ranking Chinese advisor who helped write the official published version of his speech, these specific law proposals were added after the fact by the three-man speech drafting group, and were left in by Deng and his senior advisors when the speech was published.

Major organizational actors such as the State Council and its ministries clearly account for the lion's share of these legislative proposals, between 65 and 74% in this plan.[7] Central-level Party and State Council bureaucracies (and also, presumably, provincial-level Party Committees and governments) have the resources to help focus the system's attention on what they consider 'key' problems. Their large policy staffs can also draft ready-made legislative proposals and keep them 'alive' internally for years, decades even, until they sense that the political mood is ripe for them to emerge or re-emerge on the active agenda.

It is also interesting to note the rather high percentage of legislation which was proposed by NPC and NPC Standing Committee delegates at this time. This is especially surprising because in 1983 the NPC had only begun its internal bureaucratic development (see Chapter 5), and lacked the kind of organizational and subcommittee infrastructure upon which it now relies for much of its legislative drafting work.

The increasing fluidity of agenda-setting politics is reflected in the growing number of available paths which successful entrepreneurs may use in promoting their preferred legislative proposals onto the agenda. At least three major patterns of entrepreneurship can be discerned. The 'traditional bureaucratic' path for a draft law, probably the most common if the above statistical data are any indication, is dominated by organizational patrons, such as senior policy experts in ministries, bureaus or provinces. These organizational patrons promote policy solutions which are heavily influenced by their respective organizational ideologies or missions. Yuan Baohua's low-key, low-publicity, but persistent ten-year promotion of the State-Owned Industrial Enterprises Law exemplifies this pattern. The classic Central planning official, Yuan used the power of the SEC to heighten and focus the leadership's concern on declining enterprise management efficiency. But he did not try to go outside of the normal, in-house State Council policy review systems, and preferred low publicity, low confrontation, low risk strategies for promoting the law over a decade.

In a second, 'dialectical' pattern, a draft law retains a constant place on the agenda as a result of the ongoing struggle of ideological enemies. In recent years, numerous laws have emerged or re-emerged on the agenda because two or more political actors with widely divergent, even mutually exclusive, views have all felt an interest in keeping them there. In such cases,

---

7. Of course, the high percentage of State Council sponsored legislation also reflects the subject of the plan: economic legislation, traditionally the State Council's bailiwick.

the law may go forward even without a single predominant organizational backer with enough influence to push it. Judy Polumbaum's excellent study of the development of the Chinese press law provides a dramatic example of a law which was persistently kept on the agenda by this sort of ideologically contradictory 'coalition'.[8] For several years, as many as three different groups in Beijing were pushing their own preferred drafts of a press law for China. All these drafts differed greatly on the key issue of whether the law should give greater protection to press freedom or place tighter limits on that freedom. Since, at any given time, either one side or another in this ideologically charged battle was usually on the political ascendance, the idea of drafting some kind of press law survived very well without having to be linked to one specific organizational patron, policy proposal, or even one particular draft.

Similar examples of a 'protect or restrict' battle sustaining a law on the agenda include the 1988 State Secrets Law and the 1989 Public Demonstrations Law.[9] Before the 4 June 1989 Massacre, many of China's more liberal political elements favoured a public demonstrations law which protected the public's right to peaceful protest, and a state secrets law which clarified and narrowed the range of secrecy in government. The Bureau for the Protection of State Secrets had to yield some ground on the secrecy issue when drafting its law. After Tiananmen, however, the Ministry of Public Security tried to seize on the changed political mood and pass a much more restrictive public demonstrations law than many NPC delegates had previously advocated.

During the mid-1980s, an apparently rare but still fascinating third path on to the legislative agenda began opening up for 'bureaucratic outsiders'—intellectuals and other policy advocates lacking strong, stable organizational or leadership bases. Major legislative innovations were developed and kept alive, often in newly developed policy think-tanks, and then promoted when the political mood and power balance seemed ripe for radical policy change. The hallmarks of this type of high profile, high risk entrepreneurship include careful packaging of policy proposals, dogged promotion and lobbying, adept use of publications and other mass media, and aggressive building of support coalitions both inside and outside the Beijing bureaucracy.

As shown in Chapter 7, Cao Siyuan and the Bankruptcy Law best

---

8. Polumbaum (1990).

9. On the debate over the State Secrets Law, see *China Daily*, 12 January 1988, 1; BXE, 15 Janaury 1988 in FBIS-CHI, 19 January 1988, 16; BXDS, 15 January 1988, in FBIS-CHI, 22 January 1988, 8–9; *China Daily*, 2 September 1988, 3; and '"Baomi Fa" Jin Qi Shishi' ('"Secrets Protection Law" Takes Effect Today'), *Remin Ribao*, 1 May 1989, 2. On the 1989 Public Demonstrations Law, see Polumbaum (1991); and Liu Chunhe (1990), especially 93–105. Also: BXE, 3 July 1989, in FBIS-CHI, 3 July 1989, 38–9; BXDS, 6 July 1989, in FBIS-CHI, 10 July 1989, 33–6; BXE, 30 October 1989, in FBIS-CHI, 31 October 1989, 13–14; and *Renmin Ribao*, 1 November 1989, 2.

symbolize this new style. After first conceiving the idea in 1980, Cao incessantly promoted the heretical proposal for six years, constantly repackaging it and marketing it as a 'cure-all' for whatever policy problems most concerned the organizations to whom he presented it. Seeking an organizational sponsor for the law, Cao marketed bankruptcy to the state insurance companies, then to the People's Bank of China and various industrial policy think-tanks. He repeatedly endured having the door slammed in his face, never ceasing to repackage and promote his bankruptcy proposal. Cao's persistence paid off when, in 1983–84, China's leadership was desperately searching for new, even radical solutions to the problem of state enterprise losses, and Cao had an idea ready to promote. Cao and his allies then made clever use of China's only recently re-opened mass media to build support for the idea and pull off at least a partial victory over the bureaucracy in the inter-agency review process.

In the end, Cao was every bit as successful in getting his law on the agenda as were Yuan Baohua, the Ministry of Public Security, and the other entrepreneurs looked at above, but at a dramatically higher cost and risk. Cao's highly publicized lobbying activities upset more than a few senior policy makers, earning him the famous double-edged moniker 'Cao Pochan' (Bankrupt[cy] Cao), a nickname suggesting not only his close personal association with the policy, but also a strong element of derision. Cao's public embrace of controversial policies and unwillingness to confine himself to a secure power base set him up for severe risks in case of failure. He was jailed for his high profile involvement in the 1989 Democracy Movement, and served a year. Yuan Baohua, by contrast, retired from the State Economic Committee to an honoured position at China's People's University.

All this suggests that there may be a relationship between the types of laws which finally win a place on the legislative agenda, and the paths or strategies by which they succeed. Although the high-profile new strategies of Cao Siyuan and his colleagues entail great risk to the entrepreneurs, it is not at all clear that the traditional quiet, bureaucratic strategy could ever have succeeded in promoting so radical an initiative as the Bankruptcy Law. By contrast, the Enterprise Law, and the Factory Manager Responsibility System (FMRS) which formed its base, had deep historical bureaucratic roots which dated back to China's Soviet period of the early 1950s; roots which made it easier to promote the policy within that sector of the Party-state which still bears Stalinism's strongest imprint, the State Council.[10] It seems a fair bet that the long-taboo bankruptcy law proposal, lacking any similar historical bureaucratic power base, would have died quietly in

---

10. On the history of enterprise management policy, see Andors (1977); also Donnithorne (1967); Lee Lai To (1986); and Schurmann (1968), ch. 4.

inter-ministerial review had its supporters not resorted to going outside the system to attract support through the reformist wing of the official press.[11]

Ideologically charged bills which reach the agenda through 'contradictory coalitions' can often keep a place on the agenda, but face a different kind of potential risk. Since these laws usually involve a confrontation between 'liberalizing' and 'hardline' forces, there are almost always multiple, highly opposed drafts of the law circulating at any given time. As shown above, sudden tilts in the political balance of power, such as occurred after June 1989, invariably tempt one side or the other to strike, and seek swift, unilateral advantage by passing one or another extreme version of the law 'while the iron is hot'. Such laws will invariably be counter-attacked if the opposition returns to power. The obvious losers are compromise, long-term legal stability and broad respect for the law.

Inter-agency Consensus-Building

A discernible change in process marks the transition between the stages of agenda-setting and inter-agency review. As a draft law receives attention from ever-higher levels of the system, moving towards formation of a formal drafting group or inclusion on the annual plan, the politics of the process gradually shift towards the more closed, incremental and bureaucracy-dominated politics of the inter-agency review process. From this point, it seems to be increasingly difficult for a draft to advance steadily without a clearly identified, dedicated and politically weighty patron—either a Central leader or a major Central-level organization. Conversely, after this point, it becomes increasingly difficult politically for an organizational patron to back away from the proposal. Hence, if 'outside' entrepreneurs like Cao Siyuan have not already 'married off' their legislative proposal to a major organizational patron, the pressure rapidly mounts for them to do so. For example, by the time the Bankruptcy Law was included on the 1986 Legislative Plan and presented to the NPC Standing Committee, Cao Siyuan's individual lobbying—so crucial in the early stages—no longer seems to have been a major factor in propelling the law forward. The State Economic Commission and its boldly reformist Vice-Minister Zhang Yanning had clearly taken on the role of the law's major organizational patron.

As noted, no stage of the lawmaking process is better described by one

---

11. Leadership intervention also appears to be important to such innovative departures. At several key junctures in drafting the Bankruptcy Law, when the law appeared to be stalled, the logjam was only broken by the strong intervention of Central leaders (notably Zhao Ziyang), or by a major swing in the balance of leadership politics, as occurred after the passage of the October 1984 Decision on Restructuring the Economic System.

Western policy-process model than inter-agency review is by the Organizational Politics model. The State Council usually becomes the dominant arena, Central departments and ministries are now the key actors, and the process downshifts from the swift and dexterous jockeying of competitive entrepreneurship to the slow, muddy trudge of bargaining and consensus-building. Just as the organizational politics theorists would predict, legal policy changes at this stage are largely incremental, with a constant danger of inter-ministerial stalemate or the watering down of a once-bold policy. Just as American legislative scholars commonly speak of a piece of legislation 'dying in Congressional committee', Chinese legislative scholars may speak of a draft law 'dying' in the State Council. Some of the most important forces for breaking these deadlocks are political crises, major shifts in leadership politics and strong-armed interventions by top leaders—precisely those forces whose impact on politics 'law' was supposed to mitigate.

On the other hand, the lion's share of the major deals and compromises concerning the contents of most laws appear to be made during this lugubrious phase. Owing to the prolonged period of negotiation, the drafts which emerge from inter-agency review tend to have enormous bureaucratic weight. Consequently, far fewer changes are made in the later, more open phase of 'opinion solicitation'.

Ministerial Interests, Bargaining Motivations and Tactics

The organizational politics theorists are also correct in stressing the important role which ministerial 'missions' or interests play in structuring organizational bargaining positions and tactics at this stage. But as ministries enter into bargaining over a draft law, their conceptions of their interests are shaped by a wide variety of factors in addition to their assigned tasks or 'missions'. The various strategies for pursuing a mission can be shaped by higher or lower risk tolerance, fear of losing face, or simply a desire to shepherd carefully one's potential resources for important policy battles to come. Consequently, the goals, resources and pay-offs for which these agencies bargain can be quite varied.

Many bureaucratic strategies are shaped by the ambiguous status and special characteristics of law as a policy-making vehicle—its formalism, symbolism, and purported stability and universality.[12] Given the strong historical orientation towards separate sector-by-sector administration in China, the prospect of making policy through a law which purports to universal applicability creates special fears amongst ministry bureaucrats. With tenacious defensiveness, many ministries bargain to block the adop-

---

12. I am indebted to Pitman B. Potter for his suggestions on this issue.

tion of any law or clause which might give other units a pretext for encroaching on their powers, resources or policy 'turf'. Thus, as Pitman Potter's research has shown, a law such as the Administrative Litigation Law is greatly feared by many bureaucrats, since it could potentially grant courts and other bureaucratic 'outsiders' the authority to intervene in a massive range of previously in-house ministerial activities.[13] Consequently, many agencies will trade public support for the larger draft law, even one they oppose, in return for a special exemption for their agency from the law's worst effects. These exemptions, which frequently contradict the overall thrust of the law, represent a major obstacle to expanding legal universality in China.[14]

Risk avoidance motivates many other ministries' bargaining behaviour, as they try to avoid being left to bear the uncertainties of an untested policy innovation. Sometimes ministries are willing to forego potentially important benefits in order to avoid such risks or public loss of face. One striking example of this fear was the People's Bank of China's refusal to support the Bankruptcy Law, in spite of the potential gains which the bank—China's leading creditor—might receive from increased leverage over money-losing enterprises. The PBOC feared, instead, that bankruptcy proceedings might make clear the embarrassing unsoundness of its lending practices.[15]

Ministries' pursuit of their missions and interests is not incessant and mechanistic in the manner of a wind-up toy or a pit bull, and many show considerable sophistication about shepherding their political resources, especially in the early stages, when it is still unclear if a draft will get very far through the process. Ministries sometimes appear to alter their expenditure of political capital in response to major shifts in the leadership balance of power. Rather than an acquiescence to explicit orders from above, this appears to be a case of the 'law of anticipated reactions', in which ministries are unwilling to press a fight which they anticipate could anger the central leadership.

Access and Consensus-building

In contrast to the late Maoist period, when the drafting of key policy documents was marked by bitter struggles to maintain secrecy and limit

---

13. Potter (1994a), especially 270–1, 274–5.
14. In the early stages of drafting the Bankruptcy Law, for example, several organizations, including the Ministries of Foreign Economic Relations and Trade, Light Industry, and Public Security, and the People's Liberation Army, were extremely concerned lest the law subject some of their less efficient factories to closure. A confidential report on the law as it was submitted to the State Council indicated that exemptions from the law would be granted to the notoriously unprofitable PLA 'Third Line' industries and to Public Security firearms factories, which had limited, sporadic and hence unprofitable product runs (see Chapter 7).
15. Interview with Chinese financial official, 1987.

potential rivals' access to the process, the lawmaking process now seems to be influenced by a strong norm of incorporating all or most of the major concerned parties during the early stages of drafting.[16] The State Council Legislation Bureau is the key mediator of access. Nevertheless, since the Bureau's principal task is to resolve as many inter-agency legislative disputes as possible before they clog up State Council meetings, it has a strong interest in hearing all major views early on.

Inter-agency review begins with a prolonged period of limited, defined participation by the principal concerned departments. Only much later does access expand gradually in ever-wider concentric circles, incorporating more Central departments, localities and other less-directly concerned groups and units. Since considerable redundancy is built into this multi-level consultative process, any organization which has access to the early stages can be quite confident that it will have several other opportunities to influence the draft later on.

The last phase of inter-agency review—the period of broader 'opinion solicitation'—is often much more frantic than the earlier periods of bureaucratic 'tugging and hauling'. Just before a draft law is handed over to the State Council or the Party Centre for decision, the process expands still further to consult selected mass groups, localities and basic level units (such as factories and other workplaces). Advocates and opponents of a law try to marshal their evidence, set up highly publicized meetings among like-minded mass groups, and conduct public opinion polls (often of questionable methodological calibre), all in order to build sympathetic public opinion, and sway the views of the State Council, Politburo and other Central leaders.

Even though most decisions on a given law's content have already been made by this point, the opinion-solicitation period is still fairly advantageous for those groups which feel they have been ignored or cut out of the earlier discussions. Opinion-solicitation is not simply for show, and case study evidence suggests that these meetings do indirectly influence the content of the legislation. Nevertheless, the deck is heavily stacked against those groups which are shut out of earlier negotiations.

Breaking the Bureaucratic Deadlock

One of the most important factors helping many draft laws break through the bureaucratic deadlock and move ahead in the process is the backing of a powerful, obsessively-interested Central patron who is willing to intervene forcefully, even autocratically, to speed the progress of drafting. This represents more than a mild irony, since one of Deng Xiaoping's strongest

---

16. On policy-making in the late Mao era, see Lieberthal *et al.* (1978).

justifications for building up China's legal system was that lawmaking would limit Mao-like arbitrary intervention in policy-making.[17] Relatedly, major shifts in the leadership political mood or balance of power can also drastically alter the pace of legal drafting work. For proponents of a law, however, this can be a double-edged sword, since such shifts are just as likely to stop a once promising bill dead in its tracks as they are to break a deadlock. In recent years, the December 1978 and October 1984 CCP Central Committee Plenary Sessions, the 1987 Anti-Bourgeois Liberalization Campaign, the 1987 Thirteenth CCP Congress, the June 1989 crackdown and Deng Xiaoping's winter 1991–92 Southern Trip have all dramatically affected the pace and progress of a wide variety of legislation.

As the system has moved towards more empirical policy-making, the success or failure of local experiments with a draft law have become an ever more powerful force in inter-ministerial negotiations. The success which the cities of Shenyang and Wuhan encountered in implementing their own bankruptcy regulations during 1985–86 appears to have eased Central-level fears about the possible effects of a bankruptcy law. The Enterprise Law, on the other hand, presents a more complicated case. The initial success of the Factory Manager Responsibility System in increasing productivity in some areas during late 1984 encouraged support for the more strongly reformist versions of the Enterprise Law. But later on, abuses of power by some managers experimenting with the system gave strong ammunition to those in Beijing—especially NPC Standing Committee members—who wanted the law to protect the rights and powers of enterprise Party secretaries and/or labour unions as a check against excessive managerial power.

Finally, foreign pressure has helped break a number of inter-agency legislative deadlocks by forcing agencies to reach quick consensus. Often this external pressure can greatly strengthen domestic advocates of a law, and they discreetly welcome it. In the summer of 1992, a high-ranking NPC staffer expressed gratitude for post-Tiananmen American pressure to enhance China's intellectual property protection regime, saying this pressure had been essential to his office in overcoming longstanding objections to strengthening the Copyright and Patent Laws, especially in the highly controversial area of pharmaceutical protection.

NPC Review and Debate

The most significant change in the lawmaking process since 1979 is unquestionably that the stage of NPC debate and review is no longer a perfunctory approval or a simple public show of 'socialist democracy'. Now, thanks to the activism of the senior Party officials serving in the legislature,

17. Deng Xiaoping (1984), 157–8.

few laws (except international treaties) pass through NPC review without substantive amendment, and many have their contents significantly altered.

None of this is meant to deny that by any comparative standard the NPC is a weak legislature, with tremendous limits placed upon those who would use it as a forum to influence policy. Initiative, as shown above, rests primarily with the State Council. Moreover, if a bill receives approval in principle by the Party Centre, it still requires some boldness for NPC delegates directly to oppose passing the law in some form. Consequently, while the NPC has repeatedly tabled or urged reconsideration of draft laws, only twice has it flatly voted down a law introduced by the State Council or the Party Centre (it has also voted down some major government-sponsored amendments to draft laws).[18] The NPC also cannot approve or promulgate any basic law, constitutional amendment or any major piece of political, economic or administrative legislation without prior Politburo approval, although, as shown in Chapter 4, it may now enjoy such authority concerning a few laws outside these special spheres thanks to Central Document 8.

For most laws, NPC review begins when the Committee Chairmen's Group refers the draft to one or more of the Standing Committee's eight special committees (*zhuanmen weiyuanhui*). These issue-based committees, staffed primarily with former high-ranking Party and state policy specialists on the issues under each particular committee's provenance, provide the NPC with a good deal of policy expertise and the bureaucratic connections necessary for it to review meaningfully and amend draft legislation. While more research needs to be done on these committees' exact relationship to their 'opposite number' ministries, the evidence is clear that they are not just reflexive allies or 'agents' of their members' former departments (see Chapter 5). Official special committee recommendations for revising draft legislation, published in the NPC Bulletin (*gongbao*), routinely suggest major revisions which represent setbacks for the drafting ministries. According to high-ranking NPC sources, drafting ministries now frequently face their stiffest opposition precisely from those special committee members who formerly served in their department, and who can now use their unique knowledge of ministry interests to block what they see as excessive power grabs. Upon recommendations of the appropriate special committees, the Standing Committee Party Group (acting through the Committee Chairmen's Group) determines when to list the draft for debate by either the Standing Committee or the full NPC. Again, rapidly evolving practices mean it is now quite common for the Standing Committee to discuss and revise a law twice or more before it votes on final passage.

When a draft encounters serious opposition in the NPC, the strong preference of NPC leaders is to spare the drafting department the embar-

18. Zhang Sutang and He Ping (1988).

rassment of a significant public display of 'no' votes. This usually means the NPC withholds the law from a vote while insisting on significant revisions. One such NPC bureaucratic victory was the draft Labour Law of 1984–85, submitted by the State Council and the Ministry of Labour and Personnel. According to NPC sources, the draft as submitted reflected none of the major reforms then envisaged for China's labour system. Legislative Affairs Work Committee staffers, feeling the bill was nowhere near ready for passage, rejected the State Council's request to place it on the agenda of the next NPC, and returned it to the Ministry for extensive revision.[19]

Sometimes, efforts by NPC delegates or leaders to debate a law simply represent an effort at a public referendum over a controversial policy proposal which otherwise might not get any sort of public hearing. NPC delegates have developed impressive legislative skills in forcing open policy debates through various means, including delaying tactics, tabling a draft, 'salami tactics' and manipulating a law's place on the NPC agenda. Chapters 7 and 8 illustrated one fascinating influence strategy, legislative 'hostage-taking', which was used in 1986–87 to force a reopening of the debate on the State Enterprise Law and the Factory Manager Responsibility System (FMRS). After a bitter NPC debate on the law in spring 1985, the State Council implemented the controversial FMRS on its own for almost two years under its temporary legislation authority. But in November 1986, the NPC made the State Council ransom its prized Bankruptcy Law by conditioning its implementation upon NPC approval of the Enterprise Law. Over the next sixteen months, the Enterprise Law was subjected to NPC debate and revision four more times.

The Bankruptcy Law case also illustrates that NPC officials and delegates, by requiring a debate in the NPC's more open—and often more hostile—arena, have often been able to focus widespread opposition to a law, especially amongst the large number of Party elders in the Standing Committee. By mobilizing such publicity and embarrassment, the NPC has sometimes even helped prevent a policy's implementation. When the Bankruptcy Law was first referred to the NPC in spring 1986, it had won widespread leadership and organizational support, and many objections of key constituencies had been met through careful amendment. Nevertheless, the widely televised and bitter criticisms levelled by many delegates ultimately made broad implementation of the law politically untenable when it came into effect two years later.

Critics of NPC 'obstructionism' have also charged it with deliberate use of 'legislative perfectionism' (*lifa qiuquan zhuyi*) as a delaying tactic. In numerous cases, critics allege, NPC officials have insisted on delaying a controversial reform law until 'all social conditions are ripe' or until a

---

19. Interview 26–17–13–33/TWS, Beijing, August 1992.

'relatively perfect' draft has been worked out.[20] Another variant on this tactic is to insist that a law first be implemented experimentally in a few areas for a long time in order to 'gain experience' before it may be implemented nation-wide. By slowing down a law, opponents can sometimes create the conditions to undermine its passage and implementation, or defer the battle into the indefinite future in the hope that the political climate may become inhospitable to the law. In the cyclical politics of China's reform era, opponents of a law know that delay can often be tantamount to victory.

NPC debate also provides more fertile ground for legislative entrepreneurship and the exploitation of 'decision opportunities'. When a major law has reached the final stages of NPC debate and its passage appears imminent, an array of groups may try to use it as a vehicle to promote their pet policy proposals, regardless of their intrinsic relevance to the original law. In spring 1988, when the draft State Enterprise Law had been submitted to the NPC for public discussion, many groups, including women's associations, Tibetans and other ethnic minorities, and local officials seized the opportunity, proposing numerous 'rider'-style amendments to the law, many of which were at best marginally related to its substance.

Finally, assertive opposition during NPC debates sometimes has a strong 'feedback' effect on the previous stage of the process (inter-agency review) by revitalizing and stiffening the resistance of some parties to the inter-ministerial negotiations. When many Standing Committee delegates levelled surprisingly acrimonious criticisms of the Enterprise Law during January 1985, for example, this re-invigorated Organization Department and trade union insistence on a clause defining the role of Enterprise Party Committees—insistence which they had dropped in the wake of the 1984 Third Plenum.[21]

Thus, it can be seen that since 1978, NPC delegates have shown a growing willingness to vote 'no' to a draft law. Much more often, however, delegates and officials have resorted to a range of sophisticated and effective legislative influence strategies short of the bolder, riskier step of actually voting a law down. This increased NPC activism has sometimes provoked reaction by the State Council or Secretariat. Particularly under Hu Yaobang and Zhao Ziyang, these organizations occasionally tried to take these policy issues out of the legislative system by drafting them as State Council administrative regulations or as CCP policy documents. This

---

20. I am indebted to a recent Beijing University law graduate, Yao Yixin, for the phrase 'legislative perfectionism' and for introducing me to Chinese materials which complain of the problem.

21. Interviewee 27–22–13–33/TSE, Beijing, 29 March 1989, an official who was involved in drafting the Enterprise Law, indicates that the Trade Unions and the CCP Organization Department, which had temporarily dropped their efforts to insert protections for Party and union officials in the bill, became heartened and revived their efforts with a vengeance after seeing the strength of the spring 1985 NPC opposition.

reaction to NPC activism highlights both the NPC's increased potential for influence and the political obstacles involved in trying to define and establish a stronger role for the NPC. Quite predictably, the NPC under Standing Committee Chairmen Wan Li and Qiao Shi has responded by pushing for expanded oversight of State Council legislative planning and implementation.

Drafting of Implementing Regulations and Implementation

As with Chinese policy-making in other areas, the formal adoption of a law hardly signals the end of the policy-making process. Rather, what little is known about the implementation stage of lawmaking suggests that it involves an entire 'second campaign'.[22] This time, the key actors will rejoin the battle to define how the provisions of the newly promulgated law will be interpreted and carried out, if at all. Sadly, although the last decade of research on Chinese policy-making has revealed a great deal about the general problems of implementation, there are virtually no on-the-ground studies of legal implementation. Donald Clarke's recent work on the adjudication of civil cases, a rare and excellent exception to this rule, seems to confirm the general suspicion that legal implementation, while no means completely non-existent, remains very weak and hamstrung by still-weak institutions with limited political and budgetary resources.[23]

The drafting of implementing regulations, the essential first step in actually implementing a law as policy, involves turning a law into a clearer set of guidelines which may then be communicated to lower levels. At the national level, power at this stage usually seems to revert to the State Council and the Party Centre, in particular the State Council Legislation Bureau. Despite the Bureau's claims to the contrary, my own research makes clear that it is not at all above using this stage of the process to alter the content of the original law as it was passed by the NPC.

The Bureau's dominance has not gone completely unchallenged, however. As William C. Jones' recent work on the 1987 General Principles of the Civil Law indicates, its major future rival for control over implementing regulations may be the Supreme People's Court rather than the NPC.[24] The Court's 'Opinion' on the Civil Code seems intended to serve much the same function as the Bureau's implementing regulations usually do.[25] The Court now also issues volumes containing thousands of 'example cases'

---

22. I am indebted to Stanley Lubman for this point and this apt phrase.
23. Clarke (1995).   24. Jones (1994).
25. The Court has in recent years shown more assertiveness and independence in explicating the law than in adjudicating cases based on the law. This appears to reflect the influence of Soviet training on many of its judges and staff. I am indebted to Whitmore Gray for this insight.

suggesting how laws should be interpreted and implemented. NPC officials and staff feel they still have very little influence over this final crucial stage of the process, and some regard it as the Achilles heel of NPC efforts to influence policy.

In recent years, the NPC leadership has begun to explore at least two avenues to expand its now weak influence over the implementation of laws. First, NPC officials have argued that the NPC needs to expand its oversight capacity (*jiandu*) to help it monitor State Council policy implementation, and to enable the NPC to lobby the State Council to implement laws according to its liking.[26] Secondly, the NPC has recently shown a willingness to assign the authority for drafting implementing regulations to other organizations, such as the Court, whose policy views are more in line with the NPC leadership. According to one Supreme Court staffer, during the spring 1989 debate over the Administrative Litigation Law, the NPC leadership tried to steer this authority towards the Court and away from the State Council, which had tried to undermine many efforts to impose outside legal controls on ministerial activities and administrative discretion.[27]

Conclusions

The specific conclusions of this chapter concerning the stages of the lawmaking process, the politics of the process at each stage and the general impact of these processes on policy are summarized in Table 9.2. The main conclusion is that the major changes in China's policy-making system over the last nineteen years have had an especially strong impact on lawmaking. As a result, there are now stages of the lawmaking process which are a good deal more hospitable to relatively innovative policy ideas, and are more accessible to a wide variety of non-bureaucratic groups and interests, than the Organizational Politics model might lead one to suspect. The strengthening of the NPC review stage, moreover, provides a limited 'second chance' for those groups and policy ideas which do not enjoy strong support in the State Council and the Party Centre. In certain important ways, the lawmaking system is now a good deal better suited to producing the type of innovative legal infrastructure needed to support more market-oriented economic reforms. On the other hand, certain stages of the process are now far more accessible to those groups in society who fear the risks of such reforms.

26. 'Zhuajin Lifa Gongzuo, Jiaqiang Falu Jiandu' ('Grasp Firmly Legislative Work, Strengthen Legal Oversight'), *Fazhi Ribao*, 22 March 1989, 3.
27. Interview with Supreme People's Court staffer, May 1989. The source's information is supported by a comparison of the final version of the law (published in *Fazhi Ribao*, 11 April 1989, 1) and the 24 January 1989 draft version (see 'Zhonghua Renmin Gongheguo Xingzheng Susong Fa [Cao'an]').

TABLE 9.2 Stages and processes in lawmaking

Stages	Actors	Processes and strategies	Effect on policy content
1. Agenda-setting	1. Leaders constantly redefining policital mood, balances of power, key problems, range of acceptable solutions. 2. Advisors/organizations compete to provide information on problems, relevance, feasibility availability of policy proposals. 3. Proposals may come from anywhere: permanent bureaucracy think-tanks, sometimes individual entrepreneurs (even foreigners).	1. Fluid, entrepreneurial policies bringing streams (problems, policies, moods) together. 2. 'Competitive persuasion', 'packaging', 'salesmanship'. Later, 'marrying' patrons to proposals.	1. Fluctuating, but relatively hospitable to policy innovation, reforms.
2. Inter-agency review	1. Ministries, committees, bureaus, think-tanks, CCP Central departments, provinces motivated by 'missions' and interests. 2. Periodic top leadership intervention (to break up logjams).	1. Repeated rounds of internal review and negotiations. Trading support for concessions and exemptions. 2. Motivations: 'turf' battles; 'missions'; risk avoidance; saving face; ideological concerns. 3. Agencies 'manage' political resources, assessing likelihood of proposal's passage, level of leadership support. 4. Gradually widening circle of access, from 'most concerned' to 'less concerned'.	1. Major determinant of final content. 2. Slow, incremental changes; frequent logjams and stalemate.

TABLE 9.2 (continued)

Stages	Actors	Processes and strategies	Effect on policy content
3. Top leadership decision-making	N/A	N/A	N/A
4. NPC review	1. NPC top leadership. 2. NPC Standing Committee staff. 3. Standing Committee and plenum delegates, plus incorporated interests (localities, trade unions, women's federation, minorities, etc.)	1. Top leadership: personal manoeuvring, manipulation of laws; lawmaking as symbolic struggle or search for a 'role', a conduit for personal power. 2. Staff: very modest but increasing involvement in inter-agency review. Growing independence from ministries' resources. 3. NPC leadership and delegates (Standing Committee and plenum): Some entrepreneurship and opportunism—handing proposals on available legislation.	1. Direct rejection of laws still very rare. 2. Moderate, sometimes significant effect on content—can undermine previous inter-agency consensus and deals. May slow/delay law's implementation. 3. Anti-economic reform bias(?). 4. Sometimes sparks State Council 'counter-attack' attempting to take issue out of law-making system.

		Use NPC to force 'public referendum' on key issues; media manipulation, creating image of widespread support or opposition to draft law. Bargaining: trade ratification, legitimacy of law for concessions on content, exemptions, amendments, prior passage of other laws. Tactics include: 'hostage-taking', 'salami tactics', 'perfectionism'.	
5. Explication	1. State Council Legislation Bureau, principal concerned agencies. 2. Supreme People's Court. 3. Little NPC involvement.	1. Selective interpretation, implementation of NPC ratified draft. 2. Recent, weak NPC efforts to expand involvement in explication and oversight of implementation.	1. Uncertain. Often restores earlier (pre-NPC review) inter-agency consensus.

At the same time, the two stages which probably have the greatest impact on the content of a law as policy—inter-agency review and the drafting of implementing regulations—are still dominated by state bureaucracies, especially the State Council, its Legislation Bureau and ministries. The NPC leadership in particular seems well aware of this. In its two major institutional growth plans it has targeted these stages and hopes to expand its ability to compete with the State Council by further developing its bureaucracy and subcommittees, and strengthening its oversight mechanisms. But the speed at which NPC (and Supreme Court) influence expands will be most strongly conditioned by several factors largely outside their control, including their budgetary and resource allotments, leadership attitudes towards conflictual or consultative policy-making, the continuing power of cultural attitudes towards 'law' versus 'administration', and the pace of the erosion of CCP power over the system.

10
Lawmaking Reforms and China's Democratic Prospects

Overview

Up to now, this book has taken a rather fine-grained view of Chinese lawmaking, focusing tightly on the political mechanics of the process. This chapter returns to the issues raised in Chapter 2, asking what impact the evolution of the lawmaking system and the legislature during the Deng Xiaoping era may have on China's prospects for political democratization as the nation embarks on the post-Deng Xiaoping era. Several forces attending this transition make it very likely that China's legislature will also undergo further dramatic changes, probably within the next couple of years. Historically, Leninist leadership successions have almost always been destabilizing; but Deng's death opens the door for new debates over several potentially millennial questions of Chinese governance which will affect far more than just the role of the legislature. The 'short list' of these questions would include: China's national unity, decentralization or possible division; the future of Leninism; the role of civil society and the state–society relationship in economics, law and social control; and the role of the military in politics. Obviously, the future development of the legislative system will be powerfully interwoven with and shaped by the outcome of these other debates. Neither this study, nor any other, can confidently analyse the prospects for a particular set of political institutions in the context of so many other unknowns.

This final chapter, therefore, focuses more narrowly on several important 'mid-range' issues concerning lawmaking and the prospects for democratization. First, how can changes in China's *policy-making process*, brought on by the rise of the legislative system since 1979, strengthen the prospects for a *system transition* to democratization? Secondly, how well institutionalized are the legislative changes of the Deng Xiaoping era? Do they show signs that they have sunk firm roots in the political system which will enable them to endure the uncertainties of the post-Deng transition and continue to contribute to China's transition from authoritarianism? Thirdly, within the limitations of this study, is there any evidence that changes in the lawmaking system are linking up with changes in the broader society to make this part of the political system more permeable to a variety of social interests? Finally, the chapter ends on a cautionary note by looking at some of the challenges lawmaking reform may face in the post-Deng era.

Policy Processes, Legal Transition and System Transformation

The permanent decentralization of policy-making power within an authoritarian system's top decision-making organs is a key process in the transition to a more open, consultative and ultimately democratic system. Policy-making access, influence and resources which were once highly concentrated in the hands of a very few top leaders and organizations must gradually open up to an ever wider array of elite, bureaucratic, institutional, social group and individual actors. In Leninist systems, the gradual shift away from policy-making predominantly by Party edict towards increased policy-making within state lawmaking arenas, via the vehicle of law, presents a pivotal opportunity for the process to occur.

As part of their reform movements, the leaders of these systems have yearned to rebuild the Party's popular legitimacy through a return to stability and 'rule by law' (the 'Leninist *rechtsstaat*'), slightly enhanced popular consultation and the creation of a predictable economic-legal infrastructure which would encourage investment and market growth. These forces lead to a legal transition which includes the resumption of lawmaking and the re-establishment of the legislature. Virtually all Leninist Party leaderships have attempted to keep this legal transition to policy-making via lawmaking as cosmetic as possible by trying to limit the degree to which power is decentralized in the process. They do this by trying to prevent the lawmaking organs, especially the legislature itself, from becoming a significant (and less controllable) arena for political debate and policy-making. In principle this is entirely possible, so long as the key lawmaking decisions can be made 'backstage' in the Party's Central offices, and the cleavages within the Party leadership—policy-based, factional, personal or bureaucratic—can be prevented from 'spilling out' and expressing themselves on the stage of the legislature. As long as the Party leadership can agree on how they want to script the legislative session, and can ensure that all the actors keep strictly to their parts, then the theatre in which the play is acted can remain, in principle, irrelevant to the story. And for many years this is what happened in all the Leninist systems.

But as post-Mao China and the other Leninist systems reformed themselves, the Party-state's political cleavages could not forever be kept from spilling over into the lawmaking system (or other parts of the system, for that matter). Leaders, bureaucracies, localities, social groups and other interests who did not feel their views got an adequate hearing within the traditional policy-making channels began searching for others. And at least in China's case, the Party leaders put in charge of lawmaking were searching for ways to make the institutions they headed bureaucratically strong and politically significant. As a result these once-irrelevant legislative 'theatres' were gradually transformed into highly significant 'arenas' of political struggle.

Thus, the shift to policy-making via lawmaking opened a window, which allowed more decisions—and more important decisions—to be influenced by review in the Party-state's most open, consultative and permeable policy-making arena: the legislature. Invariably, in those Leninist states where lawmaking and the legislature become more prominent, the result was a powerful trend towards more open access to the bureaucratic resources of real power: access to power holders and the mass media, control over committees, information, staffs, budgets, officials, rules and so on. Leninist legislatures such as those in Poland, Hungary, Taiwan, the former Soviet Union and China seized on this new importance as an opportunity to begin changing themselves from hollow institutional symbols of open policy-making and consultativeness into increasingly vibrant policy-making battle-grounds where these qualities gained substance. Of course in many of these systems legal and economic reform ultimately led to electoral reform, the real linchpin of legislative strengthening. But even before this, the power, assertiveness and corporate identity of these legislatures began to expand even while the key officials in these institutions were still Party members nominally subject to increasingly abstract notions of 'Party discipline'. Ranking Party members increasingly ignored organizational discipline and tried to hoard decision-making power into those organs—be they Party, state or government—within which they believed they wielded the greatest power. As a result of this internal erosion of centralized Party control, the decentralization of policy-making power in Leninist systems tended to precede and presage the collapse of one-party rule rather than follow it—an important point to remember with respect to China.

Taking its leads from both the Organizational Politics model and the Garbage Can model, this study has demonstrated an enormous decentralization and fragmentation of lawmaking power between Party, State Council and NPC organs since 1978. One of the most important and ironic aspects of this trend has been the bureaucratic development of the NPC Standing Committee which resulted from 'kingdom building' by senior Party elders whose personal and policy goals were sometimes in line with Deng's, but often very much at odds.

But, while the NPC's bureaucratic development and kingdom building, discussed in Chapter 5, is a key part of the story, the politics of the system are also becoming increasingly open to actors other than the traditional organizational 'elephants' who dominate in China's bureaucratic politics. Think-tanks, localities, intellectuals, proliferating mass media, increasingly assertive 'mass organizations', businesspeople and even small groups enjoy gradually expanding opportunities for policy entrepreneurship and influence, and many find the NPC a fine place to exercise that influence. Organizations which dominated lawmaking in the past (when there was lawmaking) have ceded power, and a wide array of previously weak organizations have asserted and strengthened themselves bureaucratically. To a greater degree than ever before, a wide array of actors are now able and willing to undertake the entrepreneurial burdens and risks of promoting policy ideas, even some radical ones, on to the agenda. And it is more likely than not that such ideas will be cast in the form of 'laws' to be considered by the NPC. Central organs and State Council ministries are still terrifically powerful policy makers, and I have stressed that point repeatedly throughout this book. But they also have lost a great deal of control over their policy agendas. And even if their inter-agency reviews are still key policy processes, the policy consensus hammered out in this process is more and more likely to be re-opened, sometimes dramatically, during an NPC review. All of these changes have made the process increasingly unpredictable and 'ambiguous', even to its experienced practitioners; but they have also made the process indisputably far more open and consultative than it was almost two decades ago.

The effects of this legal transition on consultative policy-making are especially noticeable in the economic sphere, as these systems evolve away from command-administrative systems towards the market. The Party-state must create a clearer, more predictable, contractual environment in order to lure entrepreneurs, foreign businessmen, peasants and even state factory managers into investing their capital, technology, energy, and expertise in economic development. The Party-state needs to increase its consultation with these key economic actors if this new economic-legal relationship is to succeed. Gradually, in fits and starts, and often over a long period of time, the Party-state can be disciplined into greater predictability and consultativeness as it recognizes that in a market-oriented system where both foreign investors and domestic entrepreneurs retain the option of 'exit', the Party-state's past tradition of arbitrary, unpredictable and highly secretive policy-making now carries with it enormous costs. In almost all the Leninist countries, one-Party rule actually collapsed before this process had an opportunity to reform the system into anything like a genuinely contractual state–society relationship (though the relatively peaceful transitions in Taiwan and Hungary may be exceptions). Still, even if the power of this process to 'tame' the Party-state into a much more consultative style of policy-making is not irresistible, it is still substantial.

Throughout this book, I have put forward evidence that China's lawmaking system is now much more of a multi-stage, multi-arena system than a unitary, hierarchical, top-down system. Increasingly, processes and power relationships between these arenas are losing their hierarchical definition, both formally and informally, and are evolving rapidly. Power resources are fragmented among a proliferating number of leaders and organizations, with any actor's power varying from stage to stage, and power constellations shifting from one institutional arena to another. Though Zhao Ziyang and Peng Zhen sat on the Party Politburo together, and that forum approved the Bankruptcy Law in principle, their levels of influence varied greatly in their two respective legislative arenas—the State Council system and the NPC. Consequently, despite Politburo approval, the draft fared very differently in each of these arenas. Thus, lawmaking actors try to steer key legislative proposals into the arenas where they enjoy the greatest influence, and away from those in which their adversaries predominate. The result, as the Garbage Can model would predict, is an entrepreneurial flight of powerful actors from one arena to another. Such a process simply bends any notion of coherent 'Party control over lawmaking' further out of shape, and further erodes the force of Party discipline.

In sum, the Chinese Communist Party's need to rebuild its legal system had important and probably unforeseen institutional consequences. The Party members who led the NPC favoured strengthening it bureaucratically and as a policy-debating arena, both for their own purposes and because they simply came to support its playing such a role. As a result the NPC's institutional growth and resiliency is probably greater than it would have been based solely on the Party's real commitment to abstract notions of 'rule by law'. The Party is also under increasing pressure to consult and incorporate a substantial array of interests into this lawmaking process, and many of these interests find the NPC to be one of the most hospitable access points in the system. No one should underestimate the vast distance between the current system and anything like genuine democratic accountability, nor overlook the fact that many of the life-or-death issues of the Party-state do not even get to the legislature for *pro forma* consideration. Still, the institutional politics of the NPC's growth since 1979 has, probably inadvertently, contributed significantly to decentralizing and opening up policy-making power, and continues to contribute to a possible 'quiet' transformation 'from within' the Party-state.

Establishing Roots: Beyond Cycles of Reform towards Secular Growth

But how can one be sure that the important changes made to date will not prove fleeting? The histories of many authoritarian systems are marked by alternating cycles of policy-making decentralization and recentralization; and as the works of Skinner, Tsou, Baum and others have shown, post-1949 China—both the Maoist and Dengist eras—has been a textbook example of such cycles.[1] Decades of witnessing dramatic changes interspersed with

---

1. On cycles in Chinese politics, see, for example, Skinner and Winckler (1969), Tsou Tang (1986c), Oksenberg and Dickson (1991), Dittmer (1994) Baum (1993 and 1994) and Goldman

equally dramatic setbacks have ingrained a theoretical tension in much of the discussion of long-term political reform in China, and made it difficult to distinguish ephemeral or cyclical changes from enduring, secular change. Cycles of opening up, excesses, then clampdown, followed by moribund periods which force yet another round of reform have been at the heart of many of the best discussions of reform politics in China and elsewhere.

Likewise, the pre-1978 political evolution of the NPC has often been described in terms of cycles of opening up, relatively free-wheeling debate and criticism, then crackdown and a return to a tightly controlled unitary, hierarchical style of lawmaking. The problem, of course, was always that as these cycles took place, the basic bureaucratic power relationships among organizations, particularly those among the Party Central organs, the State Council and the NPC, remained unchanged. The basic norms and 'culture' of the organization (for want of a better term) did not truly evolve; fundamental attitudes and behavioural patterns of NPC and Standing Committee delegates towards leadership, Party discipline and Party authority did not permanently move beyond submissiveness. Thus, efforts at legislative strengthening could not survive the next sudden turnaround in leadership politics and the subsequent crackdown against open politics. O'Brien has captured these cycles well in his historical-structural analysis of the NPC, *Reform without Liberalization*.[2]

But democratic transition requires the legislature and the system as a whole to undergo a series of secular changes which raise increasingly insuperable obstacles to any effort by subsequent leaders to return to a tightly hierarchical, closed, top-down style of policy-making. These include institutionalizing changes in both organizations and attitudes which deconcentrate policy-making power. Organizationally, changes in policy-making must gradually be reinforced by new official rules, unofficial norms, organizational arrangements, and balances of leadership, bureaucratic and social power which prevent reconcentration of power. Attitudinally, policy-making elites must come to value a new, more consultative style of policy-making for its own sake, even with all its novel processes, new power balances, and attendant 'messiness'. The central question, therefore, really concerns the survivability and future prospects of the Deng-era legislative changes in the potentially very unstable post-Deng political environment.

(1994). This reform vacillation is also suggested by Huntington (1968), ch. 6. On the surface, it may seem contradictory to talk about a system becoming both more 'fluid' and 'ambiguous' and more 'institutionalized'. The point is simply that a less controlled, more decentralized process with increasingly open access and less clear rules is setting down institutional roots, and is therefore more resistant to being overturned and recentralized by the top leadership. By institutionalized, however, I do not mean to suggest that the system will not become more decentralized, a prospect which seems fairly likely.

2. O'Brien (1990).

How deeply institutionalized has the NPC's growth become over the past eighteen years, and how likely are they to be able to expand and accelerate? I argue, perhaps too optimistically, that the NPC has undergone a secular evolution which I believe will sustain it into the post-Deng era, and is not simply at the high point of another cycle of change, waiting to be closed down again. The final section, however, will be sobered by an examination of several remaining major challenges and obstacles to further change, including the all-important question of direct election for the National and Provincial People's Congresses.

Perhaps one of the best simple-minded tests that long-term changes in the NPC have become 'institutionalized' and are not just high points in another unsustainable cycle is to examine how well the new arrangements have stood up to periodic 'shocks' caused by shifts in leadership politics followed by counter-attacks against political reform and liberalization. The Maoist era NPC enjoyed a brief, dramatic period of flowering, assertiveness and bureaucratic development between 1954 and 1957. Delegates put forward increasing numbers of bold legislative motions and spoke out critically. Bureaucratically, the organization expanded rapidly, adding more and more staff and legislative subcommittees. But the NPC lacked institutional staying power, and when it fell prey to the 1957 Anti-Rightist and 1959 Anti-Right Deviationist Campaigns, all these behavioural and organizational trends were abruptly wiped away.[3] There was a brief revival of these trends in the early 1960s which was completely swamped by the onset of the Cultural Revolution, and the NPC ceased to be a going concern of any kind from 1966 until about 1977.

It is now possible to get some sense of perspective on the NPC's resilience to such shocks, with almost ten years having elapsed since the suppression of the 1989 Democracy Movement unleashed the most powerful effort to crush liberalism and reassert Party control since Mao's death. As the data in Chapter 5 reveal, most of the organizational and attitudinal trends towards lawmaking decentralization established during the pre-Tiananmen years have, surprisingly, survived intact and stabilized. Some have been pushed even further. Moreover, many of the conditions which would be necessary to recentralize control over lawmaking in the future appear to be lacking.

The available data indicate that since 1979 the NPC's ability to weather such cyclical anti-liberal swings and shocks of leadership politics has improved dramatically over the Maoist era. Its delegate assertiveness, organizational development and legislative influence have all shown a capacity to persist or quickly resume their upward momentum in the face of such hostile moods. Its institutionalization is further underscored by the fact that its growth and rising influence have continued through the

---

3. On NPC activism during the Hundred Flowers, see MacFarquhar (1960 and 1974), Goldman (1981), Lieberthal (1987), and O'Brien (1990).

leadership of four NPC Standing Committee Chairmen as strikingly diverse as Ye Jianying, Peng Zhen, Wan Li and Qiao Shi (and, to date, has shown no noticeable reversal under Li Peng). Statistically, Chapter 5 showed that upward trends in indicators of delegate assertiveness (number of motions submitted), organizational development (number of staff) and delegate dissent (number of no votes and abstentions) continued, quickly resumed or even accelerated even after the three major post-Mao anti-liberal campaigns which stressed the need for Party leadership and unity (the 1983–84 Anti-Spiritual Pollution Campaign, the 1987 Anti-Bourgeois Liberalism Campaign and the 1989 crackdown after Tiananmen). The first two of these were not directed specifically against NPC delegates, as far as is known. But the NPC's durability in the face of the 1989 crackdown is especially notable because of the persecution and expulsion of NPC Standing Committee member Hu Jiwei for trying to gather signatures to convene an NPC meeting to overturn the State Council's order imposing martial law. In truth, almost a third of all NPC Standing Committee members reportedly lent their names to the petition in the famous 'signatures incident', yet Hu Jiwei was virtually the only member persecuted for it. Most importantly, this is exactly the sort of incident which in past times would have chilled and set back the assertiveness of NPC delegates.[4] This time, in fact, the opposite occurred. Over the following year delegate motions were up and high dissenting vote totals were recorded again quickly after the incident; indeed, as noted, two sources report that the Standing Committee actually voted down the Ministry of Public Security-backed draft Public Demonstrations Law at exactly the same time Hu Jiwei was under investigation. Clearly, the NPC's institutional assertiveness now shows a resilience unprecedented in its history.

Organizational Barriers to Recentralization

One of this book's principal themes is that the NPC's growth, expanding influence and resilience since 1979 have not principally been due to the Party leadership's continuing commitment to any abstract ideals of 'rule by law' or 'socialist democracy'. Even though these commitments helped set the processes in motion, the ideals themselves have proved to be weak reeds in Chinese politics; often honoured in the breech and highly susceptible to sudden anti-liberal policy reversals. Rather, the NPC has grown because of the organizational implications of this process. Its roots have been two of the hardiest perennials of the Chinese political tradition: competition among top leaders, and these leaders' subsequent obsession with building enduring 'bureaucratic empires'. The NPC's bureaucratic development has

---

4. On the signatures incident, see Hu Shikai (1993) and Goldman (1994).

Lawmaking Reforms and China's Democratic Prospects 239

given a firm foundation to its post-Mao assertiveness, and permitted this assertiveness to survive numerous cyclical shocks and setbacks to political reform far better than it did in the Maoist era. Moreover, many trends in the development of the lawmaking system's bureaucratic structure, personnel practices and institutional power balances also make significant recentralization of lawmaking power during the Jiang Zemin era appear highly unlikely. Indeed, many of these trends make further erosion of centralized Party control appear almost certain.

By the early 1990s, the erosion of Central consensus, Party discipline and Party organizational levers for controlling lawmaking from the Centre was so far advanced that the sinologist's old axiom that 'the Party controls the legislature' or that 'politically crucial decisions remain the prerogative of Party, not state, organizations'[5] had come to have less and less meaning. Increasingly, politically crucial decisions short of those concerning the imminent life-or-death of the Party-state are no longer the exclusive prerogative of any single or small set of organizations, nor are most of them 'made' once and for all in any one place. Interview data (noted in Chapter 4 and in the case studies) also indicate that top Party leaders have been increasingly unable or unwilling to reach detailed consensus on legislative issues within the Politburo or other Party decision-making organs, substantially abdicating their potential control over the lawmaking process to the NPC, its Standing Committee and the State Council. The implication of this research generally is that politically crucial decisions are now thrashed out, 'shaped' and 'reshaped' by Party members simultaneously wearing a number of different hats, acting at various stages of the decision, in a number of different arenas. Indisputably, the NPC is increasingly becoming one of those important arenas, even if its importance still pales compared with the Politburo.

As Chapter 5 showed, this process of NPC institutional growth began during the early 1980s with Deng's nominal retirement of aging, powerful conservative reformers and 'restorationists'[6] from Central Party and government posts to the traditionally quiescent NPC Standing Committee. Deng moved these elders to the NPC in part to strengthen the Congress' prestige, in part hoping that they would use the NPC to attack some of Deng's more implacable enemies (such as the 'petroleum faction'), and in part to ease out reform critics and create room for younger, better educated and more reform-oriented leaders at the top of the Party and State Council structure. With their formal conduits of power increasingly focused within the NPC, many of these elders began insisting that the NPC be seriously consulted on policy issues drafted in the form of laws. Since many of these veterans were among the last survivors of the Long March and the CCP's other great battles, they were not nearly as easily intimidated by the

5. Goldstein (1994), 721.   6. The term is from Harding (1987), 43–69.

240 The Politics of Lawmaking in Post-Mao China

Politburo and State Council (now headed by leaders with few revolutionary credentials) as the 'model workers' and non-Party luminaries who made up much of the NPC in the past. In short, since 1979 there has been an emergence of significant Party officials whose principal regular institutional affiliation is with the legislature. At the same time, the 'prestige gap' between top Party officials in the NPC and those in the traditionally more powerful Party-state offices has narrowed dramatically compared with the Maoist era. None of the Party members who serve as NPC Vice-Chairmen will ever look upon Jiang Zemin, Zhu Rongji or Li Peng with the same awe with which they viewed either Mao, Zhou Enlai or Deng Xiaoping. Neither of these trends is likely to change in the post-Deng era.

The Deng Xiaoping-era seniors bequeathed the NPC another vital institutional legacy which continues to buttress its influence even as they have left the scene. Led by Peng Zhen, Chen Pixian and Peng Chong, the seniors, precisely as any organizational politics theorist would predict, immediately set about creating an impressive bureaucratic empire of sub-committees and permanent staff offices. The excellent recent research on local people's congresses by Li Lianjiang, Laura Luerhmann and Kevin O'Brien strongly suggests a parallel process has been occurring throughout the provinces in recent years.[7] Such a combination of bureaucratically well-connected, experienced seniors with an aggressive and growing staff is exactly the traditional stuff of Chinese political power, and the NPC's day-to-day influence over the legislative agenda, legal drafting, local investigations and interdepartmental consensus-building has mushroomed as a result. Interviews and NPC personnel data indicate this organizational build-up was not halted at all after Tiananmen, and may even have accelerated under Wan Li, Qiao Shi, Tian Jiyun and Wang Hanbin.

Other organizational changes within the Party system have accelerated this erosion of centralized lawmaking power. As noted in Chapter 4, *nomenklatura* rules concerning appointments to the NPC, its Standing Committee, the Legislative Affairs Work Committee and the specialized committees did not expand Central control after 1989, despite a general policy of trying to revive Party control in other sectors.[8] Whatever overall control the Central Political-Legal Leading Group may have once exercised over lawmaking is also now ended. More generally, the norms of Party discipline upon which these organizational systems relied to exercise their control have simply lost much of their bite. The discipline of the Party member meetings which precede NPC sessions has been greatly eroded in recent years, and will almost certainly erode further so long as there continue to be few significant punishments or disincentives for Party members who choose to ignore these meetings' directives. Again in this

---

7. See O'Brien and Li (1993–94), and O'Brien and Luerhmann (1997).
8. Burns (1994) 458–91.

regard, the relatively insignificant impact of the Hu Jiwei purge and the handling of the 'signatures incident' on actual NPC delegate behaviour is important to note.

As evidence that institutionalized decentralization survived 1989, special note must be taken of Central Document Number 8 [1991]. As noted in Chapter 4, interview data and documentary analysis strongly suggests that Jiang Zemin and/or other leaders may have attempted to use the drafting of Document 8 to reassert centralized Party control over lawmaking. If so, the effort failed. Document 8, on the contrary, for the first time codified, expanded and placed the Party's highest imprimatur on the set of loose, decentralized legislative review arrangements which, according to several sources, had already become the accepted custom long before 1991. As such, it will serve as powerful ammunition for NPC leaders trying to resist future efforts at recentralizing Party control. It would make strong recentralization efforts by Jiang or other would-be successors seem an offensively bold power grab, particularly after Deng's own powerful precedent of leaving lawmaking work largely to the NPC's Party member leaders.

The NPC and Changing Elite Political Norms: The Normalization of Moderate Dissent

If the increasingly decentralized politics of lawmaking are to contribute to democratizing change, rather than just another temporary liberalizing cycle, they must also be institutionalized through changes in attitudes about what is proper in politics and policy-making. They must produce, in other words, changes in political culture or norms, particularly the elite political culture. Yet, among those observers who are most sceptical of China's prospects for democratic transition any time soon, many of the most enduring arguments focus on the persistence of the anti-democratic strains in China's political culture. In particular, these observers have stressed the oft-demonstrated power of China's political culture to overwhelm efforts to craft or import more open, democratic political institutions.

The most powerful of these cultural obstacles to democracy, well known to students of the field, are those which suppress open debate over policy issues, and which treat policy-based dissent against top leadership views as full-blown subversion. Many scholars trace these obstacles to a strong cultural imperative for ideological unity, rooted in a largely moralistic, rather than merely interest-based, view of politics.[9] Proponents of this view buttress their arguments powerfully by pointing to China's centuries-old tradition of a centralized bureaucracy, indoctrinated into the current regime's ideology (be it various strains of state Confucianism, the

---

9. Pye (1988).

Three People's Principles or Marxism-Leninism-Maoism).[10] Despite intermittent periods or cycles of ideological relaxation, no Chinese state has persistently viewed dissent or heterodox political thinking with anything other than profound suspicion. Nor has any Chinese government before late-1980s Taiwan permitted a self-confessed 'loyal opposition' to exist for long.

Very recently, Western scholars have finally had an opportunity to perform some methodologically more sophisticated tests of these assertions about Chinese political culture. One of the more notable is Nathan and Shi's inventive 1990 effort to replicate several questions from Almond and Verba's *The Civic Culture* in China.[11] Although this research has provided some grounds for optimism about future democratic prospects (and Nathan and Shi are far more optimistic than most culturalist scholars), the study has also provided strong evidence for a most disturbing point: that even after the scarring tyranny of the Cultural Revolution, both the Chinese masses and elites can still be highly intolerant of heterodox political thinking.[12]

The crucial question, however, is one of comparative politics, and concerns not just the anti-democratic character of China's historical, or even its present-day, political culture. One could concede that point and still note that many other great nations which once had powerfully anti-democratic political cultures have nevertheless established stable democracies, or at least have made major steps in that direction (Germany, Italy, Japan, Argentina, Mexico, Turkey, South Korea, South Africa and of course Taiwan spring immediately to mind).[13] The key issue concerning China is: are its anti-democratic cultural elements so strong that they can overwhelm other institutional, ideological, leadership, or socio-economic and developmental forces which might otherwise promote democratization?[14] Can China's current dictators rest safe in the knowledge that the anti-democratic cultural tradition will protect them against those non-cultural

---

10. The classic statement of the thesis is Balazs (1964), 13–27. For a critical review of these viewpoints, see Whyte (1992).   11. Nathan and Shi (1993).

12. Nathan and Shi (1993), esp. 111–13. It is possible, however, that Nathan and Shi's findings are an artifact of the particular question they asked, which focused on whether free speech should be extended to people like the infamous 'Gang of Four'. In countries with a particularly brutal historical experience of totalitarianism, even strong civil libertarians often support speech limits on certain viewpoints deemed especially dangerous to that particular system. The best example is the large number of otherwise liberal-minded Germans who supported the constitutional ban on neo-Nazi parties and the '5% rule' for legislative representation. Chinese elite and mass support of free speech for most other heterodox viewpoints may be far higher than for this particular case.

13. Martin King Whyte (1992) has argued powerfully that the characterization of China's traditional culture as overwhelmingly authoritarian is overstated, and overlooks a number of proto-democratic elements in that tradition, including the populist aspects of the notion of the 'Mandate of Heaven'.

14. For a strong argument that China's socio-economic base for democratization is as well-established as several other transitional young democracies, see Nathan (1990) 193–232.

Lawmaking Reforms and China's Democratic Prospects 243

forces which have recently impelled so many other reputedly 'authoritarian' cultures towards democratic reform? Or are Deng, Jiang and their allies, like their imperial forbears, deluding themselves that such a 'cultural great wall' will secure their tyranny?

On this point Lucian Pye, the dean of Asian political culture studies, has shown the greatest courage of his theoretical convictions, and hence the greatest pessimism, arguing that in China, political culture probably has a stronger and more enduring impact on politics than it does in most other countries.[15] And indeed, the historical record of the twentieth century is so full of failures of seemingly well-intentioned institutional efforts to encourage freer debate or decentralize and limit state power that one might well suspect that an anti-democratic 'cultural imperative' is at work. Andrew Nathan has noted six major efforts to democratize the electoral-legislative system or liberalize political and organizational rights since 1900. Each effort failed because: elections were fraudulent or suffrage too limited; legislatures were never permitted to exercise their formal powers; or political freedoms were so restricted that genuine political competition was impossible.[16] Nathan's earlier classic *Chinese Democracy* documents a failure of democratic understanding among early Chinese liberals which is so fundamental and pervasive that it seems, to me at least, to merit the label 'cultural'. The turn-of-the century democracy activists who helped build China's first legislative bodies misunderstood the enduring nature of interest-based conflict in democracy, and assumed that democratic debate would result in universal consensus around a single, scientifically 'correct' policy. Even these harshest critics of tyranny came to believe, through a flawed analogy to the ancient notion that well-governed societies will move via self-cultivation towards an era of 'Great Unity' (*Da Tong*), that the legislature, that most eternally conflictual and egalitarian of Western political institutions, would gradually bend to China's seemingly insatiable cultural need for harmony and hierarchy.[17]

But the influence between political cultures and political institutions is reciprocal, not one-way, and political cultures, like political institutions, are not immutable. This study is not, in any sense, a study of elite political culture, and it does not employ the methods necessary to make serious assertions about that culture. Nevertheless, its evidence about real lawmaking processes in the 1980s and 1990s at least suggests some ways in which the legislative practices and institutions developed over eighteen years are gradually promoting new attitudes and behaviour among Chinese political elites. These processes and institutions appear to be reshaping a

15. Pye (1988).
16. Nathan (1993). The reasons for these failures varied—from impatient tyrants, to invasion, to civil war—and hence Nathan does not conclude that a cultural imperative is necessarily at work. On the historical record, see also Zhao Suisheng (1993) and O'Brien (1990) 12–60.   17. Nathan (1985).

number of historically authoritarian political attitudes and predilections. Moreover, because many of these changes are occurring within the current communist elite, they do not depend exclusively upon the fates of some precariously-based potential democratic counter-elite or an intellectual diaspora. Nor are they rooted primarily in China's historically weak formal constitutional system. Rather, the changes appear to be the unintended result of the application of China's bureaucratic empire-building tradition to the NPC.

The interview data discussed in Chapters 4 and 5 indicate that many Party officials involved in the NPC and elsewhere in lawmaking work increasingly regard new, higher levels of open policy disagreement among various organizational, regional and social interests as a routine and desirable aspect of the policy process. It is clear to me from my interviewing that many mid-level NPC staff feel this even more strongly. At the very top of the system, former NPC Standing Committee Chairman Wan Li has come closest to expressing this viewpoint in public, arguing repeatedly since 1986 that the Party-state benefits greatly from protecting the right of legislators and policy specialists to debate openly and relay the voices of a number of social groups. Wan's successors in the NPC leadership, Tian Jiyun and Qiao Shi, also increasingly spoke this way during their tenure.[18] Li Peng, Qiao's successor as Standing Committtee Chairman, will probably also feel considerable institutional pressure to adopt similar attitudes.

Some legislative advisors interviewed for this study suggest that a sort of 'professional legislator' mentality is also developing among many (though it is not yet known how many) of the NPC's 'backbone' delegates—those who serve on the Standing Committee and the eight special committees. This mentality attaches growing value to constitutional and legal procedure, relatively free debate, the legislature's organizational autonomy and increased NPC oversight of government ministries. A far more positive view of the 'rights' enshrined in China's Constitution has also emerged among some delegates, even some whose political pasts would not predict it.[19] And even though many delegates reportedly use their NPC posts to serve as 'agents' of their former ministerial employers, many others use their rich bureaucratic expertise to oversee and check power grabs by their erstwhile organizational colleagues. The rise of such a 'professional legislator' mentality among today's NPC officials is all the more fascinating and important because, in contrast to the ill-fated legislative 'liberals' of the

18. Wan Li's (1986) views are summarized in Chapter 3. See also Qiao Shi's (1994) Speech Commemorating the 40th anniversary of the NPC's establishment. On Tian Jiyun, see Tian (1995a and 1995b). According to one NPC advisor who attended the 40th anniversary commemorative session and heard these leaders' speeches, Tian's speech, which was largely off-the-cuff and not published in full externally, was a broad-ranging and stinging attack on the anti-democratic features of China's current system.
19. See Chapter 5, especially the discussion of the NPC Special Committees.

late 1950s, today's NPC delegates have much greater traditional power bases from which to assert their legislative prerogatives.

Regular NPC and Standing Committee delegates have also indicated other significant changes in their attitudes and political assertiveness. The rise in the number of legislative motions put forward by delegates is one significant, albeit flawed, indicator of this trend. By far the most impressive indicator, discussed in detail in Chapter 5, has been the rise in the number of 'no' votes and abstentions in the NPC and its Standing Committee. Unanimous voting by the NPC, once virtually automatic, is now quite rare. Instead, dissenting votes in the range of 20 to 30%, and occasionally a good deal higher, are now far more common when the full NPC votes on draft laws, personnel appointments and other motions. Moreover, reliable NPC sources report that on at least two occasions since 1986, the NPC Standing Committee has allowed Party leadership-approved draft laws to go a formal vote and be voted down.

Even with their many limitations, these data on legislative motions and vote totals raise some serious questions about the pessimism of many culturally-based forecasts of China's political future. Since 1979, as the NPC has grown and a new, politically more meaningful lawmaking process has emerged, new attitudes towards open policy debate and disagreement have emerged among some of the current elite. Moreover, these changes are showing signs of becoming institutionalized: that is, they have shown a capacity to endure and reassert themselves even in the face of a serious crackdown. The near disappearance of unanimous voting and its replacement with annual average dissenting vote percentages in the tens, twenties and thirties indicates that moderate levels of dissent and assertiveness by NPC and Standing Committee delegates are becoming 'normal' in the Chinese system. Any such normalization of regular, moderate dissent represents a very significant evolution in the elite culture of Chinese politics, and probably indicates that the NPC is making a genuine, serious contribution towards the openness and consultativeness of the system.

'Permeability': Linking Legislative Change to Societal Change

Historically, many if not most legislatures have tended to become influential in policy-making and governance long before they become genuinely 'democratic'—that is, accessible and accountable to a wide variety of social groups and interests. In their early stages of development, legislatures often establish their power base by first incorporating not the broader society but instead some significant segment of the *ancien régime* or an emerging upper-middle segment of society. Obviously, however, the NPC (or any other legislature) cannot maximize either its power base or its contribution to democratization exclusively through building its policy-making influence, or even by 'normalizing' assertiveness and dissent. It must also establish its authority through representativeness, by becoming more 'permeable' to a growing range of emerging social groups and interests, eventually through a more direct system of election. This raises the question of how the Deng-era legislative changes, which were focused mostly at the top of the system, might link up with other potentially democratizing changes in Chinese society.

Recent experience in China and other Leninist and post-Leninist systems indicates that legislators and social constituencies can begin to forge some links with each other well before the system is opened up to genuinely competitive direct elections. As noted above, the process of drafting the legal infrastructure necessary to lure in foreign and domestic entrepreneurs forces the Party-state to consult these actors on the content of legislation. The erosion of 'Party discipline' and the other organizational and attitudinal changes described in the previous section also reveal the possibility for democratization by giving individual legislators a chance to rethink old attitudes on who in society is their true 'constituency'. Delegates and potential constituencies are becoming freer to explore and develop their links with each other, and each can seek out new ways of mobilizing the other as a source of power. The evidence from this research and other studies suggests that many NPC officials are gradually changing their constituency orientations, and increasingly taking their titles as 'representative' seriously.

As long as the leadership continues to block direct elections, these emerging legislator–constituency links could take as many different forms as there are types of constituencies. This study has revealed examples of several different patterns. Some models would probably advance democratization very little. An 'iron triangles' model, in which former Central-level bureaucrats retire to the NPC and continue representing the interests of their ministries and allied social constituencies, would suggest that the NPC's growth was doing little more than adding another layer to the phenomenon Kenneth Lieberthal has labelled 'fragmented authoritarianism'. On a more encouraging note, O'Brien has found increasing numbers of national and local people's congress officials abandoning their assigned roles as Beijing's 'agents' and taking up the role of 'remonstrators' and intermediaries between the government and a wide array of self-defined constituencies. Most of O'Brien's respondents focused not on policymaking or lawmaking, however, but on winning particularist patronage favours or individual protections and exemptions from specific government policies.[20] This particularism does indicate a step forward in representation, though it also risks getting bogged down in a 'distributive' or even a

20. O'Brien (1995).

corrupt style of politics which would advance 'rule of law' or democratization very little. At the same time, the case studies in this book clearly reveal instances of legislators working to represent the interests of a variety of mid and lower-level constituencies in broader national-level legislative issues. Trade union members of the NPC have been particularly frank about their work in this regard, though representatives of women's federations, ethnic minorities and regional governments were also prominent. A pressing item on research agendas over the next few years must be the ways in which the top-down decentralizing changes in the lawmaking system are also permitting legislators to begin establishing links with other bottom-up pre-democratic changes in China, such as the gradual rise of civil society groups.

Succession Politics and Electoral Reform

In terms of removing barriers to more radical future reforms, perhaps one of the most important forces for further legislative changes has been the recent passing of Deng Xiaoping. For just as Deng's Four Cardinal Principles defined the outer limits of reform generally, his corollary that the NPC is 'China's basic political system' and that China must never practise what he called an American-style tripartite division of powers set an insurmountable, albeit somewhat undefined, outer limit on the legislature's ability to establish its organizational autonomy from the State Council and Party Centre, or open itself to broader social forces. Even though no other Chinese leader saw fit publicly to question or modify this formulation while Deng was still alive, it seems highly unlikely that either Jiang Zemin or any other potential successor will even approach Deng's power to impose such unquestioned organizational-ideological restrictions on the legislature's role. Ultimately Deng's death will probably reopen the ideological debate on the legislature's role in Chinese politics to an even greater degree than Mao's death did.

At the same time, it must be stressed that Deng's successors would have to agree to the further reform of a truly daunting number of existing Party control institutions before the NPC could become a conduit for real pressure to change the Chinese system into one which is fundamentally more consultative, let alone begin a true democratic transition. A democratic activist's 'checklist' might include the following: the Party's prior review of legislation would have to weaken still further, eventually permitting most laws to pass or fail irrespective of Politburo wishes; remaining Central *nomenklatura* controls over the NPC Standing Committee would also have to weaken greatly, giving delegates greater real oversight of their own leaders; and the NPC Standing Committee Party Group would at a minimum have to greatly loosen its hold on lawmaking and the legislative agenda through its voting control over the NPC Committee Chairmen's

Group. This list is indeed daunting; and obviously many of these changes would presage nothing less than the complete erosion of Party leadership over policy-making.

No foreseeable reform would grant the legislature greater power of legitimacy than direct election, with more candidates than seats, for delegates to the national and provincial-level people's congresses. And no reform is also potentially so dangerous to the Party's hold on power—a point which the collapse of European Leninism dramatically illustrated, and which was surely not lost on the Chinese Politburo.[21] Since the amended People's Congress Electoral Law went into effect in 1982, China's scholarly legal and political journals, including internal NPC journals, have contained very little serious debate on this extraordinarily sensitive issue.[22] Hong Kong press reports have claimed that in early 1996 the Politburo issued a document barring any electoral reforms for several years.[23] Jiang Zemin's public pronouncements on this issue are somewhat mixed, though on balance rather conservative. His address to the Fifteenth CCP Congress indicated a desire gradually to expand the recent very promising experiments with local elections, though he clearly appeared to rule out direct election at the national and provincial levels during his October 1997 visit to Washington.[24] Still, notwithstanding Jiang's expressed resistance to proceeding in the near future, Deng's death probably removed the one leader powerful enough to enforce any absolute ban on elite-level discussion of direct election. Discussion is one thing, however. Action is quite another. And at present, with China's economy going strong, the pro-democracy forces very weak, and crime and unrest still apparently manageable, it is difficult to foresee the type of crisis which might cause the top leadership or important elements within it to consider a reform so risky as direct national elections.

Jiang Zemin may have succeeded in heading off one such scenario by his successful removal of his top rival Qiao Shi at the Fifteenth Party Congress. Prior to Deng's death, much speculation about succession scenarios implicitly assumed the struggle would take the form that the late Sovietologist Alfred Meyer once called a 'struggle *against* power' rather than a struggle *for* power. In a struggle against power, would-be successors gang up in an attempt to block the most powerful of their number from so dominating the system that he might constitute a genuine danger to the others. In the current struggle, this would mean that Jiang's Zemin's competitors would have used a number of institutional devices, including the NPC, to check and constrain his power. Qiao Shi would try to further expand the NPC's

---

21. On the inherent dangers of electoral reform, I agree with McCormick (1996).
22. For the debate before 1982, see Nathan (1985), McCormick (1990), O'Brien (1990), Tsou Tang (1986c), Liao Gailong (1980), Lin Hsin-tao (1980), Wu Jialing (1980) and Gao Wenxiang (1979). 23. See Vivian Pik-kwan Chan (1996).
24. *South China Morning Post*, 21 October 1997, 19.

Lawmaking Reforms and China's Democratic Prospects 249

autonomy, assertiveness and corporate sense of power as a vehicle for enhancing his own legitimacy as a successor or at least implicitly undermining Jiang's. Instead, Jiang decisively undermined any plans Qiao may have had to challenge the succession personally by removing his rival (as well as Wang Hanbin) from all his Central Party positions at the Party Congress. Jiang apparently failed, however, to secure the final arrangements for the new state leadership slate at the time of the Party Congress, a sign that his Fifteenth Party Congress triumph, though considerable, was not total. Thus, even though Jiang had defeated Qiao, right up to the eve of the new Congress meeting in Spring 1998, the new NPC leadership was still the object of considerable struggle within the leadership. Jiang reportedly pushed hard to appoint outgoing Premier Li Peng as Standing Committee Chairman while Qiao Shi fought a fierce battle (too late) to secure the Chairmanship for his deputy Tian Jiyun (still a Politburo member) or, as a compromise candidate, outgoing CPPCC leader Li Ruihuan (who retained a position on the Politburo Standing Committee). According to unconfirmed Hong Kong press reports, Qiao also demanded greater assurances of autonomy for NPC delegates including greater influence over the selection and oversight of State Council and NPC senior officials. Interestingly, the changed norms of delegate obedience to Party directives were reportedly a bargaining chip in the negotiations, and despite Qiao's loss of his Party posts it was suggested that if Qiao, Tian and the rest of the NPC Standing Committee were unhappy with the new state leadership arrangements, the incoming leaders might face an embarrassingly large negative vote when the NPC voted to confirm the arrangements at the spring 1998 session. These last reports had a special credibility about them, since Li Peng had never polled especially well whenever the NPC had voted to confirm his appointment to major state posts (see Chapter 5).[25] In the end, the Party leadership had to lobby hard to keep the dissenting vote on Li Peng's nomination down to a still-embarassing ten percent.

These reports that the NPC had become an object of struggle between Jiang, Li and Qiao underscore several dilemmas succession politics pose for the NPC. Most importantly, they show that the NPC is now important enough that the top leadership consider it an institution worth fighting over in a succession struggle. Further, the great increase in the NPC's organizational autonomy and the delegates' changing attitudes provide its leaders with newfound sources of leverage in this struggle. In the next few years the NPC's chances for significantly expanded influence or more radical reforms will be greatly affected by its role in the current succession struggle. But succession politics pose great potential risks as

25. The alleged struggle over the new NPC leadership was principally reported in a series of articles by journalist Willy Wo-Lap Lam in the *South China Morning Post*, 3 October 1997, 10; 15 October 1997, 9; 26 October 1997, 6; 29 October 1997, 25; 13 November 1997, 9; 16 November 1997, 6; 22 November 1997, 8; and 3 December 1997, 23.

well as rewards. The NPC could thrive if its new leadership can further transform its claim to a special popular legitimacy into a source of real power to be coveted by prospective leaders. This possibility should not be dismissed, given that of all the great national-level governing institutions in China—the Party, the Army, the Government and the people's congresses—the last emerged with its legitimacy by far the least scarred by the Tiananmen massacre. On the other hand, at present the NPC may well be perceived by Jiang Zemin and his allies as the hostile power base of a defeated rival, and they may target the organization for punishment or attempt to stack the upper levels of the Standing Committee with pliant Jiang supporters. Over the longer term, however, this chapter has argued that the NPC has gone a long way toward institutionalizing its much more influential role, and there are many organizational and attitudinal forces which would make it very difficult for Jiang or another top leader to roll back its progress significantly. It is even possible that overly bold attacks upon the NPC by Jiang might engender resentment among the other top leaders, or that the notoriously illiberal Li Peng, now that his personal power is so intertwined with the Standing Committee Chairmanship, might find himself gradually taking on more of the NPC's organizational outlook.

Conclusions and Cautions

To summarize, this chapter has argued that during the Deng Xiaoping era, the National People's Congress has made substantial progress towards institutionalizing two key changes which are essential if the legislature is to make important contributions to any potential future system transition. Thanks to the 'empire building' of several CCP elders, the NPC has built a solid permanent bureaucracy and subcommittee structure which permits it to get more heavily involved in lawmaking than ever before. The 'elite culture' of the NPC and its Standing Committee delegates, moreover, is far more assertive than in years past, as reflected in greatly increased dissenting votes and delegate motions. Most importantly, these trends have all shown great survivability in the face of sudden shocks from leadership struggles and anti-liberal political campaigns, such as occurred in 1987 and 1989. There is also evidence, though far less strong and less clear, that the legislature is becoming politically more 'permeable' to outside social interests, as legislators are freer to forge links with newly defined constituencies. Some studies suggest, however, that this permeability may for now simply mean delegates are trying to gain private favours for those they represent, rather than trying to define a broader policy consensus. Top leaders will probably continue to block direct election to the NPC and provincial people's congress for some time after Deng's death, though future succession politics or other crises may tempt some leaders to promote it. On the whole, if one focuses solely on the NPC and its place within

Lawmaking Reforms and China's Democratic Prospects 251

the traditional CCP Party-state since 1979, these trends are fairly promising, as the NPC faces the huge uncertainties of the post-Deng era.

But any such optimistic talk about China's democratic prospects must also be tempered by a forthright recognition of the serious systemic threats to a more open parliamentary system. And this chapter has proceeded on the probably heroic assumption that the NPC will face a fairly smooth, peaceful and stable transition environment. First, to succeed, any transition to a more parliamentary system must be peaceful. Fortunately, so long as China itself can resist the urge to adventurism, especially adventurism which would tempt a direct confrontation with the United States, it can probably expect to find itself in the most peaceful international environment it has faced in over a century. The leadership appears to have the ability to avoid the external violence which killed several previous liberal experiments in China during the early and mid twentieth century.

But the internal picture is far less sanguine. China's current instability, crime, ethnic and religious unrest, and bitter inter-regional rivalry all pressure the leadership away from the type of tolerance and 'rights-oriented' atmosphere needed for increased parliamentarism to flourish. Throughout twentieth-century Chinese history, whenever the leadership has seen a crime wave, it never hesitated to 'round up the usual suspects'; and regardless of the real perpetrators of the unrest, the list of 'usual suspects' has typically also included advocates of free speech, free press and free association.

The present pervasive climate of corruption presents another danger which could undermine the fragile growing confidence in the integrity of the legislative process that both elites and average citizens must feel before they will risk entrusting serious matters to the political system. Unchecked corruption creates incentives for many political actors to seek 'individual solutions' through connections with unscrupulous officials, and disincentives for them to work towards group solutions in a public forum like the legislature. Seen in this light, O'Brien's finding that NPC delegates are mostly representing their constituencies as private go-betweens and remonstrators might cause concern. A very real danger is that NPC officials will become just powerful enough that corrupt people will finally consider them worth bribing, and the institution's development will stall.

The outcome of some of these dilemmas will largely be outside the ability of the NPC and its leaders to control, though not entirely. Many of these issues also present the NPC and its leaders with challenging opportunities to enhance their legitimacy, power and influence over 'important' policies. More than any other Chinese political institution, the NPC could strike a balance between satisfying society by attacking crime and still enhancing China's elementary legal procedural protections. The NPC could provide the forum and the process for bringing diverse regional, religious and ethnic groups together. It could mobilize the public outrage needed to force a serious crackdown on corruption, and supply the organizational oversight needed to attack bureaucratic corruption within the heretofore airtight ministry system. And finally, in the current succession, NPC leaders could use the Congress' legitimizing potential to force any prospective winning candidate to show more deference to the legislature, and ultimately build his power on a far more plebicitary or parliamentary base than any previous mainland Chinese leader. (The recent Taiwanese presidential election will also create enormous pressure in this direction.) In these ways, the post-Deng NPC has some potential to shape its own political environment, not just passively accept it. To accomplish these things would of course take terrific political skill. But their value towards establishing a stable, peaceful transition towards democracy is potentially enormous.

Selected Bibliography

English Language Sources

Aberbach, Joel., Chesney, James D. and Rockman, Bert A. (1975), 'Exploring Elite Political Attitudes: Some Methodological Lessons', *Political Methodology*, Vol. 2, No. 1, 1–29.

Alford, William P. (1993), 'Double-Edged Swords Cut Both Ways: Law and Legitimacy in the People's Republic of China', *Daedalus*, Vol. 122, No. 2 (Spring), 45–69.

Alford, William P. (1995), 'Tasselled Loafers for Barefoot Lawyers: Transformation and Tension in the World of Chinese Legal Workers', *The China Quarterly*, No. 141 (March), 22–38.

Allison, Graham (1971), *Essence of Decision: Explaining the Cuban Missile Crisis* (Boston: Little, Brown and Co.)

Andors, Stephen (1977), *China's Industrial Revolution: Politics, Planning, and Management, 1949 to the Present* (New York: Pantheon)

Axelrod, Robert (1991), 'Building a Strong Legislature: The Western Experience', *PS: Political Science and Politics* (September), 474–8.

Azrael, Jeremy R. (1970), 'Varieties of De-Stalinization,' in Chalmers Johnson (ed.), *Change in Communist Systems* (Stanford: Stanford University Press)

Bachrach, Peter, and Baratz, Morton (1962), 'Two Faces of Power', *American Political Science Review*, Vol. 56 (December), 947–52.

Barnett, A. Doak (1967), *Cadres, Bureaucracy, and Political Power in Communist China* (New York: Columbia University Press).

Bartke, Wolfgang (1987), *Who's Who in the People's Republic of China* (Munich: K.G. Saur).

Bartke, Wolfgang (1991), *Who's Who in the People's Republic of China, Third Edition* (Munich: K.G. Saur).

Baum, Richard (1986), 'Modernization and Legal Reform in Post-Mao China: The Rebirth of Socialist Legality', *Studies in Comparative Communism*, Vol. XIX, No. 2 (Summer), 69–104.

Baum, Richard (1993), 'The Road to Tiananmen: Chinese Politics in the 1980s', in Roderick MacFarquhar (ed.), *The Politics of China 1949–1989* (New York: Cambridge University Press), 340–471.

Baum, Richard (1994), *Burying Mao: Chinese Politics in the Age of Deng Xiaoping* (Princeton: Princeton University Press).

Berman, Daniel M. (1966), *A Bill Becomes a Law: Congress Enacts Civil Rights Legislation* (second edition) (London: Macmillan).

Biernacki, Patrick and Waldorf, Dan (1981), 'Snoball Sampling, Problems and Techniques of Chain Referral Sampling', *Sociological Methods and Research*, Vol. 10, No. 2 (November), 141–63.

Boynton, G. R. and Kim, Chong Lim (1975), *Legislative Systems in Developing Countries* (Durham, NC: Duke University Press).

Burns, John P. (1989), *The Chinese Communist Party's Nomenklatura System* (Armonk, NY: M.E. Sharpe).
Burns, John P. (1994), 'Strengthening Central CCP Control of Leadership Selection: The 1990 *Nomenklatura*', *The China Quarterly*, No. 138 (June), 458–491.
Chamberlain, Heath B. (1987), 'Party Management Relations in Chinese Industries: Some Political Dimensions of Economic Reform', *The China Quarterly*, No. 112 (December), 631–61.
Chan, Vivien Pik-Kwan (1996), 'Officials Informed Reforms Postponed Until at Least 2002', *South China Morning Post* (25 February), 5.
Chang, Parris H. (1975), *Power and Policy in China* (University Park, Pennsylvania: Pennsylvania State University Press).
Chang, Parris H. (1978), 'Research Note: The Rise of Wang Tung-Hsing: Head of China's Security Apparatus', *The China Quarterly*, No. 73 (March), 122–36.
Chang, Parris H. (1983), *Elite Conflict in Post-Mao China (revised edition)* (Baltimore: University of Maryland School of Law Occasional Papers/Reprint Series in Contemporary Asian Studies, No. 2, (55)).
Chang, Parris H. (1987), 'China After Deng: Toward the 13th Party Congress', *Problems of Communism*, (May–June), 30–42.
Chang, Ta-kuang (1987), 'The Making of the Chinese Bankruptcy Law: A Study in the Chinese Legislative Process', *Harvard International Law Journal*, Vol. 28, No. 2 (Spring), 333–72.
Chen, David (1988), 'A Milestone for China as NPC Closes', *South China Morning Post*, (14 April), 7.
Chu, T'ung-tsu (1961), *Law and Society in Traditional China* (Paris: Mouton and Co.).
Clarke, Donald C. (1995), 'The Execution of Civil Judgements in China', *The China Quarterly*, No. 141 (March), 65–81.
Cohen, Jerome Alan (1968), *The Criminal Process in the People's Republic of China, 1949–1963: An Introduction* (Cambridge, MA: Harvard University Press).
Cohen, Jerome Alan (1978), 'China's Changing Constitution' *The China Quarterly*, No. 76, (December), 794–841.
Cohen, Michael, March, James G. and Olsen, Johan P. (1972), 'A Garbage Can Model of Organizational Choice', *Administrative Science Quarterly*, Vol. 17, No. 1 (March), 1–26.
Delfs, Robert (1987), 'Stamp of Authority: NPC Shows Signs of Some Teeth by Sending Back Proposal', *Far Eastern Economic Review* (23 April), 18.
Dicks, Anthony (1989), 'The Chinese Legal System: Reforms in the Balance', *The China Quarterly*, No. 119 (September), 540–76.
Dicks, Anthony (1995), 'Compartmentalized Law and Judicial Restraint: An Inductive View of Some Judicial Barriers to Reform', *The China Quarterly*, No. 141 (March), 82–109.
Di Palma, Guiseppe (1990), *To Craft Democracies: An Essay on Democratic Transitions* (Berkeley, CA: University of California Press).
Dittmer, Lowell (1994), *China Under Reform* (Boulder, CO; Westview Press).
Donnithorne, Audrey (1967), *China's Economic System* (New York: Praeger).
Donnithorne, Audrey (1972), 'China's Cellular Economy: Some Economic Trends Since the Cultural Revolution', *The China Quarterly*, No. 52 (October–November), 605–19.

Donnithorne, Audrey and Lardy, Nicholas (1976), 'Comment: Centralization and Decentralization in China's Fiscal Management', *The China Quarterly*, No. 66 (June), 328–54.
Domes, Jurgen (1985), *The Government and Politics of the PRC: A Time of Transition* (Boulder, CO: Westview Press).
Downs, Anthony (1967), *Inside Bureaucracy* (Boston, Little Brown and Co.).
Dreyer, June Teufel (1993), *China's Political System: Modernization and Tradition* (New York: Paragon House).
Edwards, R. Randle (1984), 'An Overview of Chinese Law and Legal Education', in Marvin Wolfgang (ed.), *China in Transition: The Annals of the American Academy of Political and Social Science* (November), 46–61.
Fairbank, John King (1983), *The United States and China, Fourth Edition, Enlarged* (Cambridge, MA: Harvard University Press).
Feinerman, James V. (1987), 'Law and Legal Professionalism in the People's Republic of China', in Merle Goldman *et al.* (eds.), *China's Intellectuals and the State* (Cambridge, MA: Harvard University Press).
Feinerman, James V. (1989), 'Backwards into the Future', *Law and Contemporary Problems*, Vol. 52, Nos. 2 & 3 (Spring and Summer), 169–84.
Feinerman, James V. (1991), 'Economic and Legal Reform in China, 1978–91', *Problems of Communism*, Vol. XL (September–October), 62–75.
Feinerman, James V. (1995), 'Chinese Participation in the International Legal Order: Rogue Elephant or Team Player', *The China Quarterly*, No. 141 (March), 186–210.
Feinerman, James V., Zweig, David, Hartford, Kathleen and Deng, Jianxu (1987), 'Law, Contracts, and Economic Modernization: Lessons from the Recent Chinese Rural Reforms', *Stanford Journal of International Law*, No. 23, 311–56.
Fewsmith, Joseph (1986), 'Special Economic Zones of the PRC', *Problems of Communism* (November–December), 78–85.
Fewsmith, Joseph (1994), *Dilemmas of Reform in China: Political Conflict and Economic Debate* (Armonk, NY: M. E. Sharpe).
Fewsmith, Joseph (1995), 'Neoconservatism and the End of the Dengist Era', *Asian Survey*, Vol. XXXV, No. 7 (July), 635–51.
Foreign Broadcast Information Service (1988), 'China's National People's Congress Session: Reform Amid Controversy', Analysis Report No. FB 88-10007 (10 June), 2–4, 23–9.
Foster, Frances Hoar (1982), 'Codification in Post-Mao China', *American Journal of Comparative Law*, Vol. XXX, No. 3 (Summer), 413–14.
Friedman, Edward (1994), *The Politics of Democratization, Generalizing East Asian Experiences* (Boulder, CO: Westview Press).
Gargan, Edward A. (1987), 'A Leader from China's Past Exerts a Growing Influence on the Nation's Future', *New York Times* (29 March).
Gasper, David (1982), 'The Chinese National People's Congress', in Daniel Nelson and Stephen White (eds.), *Communist Legislatures in Comparative Perspective* (Albany: State University of New York Press), 160–90.
Ginsburgs, George (1963), 'Theory and Practice of Parliamentary Procedure in Communist China: Organisation and Institutional Principles', *University of Toronto Law Journal*, Vol. 15, No. 1.

Gold, Thomas (1984), 'Just in Time! China Attacks "Spiritual Pollution" on the Even of 1984', *Asian Survey*, Vol. XXIV, No. 9 (September), 947–74.

Goldman, Merle (1981), *China's Intellectuals, Advice and Dissent* (Cambridge, MA: Harvard University Press, 1981).

Goldman, Merle (1994), *Sowing the Seeds of Democracy in China* (Cambridge, MA: Harvard University Press).

Goldstein, Avery (1994), 'Trends in the Study of Political Elites and Institutions in the PRC', *The China Quarterly*, No. 139 (September), 714–30.

Griffiths, Franklyn (1971), 'A Tendency Analysis of Soviet Policy-Making', in H. Gordon Skilling and Franklyn Griffiths (eds.), *Interest Groups in Soviet Politics* (Princeton: Princeton University Press), 335–78.

Gwertzman, Bernard and Kaufman, Michael T. (eds.) (1990), *The Collapse of Communism* (New York: Times Books, Random House).

Hahn, Jeffrey (1989), 'Power to the Soviets?' *Problems of Communism*, Vol. XXXVIII, No. 1 (January–February).

Hahn, Jeffrey (1990), 'Boss Gorbachev Confronts His New Congress', *Orbis*, Vol. 34, No. 2 (Spring), 163–78.

Hahn, Jeffrey (ed.) (1996), *Democratization in Russia: The Development of Legislative Institutions* (Armonk, NY: M. E. Sharpe).

Hall, Peter A., and Taylor, Rosemary C.R. (1996), 'Political Science and the Three "New Institutionalisms",' *Political Studies*, Vol. XLIV, 936–57.

Halpern, Nina P. (1986), 'Making Economic Policy: The Influence of Economists', in U.S. Congress Joint Economic Committee, *China Looks Toward the Year 2000*, Vol. One (Washington, DC: U.S. Government Printing Office).

Halpern, Nina P. (1989), 'Economic Reform and Democratization in Communist Systems: The Case of China', *Studies in Comparative Communism*, Vol. XXII, Nos. 2/3 (Summer/Autumn), 139–52.

Halpern, Nina P. (1992), 'Information Flows and Policy Coordination in the Chinese Bureaucracy', in Kenneth Lieberthal and David Lampton (eds.), *Bureaucracy, Politics and Decision-Making in Post-Mao China* (Berkeley: University of California Press).

Hamrin, Carol Lee (1990), *China and the Challenge of the Future: Changing Political Patterns* (Boulder, CO: Westview Press).

Harding, Harry (1981), *Organizing China, The Problem of Bureaucracy 1949–1976*, (Stanford: Stanford University Press).

Harding, Harry (1983), 'Competing Models of the Chinese Policy Process: Towards a Sorting and Evaluation', paper presented to the Twelfth Sino-America Conference on Mainland China, Airlie House, Warrenton, Virginia.

Harding, Harry (1987), *China's Second Revolution: Reform after Mao* (Washington, DC: Brookings Institution).

Heclo, Hugh (1977), *A Government of Strangers: Executive Politics in Washington* (Washington, DC: Brookings Institution).

Heclo, Hugh (1978), 'Issue Networks and the Executive Establishment', in Anthony King (ed.), *The New American Political System* (Washington: American Enterprise Institute), 87–124.

'Hong Kong NPC Delegates Interviewed', *Hong Kong Standard*, (23 April 1988), 11.

Hsia, Tao-tai (1978), 'Legal Development Since the Purge of the Gang of Four',

Proceeding Of The Seventh Sino-American Conference on Mainland China (Taibei: Institute for International Relations), IV.3.1–20.
Hsia, Tao-tai (1980), 'Sources of Law in the People's Republic of China: Recent Developments', *The International Lawyer*, Vol. 14, No. 1, 25–30.
Hsia, Tao-tai and Johnson, Constance Axinn (1986), *Law Making in the People's Republic of China: Terms, Procedures, Hierarchy, and Interpretation* (Washington, DC: Law Library, Library of Congress).
Hu Shikai (1993), 'Representation Without Democratization: The "Signature Incident" and China's National People's Congress', *The Journal of Contemporary China*, Vol. 2, No. 1 (Winter–Spring), 3–34.
Huntington, Samuel P. (1968), *Political Order in Changing Societies* (New Haven: Yale University Press).
Huntington, Samuel P. (1973), 'Congressional Responses to the Twentieth Century', in David B. Truman (ed.), *The Congress and America's Future, Second Edition* (Englewood Cliffs, NJ: Prentice-Hall), 6–38.
Huntington, Samuel P. (1987), 'The Goals of Development', in Samuel P. Huntington and Myron Weiner (eds.), *Understanding Political Development* (Boston: Little, Brown and Co.), 3–32.
Izdebski, Hubert (1989), 'Legal Aspect of Economic Reform in Socialist Countries', *The American Journal of Comparative Law*, Vol. XXXVII, No. 4 (Fall), 703–52.
Jennings, M. Kent (1997), 'Political Participation in the Chinese Countryside', *American Political Science Review*, Vol. 91, No. 2.
Johnson, Chalmers (ed.) (1970), *Change in Communist Systems* (Stanford: Stanford University Press).
Johnson, Constance Axinn (1990), *Chinese Law: A Bibliography of Selected English-Language Materials* (Washington, DC: Law Library of Congress, Far Eastern Law Division).
Jones, William C. (1994), 'The Significance of the Opinion of the Supreme People's Court for Civil Law in China', in Pitman B. Potter (ed.), *Domestic Law Reforms in Post-Mao China* (Armonk, NY: M. E. Sharpe), 97–108.
Jowitt, Kenneth (1975), 'Inclusion and Mobilization in European Leninist Regimes', *World Politics*, Vol. XXVIII, No. 1 (October), pp. 69–96.
Jowitt, Kenneth (1992), *New World Disorder: The Leninist Extinction* (Berkeley, CA: University of California Press).
Keith, Ronald C. (1994), *China's Struggle for the Rule of Law* (New York: St. Martin's Press).
Kim, Chong Lim, Barkan, Joel D., Turan, Ilter and Jewell, Malcolm E. (1984), *The Legislative Connection: The Politics of Representation in Kenya, Korea, and Turkey* (Durham, NC: Duke University Press).
Kingdon, John W. (1984), *Agendas, Alternatives, and Public Policy* (Boston: Little, Brown and Co.).
Klein, Donald W. and Clarke, Anne B. (1971), *Biographical Dictionary of Chinese Communism 1921–1965*, two volumes (Cambridge, MA: Harvard University Press).
Klein, James M. (1987), 'Communication: The Newly-enacted Regulations for Unemployment Insurance in State-owned Enterprises in the People's Republic of China', *China Law Reporter*, Vol. IV, No. 1, 67–70.

Kornai, Janos (1990), *The Road to a Free Economy: Shifting from a Socialist System, the Example of Hungary* (New York: W. W. Norton).
Kwan, Daniel (1994a), 'Congress Demands Power to Govern', *South China Morning Post* (13 September), 10.
Kwan, Daniel (1994b), 'Qiao Says NPC Must Clear All Party Decisions', *South China Morning Post* (16 September), 13.
La Dany, Father L. (1984), 'China's New Power Centre?' *Far Eastern Economic Review* (28 June), 38–9.
Lam, Willy Wo-lap (1995), *China After Deng Xiaoping: The Power Struggle in Beijing Since Tiananmen* (Hong Kong: P.A. Professional Consultants, Ltd.).
Lam, Willy Wo-lap (1996a), 'Qiao's Bid for the Throne', *South China Morning Post* (3 April), 21.
Lam, Willy Wo-lap (1996b), 'Qiao Seeks to Boost Power with NPC Call; Legislature Chairman Says Reform Must be Gradual', *South China Morning Post* (23 May), 10.
Lampton, David M. (1974), *Health, Conflict, and the Chinese Political System* (Ann Arbor: University of Michigan Center for Chinese Studies, Michigan Papers on Chinese Studies, No. 18).
Lampton, David M. (1983), 'Water: Challenge to a Fragmented Political System', paper presented to the Workshop on Policy Implementation in the Post-Mao Era, Columbus, Ohio, June.
Lampton, David M. (1986), 'Chinese Politics: The Bargaining Treadmill', paper presented to the Fifteenth Sino-American Conference on Mainland China, Institute of International Relations, National Chengchi University, Taibei, Taiwan.
Lampton, David M. (1987), 'Water: Challenge to a Fragmented Political System', in *Policy Implementation in Post-Mao China* (Berkeley: University of California Press).
Lee Lai To (1986), *Trade Unions in China 1949 to the Present* (Singapore: Singapore University Press).
Lees, John D. and Shaw, Malcom (eds.) (1979), *Committees in Legislatures, a Comparative Analysis*, (Durham, NC: Duke University Press).
Leng, Shao-chuan (1967), *Justice in Communist China* (Dobbs Ferry, NY: Oceana).
Leng, Shao-chuan and Chiu, Hungdah (1985), *Criminal Justice in Post-Mao China: Analysis and Documents*, (Albany: State University of New York Press).
Li, Victor (1971), 'The Evolution and Development of the Chinese Legal System', in John Lindbeck (ed.), *China: Management of a Revolutionary Society* (Seattle: University of Washington Press).
Lieberthal, Kenneth (1976), *Central Documents and Politburo Politics in China* in (Ann Arbor: University of Michigan Center for Chinese Studies, Michigan Papers in Chinese Studies, No. 33).
Lieberthal, Kenneth (1987), 'The Great Leap Forward and the Split in the Yenan Leadership', in Denis Twitchett and John K. Fairbank (general eds.) *The Cambridge History of China*, Vol. 14 (New York: Cambridge University Press), 293–359.
Lieberthal, Kenneth (1995), *Governing China, From Revolution Through Reform* (New York: W. W. Norton and Co.).
Lieberthal, Kenneth G. and Dickson, Bruce J. (1989), *A Research Guide to Central Party and Government Meetings in China, 1949–1986* (Armonk, NY: M. E. Sharpe).

Lieberthal, Kenneth, and Lampton, David (1992), *Bureaucracy, Politics and Decision-Making in Post-Mao China* (Berkeley: University of California Press).

Lieberthal, Kenneth and Oksenberg, Michel (1987), *Bureaucratic Politics and Chinese Energy Development* (Washington, DC: U.S. Department of Commerce, International Trade Administration, U.S. Government Printing Office).

Lieberthal, Kenneth and Oksenberg, Michel (1988), *Policy Making in China, Leaders, Structures, and Processes* (Princeton: Princeton University Press).

Lieberthal, Kenneth, with Tong, James and Yeung, Sai-cheung (1978), *Central Documents and Politburo Politics in China*, (Ann Arbor, Michigan: University of Michigan Center for Chinese Studies, Michigan Papers in Chinese Studies, No. 33).

Lijphart, Arend, and Waisman, Carlos H. (eds.) (1996), *Institutional Design in New Democracies: Eastern Europe and Latin America* (Boulder, CO: Westview Press).

Lindblom, Charles E. (1959), 'The Science of Muddling Through', *Public Administration Review* (Spring), 79–88.

Lindblom, Charles E. (1977), *Politics and Markets, The World's Political-Economic Systems* (New York: Basic Books, Inc.).

Linz, Juan J., and Stepan, Alfred (eds.) (1996), *Problems of Democratic Transition and Consolidation: Southern Europe, South America, and Post-Communist Europe* (Baltimore, MD: Johns Hopkins University Press).

Loewenberg, Gerhard and Patterson, Samuel C. (1979), *Comparing Legislatures* (Boston: Little, Brown and Co.).

Loewenberg, Gerhard, Patterson, Samuel C. and Jewell, Malcolm E. (eds.) (1985), *Handbook of Legislative Research* (Cambridge, MA: Harvard University Press), 273–321.

Lowenthal, Richard (1970), 'Development vs. Utopia in Communist Policy', in Chalmers Johnson (ed.), *Change in Communist Systems* (Stanford: Stanford University Press).

Lowenthal, Richard (1976), 'The Ruling Party in a Mature Society', in Mark G. Field (ed.), *Social Consequences of Modernization in Communist Societies* (Baltimore: Johns Hopkins University Press), 81–118.

Lubman, Stanley (1982), 'Emerging Functions of Legal Institutions in China's Modernization', in U.S. Congress Joint Economic Committee, *The Chinese Economy Post-Mao*, Part 2 (Washington, DC: U.S. Government Printing Office), 764–88.

Lubman, Stanley (1995), 'Introduction: The Future of Chinese Law', *The China Quarterly*, No. 141 (March), 1–21.

MacFarquhar, Roderick (1960), *The Hundred Flowers Campaign and Chinese Intellectuals* (New York: Praeger).

MacFarquhar, Roderick (1974), *Origins of the Cultural Revolution*, Vol. One (New York: Columbia University Press).

MacFarquhar, Roderick (1983), *Origins of the Cultural Revolution*, Vol. Two (New York: Columbia University Press).

Manion, Melanie (1993), *Retirement of Revolutionaries in China: Public Policies, Social Norms, Private Interests* (Princeton: Princeton University Press).

Manion, Melanie (1996), 'The Electoral Connection in the Chinese Countryside', *American Political Science Review*, Vol. 90, No. 4, 736–48.

McCormick, Barrett L. (1990), *Political Reform in Post-Mao China, Democracy and Bureaucracy in a Leninist State* (Berkeley: University of California Press).
McCormick, Barrett L. (1996), 'China's Leninist Parliament and Public Sphere: A Comparative Analysis', in Barrett L. McCormick and Jonathan Unger (eds.), *China After Socialism: In the Footsteps of Eastern Europe or East Asia?* (Armonk, NY: M. E. Sharpe), 29–53.
Medvedev, Roy A. (1975), *On Socialist Democracy* (New York: W. W. Norton and Co.).
Meyer, Alfred (1983), 'Communism and Leadership', *Studies in Comparative Communism*, Vol. 16, No. 3, 161–70.
Mills, William DeB. (1983), 'Generational Change in China', *Problems of Communism* (November–December), 16–35.
Mohr, Lawrence B. (1973), 'The Concept of Organizational Goal', *American Political Science Review*, Vol. 77, No. 2 (June), 470–81.
Nathan, Andrew (1973), 'A Factionalism Model of CCP Politics', *The China Quarterly*, No. 53 (January–March), 34–66.
Nathan, Andrew (1985), *Chinese Democracy* (New York: Alfred A. Knopf).
Nathan, Andrew (1990), *China's Crisis, Dilemmas of Reform and Prospects for Democracy* (New York: Columbia University Press).
Nathan, Andrew (1993), 'Chinese Democracy: The Lessons of Failure', *The Journal of Contemporary China*, No. 4 (Fall), 3–13.
Nathan, Andrew J. and Shi, Tianjian (1993), 'Cultural Requisites for Democratization in China: Findings from a Survey', *Daedalus* (Spring), 95–123.
Naughton, Barry (1987), 'The Decline in Central Control Over Investment in Post-Mao China', in David M. Lampton (ed.), *Policy Implementation in Post-Mao China* (Berkeley: University of California Press).
Nelson, Daniel and White, Stephen (eds.) (1982), *Communist Legislatures in Comparative Perspective* (Albany: State University of New York Press).
Norton, Phillip (ed.) (1990), *Legislatures* (Oxford: Oxford University Press).
O'Brien, Kevin Joseph (1987), 'The National People's Congress: Continuity and Change in Chinese Legislative Politics', Ph.D dissertation, Yale University (Ann Arbor: University Microfilms Inc.).
O'Brien, Kevin J. (1989), 'Legislative Development and Chinese Political Change', *Studies in Comparative Communism*, Vol. XXII, No. 1 (Spring), 57–75.
O'Brien, Kevin J. (1990a), *Reform Without Liberalization: China's National People's Congress and the Politics of Institutional Change* (New York: Cambridge University Press).
O'Brien, Kevin J. (1990b), 'Is China's National People's Congress a "Conservative" Legislature?' *Asian Survey*, Vol. XXX, No. 8 (August), 782–94.
O'Brien, Kevin J. (1994), 'Agents and Remonstrators: Role Accumulation by Chinese People's Congress Deputies', *The China Quarterly*, No. 138 (June), 359–80.
O'Brien, Kevin J. and Li, Lianjiang (1993–94), 'Chinese Political Reform and the Question of "Deputy Quality",' *China Information*, Vol. 8, 20–31.
O'Brien, Kevin J., and Luehrmann, Laura M. (1997), 'Institutionalizing Chinese Legislatures: Trade Offs Between Autonomy and Capacity', draft, forthcoming in *Legislative Studies Quarterly*.
Ogden, Suzanne (1992), *China's Unresolved Issues: Politics, Development, and Culture* (London: Prentice Hall), 184, 236–7.

Oksenberg, Michel (1970), 'Getting Ahead and Along in Communist China: The Ladder of Success on the Eve of the Cultural Revolution', in John Lewis (ed.), *Party Leadership and Revolutionary Power in China* (Cambridge: Cambridge University Press), 304–50.

Oksenberg, Michel (1976), 'The Exit Pattern from Chinese Politics and its Implications', *The China Quarterly*, No. 67 (September), 501–18.

Oksenberg, Michel (1982), 'Economic Policy-Making in China: Summer 1981', *The China Quarterly*, No. 90 (June), 165–94.

Oksenberg, Michel (1988), 'Research and Writing on Post-1949 China: An Interpretive Essay', in Denis Twitchett and John K. Fairbank (general eds.), *The Cambridge History of China*, Vol. 14 (New York: Cambridge University Press).

Oksenberg, Michel and Dickson, Bruce J. (1991), 'The Origins, Process, and Outcomes of Great Political Reform: A Framework for Analysis', in Dankwart A. Rustow (ed.), *Comparative Political Dynamics: Global Research Perspectives* (New York: Harper Collins).

Oksenberg, Michel and Goldstein, Steven (1974), 'The Chinese Political Spectrum', *Problems of Communism*, Vol. 23, No. 2 (March–April) 2–9.

Palmer, R. R. (1959), *The Age of the Democratic Revolutions, A Political History of Europe and America, 1760–1800 (Volume One), The Challenge* (Princeton: Princeton University Press).

Paltiel, Jeremy T. (1989), 'China: Mexicanization or Market Reform', in James A. Caporaso (ed.), *The Elusive State, International and Comparative Perspectives* (Newbury Park, CA: Sage Publications), 255–78.

Pan Qi (1988), 'Bankruptcy Law: A Newborn in China', *China Law Reporter*, Vol. IV, No. 4, 41–5.

Patterson, Samuel C. (1978), 'The Emerging Morphology of the World's Legislatures', *World Politics*, Vol. XXX, No. 3 (April), 469–81.

Peng Xiaohua (1987), 'Characteristics of China's First Bankruptcy Law', *Harvard International Law Journal*, Vol. 28, No. 2 (Spring), 373–84.

Perry, Elizabeth J. (1994), 'Trends in the Study of Chinese Politics: State-Society Relations', *The China Quarterly*, No. 139 (September), 704–13.

Pinard, Jeanette L. (1985), *The People's Republic of China: A Bibliography of Selected English-Language Legal Materials* (Washington, DC: Law Library, Library of Congress).

Polumbaum, Judy (1991), 'In the Name of Stability: Restrictions on the Right of Assembly in the People's Republic of China', *The Australian Journal of Chinese Affairs*, No. 26 (July), 43–64.

Polumbaum, Judy (1994), 'To Protect or Restrict? Points of Contention in China's Draft Press Law', in Pitman B. Potter (ed.), *Domestic Law Reforms in Post-Mao China* (Armonk, NY: M. E. Sharpe), 247–69.

Polyani, Karl (1944), *The Great Transformation* (Boston: Beacon Press).

Potter, Pitman B. (1986), 'Peng Zhen: Evolving Views on Party Organization and Law', in Carol Lee Hamrin and Timothy Cheek (eds.), *China's Establishment Intellectuals* (Armonk, NY: M. E. Sharpe) 21–50.

Potter, Pitman B. (1994a), 'The Administrative Litigation Law of the PRC: Judicial Review and Bureaucratic Reform', in Pitman B. Potter (ed.), *Domestic Law Reforms in Post-Mao China* (Armonk, NY: M. E. Sharpe), 270–304.

Potter, Pitman B. (ed.) (1994b), *Domestic Law Reforms in Post-Mao China* (Armonk, NY: M. E. Sharpe).
Potter, Pitman B. (1994c), 'Riding the Tiger: Legitimacy and Legal Culture in Post-Mao China', *The China Quarterly*, No. 138 (June), 325–58.
Powell, G. Bingham (1973), 'Incremental Democratization: The British Reform Act of 1832', in Gabriel Almond, Scott C. Flanagan and Robert J. Mundt (eds.), *Crisis, Choice, and Change: Historical Studies of Political Development* (Boston: Little, Brown and Co.).
Pye, Lucian W. (1981), *The Dynamics of Chinese Politics* (Cambridge: Oelgeschlager, Gunn, and Hain).
Pye, Lucian W. (1984), *China: An Introduction, Third Edition* (Boston: Little, Brown and Co.).
Pye, Lucian W. (1988), *The Mandarin and the Cadre: China's Political Cultures* (Ann Arbor: University of Michigan Center for Chinese Studies).
Pye, Lucian W. (1991), *China: An Introduction, Fourth Edition* (New York: Harper Collins).
Rahr, Alexander and Pomeranz, William (1991), 'Russian Democrats Yesterday and Today', RFE/RL Research Institute *Report on the USSR* (10 May), 16–17.
Richman, Barry M. (1969), *Industrial Society in Communist China* (New York: Random House).
Sabbat-Swidlicka, Anna (1990a), 'The Government Reaches A Turning Point', Radio Free Europe/Radio Liberty (RFE/RL) Research Institute, *Report on Eastern Europe*, (13 July), 25–31.
Sabbat-Swidlicka, Anna (1990b), 'Poland in 1989', Radio Free Europe/Radio Liberty (RFE/RL) Research Institute, *Report on Eastern Europe*, (5 January), 24–27.
Sabbat-Swidlicka, Anna (1991a), 'Solidarity's Third Congress: A New Chairman and a New Chapter', Radio Free Europe/Radio Liberty (RFE/RL) Research Institute, *Report on Eastern Europe* (22 March), 12–16.
Sabbat-Swidlicka, Anna (1991b), 'Sejm Rejects President's Proposals for Early Elections', Radio Free Europe/Radio Liberty (RFE/RL) Research Institute, *Report on Eastern Europe* (22 March), 16–21.
Saich, Tony (1981), *China: Politics and Government* (New York: Macmillan), 120–2.
Sautman, Barry (1992), 'Sirens of the Strongman: Neo-Authoritarianism in Recent Chinese Political Theory', *The China Quarterly*, No. 129 (March), 72–102.
Schmitter, Phillipe (1974), 'Still the Century of Corporatism?' in Frederick B. Pike and Thomas Stritch (eds.), *The New Corporatism* (Notre Dame: University of Notre Dame Press), 85–131.
Schulman, Paul R. (1975), 'Non-Incremental Policy Making', *American Political Science Review*, Vol. 69 (December), 1354–70.
Schurman, Franz (1968), *Ideology and Organization in Communist China* (second edition) (Berkeley: University of California Press).
Schwartz, Benjamin (1957), 'On Attitudes Toward Law in China', first published in Milton Katz (ed.), *Government Under Law and the Individual* (Washington, DC), 27–39, reprinted in Jerome Alan Cohen, (1968) *The Criminal Process in the People's Republic of China, 1949–1963: An Introduction* (Cambridge, MA: Harvard University Press), 62–70.
Shepsle, Kenneth (1988), 'Representation and Governance: The Great Legislative Trade-off', *Political Science Quarterly*, Vol. 103, No. 3 (Fall), 461–84.

Simon, Herbert A. (1957), 'A Behavioral Model of Rational Choice', in *Models of Man: Social and Rational* (New York: John Wiley), 241–260.
Simon, Herbert A. (1964), 'On the Concept of Organizational Goal', *Administrative Science Quarterly*, Vol. 9, No. 1, 1–22.
Sisson, Richard and Snowiss, Leo (1979), 'Legislative Viability and Political Development', in Joel Smith and Lloyd Musolf (eds.), *Legislatures in Development: Dynamics of Change in New and Old States* (Durham, NC: Duke University Press), 43–67.
Skinner, G. William and Winckler, Edwin A. (1969), 'Compliance Succession in Rural Communist China: A Cyclical Theory', in Amitai Etzioni (ed.), *A Sociological Reader on Complex Organizations, Second Edition* (New York: Holt, Rinehart, and Winston), 410–38.
Smith, Hedrick (1988), *The Power Game* (New York: Ballantine Books).
Smith, Joel and Musolf, Lloyd (eds.) (1979), *Legislatures in Development: Dynamics of Change in New and Old States* (Durham, NC: Duke University Press).
Solinger, Dorothy (1982), 'The Fifth NPC and the Process of Policy-Making', *Asian Survey*, No. 12 (December), 1238–75.
Solinger, Dorothy (1984), *Chinese Business Under Socialism* (Berkeley: University of California Press).
Solinger, Dorothy (1986), 'China's New Economic Policies and the Local Industrial Political Process, The Case of Wuhan', *Comparative Politics*, Vol. 18, No. 4 (July), 379–400.
Solinger, Dorothy (1992), 'Urban Entrepreneurs and the State: The Merger of State and Society', in Arthur Rosenbaum (ed.), *State and Society in China: The Consequences of Reform* (Boulder, CO: Westview Press), 121–42.
'Speak No Evil. The Party Puts a Lid on Criticism', *The Far Eastern Economic Review* (30 March 1989), 11.
Stahnke, Arthur (1967), 'The Background and Evolution of Party Policy on the Drafting of Legal Codes in Communist China', *American Journal of Comparative Law*, No. 15, 506–28.
Steele, Jonathan (1994), *Eternal Russia, Yeltsin, Gorbachev, and the Mirage of Democracy* (Cambridge, MA: Harvard University Press).
Tanner, Murray Scot (1990), 'The Organizational Evolution of Communist Party Control Over Lawmaking in China', *Facing East/Facing West: North America and the Asia/Pacific Region in the 1990s* (Kalamazoo: Western Michigan University Office of International Affairs), 218–26.
Tanner, Murray Scot (1994a), 'Organizations and Politics in China's Post-Mao Lawmaking System', in Pitman B. Potter (ed.), *Domestic Law Reforms in Post-Mao China* (Armonk, NY: M. E. Sharpe), 56–96.
Tanner, Murray Scot (1994b), 'The Erosion of Central Party Control Over Lawmaking', *The China Quarterly*, No. 138 (June), 381–403.
Tanner, Murray Scot (1994c), 'Law in China: The *Terra Incognita* of Political Studies', *China Exchange News*, Vol. 22, No. 4 (Winter), 20–4.
Tanner, Murray Scot (1995), 'How a Bill Becomes a Law in China: Stages and Processes in Lawmaking', *The China Quarterly*, No. 141 (March), 39–64.
Tanner, Murray Scot, with Chen, Ke (1998), 'China's National People's Congress: Learning to Just Say "No",' *Problems of Post Communism* (forthcoming, May).
Tanner, Murray Scot with Feder, Michael J. (1993), '"Family Politics" Elite

Recruitment and Succession: Post-Mao China in Comparative Perspective', *The Australian Journal of Chinese Affairs*, No. 30 (July), 89–120.

Teague, Elizabeth and Mann, Dawn (1990), 'Gorbachev's Dual Role', *Problems of Communism*, Vol. XXXIX (January–February), 1–14.

Teiwes, Frederick C. (1984), *Leadership, Legitimacy, and Conflict in China* (Armonk, NY: M. E. Sharpe).

Thelen, Kathleen, and Steinmo, Sven (1992), 'Historical Institutionalism in Comparative Politics', in Sven Steinmo, Kathleen Thelen and Frank Longstreth (eds.), *Structuring Politics: Historical Institutionalism in Comparative Analysis* (New York: Cambridge University Press), 1–32.

Townsend, James R. (1974), *Politics in China* (first edition) (Boston: Little, Brown and Co.).

Townsend, James R., and Womack, Brantley (1986), *Politics in China* (Third Edition) (Boston: Little, Brown and Co.).

Tsou Tang (1986a), 'Back from the Brink of Revolutionary-"Feudal" Totalitarianism', in *The Cultural Revolution and Post-Mao Reforms, A Historical Perspective* (Chicago: University of Chicago Press), 144–88.

Tsou Tang (1986b), 'Prolegomenon to the Study of Informal Groups in CCP Politics', in *The Cultural Revolution and Post-Mao Reforms, A Historical Perspective* (Chicago: University of Chicago Press), 95–112.

Tsou Tang (1986c), 'Political Change and Reform: The Middle Course', in *The Cultural Revolution and Post-Mao Reforms, A Historical Perspective* (Chicago: University of Chicago Press), 219–58.

Tyson, Ann Scott (1988), 'Chinese Go For Broke: National Parliament Poised to Approve Bankruptcy Law to Punish Debt-Ridden Companies', *Christian Science Monitor* (24 March), 1, 9.

Vinton, Louisa (1991a), 'Bielecki Confirmed as New Prime Minister', Radio Free Europe/Radio Liberty (RFE/RL) Research Institute, *Report On Eastern Europe* (25 January), 17–19.

Vinton, Louisa (1991b), 'The Sejm Confirms the New Government', Radio Free Europe/Radio Liberty (RFE/RL) Research Institute, *Report on Eastern Europe* (25 January), 25–27.

Walder, Andrew (1986), *Communist Neo-traditionalism: Work and Authority in Chinese Industry* (Berkeley: University of California Press).

Walder, Andrew G. (1995), *The Waning of the Communist State: Economic Origins of Political Decline in China and Hungary* (Berkeley, CA: University of California Press).

Wang, James C. F. (1989), *Contemporary Chinese Politics: An Introduction* (third edition) (Englewood Cliffs, NJ: Prentice Hall).

Weber, Max (1946), 'Essay on Bureaucracy', in H. H. Gerth and C. Wright Mills *From Max Weber: Essays in Sociology* (New York: Oxford University Press), 196–244.

de Weydenthal, Jan B. (1991), 'The First Hundred Days of Walesa's Presidency', Radio Free Europe/Radio Liberty (RFE/RL) Research Institute, *Report on Eastern Europe* (5 April), 9–12.

White, Stephen (1992), *Gorbachev and After* (Cambridge: Cambridge University Press).

Whyte, Martin King (1992a), 'Democratization in China', *Problems of Communism* (May–June).

Whyte, Martin King (1992b), 'Urban China: A Civil Society in the Making?' in Arthur Rosenbaum (ed.), *State and Society in China: The Consequences of Reform* (Boulder, CO: Westview Press), 77–101.
Wildavsky, Aaron (1984), *The Politics of the Budgetary Process* (fourth edition) (Boston: Little, Brown and Co.).
Womack, Brantley (1984), 'Modernization and Democratic Reform in China', *Journal of Asian Studies*, Vol. XLIII, No. 3 (May), 417–39.
Womack, Brantley (1991), 'In Search of Democracy: Public Authority and Popular Power in China', in Brantley Womack (ed.), *Contemporary Chinese Politics in Historical Perspective* (Cambridge, Cambridge University Press), 53–89.
Yin, Robert K. (1984), *Case Study Research: Design and Methods* (Beverley Hills, CA: Sage Publications, Sage Applied Social Science Research Methods Series, Vol. 5).
Zhao Suisheng (1993), 'A Tragedy of History: The Chinese Search of Democracy in the Twentieth Century', *The Journal of Contemporary China*, No. 3 (Summer), 18–37.

Chinese Language Sources in Translation

'All-China Federation of Trade Unions Circular on Implementing Enterprise Law', BXDS, 23 May 1988 (FBIS translation, unpublished copy).
An Zhiwen (1987), 'Speed Up and Deepen Reforms', *Zhongguo Jingji Tizhi Gaige*, No. 8 (23 August) 4–6, 11, in FBIS-CHI, 9 September 1987, 17–20.
'Article Views People's Congress System', *Jingji Cankao*, 17 September 1989, 4, in FBIS-CHI, 13 October 1989, 27–30.
Bao Xin (1988), 'Letter From Beijing', *Liaowang* (Overseas Edition), No. 15 (11 April), 1, in FBIS-CHI, 22 April 1988, 16–17.
Cao Siyuan (1987), 'The Bankruptcy Law is Needed for the Development of the Commodity Economy', *Jingji Ribao* (24 October), 3 (FBIS translation, unpublished, no date).
Cao Siyuan (1988), 'Economist Urges Constitutional Amendments', interview by Wu Xiaoming, *China Daily* (8 April), in FBIS-CHI, 8 April 1988, 31–32.
'CCP Central Committee Holds 2nd Plenary Session: Zhao Delivers Work Report', *Renmin Ribao* (Overseas Edition), 21 March 1988, 1, 4, in FBIS-CHI, 21 March 1988, 20–27.
'A Chapter in Blazing New Trails in Enterprise Reform—Excerpts of Speeches Who Have Won Awards for Blazing Trails in Enterprise Reform', *Renmin Ribao*, 16 February 1988, 2 (FBIS translation, unpublished copy).
Chang, Po-chun (1965), 'I Bow My Head and Admit My Guilt Before the People', in Robert R. Bowie and John King Fairbank (eds.), *Communist China 1955–1959: Policy Documents with Analysis.* (Cambridge, MA: Harvard University Press), 330–40.
Chen Pixian (1985), 'NPC Standing Committee Work Report', BXDS (14 April), in FBIS-CHI, 23 April 1985, pp. K1–7.
Chen Pixian (1986), 'NPC Standing Committee Work Report', BXDS, in FBIS-CHI, 25 April 1986, K1–4.
Chen Pixian (1988), 'NPC Standing Committee Work Report', BXDS (19 April), in FBIS-CHI, 27 April 1988, 11–19.

'Chengming Views Peng Zhen's Situation', *Chengming* (Hong Kong), No. 126, 1 April 1988, 6–9, in FBIS-CHI, 1 April 1988, 42–46.

Chi Fulin (1988), 'A Talk on Understanding of Guarantee and Supervision by Enterprise Party Organizations', *Renmin Ribao* (10 March), 10, in FBIS-CHI, 13 April 1988, 41.

China Daily Commentator (1988), 'Circular Solicits Views on Enterprise Law', *China Daily* (14 January), 4.

'Circular Details Enterprise Leadership System', BXDS, 11 January 1987, in FBIS-CHI, 15 January 1987, K20.

'Closing [NPC Standing Committee] Session Adopts Laws', BXDS, 21 January 1985, in FBIS-CHI, 22 January 1985, pp. K13–14.

'Commentator' (1986a), 'An Important Law for Promoting Economic Structural Reform', *Gongren Ribao* (3 December), 1.

'Commentator' (1986b), 'The Bankruptcy System May First Be Carried Out in Enterprises', *Renmin Ribao* (28 August) 1, in FBIS-CHI, 2 September 1986, pp. K16–17.

'Commentator' (1988a), 'Be Prepared for the Test of Market Competition—Written on the Formal Implementation of the Enterprise Law', *Renmin Ribao* (1 August) 1 (FBIS translation, unpublished copy).

'Commentator' (1988b), 'Conscientiously Implement the "Enterprise Law",' *Renmin Ribao* (16 April), 1, in FBIS-CHI, 19 April 1988, 51–52.

The Constitution of the People's Republic of China (1975), in John L. Scherer (ed.), *China Facts and Figures Annual, Volume I, 1978* (Gulf Breeze, FL: Academic International Press, 1978).

The Constitution of the People's Republic of China (1978), in John L. Scherer (ed.), *China Facts and Figures Annual, Volume I, 1978* (Gulf Breeze, FL: Academic International Press, 1978).

The Constitution of the People's Republic of China (1982), in *The Fifth Session of the Fifth National People's Congress (Main Documents)* (Beijing: Foreign Languages Press, 1983). Also available in John L. Scherer (ed.), *China Facts and Figures Annual, Volume 6, 1983* (Gulf Breeze, FL: Academic International Press, 1983).

'Counter-revolutionary Revisionist P'eng Chen's Towering Crimes of Opposing the Party, Socialism and the Thought of Mao Tse-tung', *Survey of China Mainland Magazines*, No. 639 (1967), 9–12.

'Decision of the Central Committee of the Communist Party of China on Reform of the Economic Structure', *Beijing Review*, 20 October 1984.

'Demonstration Draft Law Detailed', BXDS, 6 July 1989, in FBIS-CHI, 10 July 1989, 33–6.

Deng Xiaoping (1984), *Selected Works of Deng Xiaoping (1975–1982)* (Beijing: Foreign Languages Press).

Deng Xiaoping (1994), *Selected Works of Deng Xiaoping, Volume III (1982–1992)* (Beijing: Foreign Languages Press).

'Dossier of P'eng Chen—Big Renegade, Big Party Tyrant, and Counter-revolutionary Revisionist', Report by the 'Red Alliance' Combat Team, 2nd Corps, 3rd Red Headquarters, in *Selections from China Mainland Magazines (Supplement)*, No. 27, 8 July 1967 (U.S. Consul General, Hong Kong), 33–9.

'Draft Enterprise Law Adoption Urged', BXE, 3 April 1988 in FBIS-CHI, 4 April 1988, 36–7.

Bibliography 267

'Draft Demonstrations Law Revised', BXE, 30 October 1989, in FBIS-CHI, 31 October 1989, 13–14.
'Draft Law on Demonstrations Submitted for Debate', BXE, 3 July 1989, in FBIS-CHI, 3 July 1989, 38–9.
'Draft Law on State-Owned Enterprises', BXDS, 11 January 1988, in FBIS-CHI, 20 January 1988, 27–32.
'Drag Out Teng Hsiao-p'ing from the Black Den as a Warning to Others', *Hsin Peita* [*Xin Beida*], 25 February 1967, *Survey of the China Mainland Press (Supplement)*, No. 177, 19 April 1967 (U.S. Consul General, Hong Kong), 5.
Du Feijin, Li Su and Hong Xiaoyuan (1988), 'Perfect the Legal Entity System and Devise a Pattern for Separating Ownership and Management', *Renmin Ribao* (7 March), 5.
Editorial, 'A Vivid Manifestation of Initiative in Discussing and Participating in Politics: Roundup of Manuscripts Contributed to the Discussion on the "Bankruptcy Law",' *Gongren Ribao*, 15 November 1986, 3.
'Enterprise Managers on Enterprise Reforms', *Renmin Ribao* 16 February 1988, 2, in FBIS-CHI, 23 February 1988, 14–17.
'Entrepreneurs on Workers Rights', BXE, 7 April 1988, in FBIS-CHI, 8 April 1988, 32.
'"Explanation" of NPC's Hu Jiwei Criticized', *Renmin Ribao* (Overseas Edition), 11 July 1989, 1, in FBIS-CHI, 11 July 1989, 22–3.
Feng Lanrui (1986), 'The Positive Meaning of the Bankruptcy System', *Renmin Ribao* (22 August), 5, in FBIS-CHI, 2 September 1986, pp. K13–16.
Fu Chung (1988), 'Old Guys of the Seventh NPC "Exchange Positions", and Zhao is Firm About Dismissing Hongqi', *Ching Pao*, No. 129 (10 April), 34–38, in FBIS-CHI, 19 April 1988, pp. 39–44.
Gao Cheng (1986), 'The State Accepts No Unlimited Responsibility for an Enterprise Going Bankrupt', *Gongren Ribao* (1 November), 3.
Guan Huai (1988), 'It is Necessary to Define the Master Status of Workers in Enterprises—some Suggestions for Perfecting the "Enterprise Law",' *Gongren Ribao* (26 January), 3, in FBIS-CHI, 11 February 1988, 23–5.
'Guangdong Deputies on Enterprise Law', BXE, 1 April 1988, in FBIS-CHI, 4 April 1988, 36.
'Guangdong's Yu Fei Stresses Enterprise Law', Guangzhou Guangdong Provincial Service, 30 July 1988 (FBIS translation, unpublished copy).
He Ping and Zhang Sutang (1988), 'The Deepening of Reforms Calls for Adopting an Enterprise Law as Soon as Possible', BXDS (21 January), in FBIS-CHI, 1 February 1988, 27–9.
'Hebei Deputies on Enterprise Law', BXE, 4 April 1988, in FBIS-CHI, 7 April 1988, 18.
Hu Ge (1986), 'Bankruptcy and Unemployment are Not in Contradiction with the Principles of the Constitution', *Gongren Ribao* (1 November), 3.
Hu Jiwei (1989), 'Establish Democratic Authority', *Jingjixue Zhoubao* (*Economic Studies Weekly*), in Michel Oksenberg, Lawrence Sullivan, and Marc Lambert (eds.), *Beijing Spring, 1989: Confrontation and Conflict, The Basic Documents* (Armonk, NY: M. E. Sharpe, 1990), 138–44.
'Hu Jiwei Explanation Questioned', BXE, 5 July 1989, in FBIS-CHI, 6 July 1989, 42–7.

Jin Mosheng [Chin Mo-sheng] (1978), 'Several Proposals for Strengthening the Legal System', *Renmin Ribao* (6 December) 3, in FBIS-CHI, 14 December 1978, E23–4.
'Law Committee Chairman Reports on Draft Laws', BXDS, 9 April 1988, in FBIS-CHI, 12 April 1988, 28–31.
'Law on Demonstrations, Assemblies Examined', *Renmin Ribao*, 1 November 1989, 2, in FBIS-CHI, 8 November 1989, 25–56.
Li Quande (1984), 'Set Up a Bankruptcy System with Special Chinese Characteristics', *Liaowang*, No. 35 (27 August), 21, in FBIS-CHI, 21 September 1984, pp. K24–6.
Liao Gailong (1980), 'Historical Experiences and Our Road of Development (Part 1)', Report on CCP History Delivered to a Central Party-School Forum, *Issues and Studies* (Taibei), Vol. XVII, No. 12 (December 1981), 65–104.
'Liaoning Factory Becomes First Bankruptcy in PRC', BXE, 3 August 1986, in FBIS-CHI, 6 August 1986, S1.
'Liaowang Explains Draft Bankruptcy Law', *Liaowang* (Overseas Edition), No. 4, 27 January 1986, 10, in FBIS-CHI, 13 February 1986, K21–5.
Lin Hsin-tao (1980), 'Supreme Paramount Power—How the NPC Can be Really Worthy of its Name', *Wen Wei Po* (Hong Kong), (9 November), 3, in *JPRS China Report: Political, Sociological and Military Affairs*, No. 148, 26–8.
'List of Pre-1978 Laws Declared Invalid', *Zhongguo Fazhi Bao*, 27 November 1987, 2, in FBIS-CHI, 12 February 1988, 4.
Liu Dizhong (1984), 'Managerial Reform to Give Directors Total Responsibility', *China Daily* (8 August), 1.
Liu Zhaoxing (1986), 'Two Kinds of Worries are Unnecessary', *Gongren Ribao* (1 November), 3.
Lo, Lung-chi (1965), 'My Preliminary Examination', in Robert R. Bowie and John King Fairbank (eds.), *Communist China 1955–1959: Policy Documents with Analysis* (Cambridge, MA: Harvard University Press), 330–40.
Lu Mu (1988), 'NPC Standing Committee Holds Group Discussion to Examine Draft Enterprise Law', *Renmin Ribao* (14 January), 1, in FBIS-CHI, 19 January 1988, 17–18.
Lu Mu and Liu Guosheng (1988), 'Consolidate the Achievements of Reform, Promote Deepening of Reform—Excerpts of Speeches at the Forum on "Draft Enterprise Law",' *Renmin Ribao* (9 February), 2.
Lu Mu, Pi Shuyi and Du Feijin (1988), 'Entrepreneurs Speak on Enterprise Law— Summary of a Forum of Some Plant Directors and Managers in Beijing Sponsored by Renmin Ribao Economic Department', *Renmin Ribao* (9 January), 2, in FBIS-CHI, 21 January 1988, 20–3.
'Mayors Criticize Draft Enterprise Law', BXDS, 2 April 1988, in FBIS-CHI, 4 April 1988, 35–6.
'NPC Celebrates 40th Anniversary', Xinhua News Agency, 15 September 1994, available on NEXIS-LEXIS.
'NPC Committee Agenda Announced', BXDS, 26 August 1988, translation by FBIS, 27 August 1988, unpublished copy.
'NPC Delegates Note Defects in Enterprise Law', *China Daily*, 8 April 1988, 3.
'NPC Deputies Discuss Industry', *China Daily*, 6 April 1987, 4.

'NPC on Enterprise Draft Law, Constitution', BXE, 8 March 1988, in FBIS-CHI, 9 March 1988, 14–15.
'NPC Examines Draft Laws on Factory Directors, Secrets', *China Daily*, 12 January 1988, 1.
'NPC Examines Publicly Owned Enterprises Law', BXE, 15 November 1986, transcription by FBIS, 15 November 1986, unpublished copy.
'NPC Presidium Adopts Electoral Rules', BXE, 1 April 1988, in FBIS-CHI, 1 April 1988, 11.
'NPC Presidium Holds Fourth Meeting', BXDS, 5 April 1988, in FBIS-CHI, 5 April 1988, 11.
'NPC Press Conference Views Legislative Work', Beijing Television Service, 7 April 1987, in FBIS-CHI, 8 April 1987, K1–5.
'NPC Session Adopts Enterprise Law', BXE, 13 April 1988 (FBIS translation, unpublished copy).
'NPC Session Deliberates on Enterprise Law', BXE, 13 March 1987 in FBIS-CHI, 17 March 1987, K18–19.
'NPC Session Discusses Party Role in Enterprises', BXDS, 18 March 1987 in FBIS-CHI, 19 March 1987, K3–4.
'NPC Standing Committee Meeting Opens 16 June', BXE, 16 June 1986, in FBIS-CHI, 16 June 1986, K1–2.
'NPC Standing Committee 16th Session Begins', BXDS, 16 June 1986, in FBIS-CHI, 17 June 1986, K1–2.
'NPC Voting Tables Published', *Wen Wei Po* (Hong Kong), 30 March 1993, 2, in FBIS-CHI, 31 March 1993, 38.
Organic Law of the National People's Congress of the People's Republic of China (1954), in Albert P. Blaustein (ed.), *Fundamental Legal Documents of Communist China* (South Hackensack, NJ: Fred B. Rothman and Co., 1962), 115–26.
Organic Law of the National People's Congress of the People's Republic of China (1982), in John L. Scherer (ed.), *China Facts and Figures Annual, Volume 6, 1983* (Gulf Breeze, FL: Academic International Press, 1983).
'Peng Zhen Advocates Need for Bankruptcy Law', BXE, 29 November 1986 (FBIS translation personal copy, unpublished).
'Peng Zhen Meets Hong Kong, Macao Reporters', Beijing Television Service, 8 April 1987, in FBIS-CHI, 9 April 1987, K1–16.
'Peng Zhen's New Role as NPC Chairman Forecast', Dongxifang (East and West [Hong Kong]), 10 May 1980, 15–17, JPRS translation, undated.
'Peng Zhen Speaks on Economic Law at NPC Seminar', BXDS, 23 January 1985, in FBIS-CHI, 24 January 1985, K13–15. For a Chinese text, see 'Peng Zhen zai Renda Changweihui Juxing de Zuotanhui shang Zhichu Jingji Lifa Hen Xuyao, Tansuo, Shiyan Jieduan Buke Shao', BXDS, in *Renmin Ribao*, 24 January 1985.
'People's Congresses, Tripartite System Compared', *Renmin Ribao*, 30 October 1989, in FBIS-CHI, 27 November 1989, 20–3.
'Practising Reform Vital to Draft Enterprise Law', BXDS, 5 February 1988, in FBIS-CHI, 10 February 1988, 24.
'Professionals Discuss Draft Enterprise Law', Shijie Jingji Daobao (Shanghai), 21 December 1987, 13, in FBIS-CHI, 21 January 1988, 17–20.
'Provisional Regulations for the Workers Congresses in State-Owned Industrial Enterprises', BXE, 19 July 1981, in FBIS-CHI, 23 July 1981, K3–7.

Qian Yuan (1986), 'Will Workers Lose Their Right to Work When an Enterprise Goes Bankrupt?' *Gongren Ribao* (1 November), 3.
Qiao Shi (1994), Excerpts of Qiao Shi's Speech Commemorating the 40th Anniversary of the NPC's Establishment, BXE in BBC Summary of World Broadcasts (20 September), available on NEXIS-LEXIS.
'Qiao Shi Calls for Rule of Law', *Xinhua General News Service*, 31 March 1993, available on NEXIS-LEXIS.
'Qiao Shi Stresses Importance of Building Up Legal System', *Xinhua General News Service*, 3 July 1993, available on NEXIS-LEXIS.
'Rallies, Demonstration Law Revised', BXE 25 October 1989, in FBIS-CHI 25 October 1989, 12.
'Shenyang Enterprises Warned Against Bankruptcy', BXE, 1 August 1985, in FBIS-CHI, 9 August 1985, S1–2.
'Signature Incident Discussed', BXE, 5 July 1989, in FBIS-CHI, 5 July 1989, 27–8.
'Spokesman Gives Press Conference', at First Session of Seventh NPC, BXDS, 24 March 1988, in FBIS-CHI, 24 March 1988, 16–18.
'State Council Provisional Rules for Further Expansion of Decision-making Power of State-Run Industrial Enterprises', *State Council Bulletin*, No. 10, 30 May 1984, 323–5, in JPRS-CPS-84-087, 13 December 1984, 7–10.
'State Council to Act on 37 Draft Laws', BXE, 23 March 1988, in FBIS-CHI, 24 March 1988, 39.
'Strict Implementation of Enterprise Law Urged', BXE, 29 July 1988, in FBIS-CHI, 2 August 1988, 35.
Sun Yunling (1986), 'Establish the Enterprise Bankruptcy System, Improve the Enterprise Behaviour Mechanism', *Jingji Cankao* (21 June), 6 (FBIS translation, unpublished, no date).
'Ta Kung Pao on CPC Plenary Session', *Ta Kung Pao* (Hong Kong), 29 September–5 October 1988, 2, reprinted in FBIS-CHI, 29 September 1988, 23.
Tao Guofeng (1986), 'Report on passage of Enterprise Bankruptcy Law', *Jingji Ribao* (3 December), 1 (FBIS translation, unpublished copy).
Tian Jiyun (1986), Speech to the '8,000 Cadres Conference' on 6 January, in FBIS-CHI, 13 January 1986, K5–20.
'Tibetans Want More Favorable Policies', BXE, 5 April 1988, in FBIS-CHI, 6 April 1988, 21.
'Wan Li Addresses Committee', *Renmin Ribao*, 30 June 1989, 1, in FBIS-CHI, 3 July 1989, pp. 25–7.
'Wan Li on Tasks of the NPC', BXE, 13 April 1988 (FBIS translation, unpublished copy).
'Wang Han-pin [Wang Hanbin]—Secretary General of the NPC Standing Committee', *Issues and Studies* (Taibei), May 1987, 150–2.
Wang Yongqing (1986), 'Joining the Discussion that Laws Must Protect the People's Interests', *Gongren Ribao* (1 November), 3 (FBIS translation, unpublished, no date).
Who's Who in China: Current Leaders, 1994 Edition (bilingual edition, also entitled *Zhongguo Renming Dacidian, Xianren Dangzhengjun Lingdao Renwo Juan*) (Beijing: Foreign Languages Press, 1994).
Wu Jialing (1980), 'How to Bring into Full Play the Function of the National

People's Congress as the Organ of Supreme Power', *Guangming Ribao* (30 October), in FBIS-CHI, 25 November 1980, L32.
Wu Jiaxiang (1989), 'Commenting on Neo-Authoritarianism', *Shijie Jingji Daobao* (*World Economic Herald*, Shanghai), in Michel Oksenberg, Lawrence Sullivan and Marc Lambert (eds.), *Beijing Spring, 1989: Confrontation and Conflict, The Basic Documents* (Armonk, NY: M. E. Sharpe, 1990), 130–4.
'Wuhan Government Warns Enterprises on Bankruptcy', BXE, 10 August 1986, in FBIS-CHI, 11 August 1986, P4.
Yang Shangkun (1983), 'NPC Standing Committee Work Report', BXDS, (25 June), in FBIS-CHI, 27 June 1983, K9–14.
Yuan Baohua (1985), 'Reform the Management of Enterprises and Promote Modernization of Enterprise Management', *Jingji Ribao* (27 March), 3, in FBIS-CHI, 4 April 1985, K18–22.
'Yuan Baohua Addresses National Economic Forum', BXDS, 14 February 1985, in FBIS-CHI, 19 February 1985, K7–9.
'Yuan Baohua on State Firms Law', ZGXWS, 15 January 1985, in FBIS-CHI, 17 January 1985, K7–8.
'Yuan Baohua on State Firms Law', BXDS, 15 January 1985, in FBIS-CHI, 22 January 1985, K4–6.
Zhang Sutang and He Ping (1993), 'The Light Boat Has Swiftly Passed Through the Mountains—Looking Back on the Seventh National People's Congress', BXDS (8 March), in FBIS-CHI, 9 March 1993, 14–17.
'Zhang Yanning Remarks on Bankrupt Enterprise', BXDS, 26 July 1988, in FBIS-CHI, 2 August 1988, 35.
Zhao Ziyang (1983), 'Report on the Work of the Government' (delivered at the First Session of the Sixth National People's Congress on 6 June), *Beijing Review*, No. 27 (4 July), special section, I–XXIV.
Zhao Ziyang (1986), 'Report on the Seventh Five Year Plan at the Fourth Session of the Sixth National People's Congress', BXDS (25 March), in FBIS-CHI, 28 March 1986.
Zhao Ziyang (1987), 'Advance Along the Road of Socialism with Chinese Characteristics—Report Delivered at the Thirteenth National Congress of the Communist Party of China on October 25, 1987', *Beijing Review* (9–15 November), 23–49.
Zeng Pu (1986), 'Discussion of Legislative Issues in Newspapers Can Do Much Good', *Gongren Ribao* (15 November), 3.

Chinese Language Sources

Beijing University Law Department (ed.) (1989), *Gaige yu Fazhi Jianshe* (*Reform and the Construction of the Legal System—A Collection of Essays on Legal Studies to Commemorate the 90th Anniversary of Beijing University*) (Beijing: Guangming Ribao Chubanshe).
Cao Haiquan (1985), *Dui 'Qiye Pochan Fa' Dagang Yaodian de Gouxiang* (*Structure and Essential Outline of 'The Enterprise Bankruptcy Law'*), *Tizhi Gaige Tansuo* (Chongqing Sichuan: [Sichuan Provincial Economic Structure Reform Office publication?]), No. 4, 12–16. (Note: Given the topic and the physical similarity of the Chinese characters, 'Cao Haiquan' may in fact be either a misprint or a pseudonym for Cao Siyuan.)

Cao Siyuan (1980), 'Zai Jingzheng Zhong Fahui Baoxian Gongsi Zuoyong de Shexiang' ('An Idea for Giving Full Play to the Role of Insurance Companies in Competition'), *Caiyi Jingji* (Beijing: Zhongguo Shehui Kexueyuan Gongye Jingji Yanjiu Suo), No. 5, V47–9.

Cao Siyuan (1983), 'Shixing Pochan Fa, Zhengqu Gao Xiaoyi: Guanyu 'Qiye Pochan Zhengdun Fa' de Fangan Shexiang' ('Carry Out the Bankruptcy Law, Strive for High Efficiency: An Idea Concerning the Matter of an "Enterprise Bankruptcy Consolidation Law"'), *Jishu Jingji Yanjiu Ziliao* (State Council Technical Economic Research Center), No. 9 (September), General No. 125, 1–12.

Cao Siyuan (1984a), 'Guanyu Zhiding Pochan Fa de Jianyi' ('Concerning a Suggestion for Drafting a Bankruptcy Law'), *Shehui Kexue* (Beijing), No. 11, 42–6.

Cao Siyuan (1984b), 'Zengqiang Qiye Huoli de Falu Cuoshi' ('Legal Measures for Increasing the Vitality of Enterprises'), *Minzhu yu Fazhi* (Beijing: PRC Ministry of Justice) (November), 7–11.

Cao Siyuan (1985), 'Pochanfa yu jingji tizhi gaige' ('The Bankruptcy Law and Economic Structural Reform'), *Zhong Qingnian Jingji Luntan* (*Young Chinese Economists Discussions*) (Tianjin), No. 1, 16–17.

Cao Siyuan (1986), *Jingji Fazhan yu Tizhi Gaige* (*Economic Development and Structural Reform*) (Beijing: Chinese Economic Structural Reform Research Institute & Beijing Young Economists Study Society Joint Publication), No. 5, 32–40.

Cao Siyuan (1988a), *Sitong Shehui Fazhan Yanjiu Suo Suozhang Cao Siyuan Jianli* (*Resume of Cao Siyuan, Director of the Sitong Corporation* [aka Stone Corporation] *Social Development Research Institute*) (Beijing: Sitong Corporation) (November).

Cao Siyuan (1988b), *Zhongguo Qiye Pochan Fa Zhinan* (*A Primer on China's Enterprise Bankruptcy Law*) (Beijing: Jingji Chubanshe).

Cao Zhi (1995), 'Zai Xiugai Xuanjufa he Difang Zhuzhifa Zuotanhui shang de Jianghua', ('Speech at a Symposium on Revising the Election Law and the Local Organizational Law'), *Renda Gongzuo Tongxun*, No. 4, 17–21.

CCP Central Secretariat Research Office (1986), *Dang de Shiyijie Sanzhong Quanhui Yilai Dashiji* (*A Chronology of Major Events Since the Third Plenum of the CCP's Eleventh Central Committee*), (Beijing: Hongqi Chubanshe).

Chen Yongjie and Sun Tao (1985), 'Shenyang Shi Jiti Gongye Qiye Pochan Wenti Diaocha' ('Investigation into Questions of Bankruptcy in Shenyang City Collective Industrial Enterprises'), in *Jingji Fazhan yu Tizhi Gaige* (*Economic Development and Structural Reform*) (Beijing: Chinese Economic Structural Reform Research Institute & Beijing Young Economists Study Society Joint Publication), No. 5, 1–9.

Chinese Economic Law Society (Beijing Branch) and Beijing City People's Government Electrical Engineering Office (joint publication) (1988), *Zenyang Zhengque Shishi 'Qiye Fa'* (*How to Correctly Carry Out 'The Enterprise Law'*) (Beijing: Xinshidai Chubanshe).

Deng Xiaoping (1987), *Jianshe you Zhongguo Tese de Shehuizhuyi [zengding ben]* (*Build Socialism with Chinese Characteristics [revised edition]*) (Hong Kong: Joint Publishing Company).

'Di Yi, Er, San, Wu, Liu, Qi jie Quanguo Renmin Daibiao Dahui Lici Huiyi Ti'an [Yi'an he Jianyi, Piping, Yijian] Qingkuang Biao' ('Table of Motions [inc.

Legislative Motions, Suggestions, Criticisms, and Opinions] Put Forward at the Successive Meetings of the First, Second, Third, Fifth, Sixth, and Seventh National People's Congresses'), in *Quanguo Renda Changweihui Bangongting Yanjiushi, bian (1990), Zhongghua Renmin Gongheguo Renmin Daibiao Dahui Wenxian Ziliao Huibian, 1949-1990* (Beijing: Zhongguo Minzhu Fazhi Chubanshe), 855-7.

Dong Fureng (1986), 'Tantan Qiye Pochan Zhi' ('Discussing the Enterprise Bankruptcy System'), *Renmin Ribao* (10 October), 5.

Du Xichuan and Zhang Lingyuan (eds.) (1988), *Zhonghua Renmin Gongheguo Quanmin Suoyouzhi Gongye Qiye Fa Zhishi Shouce (A Handbook of Information on The State-Owned Industrial Enterprise Law of the People's Republic of China)* (Beijing: Zhongguo Zhengfa Daxue Chubanshe).

Economic Legislation Research Centre, '1982-1986 Nian Jingji Lifa Guihua (Cao'an)' ('1982-1986 Economic Legislative Plan [Draft]'), in the ELRC internal journal *Jingji Fagui Yanjiu Ziliao* (photocopy, issue number and date missing, approximate date, spring 1983), 3-16.

Economic Legislation Research Centre (1988), 'Guanyu Guowuyuan Jingji Fagui Yanjiu Zhongxin Chengli Yilai Gongzuo Qingkuang de Huibao' ('Report on the Work Situation of the State Council Economic Legislation Research Centre Since its Establishment') in *Jingji Fazhi* (Beijing) No. 3, 22-25. (Note: This Report reprints Zhao Ziyang's brief positive comments *(pishi)* on the ELRC's work.)

Gao Shangquan (1988), '"Qiye Fa" Chutai Shiji Yi Chengshu' ('The Time is Already Ripe for the Emergence of the "Enterprise Law")', *Shijie Jingji Daobao* (Shanghai) (7 March), 15.

Gao Wenxiang (1979), 'Luelun Falu yu Zhengce de Guanxi' ('A Brief Discussion of the Relationship Between Law and Policy'), *Minzhu yu Fazhi*, No. 1, 45-8.

Gu Ming (1986), 'Wei Shenmo Shehui Zhuyi Guojia Hai Yao Li Pochan Fa?' ('Why Must a Socialist Country Still Want to Establish a Bankruptcy Law?'), *Jingji Ribao* (11 November), 3.

Gu Ming (1988), 'Huigu yu Zhanwang: Gu Ming Tongzhi Tan Qiye Fa Caoan de Qicao he Taolun Qingkuang' ('Retrospective and Prospect: Comrade Gu Ming Talks About Drawing Up the Draft Enterprise Law and Discusses its Situation'), *Fazhi Ribao*, No. 2, 24.

Guo Daohui (1988), *Zhongguo Lifa Zhidu (China's Legislative System)* (Beijing: Renmin Chubanshe).

Guojia Jingwei Jingji Fagui Ju (State Economic Commission Legal Bureau) (1988), 'Woguo Jingji Fazhi Jianshe Chujian Chengxiao' ('The Construction of Our Nation's Economic Legal System is Showing Initial Success'), *Jingji Gongzuo Tongxun* (Beijing), No. 5, 15.

'Guojia Xingzheng Jiguan Gongwen Chuli Zhanxing Banfa' ('Provisional Methods for Handling Official Documents of State Administrative Organs'), State Council Document No. 5 (1981), *Guowuyuan Gongbao (State Council Bulletin)*, No. 352, 152-7.

Guowuyuan Fazhiju Yanjiushi (State Council Legislation Bureau Research Office) (1988), 'Yiding Yao Jianli You Zhongguo Tese de Qiye Zhidu' ('We Definitely Must Establish an Enterprise System with Special Chinese Characteristics'), *Fazhi Ribao*, (11 July), 2.

Guowuyuan Jingji Fagui Yanjiu Zhongxin (State Council Economic Legislation

Research Center, ed.) (1984), *Kaizhuang Jingji Fazhi Gongzuo de Xin Jumian: Diyici Quanguo Jingji Fazhi Gongzuo Jingyan Jiaoliu Huiyi Cailiao Xuanbian* (*The New Situation in the Work of Opening Up the Economy and the Legal System: Selected Materials of the First Conference on Exchanging Experiences in Economic Law Work*) (Beijing: Falu Chubanshe).

Huang Qinnan (1988), '"Qiye Fa" Yiding Yao Fuhe Woguo Guoqing he Qiye de Shiji' ('"The Enterprise Law" Must Accord With Our Country's National Situation and the True Situation of Enterprises'), *Gongyun Yanjiu* (Beijing), No. 3, 19–21.

Jiang Zemin (1990a) 'Guanyu Jianchi he Wanshan Renmin Daibiao Dahui Zhidu' ('On Maintaining and Perfecting the People's Congress System'), (18 March), in Quanguo Renda Changweihui Bangongting Yanjiushi, bian (1990), *Zhongghua Renmin Gongheguo Renmin Daibiao Dahui Wenxian Ziliao Huibian, 1949–1990* (Beijing: Zhongguo Minzhu Fazhi Chubanshe) 623–5.

Jiang Zemin (1990b), 'Zai Qingzhu Zhonghua Renmin Gongheguo Chengli Sishi Zhounian Dahui shang de Jianghua [jiexuan]' ('Excerpts from a Speech at the Celebration of the Fortieth Anniversary of the Establishment of the People's Republic of China'), in Quanguo Renda Changweihui Bangongting Yanjiushi, bian (1990), *Zhongghua Renmin Gongheguo Renmin Daibiao Dahui Wenxian Ziliao Huibian, 1949–1990* (Beijing: Zhongguo Minzhu Fazhi Chubanshe), 622.

'Jingji Fagui Yanjiu Zhongxin Changwu Ganshi Yanjiu Bushu Jinian Gongzuo' ('The ELRC Directorate Meeting Studies and Arranges This Year's Work'), *Jingji Fagui Yanjiu Ziliao* (approximate date, March 1982), 38–40.

Lei Fa (1985), 'Guanyu Guoying Gongye Qiyefa de Jiegou' ('On the Structure of the State-Managed Industrial Enterprise Law'), *Shehui Kexue* (Shanghai), No. 2, 49–51.

Li Tao (1988), 'Zhongguo Kexie Guanli Xiandaihua Yanjiuhui Zhaokai Zuotanhui, Taolun "Zhonghua Renmin Gongheguo Quanmin Suoyouzhi Gongye Qiye Fa (Cao'an)" de Xiugai Yijian' ('The Management Modernization Research Society of the Chinese Science Association Convenes a Symposium, Discusses Views on Revision of "The Law of the People's Republic of China on State-Owned Industrial Enterprises (Draft)",'), *Faxue Yanjiu Dongtai* (Beijing), No. 5 (5 March), 7–9.

Lian He (1988), '"Qiye Fa" Qianqian Houhou' ('The Whole Story About "The Enterprise Law"'), *Xiandai Qiye Daokan* (Beijing), No. 4, 5–10.

Lin Songgen (1986), 'Guanyu Qiye Pochan de Lifa Wenti' ('On Problems of Legislating Enterprise Bankruptcy'), *Shehui Kexue Yanjiu Cankao Ziliao* (Sichuan Shehui Kexue Yuan), No. 26 (11 September), 2–5.

Liu Chunhe (ed.) (1989), *Zhonghua Renmin Gongheguo Jihui Youxing Shiwei Fa Jiangjie* (*An Explanation of the Public Demonstrations Law of the People's Republic of China*) (Beijing: Qunzhong Chubanshe).

Liu Shengping (1988), 'Lun Wo Guo Lifa Zhidu' ('On Our Country's Legislative System'), *Renmin Ribao* (29 August), 5.

Liu Xiuping (1986), 'Tantan Woguo Pochanfa de Tuchu Tedian' ('Outstanding Points of Our Country's Bankruptcy Law'), *Jingji Fagui Yanjiu Ziliao*, No. 3, 20–5.

'Lu Dong Zai Zuo Guanyu Qiye Fa Cao'an Shuoming Shi Zhichu: Xuyao Jinkuai Banbu he Shishi Qiye Fa' ('Lu Dong, While Giving an Explanation of the Draft

Enterprise Law Points Out: We Must Promulgate and Carry Out the Enterprise Law as Quickly as Possible'), *Renmin Ribao*, 1 April 1988, 2.

Lu Mu (1988), 'Shinian Yunyu, Hunxi San "Fen". "Qiye Fa" Dansheng Ji' ('After Ten Year's Gestation, Its Spirit Rests on Three "Divisions". A Record of the Birth of the "Enterprise Law"'), *Renmin Ribao* (14 April), 4.

Meng Liankun (1995), 'Qunian Gongzuo Huigu he Jinnian Gongzuo Shexiang' ('A Look Back on Last Year's Work and a Prospectus on This Year's Work'), *Renda Gongzuo Tongxun*, No. 1, 6.

Pang Song and Han Gang (1987), 'Dang he Guojia Lingdao Tizhi de Lishi Kaocha yu Gaige Zhanwang' ('The Party and State Leadership System: An Historical Investigation and the Outlook for Reform'), *Zhongguo Shehui Kexue*, No. 6, 3–20.

Peng Chong (1987), 'Guanyu Jianquan Renda Jiguan he Jigou de Baogao' ('Report On Perfecting the Work and Structure of the NPC's Work Organs'), Report to the NPC Standing Committee Chairmen's Group, 7 July, in Quanguo Renda Changweihui Bangongting Yanjiushi, bian (1990), *Zhongghua Renmin Gongheguo Renmin Daibiao Dahui Wenxian Ziliao Huibian, 1949–1990* (Beijing: Zhongguo Minzhu Fazhi Chubanshe), 470–3.

Peng Chong (1992), 'Quanguo Renmin Daibiao Dahui Changwu Weiyuanhui Gongzuo Baogao' ('Work Report of the NPC Standing Committee'), in *Quanguo Renmin Daibiao Dahui Changwu Weiyuanhui Bangongting (A Collection of Documents from the Fifth Meeting of the Seventh National People's Congress of the PRC)* (Beijing: Renmin Chubanshe), 172–80.

Peng Zhen (1980), 'Peng Zhen Tongzhi Zai Quanguo Ge Sheng, Zizhiqu, Zhishushi Renda Changweihui Fuze Tongzhi Di Yi Ci, Zuotanhui shang de Jianghua Jiyao' ('Essentials of Comrade Peng Zhen's Speech to the Responsible Comrades of the People's Congress Standing Committees of Each Province, Autonomous Region, and Directly Administered City'), NPC internal document dated 'afternoon of 18 April'.

Peng Zhen (1981), 'Peng Zhen Tongzhi Zai Quanguo Ge Sheng, Zizhiqu, Zhishushi Renda Changweihui Fuze Tongzhi Di Er Ci, Zuotanhui shang de Jianghua Jiyao' ('Essentials of Comrade Peng Zhen's Speech to the Responsible Comrades of the People's Congress Standing Committees of Each Province, Autonomous Region, and Directly Administered City'), NPC internal document dated 'morning of 7 March'.

Peng Zhen (1983), 'Jinyibu Shishi Xianfa, Yange Anzhao Xianfa Banshi' ('Further Carry Out the Constitution, Handle Affairs Strictly in Accord with the Constitution'), Speech dated 3 December 1983, reprinted in *Faxue Yanjiu*, No. 1 (1984), 1–4.

Peng Zhen (1984a), 'Zai Quanguo Renda Changweihui Zai Jing Weiyuan Zuotanhui shang de Jianghua Yaodian' ('Essential Points of a Speech to a Seminar of NPC Standing Committee Members in Beijing'), NPC internal document dated 24 January.

Peng Zhen (1984b), 'Zai Sheng, Zizhiqu, Zhishushi Renda Changweihui Fuze Tongzhi Zuotanhui shang de Jianghua Yaodian', ('Essential Points of a Speech to Responsible Comrades of the People's Congress Standing Committees of the Provinces, Autonomous Regions, and Directly Administered Cities'), NPC internal document dated 'morning of 13 March'.

Peng Zhen (1986a), 'Lixiang, Minzhu, Fazhi' ('Ideals, Democracy, and the Legal System'), *Shiyijie Sanzhong Quanhui yilai Zhongyao Wenxian Xuandu [Xia Ce] (Selected Important Documents Since the Third Plenum of the Eleventh Central Committee, [Final Volume])* (Beijing: Renmin Chubanshe), 1182–8.

Peng Zhen (1986b), 'Peng Zhen Weiyuanzhang Zai Quanguo Renda Changweihui Di Shiba Ci Huiyi Lianzu Hui Shang de Jianghua Yaodian' ('Essential Points of Standing Committee Chairman Peng Zhen's Remarks to the Joint Group Meeting at the Eighteenth Session of the [Sixth] NPC Standing Committee'), 29 November (xerox copy from an unnamed NPC internal journal).

Peng Zhen (1987), 'Yi Buyao Shizhi, Er Buyao Yueguan' ('First, Do Not Neglect One's Duty. Second, Do Not Exceed One's Authority'), Portions of a Speech by Comrade Peng Zhen to a Joint Group Meeting of the 21st Session of the Sixth NPC Standing Committee, 22 June, in Quanguo Renda Changweihui Bangongting Yanjiushi, bian (1990), *Zhongghua Renmin Gongheguo Renmin Daibiao Dahui Wenxian Ziliao Huibian, 1949–1990* (Beijing: Zhongguo Minzhu Fazhi Chubanshe), 607–8.

Peng Zhen (1989), *Lun Xin Shiqi de Shehuizhuyi Minzhu yu Fazhi Jianshe (On the Construction of Socialist Democracy and the Legal System in the New Period)* (Beijing: Zhongyang Wenjian Chubanshe).

Peng Zhen (1991), *Peng Zhen Wenxuan (Selected Works of Peng Zhen)* (Beijing: Zhongyang Wenxian Chubanshe), 560–71.

Peng Zhen (1992), *Lun Xin Zhongguo de Zhengfa Gongzuo (On Political-Legal Work in the New China)* (Beijing: Zhongyang Wenxian Chubanshe).

Qian Jianping et al (eds.) (1985), *Jianguo Yilai Fazhi Jianshe Jishi (Chronicle of Events in the Building of the Legal System Since the Founding of the Country)* (Shijiazhuang: Hebei Renmin Chubanshe).

Qiao Shi (1995a), 'Jiakuai Lifa, Yange Zhifa, Tuijin Gaige, Xiaochu Fubai' ('Speed Up Lawmaking, Toughen Legal Enforcement, Push Reform Forward, Eliminate Corruption'), Comments to a group of German reporters, *Renda Gongzuo Tongxun*, No. 3, 3–5.

Qiao Shi (1995b), 'Zai Bajie Quanguo Renda Sanci Huiyi shang de Jianghua' ('Speech at the Third Session of the Eighth National People's Congress'), *Renda Gongzuo Tongxun*, No. 6, 3–4.

Qiao Shi (1995c), 'Zai Bajie Quanguo Renda Changweihui Dishisanci Huiyi shang de Jianghua' ('Speech at the Thirteenth Meeting of the Eighth National People's Congress Standing Committee'), dated 10 May, *Renda Gongzuo Tongxun*, No. 9, 3–4.

Qiao Shi (1995d), 'Genghaode Yunyong Falu Shouduan Zujin Jingji Xiaoyi de Tigao' ('Do a Better Job of Using Legal Methods to Accelerate the Increase in Economic Efficiency'), *Renda Gongzuo Tongxun*, No. 10, 3–4.

'Qiye Fa He Zhongwai Hezuo Jingying Qiye Fa Cao'An Jiben Chengshu' ('The Draft Enterprise Law and Law on Sino-Foreign Cooperative Enterprises are Basically Complete'), *Renmin Ribao*, 10 April 1988, 2.

'Qiye Fa Jiben Chengshu Jianyi Tongguo Shishi' ('The Enterprise Law is Basically Ready. It Should Be Passed and Implemented') (Explanation of Song Rufen Regarding the Revision of the Enterprise Law), *Renmin Ribao* (6 March), 2. (Note: A similar report by BXDS is translated in FBIS-CHI, 7 March 1988, 55–6).

Bibliography 277

'Qiye Pochanfa (Cao'an) Jianjie' ('A Brief Introduction to the Enterprise Bankruptcy Law [Draft]'), *Jingji Fagui Yanjiu Ziliao*, No. 3 (1986), 15–19.

'Qiye Zizhiquan yao Kao Falu Baozhang' ('Enterprise Autonomy Must Rely Upon Law for its Guarantee'), *Renmin Ribao*, 11 October 1986, 2.

Quanguo Renda Changweihui Bangongting Yanjiushi (NPC Standing Committee General Office Research Office, ed.) (1990), *Zhongghua Renmin Gongheguo Renmin Daibiao Dahui Wenxian Ziliao Huibian, 1949–1990* (*Collection of Selected Documents of the PRC National People's Congress 1949–1990*) (Beijing: Zhongguo Minzhu Fazhi Chubanshe). (Source Note: This extraordinary volume [1,058 pages] contains a wealth of documentation on the NPC, its organization, and history, including all of the Standing Committee Work Reports, and hundreds of previously unpublished leadership speeches, internal NPC reports and regulations, and data tables dating back to 1954. Though designated 'internal circulation' (*neibu faxing*), it is available for purchase.)

Quanguo Renda Changweihui Bangongting Yanjiushi (NPC Standing Committee General Office Research Office, ed.) (1991), *Renmin Daibiao Dahui Zhidu Jianshe Sishinian* (*Forty Years of Building the People's Congress System*) (Beijing: Zhongguo Minzhu Fazhi Chubanshe).

Quanguo Renda Changweihui Bangongting Yanjiushi (NPC Standing Committee General Office Research Office, ed.) (1992), *Renmin Daibiao Dahui Wenxian Xuanbian* (*Selected Documents on People's Congresses*) (Beijing: Zhongguo Minzhu Fazhi Chubanshe).

Quanguo Renmin Daibiao Dahui Changwu Weiyuanhui Bangongting (NPC Standing Committee General Office, ed.) (1992) *Zhonghua Renmin Gongheguo di qi jie Quanguo Renmin Daibiao Dahui di wu ci Huiyi Wenjian Huibian* (*A Collection of Documents from the Fifth Meeting of the Seventh National People's Congress of the PRC*) (Beijing: Renmin Chubanshe).

'Quanguo Renmin Daibiao Dahui ji qi Changwu Weiyuanwei de Lifa Gongzuo' ('The Legislative Work of the National People's Congress and its Standing Committee'), *Law Yearbook of China*, 1987 (Beijing: Falu Chubanshe), 1–3.

'Quanguo Renmin Daibiao Dahui ji qi Changwu Weiyuanwei Gongzuo Jigou de Lishi Yange' ('The Historical Evolution of the Work Organs of the National People's Congress and its Standing Committee') in Quanguo Renda Changweihui Bangongting Yanjiushi, bian (1990), *Zhongghua Renmin Gongheguo Renmin Daibiao Dahui Wenxian Ziliao Huibian, 1949–1990* (Beijing: Zhongguo Minzhu Fazhi Chubanshe), 924–5.

'"Renda Changweihui" Heyi She Fazhi Weiyuanhui?' ('How Did the NPC Standing Committee Come to Establish the Legislative Affairs Committee?'), *Studies in Chinese Communism* (Taibei), No. 3 (1979), 77–83.

'Renda Changwei Hui Juxing Ershisi Ci Huiyi' ('The NPC Standing Committee Convenes its Twenty-Fourth Meeting'), *Renmin Ribao*, 12 January 1988, 1.

Renmin Daibiao ('People's Delegates' [Wen Yuankai, *et al.*]) (1984), *Guanyu Zhiding 'Qiye Pochan Zhengdun Fa' de Ti'an* (*A Proposal for Drafting an 'Enterprise Bankruptcy Consolidation Law'*), proposal to the Presidium of the National People's Congress, 17 May 1984.

Shandong Sheng Renda Changweihui Yanjiushi (Shandong Provincial People's Congress Standing Committee Research Office, ed.) (1989), *Renda Gongzuo*

Wenxian Ziliao Huibian (*Collection of Materials and Documents on People's Congress Work*) (Jinan, Shandong: Shandong Renmin Chubanshe).
'Shixing Pochan Zhidu Zujin Qiye Zizhu Jingying' ('Carrying Out the Bankruptcy System Will Accelerate the Autonomous Management of Enterprises'), Remarks by a 'Responsible Person' of the NPC Legislative Affairs Commission to Reporters, *Renmin Ribao*, 7 December 1986, 2.
Song Rufen (1995), *Canjia Lifa Gongzuo Suoji* (*Scattered Recollections on My Participation in Lawmaking Work*, two volumes (Beijing: Zhongguo Fazhi Chubanshe).
State Council General Office (1981), 'Guojia Xingzheng Jiguan Gongwen Chuli Zhanxing Banfa' ('Provisional Measures on the Handling of Official Documents in State Administrative Organs'), *Zhonghua Renmin Gongheguo Guowuyuan Gongbao* (*PRC State Council Gazette*) (15 May), 152–8.
State Council Legislation Bureau Research Office (1988), 'Yiding Yao Jianli Juyou Zhongguo Tese de Qiye Zhidu' ('We Must Definitely Establish an Enterprise System with Chinese Characteristics'), *Fazhi Ribao* (11 July), 2.
Sun Chenggu (1983), *Lifa Quan yu Lifa Chengxu* (*Legislative Authority and Legislative Procedure*) (Beijing: Renmin Chubanshe).
Sun Guohua (1979), 'Dang de Zhengce Yu Falu de Guanxi' ('The Relationship Between Party Policy and Law'), *Guangming Ribao* (24 February), 3.
Sun Yaming (1986), 'Zhiding Qiye Pochan Fa Shi Yousheng Lietai Guilu de Keguan Yaoqiu' ('Drafting the Enterprise Bankruptcy Law is an Objective Demand of "Letting the Excellent Win and Letting the Inferior Fall by the Wayside"'), *Fazhi Jianshe*, No. 6, 5–9.
Tian Jiyun (1995a), 'Zai Quanguo Renda Jiguan Ganbu Dahui shang de Jianghua' ('Speech at a Meeting of Cadres in the NPC Organs'), made on 8 February, *Renda Gongzuo Tongxun*, No. 5, 5–12.
Tian Jiyun (1995b), 'Quanguo Renmin Daibiao Dahui Changwu Weiyuanhui Gongzuo Baogao' ('National People's Congress Standing Committee Work Report'), delivered at the Third Session of the Eleventh NPC, 11 March, *Renda Gongzuo Tongxun*, No. 6, 6–13.
Tian Jiyun (1995c), 'Tian Jiyun Fuweiyuanzhang jiu Jiakuai Jingji Lifa Da Zhongyang Dianshitai Jizhe Wen' ('Vice-Chairman Tian Jiyun Answers Questions of the Central Television Network on Accelerating Economic Legislation'), *Renda Gongzuo Tongxun*, No. 3, 6–7.
Tao Hejian (1986), *Jingjifa Jichu Lilun* (*Basic Theory of Economic Law*) (Beijing: Falu Chubanshe).
Tao Xijin (1981), 'Guanyu Minfa Qicao Gongzuo zhong de Jige Wenti' ('On Several Issues in Drafting the Civil Code'), *Minzhu yu Fazhi*, No. 9, 2–7.
Tao Xijin (1988), *Xin Zhongguo Fazhi Jianshe* (*Building New China's Legal System*), (Tianjin: Nankai Daxue Chubanshe).
Wan Li (1986), 'Making Decision Making More Democratic and Scientific is an Important Part of Reforming the Political System', *Renmin Ribao* (15 August), 1.
Wan Li (1988a), 'Zai Qijie Quanguo Renda Yici Huiyi shang de Jianghua' ('Speech at the First Session of the Seventh NPC') in Quanguo Renda Changweihui Bangongting Yanjiushi, bian (1990), *Zhongghua Renmin Gongheguo Renmin Daibiao Dahui Wenxian Ziliao Huibian, 1949–1990* (Beijing: Zhongguo Minzhu Fazhi Chubanshe), 615–6.

Bibliography 279

Wan Li (1988b), 'Zai Qijie Quanguo Renda Changweihui Di Yici Huiyi shang de Jianghua' ('Speech at the First Session of the Seventh NPC Standing Committee') in Quanguo Renda Changweihui Bangongting Yanjiushi, bian (1990), *Zhongghua Renmin Gongheguo Renmin Daibiao Dahui Wenxian Ziliao Huibian, 1949-1990* (Beijing: Zhongguo Minzhu Fazhi Chubanshe), 616-8.

Wan Li (1990), 'Wan Li Zai Qijie Quanguo Renda Changweihui Dishisanci Huiyi shang de Jianghua' ('Wan Li's Speech at the Thirteenth Meeting of the Seventh NPC Standing Committee'), in Quanguo Renda Changweihui Bangongting Yanjiushi, bian (1990), *Zhongghua Renmin Gongheguo Renmin Daibiao Dahui Wenxian Ziliao Huibian, 1949-1990* (Beijing: Zhongguo Minzhu Fazhi Chubanshe), pp. 622-3.

Wan Li (1992), 'Zai Qijie Quanguo Renda Changweihui di Ershiliuci Huiyi shang de Jianghua' ('Speech at the Twenty-Sixth Meeting of the Seventh NPC Standing Committee'), dated 1 July, in CCP Central Committee Document Research Office (1993), *Shisanda Yilai Zhongyao Wenxian Xuanbian [Xia]* (*Selected Important Documents Since the Thirteenth Party Congress, Third Volume*), 2121-2.

Wang Baoshu (1988), 'Lun "Quanmin Suoyouzhi Gongye Qiye Fa" Zai Qiye Lifashang de Tupo' ('A Discussion of the Legislative Breakthroughs in "The Law on State-Owned Industrial Enterprises"'), *Zhongguo Faxue* (Beijing), No. 4, 3-10.

Wu Daying (1981), 'Lun Lifa Jishu' ('On Legislative Techniques'), *Beifang Luncong* (Harbin), No. 1, 14-9.

Wu Daying et al. (1984), *Zhongguo Shehuizhuyi Lifa Wenti* (*China's Socialist Legislative System*) (Beijing: Qunzhong Chubanshe).

Wu Daying et al. (eds.) (1987), *Zhongguo Shehuizhuyi Falu Jiben Lilun* (*Basic Theory of China's Socialist Legal System*) (Beijing: Falu Chubanshe).

Xiang Chunyi (1984), 'Wo Guo de Lifa Zhidu he Lifa Chengxu' ('Our Country's Legislative System and Legislative Procedure'), speech at Peking University, March (Beijing: Ministry of Justice and NPC Legislative Affairs Commission Joint Legislative Cadres Training Class).

Yang Hong and Wang Jinzhong (1981), 'Yao Jiaqiang Jingji Lifa de Gongzuo' ('We Must Strengthen the Work of Economic Legislation'), *Renmin Ribao*, (14 May), 5.

Yang Zixuan (ed.) (1986), *Gongye Qiye Fa Jiaocheng* (*A Curriculum on Industrial Enterprise Law*) (Beijing: Falu Chubanshe).

'Yi Fa Guanli Shi Qiye Biyou Zhi Lu: Qiao Shi Shou Qiye Fa Jiang wei Gaige Zhiming Fangxiang' ('Reliance on Law in Management is the Road Which Enterprise Must Follow: Qiao Shi Says the Enterprise Law Will Point the Way for Reform'), *Renmin Ribao*, 9 January 1988, 1.

Yu Jianping et al (1985), *Jianguo Yilai Fazhi Jianshe Jishi* (*Major Events in the Construction of the Legal System Since the Founding of Our Country*) (Shijiazhuang, Hebei: Hebei Renmin Chubanshe).

Yuan Baohua (1988), 'Jianding Buyide Guangqie Zhixing "Qiye Fa"' ('Resolutely, Unwaveringly, and Thoroughly Implement the "Enterprise Law"'), *Renmin Ribao* (23 May), 5.

'Yuan Baohua Dui "Qiye Fa" de Xiugai Zuo Shuoming' ('Yuan Baohua Gives an Explanation of the Revision of the "Enterprise Law"'), *Renmin Ribao*, 12 January 1988, 2.

'Yuan Baohua Jiu Quanmin Suoyouzhi Gongye Qiyefa Cao'an Zuo Shuoming' ('Yuan Baohua Gives an Explanation of the Draft State-Owned Industrial Enterprises Law'), *Renmin Ribao*, 16 November 1986, 1.

Yuan Mu (1986), 'Guanyu Zhiding Qiye Pochan Fa de Ji Dian Renshi' ('Looking at a Few Points Concerning the Drafting of the Enterprise Bankruptcy Law'), *Renmin Ribao* (6 December), 2.

Zhang Jin (1979), 'Falu yu Zhengce youle Maodun Zenmo Ban?' ('What Should be Done When Law and Policy are in Contradiction?'), *Minzhu yu Fazhi*, No. 5, 20–1.

Zhang Sutang and He Ping (1988), 'Gaige Huhuanzhe Qiyefa Jinkuai Chutai' ('Reform Cries Out for the Immediate Emergence of the Enterprise Law'), *Liaowang*, No. 5, 4–7.

Zhang Yanning (1988), Interview, 'Yunyong "Qiye Fa" Tuijin Qiye Gaige' ('Use the "Enterprise Law" to Push Enterprise Reform'), *Renmin Ribao* (31 July), 2.

Zhang Youyu (1983), 'Renmin Daibiao Dahui Zhidu de Xin Fazhan' ('The New Development of the NPC System'), *Renmin Ribao* (14 January), 5.

'Zhonggong Zhongyang Guanyu Guanche Zhixing Qiye Fa de Tongzhi' ('Notice of the CCP Central Committee on Thoroughly Implementing the Enterprise Law'), *Renmin Ribao*, 11 May 1988, 1.

'Zhonggong Zhongyang Guanyu Jiaqiang dui Lifa Gongzuo Lingdao de Ruogan Yijian' ('Several Opinions of the CCP Central Committee on Strengthening Leadership Over Lawmaking Work'), Chinese Communist Party Central Committee Document Number 8, 1991 (Zhongfa Ba hao [1991]), personal copy.

Zhongguo Shehui Kexue Yuan Gongye Jingji Yanjiusuo (Chinese Academy of Social Science, Institute of Industrial Economics, ed.) (1986), *Shiyijie Sanzhong Quanhui yilai Jingji Zhengce Wenxian Xuanbian* (*A Collection of Selected Documents on Economic Policy Since the Third Plenum of the Eleventh Central Committee*) (Beijing: Zhongguo Jingji Chubanshe).

'Zhonghua Renmin Gongheguo Qiye Pochan Fa (Shixing)' ('Enterprise Bankruptcy Law of the People's Republic of China [for Trial Implementation]'), *Renmin Ribao*, 3 December 1986, 2.

'Zhonghua Renmin Gongheguo Quanmin Suoyouzhi Gongye Qiye Fa Cao'an' ('Draft Law of the People's Republic of China on State-Owned Industrial Enterprise'), *Renmin Ribao*, 12 January 1988, 2.

'Zhonghua Renmin Gongheguo Quanmin Suoyouzhi Gongye Qiye Fa' ('Law of the People's Republic of China on State-Owned Industrial Enterprise'), *Renmin Ribao*, 16 April 1988, 2.

Zhonghua Renmin Gongheguo Xingzheng Susong Fa (Cao'an) (Administrative Litigation Law of the PRC [Draft]), unpublished revised draft dated 24 January 1989.

Zhonghua Renmin Gongheguo Xingzheng Susong Fa (Administrative Litigation Law of the PRC), *Fazhi Ribao*, 11 April 1989, 1.

'Zhongyang Zhengzhiju Zhaokai Di San Ci Huiyi, Yuanze Tongyi "Qiye Fa Cao'an"' ('The CCP Politburo Convenes Third Plenary Meeting, Approves in Principle the "Draft Enterprise Law"'), *Renmin Ribao*, 10 January 1988, 1.

Zhou Wangsheng (1989), *Lifa Xue* (*The Study of Lawmaking*) (Beijing: Beijing Daxue Chubanshe).

Zhou Wangsheng (1994), *Lifa Lun* (*On Legislation*) (Beijing: Beijing Daxue Chubanshe).
Zhou Xinming (1984), 'You Zhongguo Tese de Shehuizhuyi Lifa Wenti' ('Issues in the Socialist Legal System with Chinese Characteristics'), *Faxue Zazhi*, No. 3, 13–15.
'Zhuajin Lifa Gongzuo, Jiaqiang Falu Jiandu' ('Firmly Grasp Legislative Work, Strengthen Legal Supervision') *Fazhi Ribao*, 22 March 1989, 3.
'Zhuanmen Weiyuanwei Gongzuo You Qise' ('In Their Work, Special Committees Have Shown Their Colours'), *Fazhi Ribao*, 22 March 1989, 3.
'Zhuming Faxuejia Zhang Youyu Tan "Qiye Fa"' ('Famous Legal Scholar Zhang Youyu Discusses the "Enterprise Law"'), *Qiyejia* (*Entrepreneur Magazine*) (Wuhan), No. 7 (1988), 6–9.

Index

Administrative Litigation Law [1989] 131, 219
All-China Federation of Trade Unions (ACFTU) 144–5, 154, 174, 176, 178–9, 182, 184–7, 193–4, 197, 202–3, 224, 247
All-China Women's Federation 198
Allison, Graham 14, 109
Almond, Gabriel 242
Anti-Bourgeois Liberalism Campaign (1987) 92, 221, 238
Anti-Right Deviationist Campaign (1959) 122, 237
Anti-Rightist Campaign (1957) 18, 43, 80, 94, 113, 122, 237
Anti-Spiritual Pollution Campaign (1983) 80, 238
An Zhiwen 193
Auditing Law 116

Banking Law 116
Bankruptcy Law, *see* Enterprise Bankruptcy Law
Baum, Richard 235
basic laws (jiben fa) 45–6, 167, 172, 222
Bo Yibo 177
Budgeting Law 116

Caimao Jingji 136
Cao Siyuan 134–43, 149–52, 154–6, 166, 170, 211–12, 215–17
Cao Zhi 59
Central Work Conference (1978) 168–9
Chen Junsheng 124
Chen Muhua 98
Chen Pixian 33, 64, 98, 156, 163, 190–1, 199, 210, 240
Chen Yun 176
China Democracy & Legal System Press 112
Chinese Academy of Social Sciences 136, 196
Chinese Communist Party (CCP) 15, 44–9, 51, 56, 64–8, 209, 214
 13th Party Congress (1987) 63, 192, 221
 15th Party Congress 248–9
 erosion of lawmaking control 10, 39, 48, 59–61, 131, 230, 233, 235, 239, 240, 246
 Party Groups (*dangzu*) in NPC 58–61
 relationship with NPC 54–70, 222, 231–52
Chinese Communist Party Central Committee (CCPCC) 44, 174, 176, 178–9, 180
 Central Advisory Commission 97
 Central Document Number 8 [1991] 51, 61, 64–70, 114, 222, 241
 Central Committee General Office 96, 180
 Central Organization Department 174–5, 178–9, 183–4, 186, 193–4, 202, 224
 Central Political-Legal Leading Group (CPLG) 43, 56, 61–4, 96, 112, 145, 169, 240
 Constitution of 184
 Financial and Economic Leading Group 64, 159
 Politburo 44, 47–8, 68, 157, 160, 164–5, 193, 195, 199, 240
 Secretariat 44, 64, 145, 179–80, 183–4, 187, 192, 224
 Third Plenum of 11th CCPCC (1978) 6, 43, 45, 72, 122, 221
 Third Plenum of 12th CCPCC (1984) 147–8, 182–3, 221
Civil Law, General Principles of 225
civil society 35, 231, 245–7
Clarke, Donald 225
codification of law, post-Mao trend toward 45, 95, 185, 189, 198
Cohen, Jerome Alan 13
Cohen, Michael 28–30
comparative legislatures 5–6, 73
Constitution, PRC State 4, 44–7, 68–70, 94, 105, 132, 186, 189, 196, 212, 222, 244
Copyright Law 116, 221
Criminal Law 21, 46
Cultural Revolution (1966–76) 12, 19, 36, 52, 80, 94, 96, 113, 122, 239, 242

Decision of the CCP Central Committee on the Restructuring of the Economic System 148, 181–2, 186, 188–9
Democracy & the Legal System 147, 149
Democracy Movement (1989) 7, 57, 166, 242–3
democratization 9–11, 35–40, 70–1, 75–9, 92–4, 231–52
Deng Liqun 167
Deng Xiaoping 3, 21, 33, 36, 43, 48, 50, 97, 101, 132, 167–9, 171, 193, 211, 213–14, 220–21, 231, 239–41, 243, 247

Economic Contracts Law 142
electoral reform 247–50
Enterprise Bankruptcy Law [1986] 6, 10, 11, 19, 34, 65–6, 90, 135–66, 187, 212, 215–17, 219, 223, 235

284 Index

Enterprise Bankruptcy Relief Methods 154, 162
enterprise reform 147–8, 151, 158–9, 181–2
entrepreneurship, political 30–31, 214–15

Factory Manager Responsibility System 139, 172–3, 180–98, 221–3
Foster, Frances Hoar 12

Gang of Four 167
Gao Shangquan 197
Geng Biao 98
Great Leap Forward 43, 80, 96
Gu Linfang 63–4
Gu Ming 123–4, 144, 146, 150, 177, 182
Guan Huai 197
Guo Daohui 161

Hu Jiwei 57, 61, 80, 90, 114, 238, 240
Hu Qiaomu 169
Hu Qili 156
Hu Yaobang 160, 169, 179–80, 183, 188, 191, 224
Hua Guofeng 21, 168
Hundred Flowers Campaign (1956–7) 18, 77, 79–80, 94, 237

implementing regulations 129–31, 225–6
'Inadvertent transition' and democratization 35–40, 232–5
Institutionalization of NPC changes 74–93, 235–45
'Iron Triangles' 107–9, 246

Ji Denkui 168–9
Jiang Ping 202
Jiang Zemin 3, 4, 21, 33, 36, 54, 66–7, 240–41, 243, 247–50
Jingji Ribao 159–61
Jones, William C. 225

Kang Sheng 96
Kingdon, John 29–30

labour Law 169, 176, 223
Lampton, David 24–5
lawmaking
  CCP, role in 15, 44–9, 51–71, 209–14
  CPLG, role in 56, 62–4
  decentralization of power 52–3, 55, 70–1, 232
  Legislation Bureau, role in 124–31
  Leninist system of 8, 9, 36, 38, 232–4
  NPC, growing influence 10, 72–119, 222–5, 250–52
  NPC, role in 10, 15, 44–51, 61, 74, 77–8, 177–9, 209, 214, 221–6, 234
  Politburo, role in 55, 209–10, 212, 214, 220, 225–6, 234–5

political power trends in 21, 43–50, 127–32, 167, 188, 212, 217–19, 230, 239–40, 247–50
State Council, influence 120–29
State Council, role in 44–51, 120–32, 209, 211, 214, 218, 220, 225–6, 230, 234
lawmaking processes and stages 5, 7–8, 10–11, 32–4, 64–6, 126–9, 209–30
  agenda-setting 135–144, 168–71, 177–9, 187, 209–17, 233–4
  CCP Center erosion of influence 10, 39, 48–71, 230, 233
  explication/implementation 204–5, 209, 225–6, 230
  interagency review/consensus-building 135, 144–53, 170–203, 210, 217–21, 224, 230, 239
  NPC review 135, 155–66, 170–203, 209–10, 221–6, 239
  top leadership decision-making 135, 153–5, 209–10
lawmaking system, defined 44
legal system
  post-Mao 38, 43–50, 52–3, 123–4
  transition in 8, 9, 11, 13, 35–40, 51–55
legislative plans, annual and five-year 115–17, 123–127, 217
Legislative Work Conference (1992) 116
Li Changchun 147
Li Lianjiang 240
Li Peng 21, 37, 57, 121, 128, 200, 240, 249–50
Li Ruihuan 249
Li Quande 147
Li Xiannian 165
Lieberthal, Kenneth 21, 25, 37–8, 246
Lu Dong 139, 200
Luerhmann, Laura 240

Ma Hong 138–40, 142
Mao Zedong 240, 247
March, James 13, 28–30
Meyer, Alfred 248
Ministry of Agriculture, Animal Husbandry and Fisheries 109
Ministry of Civil Affairs 106
Ministry of Finance 144, 146
Ministry of Foreign Economic Relations and Trade 144, 146
Ministry of Justice 106
Ministry of Labour and Personnel 140, 144–6, 154–5, 223
Ministry of Light Industry 143, 145
Ministry of Public Security 12, 106, 109, 115, 215–16, 238
Ministry of State Security 106
Ministry of Supervision 106
Ministry of Transportation 109

Index 285

Nathan, Andrew 242–3
National People's Congress (NPC) 4, 33, 43–50, 58–61, 65, 68–72, 83, 113–17, 125, 131–2, 142, 150, 154–5, 157–8, 161–2, 165, 175, 179, 184–5, 191, 200, 235, 237
  1st Plenary Session of 7th 196
  2nd Plenary Session of 7th (1989) 131
  5th Plenary Session of 6th (1983) 138
  Administrative Office 95
  Advisors Office 95
  bureaucratic development 13, 38, 94–118, 233, 238–9
  changing attitudes and behaviour 74–94, 161–2, 238, 241, 245
  changing role of 33, 44–7, 83, 221–5, 230–52
  changing voting patterns 83–93, 161–2, 238, 241
  Committee Chairmen's Group 44, 99, 112, 158, 162, 186, 190, 195–6, 202–3, 222, 247
  election to 199–200, 237, 240, 250
  emergence of powerbase 72–4, 97–118, 250
  International Legislatures Office 95
  Language Office 95
  Law Office 95
  Nationalities Office 95
  News Bureau 112
  organizational structure 94–112
  Personnel Bureau 112
  relationship with Legislation Bureau 129–31
  Research Office 95, 103
  Secretariat 94, 103
  streamlining bureaucracy 95–7, 109–13
  Translation and Compilation Office 95
NPC Legislative Affairs [Work] Committee (LAC/LAWC) 45, 47, 59, 97, 101–3, 105–6, 110–12, 115, 131, 157–64, 172, 199, 205, 211, 223, 240
  Civil Law Office 103
  Criminal Law Office 103
  Economic Law Office 103
  Enterprise Law Investigation Group 172–80, 182–185
  General Office 103
  Research Office 103
  State and Administrative Law Office 103
NPC Standing Committee (NPC\SC) 38, 44–55, 57, 68–70, 83, 91–4, 97–101, 106, 114–16, 154, 157–161, 183–4, 187–9, 194–6, 211, 217, 224, 238
  16th Session of 156–7
  17th Session of 159–60, 162
  18th Session of 164, 188
  18th Session of 6th 165
  Education, Science, Culture and Public Health Committee 105, 113

Environmental Protection Committee 105
  Finance and Economics Committee 104, 158–60, 162, 185
  Foreign Affairs Committee 105
  General Office 95, 96, 97, 103, 110–12
  Internal and Judicial Affairs Committee (IJAC) 104, 106, 112, 114
  Law Committee 104–6, 158–160, 185
  Nationalities Committee 104, 113
  Organs Party Group 58
  Overseas Chinese Affairs Committee 105
  Party Group 58, 83, 112, 221, 246
  Party Member's Group 156, 159
  Special Committees 98, 104–112, 221, 239
Ni Zhifu 98
nomenklatura system 15, 23, 56–8, 92, 239, 246

O'Brien, Kevin 6, 7, 18, 235, 239, 245, 256
Oksenberg, Michel 21, 25
Olsen, Johan P. 13, 28–30
organizational politics theories 22–31, 107–10, 208–29

Patent Law 7
Peng Chong 63, 75, 98, 106, 111–13, 116–17, 209, 239
Peng Qingyan 188
Peng Zhen 21, 33, 45, 53–4, 64, 73–4, 95–101, 110, 123, 141, 157, 161–3, 170–2, 174, 176–8, 181–2, 189–90, 198, 209, 234, 237, 239
People's Bank of China 143, 145, 218
People's Daily 121, 159, 194, 203
policy process models 10, 13–5, 232
  Command model 10, 13–9, 25
  Garbage Can model 10, 13–4, 28–35, 50, 130–4, 137–8, 197, 209, 232–4
  Leadership Struggle model 10, 13–4, 19–22, 24, 32
  Organizational Politics model 10, 13–4, 22–7, 31–2, 35, 134–5, 154, 209, 217, 225, 232
Polumbaum, Judy 214
Potter, Pitman 218
Press Law, debates over 7, 214
Price Law 115
Public Demonstrations Law [1989] 7, 90, 115, 214, 237
Pye, Lucian 242

Qiao Shi 3–4, 21, 33, 59, 209, 224, 237, 239, 243, 247–8

Renmin Ribao, see *People's Daily*
rule by law 6, 8–9, 40, 53, 167, 231
rule by man 167
rule of law 8, 122, 246

286 Index

Shepsle, Kenneth 118
Shi Tianjian 242
Shi Liang 102
Skinner, William 235
Solinger, Dorothy 12, 20, 74
Song Chengzhi 189
Song Rufen 161, 190, 193–4
State Council 5, 43–50, 116–17, 120–132, 136, 142–3, 150–52, 154–5, 157–8, 163–4, 174, 184, 216, 223–4, 240
   Bankruptcy Law Drafting Group 147, 150–51
   Bureau for Protection of State Secrets 215
   departmentalism as a problem in 121–3
   Economic Legislation Research Center (ELRC) 121–5, 144–7, 163, 178, 211
   General Administration of Industry and Commerce 144, 146
   General Office 180
   lawmaking organs 120–29
   Legislation Bureau 44, 47, 49 62, 63, 121–2, 124–9, 166, 187, 204–5, 216, 220, 225, 230
   Legislative Co-ordination Bureau 63
   Standing Committee of 44, 121, 124–5, 150, 153, 173, 180, 189–90
State Commission for Restructuring the Economic System 153, 192
State Economic Commission 139–40, 142, 144, 146, 153, 159–60, 163, 170, 172–7, 179, 182–4, 186, 188–90, 214, 217
State Enterprise Commission 213
State Planning Commission 144
   Technical Economic Research Center (TERC) 136–7, 142–4, 146–7, 153, 212
State-Owned Industrial Enterprises Law [1988] 10–11, 19, 205, 213–14, 215, 221, 223–4
State Secrets Law [1988] 215
structural-functionalism 5, 16
succession politics, and NPC role 246–9
Sun Wanzhong 203
Supreme People's Court 106, 144, 146, 225
Supreme People's Procuratorate 106

Tao Guofeng 161
Tao Xijin 62, 121–2

Tian Jiyun 124, 156, 210, 240, 244, 249
Tiananmen massacre (1989) 7, 21, 31, 53, 66–7, 72, 77, 80, 92, 113–5, 215–16, 221, 237–8
Tsou, Tang 235
Twenty Articles on Industry [1975] 167

Verba, Sidney 242

Walder, Andrew 36
Wan Li 33, 48, 54, 59, 66, 199, 202, 210, 225, 238, 240, 244
Wang Dongxing 21, 167–8
Wang Feng 107
Wang Hanbin 106, 111, 157, 161, 201, 210, 240, 249
Wang Zhen 64
Weber, Max 18
Wei Guoqing 98
Wen Yuankai 142, 212
Wu Fuzhao 191
Wu Juetian 189

Xi Zhongxun 106
Xue Ju 106
Xue Muqiao 183

Yao Yilin 156–77
Ye Jianying 238
Yu Shutong 107
Yuan Baohua 139, 170–71, 173, 177, 179, 184, 187–8, 193, 211, 213–14, 216
Yuan Mu 159

Zhang Jingfu 139
Zhang Ruiying 196
Zhang Yanning 157, 166, 217
Zhang Zhizhai 189
Zhao Cangbi 62
Zhao Ziyang 3, 6, 21, 37, 48, 63–5, 121–2, 124, 127–8, 135–6, 138, 140, 151, 155–6, 160, 164–6, 171, 173, 175, 179–81, 191–3, 199–200, 224, 235
Zhou Enlai 43, 96, 121, 240
Zhu Rongji 240
Zou Yu 107